THOMAS JEFFERSON: MORALIST

Thomas Jefferson: Moralist

M. Andrew Holowchak

McFarland & Company, Inc., Publishers
Jefferson, North Carolina

ISBN (print) 978-1-4766-6924-3
ISBN (ebook) 978-1-4766-2817-2

LIBRARY OF CONGRESS CATALOGUING DATA ARE AVAILABLE

British Library cataloguing data are available

© 2017 M. Andrew Holowchak. All rights reserved

No part of this book may be reproduced or transmitted in any form or by any means, electronic or mechanical, including photocopying or recording, or by any information storage and retrieval system, without permission in writing from the publisher.

Front cover image of a statue of Thomas Jefferson in Virginia © 2017 Kyle McMahon/iStock

Printed in the United States of America

*McFarland & Company, Inc., Publishers
Box 611, Jefferson, North Carolina 28640
www.mcfarlandpub.com*

To Charles,
amicus constans omnium horarum

Table of Contents

Preface	1
1. "The ennui … of a tedious sermon": Head versus Heart in a Love Letter to Maria Cosway	7
2. "Art appears too much": Jefferson and the Moral and Aesthetic Senses	34
3. "Expediency can never contend with virtue": Jefferson's Ancient Philosophy Sources	63
4. "The law of nature … cannot be stationary": Jefferson's Curious Immixture of Modern Moralists	95
5. Ethicizing Through Truth and Untruth: The Lessons of History and Useful Fiction	128
6. The Politics of Progress: The Lessons of Government by the Few	145
7. Duty to God and Duty to Man: Jefferson on Religion, Sectarian and Natural	161
8. Government by the Natural *Aristoi:* Education and the Problem of Virtuous Politicians	191
9. The (Stoic) Sage of Monticello: "Truth [as] a branch of morality"	207
Chapter Notes	227
Bibliography	247
Index	255

Preface

Jefferson tells his daughter Martha (11 Dec. 1783) that it is critical always to be prepared for the end of the world or one's death, and the best way to do that is "never to do nor say a bad thing." He adds: "If ever you are about to say any thing amiss or to do any thing wrong, consider before hand. You will feel something within you which will tell you it is wrong and ought not to be said or done: this is your conscience, and be sure to obey it. Our maker has given us all, this faithful internal Monitor, and if you always obey it, you will always be prepared for the end of the world: or for a much more certain event which is death." The letter, in gist Stoical, suggests acceptance of things outside of one's control—*viz.*, the end of the world or the time of one's death—and responsibility of things within one's control—*viz.*, one's thoughts and actions. Each person has been given an "internal Monitor"—a moral sense—and each is responsible for appropriate use of it.

Jefferson's writings on morality and the moral sense are generally ignored by scholars, if only because his thoughts are believed to be unsystematic, inchoate, or confused. There seems to be rough agreement among the few scholars that have written on Jefferson views on morality and the moral sense that he was a Stoic in his youth and became a Utilitarian/Epicurean in mature years. Perusal of his writings and the works he read and recommended to others on ethics shows that that thesis is, at best, strained. Though his thoughts did mature over time, there was never a change of course. Jefferson grew up embracing a Stoicized moral-sense ethics—influenced heavily by contemporaries such as Lord Bolingbroke, A.L.C. Destutt de Tracy, Francis Hutcheson, Lord Kames, and even David Hume and a deterged view later in life of the life and teachings of Jesus—and embraced that view till his death.

This book is the first comprehensive account of Jefferson's ethical views through study of his accounts of the moral sense, morality in general, and human flourishing. Though Jefferson never makes the moral sense the topic of a formal, published treatise, his writings, especially his letters to friends and family members, allow for more than a general sketch of what the moral sense is and how it functions. In addition, they allow us to say much on his views of good living.

The motivation for the book is one of Jefferson's own rules of conduct for right living—"Take things always by their smooth handle"—put into an advisory letter to a young namesake, Thomas Jefferson Smith. The source is doubtless the Roman philosopher and former slave Epictetus, who at *Enchiridion* §43, writes, "Every matter has two handles—one by which it ought to be carried; the other by which it ought not to be carried." Taking hold of the wrong handle when unjustly wronged by your brother, says Epictetus, one forms the false judgment of being unjustly wronged (one grabs the wrong handle) and fails to consider who the wrongdoer is and that he has been brought up with you (the right handle).[1]

The breakdown of the book is as follows. Chapter 1 explicates Jefferson's view of the moral sense through his love letter to Maria Cosway. The second chapter explains what the aesthetic sense is for Jefferson and how it interacts with the moral sense. Chapters 3 and 4 examine the role of ancient and modern ethical thinking on Jefferson's views of morality and are more expository than critical. The fifth chapter is an elaboration of history and "useful" fiction in developing the moral sense. Chapter 6 argues that Jefferson's political views, essentially progressive, are founded on his moral views, essentially progressive. Chapter 7 explains the relationship between religion and morality for Jefferson. The eighth chapter discusses the role of education in shaping a prosperous Jeffersonian republic. The final chapter argues that Jefferson, in spite of expressed discipleship of Epicurus, was by thought and temperament a living Stoic.

One of the most significant discoveries I have made over time—both through reading Jefferson's writings, his own version of the Bible, and the numerous books he collected or recommended on morality and ethics and through noting the persons with whom he interacted intimately and held in highest esteem—is that he had prodigious regard for morality and for personal moral improvement, and utmost respect for moral exemplars. One might even say that his writings indicate an obsession about acting with regard for moral correctness, and he expected others to have similar regard. That is not to say Jefferson never strayed from the virtuous course. Numerous writings, especially during his years as president, suggest otherwise. It is to say, however, that morality for Jefferson was something to be integrated into everyday life, not something to be read to pass the time or because it was chic. According to Jefferson, works like Cicero's *Tusculan Disputations*, Comte de Volney's *Les Ruins*, Tacitus's *Histories*, Lord Kames's *Essays on the Principles of Morality and Natural Religion*, the sermons of Jean Bapiste Massillon, the New Testament, and even novels like Laurence Sterne's *A Sentimental Journey* were to be read, and reread, for personal enrichment and ethical betterment. Persons such as Professors William Small and George Wythe were to be befriended not only on account of their knowledge, but also on account of their virtue. Jefferson was many persons—scientist, politician, diplomat, farmer, and family man, among many other things—but, I argue throughout, he was axially a moralist.

This depiction of Jefferson runs counter to two distinct trends in the historical literature.

First, it runs counter to the notion of Jefferson as rationalist. The emphasis on Jefferson the rationalist occurs in so many sources—especially early twentieth-century sources—that enumeration would be bootless. It is not that Jefferson did not embrace reason. He did. Yet he consistently maintained that reason amounted to nothing if it was not in the service of moral aims. Hence, Jefferson's preference for a practical education—an education suited to the needs of the people—was at once recognition that the people in general could use moral sensitivity to "decide" for themselves what they would need to know.

Second, and more importantly, it runs counter to the notion of Jefferson as immoralist. The emphasis on Jefferson as immoralist—Jefferson as "racist,"[2] "opportunist,"[3] "hypocrite,"[4] "the contradiction,"[5] "monster of self-deception,"[6] "limousine liberal,"[7] a person of "monumental confusion,"[8] and even spiritual founder of the KKK—occurs customarily in today's secondary literature.[9] In my years of study of the man and his writings, I have never, I confess, found Jefferson to be any of such things.

This book has been crafted in large part to rectify the two mistaken depictions of Jefferson. The former, which presupposes that Jefferson was predominantly a rationalist and not a moralist, is a mistake of emphasis, or in moral terms, a peccadillo. The latter, which builds an argument for Jefferson as miscreant by a tendentious use of Jefferson's writings, is a mistake of overreaction, or in moral terms, a peccancy.

Yet to dub Jefferson as moralist is not to return to the saintly Jefferson of hagiographers of the early to mid-twentieth century for whom Jefferson could do no wrong. One can have great regard for morality without being morally immaculate, and Jefferson, like any other person, was morally maculate.

Yet antipodal depictions of Jefferson—e.g., Jefferson the deep-dyed hypocrite and Jefferson the plaster saint—predominate in the secondary literature. Why is there such rife disagreement among scholars? Why does he seem to invoke undue praise or undue condemnation? Why cannot scholars find a middle ground?

Joseph Ellis argues that Jefferson was a man of perplexity and numerous contradictions.[10] Peter Onuf states that scholars' confusion is a result of the inaccessibility of Thomas Jefferson.[11] Such views are shared by numerous other scholars—even the great Jeffersonian scholar Merrill Peterson calls Jefferson a "baffling series of contradictions."[12] Thomas Jefferson, though not a man of contradictions, is a perplexing figure, and his writings, though not inaccessible, are difficult to discern. Such are the weighty obstacles that confront all Jeffersonian scholars and make challenging an understanding the man and his views.

Yet as Peterson notes, it is wrong to situate the confusion in Jefferson. Scholars, he asserts, seem to come to Jefferson through the colored lens of prejudice. There is no lack of information concerning Jefferson. The difficulty concerns scholars' use of knowledge. The image of Jefferson shatters when they arrive "through the doors of partisan, and perhaps hereditary, prejudice to the interpretation of the facts."[13] Jefferson is, in his estimation, a man of "fundamental harmony" and "clarity of purpose." He adds, "The apparent ironies, paradoxes, and contradictions in Jefferson's life and thought, so much dwelled upon by latter-day scholars, [matter] little in the light of this fundamental harmony and clarity of purpose."[14]

Peterson is, I maintain, correct. If we come to Jefferson's writings without our conclusions preformed and if we work studiously over time through his voluminous writings, our discomfiture and befuddlement lessen and the protean Jefferson disappears. The many fuzzy images of Jefferson merge into one clear, or relatively clear, image. That image, I argue, is of Jefferson as moralist.

It is with that in mind that I have written *Thomas Jefferson, Moralist*. Following Epictetus and Jefferson, I maintain that Jeffersonian scholarship too has two handles. Grasping the wrong handle, we begin on assumption that knowing Jefferson is a Byzantine task, which allows for indefinite scholarly plasticity, or we approach Jefferson with judgments preformed and then we seek out evidence from the mass of his writings to confirm our judgments. Grasping the "smooth handle," we begin on assumption that knowing Jefferson is possible, and we confront Jefferson's corpus as a whole and essay to tease out a consistent rendering of the life of the man and of his thinking. The former task is relatively easy and theoretically immune to criticism; the latter is laborious and invites the possibility of considerable scholarly criticism. The latter task, however, is the only one that promises any sort of substantive scholarly return.

Concerning his moral thinking and his thoughts on good living, I have tried to take on Jefferson by grasping the smooth handle. The result, driven by the finding that morality was focal in his life, is a depiction of a morality and a man that are greatly shaped by reading and assimilation of Stoic thinking, and to a lesser extent, the life and teachings of Jesus as well as the thoughts of contemporary Scottish moralists, coetaneous sermonizers, ancient historians, and even moralizing novelists.

Three caveats are in order.

First, I have in the main chosen not to add *sic* to misspellings (e.g., "Kaims" and "vertue"), grammatical infelicities (e.g., failure to begin the first word a sentence with a capital letter as Jefferson often and intentionally does), or linguistic conventions that differed in Jefferson's day (e.g., "it's," "tranquillity," and "traveller"). I merely trust that they will be readily recognizable to readers, once suitably acclimated to Jefferson's writings.

Next, I have adopted the convention here, as in other publications, of labeling Jefferson's epistolary writings by reference only to his correspondent and to the date of the letter, if known, thereby giving readers the opportunity to refer to the edition of Jefferson's writings that is most readily available to them.[15] Non-epistolary writings, in contrast, are fully referenced throughout this book.

Finally, this book is more expository than critical. No one has ever attempted to flesh out Jefferson's moral views in a book-length manuscript, so the task of spelling out fully those views and doing so in relation to his views on the aesthetic sense, politics, education, and religion is no small beer. Moreover, though the secondary literature on Jefferson and morality is sparse, there are, I have found, persistent problems in that literature—e.g., the posits that Jefferson was fundamentally an Epicurean, that Jefferson's moral views changed over time, and that Jefferson was a moral relativist—that demand rectification. It is my hope that the rectification that I offer will withstand the test of time.

1

"The ennui of ... a tedious sermon"

Head versus Heart in a Love Letter to Maria Cosway

> "Let the gloomy monk, sequestered from the world, seek unsocial pleasures in the bottom of his cell! Let the sublimated philosopher grasp visionary happiness while pursuing phantoms dressed in the garb of truth!"
>
> —Jefferson to Maria Cosway

Thomas Jefferson's Head-and-Heart letter to Maria Cosway (12 Oct. 1786) has received considerable attention by scholars, most of whom grasp that the letter is much more than an expression of Jefferson's soul-searching feelings for Cosway at the time of its composition. While Jefferson certainly displays his affection for Cosway in his inimitable tug-of-war manner in the letter, perusal of it indicates that it is a heated philosophical discussion, perhaps even a philosophical debate, between reason and emotion—more narrowly, between reason and the moral sense. What unfortunately is often missed is the extent to which the love letter gives a marrowy, enduring expression of Jefferson's views of issues such as man in the cosmos, what the moral sense is and how it works, and the relationship between the moral sense and reason.

Furthermore, there is considerable scholarly disagreement on key issues. Are Head and Heart really debating? If so, about what are Head and Heart debating? Is the "divided empire" over which each rules an indication that each faculty is master of its own province? If so, are the two constantly warring or is one faculty superior to the other?

In this chapter, I offer a critical analysis of the *billet doux* as a means of making sense of Jefferson's moral sense. Exploring the philosophical implications of the letter and attending on what we learn about the moral sense and its relationship to reason here and in other letters, I show that Jefferson's term "divided empire" is horribly misleading. For Jefferson, reason is always at the beck and call of emotion. The empire of reason is a satellite of morality, as the successes of reason are successes only insofar as they advance the cause of human flourishing.

Intentions Behind the Letter

There is little agreement in the secondary literature concerning Jefferson's intentions in his love letter.

Some scholars are perplexed by the letter.

Dumas Malone finds the dialog enigmatic. "As a love letter this is full of vexing qualifications, and probably it should not be singled out on its own account as literature." Still it offers scholars, he thinks, a depiction of the tormented mind of Jefferson at the time of its writing. "It is not a debate between virtue and vice, but intelligence and the emotions, between reasoned conduct and spontaneity." He adds, "The very arguing of the case made him sound cold-blooded, but the most significant conclusion that emerges from the dialogue is that this highly intellectual man recognized in human life the superior claims of sentiment over reason."[1]

Douglas Wilson admits that the letter is self-revelatory, yet "as to what is revealed, there seems to be no real agreement." One thing seems certain. Jefferson "is trying in this letter to prove to Maria Cosway that he has a heart." By placing his strong feelings on display, he is essaying to remove his veil. Wilson too acknowledges that part of Heart's agenda is to show that moral considerations are not a matter of the head.[2]

Norman Risjord claims that the "ardor of Jefferson's message probably embarrassed and may have frightened the lady."[3]

R.B. Bernstein, calling the dialog "half-flirtatious and half-philosophical," sees a collision of interests.[4]

Alf Mapp, comparing this letter with one to boyhood friend John Page apropos of Jefferson's early interest in Rebecca Burwell (25 Dec. 1762), calls the letters "epistolary threnodies," with the exception of Head's counterpoint in the letter to Cosway. The threnody to Cosway, however, is written with great attention to the belletristic style of the day, without "ostentatious display of linguistic erudition."[5]

Other scholars consider the exchange between Head and Heart to be a sort of debate.

In *American Sphinx*, Joseph Ellis writes that the letter is a labor of love in which Heart triumphs over Head in debate. "Twelve pages and more than four thousand words long, Jefferson labored over the letter with the same intensity he had brought to the Declaration of Independence.... Though the announced intention of the letter is to offer Cosway a problematic picture of the internal battle within Jefferson between reason and emotion, it is a love letter, and therefore the powers of the heart are privileged. The heart has the last word as well as the best lines."[6]

Andrew Burstein in *The Inner Jefferson* gives a robust depiction of the dialog between Head and Heart. He acknowledges, "The Heart is best suited to resolve questions of morality, to do good and produce genuine happiness." He too admits that Heart wins the debate. The pleasures of love outweigh the pains.[7]

Robert Dawidoff calls the letter a conceit. "At the core of this letter, beneath the charming skein of its conceit—whatever Jefferson's real relations with Mrs. Cosway—we see there is no serious way in which even his excited Heart can compete for Jefferson's attention with his Head." For evidence, Dawidoff cites Jefferson's view of literature, which he says Jefferson tended to value little.[8]

Julian Boyd agrees. Yet he maintains that Head gets the better of the exchange, since Head was "a sovereign to whom the heart yielded a ready and full allegiance."[9]

Daryl Hale argues that the dialogical exchange for Jefferson, who "gives equal weight to each side of the argument," is a stalemate. "Jefferson makes a strong case for each side, using the occasion of his new love in his life to provide passionate support for his intellectual grasp of the basic Epicurean positions."[10]

Finally, Lee Quinby maintains that the letter is evidence of an "aesthetics of virtue"—*viz.*, "a fusion of arts and morals" that allows for a "virtuous harmony" between reason and morality.[11]

Thus, the secondary literature is, so to speak, such an *omnium gatherum* of opinions that consensus seems impossible. What is salvageable? Answering that question requires a thorough synopsis of the letter.

Epitome of the Letter

"Having performed the last sad office of handing you into your carriage at the Pavillon de St. Denis, and seen the wheels get actually into motion," Jefferson begins his *billet doux*, "I turned on my heel and walked, more dead than alive, to the opposite door, where my own was awaiting me. Mr. Danquerville was missing. He was sought for, found, and dragged downstairs. We were crammed into the carriage, like recruits for the Bastille, and not having soul enough to give orders to the coachman, he presumed Paris our destination, and drove off." Once back to his Paris residence, he says, "Seated by my fireside, solitary and sad, the following dialogue took place between my Head and my Heart."

The opening scene of the letter depicts a saturnine Jefferson, perhaps slumping before a die-on-the-vine fire. Head begins the dialog in some attempt to alleviate the suffering of Heart, for as the dialog moves forward, it becomes clear quickly that Heart is responsible for its own dejection. "These are the eternal consequence of your warmth and precipitation," says Head. "You confess your follies indeed: but still you hug and cherish them, and no reformation can be hoped, where there is no repentance." From the perspective of Head, it is a matter of floundering in one's suffering or withdrawing from human intimacy. Yet Heart enjoins Head to spare such critical advice. Heart asks for soothing words, not further torments. Head replies, "Harsh therefore as the medicine may be, it is my office to administer it." The suggestion is that it is dwelling on matters of the heart brings more sorrow than joy. Head advises that it is best to steer clear of new friends, especially singular persons, because the pain on parting with them is proportional to their talents and merits.

Heart is unwilling to accept blame, but implicates Head for agreeing to meet with the architects Legrand and Molinos in order see the Halle aux Bleds, with its grand, new-constructed dome. It was there where Jefferson was introduced to the Cosways. "You then, Sir, and not I, have been the cause of the present distress."

Head then discusses the prevarications that Heart contrived to cancel engagements of the rest of the day so as to spend the time with the Cosways. Those contrivances, Heart replies, were well worth the mendacity, for the events of the day, when recalled the next morning, were warm and seemed to be a month's worth. Heart recalls also the trip to St. Germains with the Cosways and the many beautiful things that were observed. "The wheels of time moved on with a rapidity of which those of our carriage gave but a faint idea, and yet in the evening, when one took a retrospect of the day, what a mass of happiness had we travelled over!" From the perspective of Heart, the orectic benefits of intimacy outweigh its sufferings as well as the anesthesia of withdrawal.

Head again reminds Heart that the suffering upon separation is in proportion to the merits and charms of the persons from which one has separated. "But they [the Cosways] told me they would come back again the next year," chimes Heart. The contingencies on which their return rests are so many, replies Head, that "you should abandon the idea of ever seeing them again." Heart retorts recalcitrantly, "May heaven abandon me if I do!"

Ever an optimist, Heart is sanguine about the possibility of their return to Paris and even a trip to America. "I see things wonderfully contrived sometimes to make us happy." There follows a lengthy paean to America—an obvious attempt to lure the Cosways, Maria the artist especially, to Virginia.[12]

Heart continues. The lady, upon seeing the objects of America, will find landscapes of incomparable beauty. There are sights—the falls of Niagara and the Natural Bridge—worth immortalizing through sketch. Heart turns to Jefferson's beloved Monticello. "And our own dear Monticello, where has Nature spread so rich a mantle under the eye? mountains, forests, rocks, rivers. With what majesty do we there ride above the storms! How sublime to look down into the workhouse of nature, to see her clouds, hail, snow, rain, thunder, all fabricated at our feet! And the glorious Sun, when rising as if out of a distant water, just gilding the tops of the mountains, and giving life to all nature!—I hope in god no circumstance may ever make either seek an asylum from grief!"

Heart, bemoaning its "effusion of woes," deviates. "Deeply practiced in the school of affliction, the human heart knows no joy which I have not lost, no sorrow of which I have not drank! Fortune can present no grief of unknown form to me!" He is best prepared to bind up the wound of another who has felt the same would himself. Heart, admitting its deviation, lets Head speak.

Head follows up on Heart's paean to America by noting that the possibility of a visit to America is made less likely by the lies and misrepresentations of London's newspapers. The two agree that America is the most tranquil nation because of the mildness of its laws, easily obeyed. American citizens are self-sufficient and American government is relatively nonintrusive. Travelers are well-received and treated with great hospitality and sacred respect. The energy of citizens is put to use in opening rivers, digging canals, making roads, building schools and academies, honoring great men, fighting for free religious expression, abolishing sanguinary punishments, and revising and bettering extant laws. So ends the paean to America.

Thus far, there are two parts to the letter. First, Head presents Heart with a dilemma: exposure to intimacy and its attendant suffering or withdrawal from intimate affairs as a buffer from suffering. One is inclined here to see Heart mulling over the dilemma. Heart does no mulling. Heart asks for words of reassurance as a kind of analgesic, but never entertains the thought that withdrawal could ever be preferable to involvement. That is a point worth underscoring. Second, there is the paean to America, about which Head and Heart are in complete agreement. About America's virtues, there is nothing to debate.

There follows Head's schoolmasterist "lecture" on investing emotion in objects that must soon be lost. Head's advice is bluntly Epicurean. Move forward by balancing the anticipated pains and pleasures of actions. "This is not a world to live at random in as you do," says Head. "To avoid those eternal distresses, to which you are forever exposing us, you must learn to look forward before you take a step which may interest our peace. Everything in this world is a matter of calculation. Advance then with caution, the balance in your hand. Put into one scale the pleasures which any object may offer; but put fairly into the other the pains which are to follow, & see which preponderates." The advice of deliberation before deed is straightforward enough, but it is worth emphasizing here that the advice is not mere paternalistic intrusion: The sufferings of Heart influence Head—at least through obstruction. When Heart wallows in its lachrymal reminiscences, it is difficult for Head to enjoy its intellectual indulgences.

Head continues its Epicurean peroration. "Do not bite at the bait of pleasure till you know there is no hook beneath it. The art of life is the art of avoiding pain: & he is the best pilot who steers clearest of the rocks & shoals with which he is beset. Pleasure is always before us; but misfortune is at our side: while running after that, this arrests us."

Yet Head advises more than deliberatively balancing pleasures and pains in one's activities. Head advocates withdrawal.

> The most effectual means of being secure against pain is to retire within ourselves, & to suffice for our own happiness. Those, which depend on ourselves, are the only pleasures a wise man will count on: for nothing is ours which another may deprive us of. Hence the inestimable value of intellectual pleasures. Even in our power, always leading us to something new, never cloying, we ride serene & sublime above the concerns of this mortal world, contemplating truth & nature, matter & motion, the laws which bind up their existence, & that eternal being who made & bound them up by those laws. Let this be our employ. Leave the bustle & tumult of society to those who have not talents to occupy themselves without them.

Withdrawal makes sense only on supposition that one cannot live well by balancing pleasures and pains—i.e., there are more pains than pleasures in humans' involvements with each other.

Withdrawal is at the core of Epicurean philosophy, which is essentially a manual for good living through achieving what Epicurus called *ataraxia*—

viz., equanimity. As immersion in social and political affairs is chiefly responsible for unhappiness through instilling and reinforcing the notions that the gods involve themselves in human affairs, that death is something to fear, and that there is no limit to human emotions, the Epicurean remedy for unhappiness is simple: withdrawal from social and political concerns and immersion in the study of Epicurean philosophical principles, aimed at *ataraxia*. Head sums rhetorically, "Is there so little gall poured into our cup that we must needs help to drink that of our neighbor?" There is no need of friends.[13]

Heart replies with a lengthy defense of its way of life, the gist of which is to show that withdrawal from human affairs is pleasure lost. What appears to Head as pain is great pleasure. "What more sublime delight than to mingle tears with one whom the hand of heaven hath smitten! to watch over the bed of sickness, & to beguile it's tedious & it's painful moments! to share our bread with one to whom misfortune has left none! This world abounds indeed with misery: to lighten it's burthen we must divide it with one another." The argument might be cashed out as the argument from commiseration. Roughly:

1. The world abounds with misery.
2. Humans can lighten that misery through helping others.
3. The world is a better place when its misery is reduced.
4. So, humans ought to lighten the misery of others [1–3].

Heart next turns to Head's assumption that the pains of integrative living outbalance the pleasures. "Let us now try the virtues of your mathematical balance, & as you have put into one scale the burthen of friendship, let me put it's comforts into the other." Heart uses Head's illustration of friendship being more of an hindrance than a boon. Here the focus is not helping others in need, but being helped by others when in need.

> When languishing then under disease, how grateful is the solace of our friends! how are we penetrated with their assiduities & attentions! how much are we supported by their encouragements & kind offices! When heaven has taken from us some object of our love, how sweet is it to have a bosom whereon to recline our heads, & into which we may pour the torrent of our tears! Grief, with such a comfort, is almost a luxury! In a life where we are perpetually exposed to want & accident, yours is a wonderful proposition, to insulate ourselves, to retire from all aid, & to wrap ourselves in the mantle of self-sufficiency! For assuredly nobody will care for him who cares for nobody.

The final sentence, parturient, gives birth to the following implicit argument—the argument from withdrawal (brackets indicative of an implicit claim).

1. Nobody will care for one who has only cared for himself.
2. [Those persons who care only for themselves will likely have their day when they can no longer care for themselves.]
3. [So, when the day comes, they will be without the care of others.] (1 & 2).

The argument is meant to show that those persons who withdraw from the company and affection of others might get along capably for most of their life, but if they outlive their capacity to care for themselves, they will assuredly live out wretchedly the remainder of their lives.

Heart has more to say on friendship. "Friendship is precious, not only in the shade but in the sunshine of life; & thanks to a benevolent arrangement of things, the greater part of life is sunshine." Heart offers as proof "the days we have lately passed" with Maria Cosway. Every part of the face of nature appeared gay because of "our charming companion." Heart adds: "They were pleasing, because she seemed pleased. Alone, the scene would have been dull & insipid: the participation of it with her gave it relish."

Withdrawal, Heart asserts, is for the "gloomy monk" and the "sublimated philosopher." Their "supreme wisdom is supreme folly," since they "mistake for happiness the mere absence of pain." Speaking through Heart, Jefferson, who claims to be a disciple of Epicurus many years later,[14] here starkly disavows Epicurean hedonism. "Had they ever felt the solid pleasure of one generous spasm of the heart, they would exchange for it all the frigid speculations of their lives, which you have been vaunting in such elevated terms." It is a "miserable arithmetic" that reckons friendship to be nothing.

Heart follows by stating it has listened to the counsel of Head not because of the substance of its arguments, but out of respect. "Respect for you has induced me to enter into this discussion, & to hear principles uttered which I detest & abjure. Respect for myself now obliges me to recall you into the proper limits of your office."

What follows is the divided-empire passage. "When nature assigned us the same habitation, she gave us over it a divided empire," says Heart. Head's field is science—i.e., knowledge. It functions in such recondite, impractical actions as squaring the circle, tracing the orbit of a comet, and investigating the arch of greatest strength or the solid of least resistance. Heart's field is morality. Controlling the feelings of sympathy, benevolence, gratitude, justice, love, and friendship, it is concerned with the lion's share of human activities. "Morals were too essential to the happiness of man to be risked on the uncertain combinations of the head. She laid their foundation therefore in sentiment, not in science. That she gave to all, as necessary to all: this to a few only, as sufficing with a few." The implication is sufficiently clear: All men are capable of happiness, but few only are capable of science. The suggestion, in keeping with Jefferson's equalitarian sympathies, is that morality, because it is democratic, is a more fundamental and significant discipline than science.[15]

Heart now rebukes Head. "I know indeed that you pretend authority to the sovereign controul of our conduct in all its parts: & a respect for your grave saws & maxims, a desire to do what is right, has sometimes induced me to conform to your counsels." Nonetheless, when following the saws and maxims of Head, Heart is always, or nearly so, misled. Heart illustrates. First, there was the "poor wearied souldier [*sic*] whom we overtook at Chickahomony with his pack on his back." The soldier pleaded to be taken up on the wagon, but Head intervened, and ascertaining that the road was full of soldiers and that to take up every one would kill the horses, it insisted that they bypass the pleading soldier. They did. Heart soon convinced Head that "tho we cannot relieve all the distressed we should relieve as many as we can," and Jefferson turned around the cart to retrieve the soldier, who was not to be found. Second, there was the beggarly slattern in Philadelphia, who asked for money. Head figured her for a drunkard and refused. "Those who want the dispositions to give, easily find reasons why they ought not to give." Again, he sought her out to give her money. When he did, she employed the money toward placing her child at school. Finally, the American Revolution, Heart says, was fought and won only because Americans were led by their hearts, not their heads. Were it a matter of calculating wealth and numbers, there would have been no revolution. Heart boldly dismisses any notion about its answerability to Head in matters of morality. "In short, my friend, as far as my recollection serves me, I do not know that I ever did a good thing on your suggestion, or a dirty one without it. I do forever then disclaim your interference in my province. Fill papers as you please with triangles & squares: try how many ways you can hang & combine them together. I shall never envy nor controul your sublime delights. But leave me to decide when & where friendships are to be contracted."

Heart considers its present situation, where it "feels more fit for death than life" on account of Jefferson's separation from Cosway. There is no rose without thorn and no pleasure without alloy. "It is the law of our existence; & we must acquiesce. It is the condition annexed to all our pleasures, not by us who receive, but by him who gives them." Yet instead of mawkishly wallowing in the thought of separation, Heart finds comfort in the hope of the Cosways' return. "Hope is sweeter than despair."

Heart ends its apologia by imploring Head to stay out of moral matters. Heart after all willingly stays out of matters of Head. Matters of Heart—i.e., moral concerns—are skewed by the intrusions of Head, for morally correct action is impeded by rational calculation.

The dialog between Head and Heart closes. Jefferson apologizes to Cosway for his prolixity—that is, for not having spared Maria the "ennui of such a tedious sermon." He then expresses his love for Maria—"je t'aime"—and concludes politely with a few trite observations and pleasantries.

"A divided empire"

In analyzing the letter, I begin by noting Jefferson's own choice of "dialogue" at the beginning of the exchange between Head and Heart. He does not use "debate," and that is critical. As we have seen, Head's exchanges with Heart are mostly paternalistic and exhortatory, and lead neatly to the view that the exchanges make for a debate. Yet that is merely façade, for Heart is an unwilling debater. Heart simply needs to vent. Heart often seems to lapse into soliloquy, for it often seems of no great consequence whether Head is there to listen or not. The counsel Head continually offers Heart never considers. Head and Heart rule over separate provinces and Head's admonitions are mere intrusions. For the most part, Head is an unsympathetic annoyance, whose utterances to Heart are mostly empty. Heart listens on account of civility.

That said, I turn to three points on the philosophical dimension of the *billet doux*.

First, the love letter tells us much about Jefferson's views of man and the world in which he lives.

In keeping with Aristotle's statement of humans' social essence—"Man is by nature a social animal (*politikon zōon*)"[16]—humans for Jefferson are essentially social creatures. "Man was destined for society," he writes to Peter Carr (10 Aug. 1787). To John Adams (14 Oct. 1816), he says a wise Creator must have seen it necessary for man to live in society. Hence, withdrawal is not an option for peace of mind.

Why, then, does Head advocate withdrawal? Head is steadfast in its belief that human living is fraught with suffering, and withdrawal is the best means of mitigating suffering. Heart, parrying the notion of withdrawal, never disavows the notion that human life is fraught with suffering. "This world abounds indeed with misery," says Heart, "to lighten its burden we must divide it with one another." Heart merely challenges Head's arithmetic. Withdrawal follows only on conclusion that there is more pain than pleasure in living. Head suffers under the delusion that to "share our bread with one to whom misfortune has left none" is itself painful, yet recall that Heart thinks it is "sublime delight" to mingle tears with the misfortunate. Head, having offered counsel in issues about which it is unknowing, has overreached. "Knowing then my determination," says Heart, "attempt not to disturb it."

Taking the position of Heart on moral concerns, Jefferson very likely makes purchase of the view that there is in balance more pleasure than pain in human living, hence there is no need to withdraw from human involvement. We need only to consider Head's confusion about commiserating with those persons in need. That there is more pleasure than pain in living is a point Jefferson also makes to John Adams (8 Apr. 1816), "I think with you, that it is a good world on the whole; that it has been framed on a principle of benevolence, and more pleasure than pain dealt out to us," and that point is iterated almost a decade later in another letter to Adams (18 Dec. 1825).

Jefferson also argues it is morally appropriate to help those in need. It helps to alleviate their suffering, is itself sublime delight, and gives insurance that others will come to one's aid when one is in need.

Second, the love letter tells us much about Jefferson's views of the moral sense and reason.

All persons, Jefferson believes, have a moral sense which functions relatively equally. "That [Nature] gave to all," says Heart, "as necessary to all." The universality of the moral sense is reinforced in other letters. "Our maker has given us all, this faithful internal Moniter," Jefferson writes to his daughter Martha (11 Dec. 1783). "The Creator would indeed have been a bungling artist, had he intended man for a social animal, without planting in him social dispositions," he writes to Thomas Law (13 June 1814). Exceptions exist—some like Napoleon seem to be born without a moral sense[17]—but they are like the exceptions of blindness or deafness—extant, but uncommon.

In contrast, Jefferson thinks few persons have a capacity for heightened rational activity. "This [Nature gave] to a few only," says Heart, "as sufficing with a few."

Next, recall Jefferson states that reason and the moral sense rule over different empires: Head, the field of science; Heart, the field of morals. Elsewhere, Jefferson writes to Peter Carr (10 Aug. 1787): "He who made us would have been a pitiful bungler, if he had made the rules of our moral conduct a matter of science. For one man of science, there are thousands who are not."[18]

Again, and this point attends on the last, when reason essays to calculate moral ends to decide morally correct action, the results are almost always cataclysmal. "In short, my friend, as far as my recollection serves me, I do not know that I ever did a good thing on your suggestion, or a dirty one without it." Deliberation before action to maximize pleasure through avoidance of pain is the gist of Epicurean moral psychology—the position of Head. That is sufficient[19] to disprove the assertion of some scholars that Head represents Stoicism and Heart represents Epicureanism[20] and the statement that the advice of Head is "in Stoic vein."[21]

Third, the love letter has some unobvious implications.

The notion of a divided empire is misrepresentative, since the faculties of reason and the moral sense are not on equal footing. *Pace* Boyd, the moral sense is a faculty superior to rationality. To nephew Peter Carr (19 Aug. 1785), he says: "I can assure you, that the possession of [science] is, what (next to an honest heart) will above all things render you dear to your friends, and give you fame and promotion in your own country.... An honest heart being the first blessing, a knowing head is the second." To John Adams (25 Feb. 1823), he writes, "the moral sense [is] the first excellence of well organised man."[22]

Why is the moral sense superior to reason? That is because the great majority of everyday-life actions answer to the moral sense; only few answer wholly to reason or are adiaphorous (e.g., counting the stars in the nighttime sky or examining the Halle aux Bleds to entertain Head's mathematical sense of proportionality[23]). Perusal of Jefferson's writings with educational content shows a decided preference for practical or heterotelic learning.[24] Why? Such learning is in the service of human betterment—i.e., human happiness—which is a normative or moral end. "Everything is useful which contributes to fix in the principles and practices of virtue,"[25] Jefferson writes to Robert Skipwith (3 Aug. 1771). Thus, purely autotelic rational actions are of questionable worth.

To illustrate the superiority of Heart to Head, let us merely consider again the tasks of reason that Jefferson limns in the letter to Cosway: squaring the circle, tracing the orbit of a comet, and investigating the arch of greatest strength or the solid of least resistance. All are in some sense autotelic, undertaken to slake human curiosity. As David Hume writes, "In the operation of reasoning, the mind does nothing but run over its objects, as they are supposed to stand in reality, without adding any thing to them, or diminishing any thing from them."[26] Nonetheless, some have obvious consequences for human flourishing—e.g., finding the arch of greatest strength—or at least conceivable consequences—e.g., investigating the solid of least resistance—and thus, might have moral implications. Thus, Head again answers to Heart. In contrast, it is difficult to think up "judgments" of Heart that could have implications for Head, other than something like a decision to end one's life.

Subservience and answerability to Heart does not mean that the moral sense is second-order—i.e., that it sits above and superintends on reason. Here the divided-empire analogy *is* aidful. For Jefferson, the moral sense sits beside reason and guides it in the sense of a satellite sitting beside its mother country.

It follows that Jefferson, as a eudemonist of some persuasion, is not a eudemonist in the traditional sense—e.g., Plato, Aristotle, or the Stoics for whom morally correct activity is a function of the rational faculty and for whom rationality is the ruling faculty.[27] For Jefferson, reason is not to intrude directly in the moral domain.

A Dead Lift?

There is an imbroglio. "Men living in different countries, under different circumstances, different habits and regimens, may have different utilities," Jefferson writes to Thomas Law (13 June 1814), "the same act, therefore, may be useful, and consequently virtuous in one country which is injurious and vicious in another differently circumstanced." To John Adams (14 Oct. 1816) two years later he writes:

> The non-existence of justice is not to be inferred from the fact that the same act is deemed virtuous and right in one society, which is held vicious and wrong in another; because as the circumstances and opinions of different societies vary, so the acts which may do them right or wrong must vary also: for virtue does not consist in the act we do, but in the end it is to effect. If it is to effect the happiness of him to whom it is directed, it is virtuous, while in a society under different circumstances and opinions, the same act might produce pain, and would be vicious. The essence of virtue is in doing good to others.

Those passages suggest that morally correct action is a matter of deliberating among alternative possible courses of action and deciding on the course of action that maximizes pleasure and mitigates pain. Moreover, an act might be pleasant, and thus, virtuous in one society, but unpleasant, and thus, vicious in another. That suggests embrace of cultural relativism with an Epicurean (hedonistic) twist.[28] Yet that is entirely contrary to what Jefferson says in his letter to Cosway.

Given that the letters cited above were penned relatively late in Jefferson's life, some scholars have opted for a shift in Jefferson's thinking in his mature years. For instance, Gilbert Chinard maintains that Jefferson was a Stoic early in life, but later "transferred his moral allegiance to Epicurus."[29] Adrianne Koch thinks Jefferson's ethics—a mishmash of Epicureanism, Jesus's precepts, and moral-sense intuitionism—only became salvageable with the late addition of utilitarianism. "Only utilitarianism could be relied on to cut the suggestion of absolutism out of these more single-valued philosophies, making room for that variability of moral judgement which Jefferson's historic sense made him acknowledge as one segment in the development of man in society." Jesus's precepts were plain and universally binding, and therefore, they lacked context-sensitivity. Utilitarianism gave them context-sensitivity.[30] Jean Yarbrough argues that late in life Jefferson recognized that the moral sense was "too weak and diffuse" to ascertain right action in different or complex circumstances. Reason, thus, came to have a more prominent role in moral scenarios.[31] Eugene R. Sheridan posits no change, but merely states that, on account of a purchase of social utility, "the moral standards prescribed by this faculty varied from age to age and culture to culture—a species of relativism Jefferson accepted with equanimity."[32] Johann Neem maintains that Jefferson's 1819 Epicurean letter to William Small shows Jefferson's commitment to Epicurean hedonism, where utility is the standard of morally right action. "Reason was necessary to guide people to their greatest happiness, and to enable them to question authority."[33] Ari Helo too seems to think moral judgments essentially were reason-aided for Jefferson. "All in all, Jefferson's moral sentimentalism was grounded in the idea that natural passions and affections only gradually turn into personal moral sentiments via individual reflection. All moral judgments, in turn, involved active deliberation about the different means of promoting justice and benevolence.... Thus, practical reasoning, or deliberation, seems a crucially important element in Jefferson's virtue ethics."[34]

This sample from the secondary literature shows a considerable degree of confusion, much driven by the letters to Law and Adams, concerning how the moral sense functions in complex social settings. Was Jefferson a moral relativist, an Epicurean, or roughly a modern-day utilitarian? Did his moral thinking evolve substantially or change over time? Did he come to see that reason was crucially involved in moral decision making in complex scenarios?

Yet the scenario is not the dead lift it seems to be. Jefferson began as a Stoic intuitionist and remained loyal to Stoic intuitionism throughout his life. The letters to Law and Adams mark no shift in his thinking and can be grasped by an appropriation of a Stoic orientation[35] to the issue of morally correct action for Jefferson—*viz.*, intention and outcome are mutually entailing, minus any suspicion that rationality factors prominently into moral decisions as is the case with the Stoics, for whom the human soul is monolithically rational. That makes unneeded any postulation that Jefferson moved from an intention-orientation of morally correct action to an outcome-orientation. Thus, the statements—"The answer is that nature has constituted utility to man the standard and test of virtue" (letter to Law) and "Virtue does not consist in the act we do, but in the end it is to effect" (letter to Adams)—are reconcilable with a Stoical Jefferson.

Jefferson avidly read Cicero's moral works and *On Duties*, covered fully in Chapter 3, was one of his favorite Ciceronian treatises.[36] In the work, Cicero discusses the Stoic Panaetius's view that morally correct action (*honestum*) is neither exclusively measured only by consequences (*utilitas*), nor is it exclusively independent of consequences. Virtuous action, rightly grasped, always is expedient, and what is expedient, rightly grasped, always is virtuous. *Dubitandum non est, quin numquam posit utilitas cum honestate contendere,* says Cicero concerning Panaetius's position.[37]

Panaetius considers the following scenario to illustrate the thesis. Consider a good man, selling his house, which looks sound, but suffers structural defects. Does the seller have a moral obligation to inform the potential buyer of the structural defects, if the potential buyer never asks about them? Diogenes the Stoic argues that dissimulation is not dishonesty, for the potential buyer did not ask about the house's structure. Antipater the Stoic argues that dissimulation is dishonesty, for the seller is wittingly selling an inferior product to an unwitting buyer. Panaetius, in agreement with Antipater, sums, "To commit wrong deeds is never expedient (*utile*), because it is always wicked, and it is always expedient to be good, because it is always good for a man to be virtuous (*honestum*)." In sum, what is expedient is always virtuous and what is virtuous is always expedient, and dissimulation is neither expedient nor virtuous. As Jefferson says in a letter to George Logan (12 Nov. 1816), "Virtue and interest are inseparable."

Jefferson never rejected the view that purity of intention in moral judgments was essential. In Summary View of the Rights of British Americans (1774), he lectures King George III on moral governing: "The whole art of government consists in the art of being honest. Only aim to do your duty, and mankind will give you credit where you fail."[38] Years later, he advises nephew Peter Carr (10 Aug. 1787) on deciding for himself matters of religion. "Your own reason is the only oracle given you by heaven, and you are answerable, not for the rightness, but uprightness of the decision." Moral integrity and right intention are more important than outcome. In his "Syllabus," included in a letter to Benjamin Rush (21 Apr. 1803), Jefferson claims that the superiority of Jesus's teaching to that of the Jews or ancient philosophers consists in due regard for intentions. "The precepts of philosophy, & of the Hebrew code, laid hold of actions only. He pushed his scrutinies into the heart of man; erected his tribunal in the region of his thoughts, and purified the waters at the fountain head." In his 1814 letter, cited as evidence by Koch and Yarbrough for an outcome-orientation, to Law, Jefferson states: "Virtue does not consist in the act we do, but *in the end it is to effect* [my italics]. If it is to effect the happiness of him to whom it is directed, it is virtuous." Note the wording is not "in the end," but "in the end it is to effect," which implies intentionality.[39]

Thus, contrary to the views of scholars like Sheridan, Neem, Koch, Yarbrough, and Helo, Jefferson never changed him mind about morally correct action being independent (or mostly so) of rational deliberation. To grandson Thomas Jefferson Randolph (24 Nov. 1808), he writes that moral perplexities are dissolved not by use of reason, but by reflection on what moral cynosures might have done.[40] "Under temptations and difficulties, I would ask myself what would Dr. Small, Mr. Wythe, Peyton Randolph do in this situation? What course in it will insure me their approbation? I am certain that

King George III. In his Summary View on the Rights of British America (1774), Jefferson has the effrontery to castigate the king of England (courtesy Pixabay).

this mode of deciding on my conduct, tended more to correctness than any reasoning powers I possessed. Knowing the even and dignified line they pursued, I could never doubt for a moment which of two courses would be in character for them. Whereas, seeking the same object through a process of moral reasoning, and with the jaundiced eye of youth, I should often have erred."

This reference to moral cynosures to assist or reinforce the judgments of the moral sense shows again the influence of the Stoics, for whom there are no inviolable principles of right actions.[41] To the Rev. James Fishback (27 Sept. 1809), just a few years before his letters to Law and Adams, Jefferson writes, "The practice of morality being necessary for the well-being of society, [deity] has taken care to impress it's precepts so indelibly on our hearts that they shall not be effaced by the subtleties of our brain." Even in the 1814 letter to Law, cited as evidence of a Utilitarian strain, Jefferson says, "How necessary was the care of the Creator in making the moral principle so much a part of our constitution as that no errors of reasoning or of speculation might lead us astray from its observance in practice." Only when the moral sense is wanting in humans, he adds, do "appeals to reason and calculation" help a defective individual behave in conformance with right action. Yet the implication clearly is that such actions in conformance with right action are not right actions, because they are prompted by reason, not sentiment. Thus, there is no reason to believe Jefferson suffered a change of mind on non-rationality of moral judgments of the moral sense. There is no reason to believe Jefferson wavered on the notion that the moral sense worked meticulously and effectively without the input of reason. He never adopted rational calculation as the measure of morally correct action.

To explicate how the moral sense forms judgments independently of reason, it is helpful to note Jefferson makes purchase of two senses of moral progress. First, there is the rather obvious sense of moral progress made by each individual who seeks moral betterment. Second, there is moral progress that the human species makes over time. He writes, for example, to James Madison vis-à-vis the last: "To say in excuse that gratitude is never to enter into the motives of national conduct, is to revive a principle which has been buried for centuries with it's kindred principles of the lawfulness of assassination, poison, perjury, &c. All of these were legitimate principles in the dark ages which intervened between antient & modern civilization, but exploded & held in just horror in the 18th century" (28 Aug. 1789).[42]

When Jefferson writes of the same act being right in one society and wrong in another, he is merely being morally sensitive to differing rates of moral progress in different cultures and not adopting a stance of stultifying moral relativism.[43] Though all persons roughly possess the moral sense to the same degree, inasmuch as all persons possess the organ of sight, not all cultures have refined the moral sense to the same degree—i.e., some cultures are morally retarded. As a student in college, I recall reading of certain tribal people, who, having been exposed to open space after having spent the whole of their lives in a jungle, could not fathom that objects in an open space did not really diminish in size when they moved away from them and increase in size when they moved toward them. Their perceptions were straightforward. They merely lacked knowledge to form the correct judgment of size constancy. It is in some sense the same with the moral sense. Torturing or even killing captives in war is immoral, Jefferson notes,[44] but it was still a common practice of several cultures in Jefferson's day—e.g., certain tribes of American Indians. Hence, there is need for cultural sensitivity when interfacing with members of such tribes. Here reason must come to the aid of the moral sense not to express moral approbation or disapprobation, but to allow for some degree of understanding of that culture's retardation. Express disapprobation in another culture of the practice of torturing or killing prisoners of war is likely to be met with staunch resistance by members of that culture. In such a case, it will be more difficult in the long term to change their scrofulous practices concerning prisoners of war. There is no embrace of treadmill relativism here—relativity as subjectivity. Jefferson was always a diehard progressivist apropos of science, politics, and morality, and progress makes no sense without a substantive notion of advancement toward some end—e.g., in natural science, correct understanding of the laws of the physical universe.[45]

Note here that complexity is not the issue. The moral sense can "decide" right action in a given social scenario with relative ease. Consider Jefferson's illustration of the Revolutionary War. Careful analysis of the circumstances showed the improbability of Americans' success. Still Heart knew that going to war was the right thing to do, hence the war occurred and was sustained, in spite of numerous setbacks or any admonitions of reason. Slavery is another helpful example. The institution of slavery, Jefferson always admitted, was a moral abomination. Yet it was clear to him that pushing for emancipation would have had deleterious results had he pushed for it at the wrong time. It would have torn the nation asunder. Thus, emancipation was the right thing to do, but it was the wrong time to do the right thing. "I can scarcely contemplate a more incalculable evil than the breaking of the union into two or more parts," writes Jefferson to George Washington (23 May 1792). To James Heaton (20 May 1826), shortly before his death, Jefferson writes: "The subject [slavery] of your letter of April 20, is one on which I do not permit myself to express an opinion, but when time, place, and occasion may give it some favorable effect. A good cause is often injured more by ill-timed efforts of its friends than by the arguments of its enemies. Persuasion, perseverance, and patience are the best advocates on questions depending on the will of others." Thus, it is clear that morality sometimes must yield to political expediency—i.e., political expediency must often be factored into moral decisions. In such cases, compromise is needed, and here reason does come to the aid of the moral sense. Otherwise, moral progress in the long term is encumbered.

Reason has other, indirect roles in aiding the moral sense. As with Adam Smith, reason is likely involved in the shaping of general, though not inviolable, moral rules through enumerative induction. For Smith, humans have first perceptions of right and wrong action, based in "immediate sense and feeling," and from those perceptions over time, rules are fashioned. While the rules of prudence, charity, generosity, gratitude, and friendship are "loose and inaccurate," those of jurisprudence are fairly strict.[46] Moreover, given that the moral sense is strengthened with use and weakened with disuse, it is up to reason to see to it that the moral sense is and remains strong so that it can sense morally correct action. Like a limb that is made more dexterous with practice at certain types of activity (e.g., swinging an axe or scythe), in a like manner, right use of the moral sense in varying circumstances makes it more adaptable to other, similar scenarios, and in time, to complex scenarios. Such edification is necessary, especially for the young. That is why Jefferson advocates the reading of the right sort of history, when young. That too is reason's role. Thus, it is reason's role to see to it that the moral sense neither weakens nor loses its "resourcefulness" through desuetude.[47]

Hume v. Kames

Jefferson read both the writings of Lord Kames and David Hume on morality and was influenced much by both—especially Kames. Thus, it is profitable to say something about the moral thinking of each to shed additional light on Jefferson's inchoate thinking.

I have elsewhere used Hume's views of the relationship of reason and moral sentiment to help to illustrate what I take to be the relationship for Jefferson between reason and the moral sense. For both, the moral faculty is much more important for human functioning than reason.[48] Hume thought through the notion of morality, being grounded in sentiment, and proffered a full explanation of the "foundation" of moral judgments. Jefferson never did, and one wishes he would have done so.

In a short essay titled "The Sceptic," David Hume says, "There is nothing, in itself, valuable or despicable, desirable or hateful, beautiful or deformed." Such attributes are a result of "the particular constitution and fabric of human sentiment and affection."[49] When the mind forms judgments of praise or blame, it does so not from qualities that are in the objects, the judgment is of a sentiment of the mind. Vary the fabric of the mind—"and the tempers of mind [are] very different"—and the judgment will vary.[50]

Nonetheless, Hume states that the happiest human life is not the life of pleasure, incapable of being sustained, but a virtuous life—a life that leads to "action and employment, renders us sensible to the social passions, steels the heart against the assaults of fortune, reduces the affections to a just moderation, makes our own thoughts an entertainment to us, and inclines us rather to the pleasures of society and conversation."[51] Still not all humans are suitably disposed to virtue, and the conditions of life, often varying considerably from person to person, are judged favorable or unfavorable by the disposition of mind.

Yet men are not so opportunely formed that they can alter their minds to be happily disposed to changing conditions. It is easier for the wise and thoughtful than for the ignorant and thoughtless, but neither is guaranteed success. "Mankind are almost entirely guided by constitution and temper, and ... general maxims have little influence, but so far as they affect our taste or sentiment."[52] Sciences and the arts can "soften and humanize the temper." So too can education and habit. However, temper refines "insensibly," but it has no "great influence," and the "exhortations and consolations" that are the philosophical vogue are of dubious worth, because they are so often at odds with culture.[53]

Why is philosophy of dubious value? First, if views of living happily are natural and obvious, then philosophy is superfluous. If they are not natural and obvious, they cannot have much influence on the affections.[54] Second, the "air of philosophy," above the winds and clouds, is rarefied and "too fine to breathe in." Thus, "the reflections of philosophy are too subtle and distant to take place in common life, or eradicate any affection."[55] Finally, it is likely that extinguishing vicious passion will also extinguish virtuous passion, thereby rendering a person "totally indifferent and unactive."[56]

In all, "human life is more governed by fortune than by reason; is to be regarded more as a dull pastime than as a serious occupation; and is more influenced by particular humour,[57] than by general principles"[58] which generally incite the vicious passions. Hume glumly sums, "Though virtue be undoubtedly the best choice, when it is attainable; yet such is the disorder and confusion of human affairs, that no perfect or regular distribution of happiness and misery is ever, in this life, to be expected."[59]

In "Of the Standard of Taste," Hume makes the case that the judgments of sentiment, of which morality consist, are in a sense indubitable, "because sentiment has a reference to nothing beyond itself, and is always real," while the "determinations of the understanding are not right," since they answer to real matters of fact, and often fail to conform to that standard. Thus, "a thousand different sentiments, excited by the same object, are all right: Because no sentiment represents what is really in the object." What it marks is conformacy of the object to the sensory organ of reception.[60] Nonetheless, though moral judgments and judgments of taste are not grounded in the objects themselves, "it must be allowed, that there are certain qualities in objects, which are fitted by nature to produce those particular feelings."[61]

Hume has us consider Sancho Panza from Cervantes's *Don Quixote*. Sancho speaks of two kinsmen, each of whom professes to have good judgment of wines. Each is asked to judge the wine of a hogshead. Both give a favorable verdict. One says there is a slight taste of leather; the other, a slight taste of iron. Both are ridiculed until, when the hogshead is emptied, there is found at its bottom a key with a leather thong affixed to it.[62] The instance has its lesson. Though it is best to say that in deciding that a person is wise, the wisdom is in our mind and not in the person, there is something in the person that elicits the verdict. Ethical judgments are not inevasibly subjective. Ethics is not an uncultivatable subject.

Hume's take on moral judgments is much richer than Jefferson's, as it answers to a well-thought-out epistemology. Why did Jefferson not adopt a Humean stance?

First, it must be acknowledged that Jefferson was no Hume. That goes a long way toward answering the question.

There is more to say, however. Each had a different take on reason. For both, reason was limited in its application and of use to not all, but merely a few, persons. "The more principle any person possesses, the more apt is he, on such occasions, to neglect and abandon his domestic duties."[63] Still, for Hume, though benevolent human actions were spontaneous, reason was needed in forming full moral judgments concerning matters of justice and fidelity, for moral praise, even though a matter of the heart, was driven by the "usefulness of any quality or action."[64] For Jefferson, as we have seen, moral judgments were immediate. Moreover, reason's employment in science for Jefferson was invaluable; for Hume, science was a discipline of limited worth.

For Hume, scientific reasoning answers to matters of fact and the "thousand different opinions which different men may entertain of the same subject" have only one answer.[65] Hume, however, gives little reason to believe that human efforts will ever disclose that answer. Humans might "avow a certain criterion in science and deny it in sentiment, the matter is found in practice to be much more hard to ascertain in the former case than in the latter." He adds: "Theories of abstract philosophy, systems of profound theology, have prevailed during one age: In a successive period, these have been universally exploded: Their absurdity has been detected: Other theories and systems have supplied their place, which again gave place to their successors: And nothing has been experienced more liable to the revolutions of chance and fashion than these pretended decisions of science."[66] In contrast, judgments of art and morality "maintain an universal, undisputed empire over the minds of men," as they appeal to sentiments relatively unchanged.[67] While the judgments of the arts and morality are relatively sustainable over time, the theories of philosophers and religionists are ever in flux. Thus, reason is mostly unavailing.

For Jefferson, though he acknowledges that few persons have the capacity for science, science is truth-engendering and critical to his experiment of republican governing. "Science is more important in a republican than in any other government," he states to a correspondent unknown (28 Sept. 1821). "And in an infant country like ours we must depend for improvement on the science of other countries, longer established, possessing better means, and more advanced than we are." It held the promise of solving the riddles of the cosmos. More importantly, it held the promise of easing the burden of human living.[68]

Yet concerning moral assessment, Jefferson went more in a Kamesian direction than a Humean direction, as both Kames and Jefferson made purchase of the progress and value of science and of morality. Moreover, both stated that morality was not merely rooted in sentiment, as did Hume, but in a sensory faculty—the moral sense. Lord Kames's *Essays on the Principles of Morality and Natural Religion*, published anonymously in 1751 and revised in 1758 and 1779, is a blow-by-blow reply to the stultifying skepticism of David Hume.

The way out of the metaphysical labyrinth of Humean skepticism is to disregard reason[69] and follow a method "entirely suited to the nature of man": intuitive perception. Intuitive perception is "the faculty of perception, working silently, and without effort"—*viz.*, a sort of immediate grasp of some truth or conveniency[70] that is guided by sensory data. By intuitive perception, not reason, we come immediately to see our moral duties, our continued identical existence over time, the self-existence and benevolence of deity, and the uniformity and causal framework of the cosmos.[71] Intuitive perception, it seems, makes mince-meat of all the meaty philosophical issues.

Men are by nature disposed to have affection for some emotions and aversion to others. At birth, affection and aversion relate only to self-love or self-preservation.[72] As they mature, men develop a sense of other-regard. "Nature, which designed us for society, has linked us together in an intimate manner, by the sympathetic principle, which communicates the joys and sorrow of one to many." Mutual sympathy, he says Stoically, is the "great cement of human society," as misfortune abounds and sympathy greatly excites the security and happiness of mankind.[73]

Sympathy occurs because of humans' moral sense, which functions intimately with aesthetic appreciation. Objects of perception are naturally deemed beautiful or ugly, or neither. Perception of beauty—e.g., seeing some object fitted to some use or related to some end—gives pleasure and is *approbation*. The perception of ugliness—e.g., seeing a beautiful-looking object that is ill-suited for its end—gives pain and is *disapprobation*. There is also beauty and ugliness of actions that relate to intention, deliberation, and choice. Some are "*fit, right,* and *meet* to be done"; others "*unfit, unmeet, and wrong* to be done." Fitness applies to the means; rightness to the end; and meetness to the intention of the agent. Those perceptions are simple—i.e., incapable of definition. Hence, there are moral beauty and moral deformity, and the "power or faculty by which we perceive this difference among actions, passeth under the name of the *moral sense.*"[74]

The moral sense is not a principle of human action, as are passions, but a "guide and director"—"the voice of God within us which commands our strictest obedience." A second mover, it naturally regulates our appetites and passions by approving or disapproving human actions. It is an instinctual or appetitive faculty, not a rational faculty, though it is not entirely independent of reason.[75]

The moral sense is a natural and not an artificial faculty.[76] It was with humans even in the brutish, pre-social state of nature, unpropitious for moral refinement. The state of nature engendered men's fears, not their virtues. The security provided by regular society expunged men's fears and the social virtues, through fit use of the moral sense, developed. "Their defect … lies in the weakness of their general principles of action … directed upon objects too complex for savages readily to comprehend." Mired in their perception of particular objects and in selfish passions, savages cannot easily forge general, complex ideas like that of the public good, usefulness to others, and love of country. Yet desuetude of the moral sense is remediable by enculturation, especially education.[77]

Thus, improvements in social settings toward sympathetic interactions allow for moral progress in the species of men, a sentiment consonant with many Enlightenment thinkers. "The law of nature, which is the law of our nature, cannot be stationary. It must vary with the nature of man, and consequently refine gradually as human nature refines." And so, practices given the consent of the moral sense centuries ago, like putting to death an enemy in cold blood or fighting with poisonous weapons, are presently condemned as vicious acts.[78]

Fit, right, and meet actions are virtuous, and there are primary and secondary virtues. The primary virtues—e.g., justice (restraint from harming others and keeping promises and covenants) chief among them—are essential for the subsistence of society and more universal. "Entirely withdrawn from our election and choice," we are duty-bound and indispensably obliged to follow them. Transgression of primary virtues is attended by "severe and never-failing punishment" and pain, while obedience conduces to lesser pleasure.[79] The secondary virtues—e.g., generosity, heroism, benevolence, friendship, and mildness of manners—contribute to the improvement of society, but are not necessary for social stability. They are within our choice and we have no duty in the strictest sense to follow them.[80] Failure to act in accordance with secondary virtues effects no guilt. Though not the first in order of utility, the secondary virtues are "objects of the strongest perceptions of moral beauty" and excite greatest praise.[81] Circumstances, however, do intervene. One has no duty strictly speaking to be benevolent to make another happy, yet one might be morally moved to be benevolent to relieve another from distress.[82]

What of will? In his essay "Liberty and Necessity," Kames addresses the issue of free will, which is incongruent with the strict determinism of the Newtonian physical world. He distinguishes between the material world, where all things proceed in a fixed and unalterable train of causes and effects, and the moral world, where man, guided by will and choice, determines his own path.[83] The two worlds are reconcilable, because liberty, rightly grasped, is reconcilable with necessity. Humans recognize, upon examination, that every action, however arbitrary, is determined by a motive, which in many instances could have been otherwise. Every person, indecisive in a course of action, eventually acts pursuant to his strongest motive, whether rational or passionate in nature. Thus, though we act by will and choice, motive determines will and will determines choice.[84]

Motives are fixed, not free, for every motive is rooted in desire. We desire some end and then act to bring about that end. Still desire is not our own—"not under our own power." Thus, "if our desires are not under our own power, neither can our actions be under our power."[85]

Yet "liberty ... if it have any meaning, must signify a power to act in contradiction to desire; ... a power to act in contradiction to any view, purpose, or design, we can have in acting." Such a conception, though, is absurd. Humans act not according to liberty, but according to moral necessity. They will and choose what they desire, though desire is not up to them.[86]

What of the strong sense of contingency apparent in human actions? Deity, Kames states, formed humans not that they could readily grasp the nature of things *per se*, but that their impressions and the notions of them are of utmost use. The senses are not so much for "discovery of the intimate nature and essences of things," but more for "the uses and conveniences of life." Humans perceive color in objects, but learn that color is not a property of objects, but of light. They believe the precise moment of their death is unfixed, though it is strictly determined. Hence, "contingency in this view may justly be considered as a secondary quality, which hath no real existence in things; but, like other secondary qualities, is made to appear as an attribute of events, in order to serve the purposes of human life." He adds, "To make way ... for the sense of contingency, the necessary connection betwixt desire and will is kept out of sight; and by this contrivance it is, that we are not sensible of being necessary agents." Consequently, liberty and necessity are reconciled. Though humans are determined animals, they perceive themselves to be free.[87] Deity, thus, thought it best to be so.

It is unquestionable that Jefferson's notion of the working of the moral sense, in general sketch, owed much to Kames. Jefferson's notion of the relative infallibility of moral judgments owes much to Kames's notion of intuitive perception. Nonetheless, it seems unlikely that Jefferson made purchase of intuitive perception to solve with legerdemain all the thorny metaphysical matters to which Kames puts it to use—such as the nature of mind and life after death—since Jefferson shows a preference for the writings of Locke, Tracy, and Steward on such Byzantine issues.[88] Furthermore, Jefferson gives no evidence of every having thought through the necessity/free-will argument as did Kames. His disrelish in varied writings of key tenets of Calvinism—e.g., trinitarianism, divine foreordination and predestination, and the unlawfulness of reason[89]—and Kames's express embrace of Calvinism in an appendix to "Liberty and Necessity"[90] show that Jefferson probably would have found Kames's reconciliation of liberty with necessity unacceptable, though such a view would have fit neatly with Jefferson's own materialist cosmology, deity among the material entities, and his acceptance of a divine hand in the advance of human moral affairs over time.

Such things conceded, it is not clear that Jefferson had anything to gain by rooting morality in a moral sense instead of human sentiment. As Adam Smith writes, there is no need to posit any additional, heretofore unknown sensory faculty to explain moral actions. "Nature ... acts here, as in all other cases, with the strictest oeconomy, and produces a multitude of effects from one and the same cause; and sympathy, a power which has always been taken notice of, and with which the mind is manifestly endowed, is ... sufficient to account for all the effects ascribed to this peculiar faculty."[91]

Afterword

Before sending off his love letter, Jefferson adds to it another letter, dated one day later (13 Oct. 1786). In this letter, he acknowledges receipt of a missive, just received from Cosway, comprising four meager lines. "In fine after reading a little and examining the signature, alternately, half a dozen times, I found that your name was to four lines only instead of four pages. I thank you for the four lines however because they prove you think of me. Little indeed, but better a little than none." He then bids Cosway to read his lengthy *billet doux* in six doses over six days.

Cosway answers Jefferson on October 30. She admits to being overwhelmed and bewildered. "How I wish I could answer the dialogue!" she begins. Her earliest lines, written in English, are discursive. "I did not know what I was doing, I should like to write it over again [in Italian]," she concedes. She also concedes a certain sense of inferiority, which might be a way of the coquette distancing herself from Jefferson. "Oh, Sir, if my correspondence equaled yours how perfect it would be!" She admits to transgressing Jefferson's injunction and reading his love letter in one dose. Though acknowledging that she could consider every word for an hour and that she could write a volume in reply to every sentence, nothing she writes offers a suspicion that she grasps anything of the philosophical significance of Jefferson love letter. Moreover, she seems somewhat oblivious to Jefferson's amour. Her mind soon turns away from Jefferson's letter, and she writes of her voyage home, the weather, her health, the "fog and smoke" of London, and the sadness of Londoners, among other things.

Jefferson does not write again till November 19. The passion and prolixity are gone. Writing now with his maimed right hand[92]—perhaps significant of his pain on realization of unrequited love—he adds, "You are saved by a cruel cramp in my hand which admonishes me in every line to condense my thoughts and words." The pain soon causes him to end his letter, or so he says. "Mercy, cramp! That twitch was too much. I am done, I am done." One senses lack of passion for writing Cosway—the depletion of a beaten man. He did, after all, write the entire Head-and-Heart letter with his unmaimed left hand.

On November 29, Jefferson writes: "When I pass the same moments in review, I recollect nothing but the agreeable passages, and they fill me with regret. Thus, present joys are damped by a consciousness that they are passing from us; and past ones are only the subjects of sorrow and regret." He asks Cosway whether she will ever come again and then adds: "I dread the answer to this question, and that my poor heart has been duped by the fondness of its wishes. What a triumph for the head!" The admonitions of Head, to which Heart turned a deaf ear in his letter of October 12, now peal loudly in Jefferson's joyless heart. Jefferson, in this brief letter, allows Epicurus a momentary triumph over the Stoics.

2

"Art appears too much"
Jefferson and the Moral and Aesthetic Senses

> "Those despotic governments, which are founded on the passions of men, and principally upon the passion of fear, keep their chief as much as may be from the public eye."
> —Edmund Burke, *The Sublime and the Beautiful*

Aesthetic sensibility is a topic about which Jefferson says scarcely anything in any systematic way. There is so little from which to draw in his writings that to forge an account would be tantamount to working from surmise. Nonetheless, to overpass the aesthetic sense entirely would leave a gap in Jefferson's thinking on the interworking of the moral sense, reason, and the aesthetic sense, so we must do what we can, through appeal to his writings as well as appeal to other authors, to whom he refers and who have written on the aesthetic sense, to try to offer a plausible account of the aesthetic sense and how it functions.

In this chapter, I begin with a particular problem for aesthetic sensibility for Jefferson: the paradox of aesthetic cultivation. I next turn to exposition of three works on aesthetics, recommended by Jefferson to Robert Skipwith in 1771—William Hogarth's *The Analysis of Beauty*, Edmund Burke's *On the Beautiful and the Sublime*, and Lord Kames's *The Elements of Criticism*. I then attempt a reconstruction of Jefferson's view of "the beautiful" and "the sublime" through analysis of his use of the terms and their cognates in his writings. I end with some thoughts on the role both of aesthetic sensibility as it relates to a life well lived for Jefferson and of the likely influence of Hogarth, Burke, and Kames on Jefferson's view of aesthetic sensibility.

Paradox of Aesthetic Cultivation

Jefferson, evidenced by his bills on educational reform over the years, wished to change the American educational system by instantiating local reforms in keeping with his participatory republicanism. It is clear that such local reforms were meant, at least early on, to be a blueprint for a system of progressive education for all states, wishing to be model Jeffersonian republics.

Jefferson writes to John Banister (15 Oct. 1785) of the many disadvantages—"to enumerate them all, would require a volume"—of sending an American youth to be educated oversees. Being educated in Europe—and here his description of European dissipation is chiefly a description of the degeneracy observed in France, the country with which he had greatest familiarity—he acquires fondness of luxury and its resultant dissipation and "contempt for the simplicity of his own country." He becomes fascinated by the privileges of the aristocracy and comes to despise the "lovely equality" the poor and rich enjoy in America. He forms foreign friendships of no use and loses that "season of life" for forming faithful and lasting friendships in his own country. "Fidelity to the marriage bed" comes to seen as something ungentlemanly, and thus, he is led into a "spirit for female intrigue," conducive to unhappiness for all, or a "passion for whores," conducive to unhealth. He recalls with excitement the "voluptuary dress and arts of European women" and "pities and despises the chaste affections and simplicity" of America. Upon returning to America, he is no longer an American. Jefferson sums, "An American coming to Europe for education, loses in his knowledge, in his morals, in his health, in his habit, and in his happiness."

Yet there are plusses to a European education. In Rome, for instance, a scholar will grow from living in a "spot so classical and celebrated," learn the true pronunciation of Latin, gain familiarity with "objects and processes of agriculture," live in a healthy climate, and acquire a "just taste in the fine arts, more particularly those of painting, sculpture, architecture, and music." That point he iterates to Charles Bellini and George Wythe. He writes to Bellini (30 Sept. 1785): "Were I to proceed to tell you how much I enjoy [European] architecture, sculpture, painting, music, I should want words. It is in these arts they shine." While traveling through southern France and northern Italy, he observes to Wythe (16 Sept. 1787), "In architecture, painting, sculpture, I found much amusement."

Nonetheless, appreciation for European art does not show a desire to imitate Europeans. Jefferson makes it clear that his vision for assimilation of the arts for America is a welding together of what is beautiful with what is practical—hence, his interest in gardens and architecture in preference to painting and sculpture.[1] In his "Travel Journals," he writes of a tour of the gardens of England and continually carps on the excessive luxury of many gardens—"too much art" and many "useless" garnishments.[2] In "Travelling Notes for Mr. Rutledge and Mr. Shippen," Jefferson lists agriculture, mechanical arts, lighter mechanical arts and manufactures, gardens, and architecture ahead of painting and statuary. He advises study of European gardens, with the proviso that in America we shall "cut out the superabundant plants." He especially advises attention to architecture—"it is among the most important arts"—because of rapid American populational growth, the American tendency to build with perishable materials, and the need to "introduce taste into an art which shows so much." He states that painting and statuary are "too expensive for the state of wealth among us." He adds: "It would be useless … and preposterous, for us to make ourselves connoisseurs in those arts. They are worth seeing, but not studying."[3] To James Madison (20 Sept. 1785), Jefferson complains of the lack of taste in American architecture. "How is a taste in this beautiful art to be formed in our countrymen, unless we avail ourselves of every occasion when public buildings are to be erected, of presenting to them models for their study and imitation?" In all such instances, Jefferson's focus is on useful beauty. America is not to be a plushy or lavish country.

What is so undesirable about extravagance? Jefferson's concern is that aesthetic overindulgence will work against his republican political reforms and moral aims.[4] Aesthetic indulgence—too much art and too many useless items—is a luxury in which only the wealthy can indulge, and when doing so, they do so at the expense of the unwealthy, which are the majority. Jefferson's political reforms, in keeping with his moral aims, are targeted at an equitable distribution of wealth that does not privilege the wellborn or the progeny of the wealthy. His aim is to allow for a rough equality of opportunity, where virtue and talent, not wealth and good birth, will rise.

The notion that aesthetic indulgence works against republican government is a sentiment which might be dubbed the paradox of aesthetic cultivation and was shared by many American's of republican bent. "The more elegance," wrote John Adams to his wife, "the less virtue, in all times and countries." Though the arts were capable of refining taste and enhancing understanding, they could also, if overdone or done badly, "seduce, betray, deceive, deprave, corrupt, and debauch."[5] In short, over-cultivation of aesthetic sensibility can readily lead to political instability and moral obliquity. Over-cultivation was also indicative of superfluous wealth and luxury, and thus was, in keeping with the four-stage theory of social maturation accepted during the time, symptomatic of social decay.[6] Yet because Jefferson says so little on the aesthetic sense, it is best first to turn to the work of others Jefferson read and recommended before expatiating on the paradox.

Three Critical Works on the Fine Arts

In a 1771 letter to friend Robert Skipwith (Aug. 3), Jefferson replies to a request from his friend to recommend a catalog of books to accommodate a modest expenditure of money. Jefferson finds the task of framing a library in pursuance of a limited expenditure to be impossible. Instead he recommends "such a general collection as I think you would wish and might in time find convenient to procure." Under "Criticism on the Fine Arts," he lists three influential works of the day: Lord Kames's *Elements of Criticism*, William Hogarth's *Analysis of Beauty*, and Edmund Burke's *On the Beautiful and the Sublime*. In the next few sections, I offer a précis of each. In each, we find in keeping with the sentiment of the time, a fairly tight conjunction between aesthetic sensibility and moral sensibility. Analysis of such works will help to tease out Jefferson's own views of aesthetic sensibility.

William Hogarth: The "line of beauty"

William Hogarth's *The Analysis of Beauty* (1753) begins, "For though beauty is seen and confessed by all, yet, from the many fruitless attempts to account for the cause of its being so, enquiries on this head have almost been given up; and the subject generally thought to be a matter of too high and too delicate a nature to admit of any true or intelligible discussion."[7] The reason for the confusion, it seems, is that all expositions of beauty have been highbrow, when the subject admits of simpler explication. Men of letters, on the "more beaten path of moral beauty," have been "continually discoursing of effects instead of developing causes." Having assumed that beauty can be apprehended through sculpture alone, they have ignored the art of painting.[8]

Hogarth quotes a passage from a work by Gian Paolo Lamozzo vis-à-vis a certain discovery of Michelangelo. "*Michael Angelo* upon a time gave this observation to the Painter *Marcus de Sciena* his scholler; *that he should alwaies make a figure Pyramidall, Serpentlike, and multiplied by one, two and three. In which precept (in mine opinion) the whole mysterie of the arte consisteth." The greatest grace and life of a picture comes through its expression of motion and no form expresses motion so well as fire—the most active of all material elements. Fire "hath a *Conus* or sharpe pointe wherewith it seemeth to divide the aire, that so it may ascende to his proper sphere ... [and] a picture having this forme will bee most beautifull."[9] Winding lines, then, and pyramidal figures are the keys to beauty. He refers to the picture on his frontispiece of his book, a serpentine line within a glassine pyramid lying on a painter's pallet, with these words under it: the "Line of Beauty."[10] He adds, "There is scarce an Egyptian, Greek, or Roman deity, but hath a twisted serpent, twisted cornucopia, or some symbol winding in this manner to accompany it."[11]

Overall, the project Hogarth proposes is a sort of democratization of the appreciation and understanding of beauty and grace. Aesthetic sensibility is not just for the elite—those practiced in the arts. "The more prevailing the notion may be, that painters and connoisseurs are the only competent judges of things of this sort; the more it becomes necessary to clear up and confirm ... that no one may be deterred, by the want of such previous knowledge, from entering into this enquiry."[12] The principles of beauty and grace, like the principles of bodily motion, are in nature and discoverable by all persons, not merely men of letters. That is a "democratic" point that Jefferson doubtless found appealing.

Hogarth writes of a certain conceit. In its simplest illustration, he asks readers to imagine a sphere that emanates from a point, which can be assumed as the eye, from which "an infinite number of straight rays of equal lengths, issuing from the center, as from the eye, spreading every way alike." The ends of each line are "circumscribed or wound about at their other extremities with close connected circular threads, or lines, forming a true spherical shell." In such a manner, we are to imagine all other, non-spherical objects.[13] Employment of such a conceit enables observers to "obtain the true and full idea of what is called the *out-lines* of a figure." "In the example of the sphere given above, every one of the imaginary circular threads has a right to be considered as an out-line of the sphere, as well as those which divide the half, that is seen, from that which is not seen; and if the eye be supposed to move regularly round it, these threads will each of them as regularly succeed one another in the office of out-lines, (in the narrow and limited sense of the word:) and the instant any one of these threads, during this motion of the eye, comes into sight on one side, its opposite thread is lost, and disappears on the other." Thus, observers must get into the habit of considering every object "as if his eye were placed in it."[14]

There are six fundamental principles, Hogarth continues, by which elegance and beauty are to be judged. They are fitness, variety, uniformity, simplicity, intricacy, and quantity—"*all which co-operate in the production of beauty, mutually correcting and restraining each other occasionally.*"[15]

Fitness concerns bulk and propriety, and it is duly exemplified by considering the size and proportion of tables, chairs, other items of furniture, and utensils. The size of a building in a work of art determines, thus, the size of its windows, window seats, steps of stairs, and doors.[16] Yet fitness has more than just formal features. Like Aristotle's *eidos* (the form of an object), fitness concerns not only shape, but also function. "In nature's machines, how wonderfully do we see beauty and use go hand in hand!" Nature has made beauty of proportion and beauty of movement "necessary to each other."[17]

Hogarth introduces variety by appealing to nature. "The shapes and colours of plants, flowers, leaves, the paintings in butterflies wings, shells, etc., seem of little other intended use, than that of entertaining they eye with the pleasure of variety." Variety is to be balanced by sameness, for a glut of the one or the other is repugnant to the eyes and ears. Moreover, variety must be a composed variety, "for variety uncomposed, and without design, is confusion and deformity." Aesthetically pleasing instances of variety are "a gradual lessening," in the instances of pyramids and in the front of a ship, going out to sea, and becoming smaller by degrees from its rear.[18]

Uniformity, the third element, is believed by many to be the key principle of beauty, yet if that were so, then the greater the uniformity a work of art in relation to its object, the greater the pleasure of the eye. Yet aesthetic pleasure is not in strict proportion to uniformity. Hence, uniformity is not the chief principle of beauty. Uniformity, however, answers to fitness. "Whence it is clear, the pleasure does not arise from seeing the exact resemblance, which one side bears the other, but from the knowledge that they do so on account of fitness, with design, and for use." The head of a fine woman is most graceful, when it is turned a little to the side and reclined somewhat, not when there is exact similarity of the two halves of the face.[19]

The fourth element is simplicity. "Simplicity, without variety, is wholly insipid," Hogarth begins. With variety, it easily pleases. "There is no object composed of straight lines, that has so much variety, with so few parts, as the pyramid: and it is its constantly varying from its base gradually upwards in every situation of the eye, (without giving the idea of sameness, as the eye moves round it) that has made it been esteemed in all ages, in preference to the cone, which in all views appears nearly the same, being varied only by light and shade."[20] The sculpture Laocoon and his Sons, attributed to three Rhodian artists, is a work that exemplifies pyramidal design insofar as the piece readily admits a pyramidal casing as a cover. Odd numbers, replete in nature, are simpler than even numbers, and they exemplify variety more than uniformity.[21]

Intricacy, the fifth element, Hogarth introduces as a sort of spice of life. Difficulties give a spring to the mind, enhance pleasure, and take what would otherwise have been toilsome and laborious and make it sporting and recreational. Love of pursuit, an illustration of intricacy, is implanted in the nature of men. He says, "Intricacy of form, therefore, I shall define to be that peculiarity in the lines, which compose it, that *leads the eye a wanton kind of chace*, and from the pleasure it gives the mind, intitles it to the name of beautiful." Thus, there arises people's love of sport. Intricacy, next to variety, is the most immediate cause of grace. Hogarth exemplifies by stating his pleasure as a youth in watching a certain graceful woman at a country dance. The "windings of the figure" were "bewitching to the sight," and his "imaginary ray ... was dancing with her all the time," and the eye was willy-nilly in a kind of chase.[22]

Finally, there is quantity, which is bedfellow of the sublime. Hogarth explicates by appeals to illustrations. "Huge shapeless rocks have a pleasing kind of horror in them, the wide ocean awes us with its vast contents." Yet when beauty is present in quantity, "horror is softened into reverence." Elephants and whales "please us with their unwieldy greatness." So too do large personages, and deficiencies of figure can often be overcome by largeness. Quantity adds greatness to grace, but excesses are to be avoided, as "quantity will become clumsy, heavy, or ridiculous."[23] He illustrates excess by a face of a fat man, who wears a child's cap and a child's clothing under his chin. Such lack of appropriateness invites laughter. One could imagine Hogarth's impression of Chaplin's tramp—a small and thin man, wallowing in large baggy pants and shoes too big and, with cane, having an air of dignity while wallowing in poverty. Hogarth illustrates the fundamental principles throughout the remainder of the book, chapters 6 through 17, by expatiation on lines; pleasing forms; compositions with the waving line, the "line of beauty," and the serpentine line, the "line of grace"—"the two lines are the lines most varied in form, and they contribute most to producing beauty"—proportion, light and shade; composition (light, shade, and colors); coloring; the human face; human attitude; and human action.

Edmund Burke: "Ideas of a very different nature"

Edmund Burke's *A Philosophical Enquiry into the Origin of Our Ideas of the Sublime and Beautiful* (1756) is an excursion into the origins of the ideas of the sublime and the beautiful. Burke's analysis is descriptive, not normative. He writes nothing of how beauty or the sublime are to be cultivated, as they are mere qualities that act mechanically through the senses on the mind. The account, in modern terms, is strictly physiological.

Burke begins by noting the general confusion in distinguishing "the beautiful" and "the sublime." The remedy of such defects requires a "diligent examination of our passions in our own breasts [and] a careful survey of the properties of things which we find by experience to influence those passions and a sober and attentive investigation of the laws of nature by which those properties are capable of affecting the body and thus of exciting our passions."[24] The remainder of the book is an attempt to disambiguate sublimity and beauty.

There are two main groups of passions: the self-preservative and the social passions.

First, "the passions which concern self-preservation," Burke writes, "turn mostly on pain or danger. "Whatever is fitted in any sort to excite the ideas of pain, and danger, that is to say, whatever is in any sort terrible, or is conversant about terrible objects, or operates in a manner analogous to terror, is a source of the *sublime*."[25] Since self-preservative passions, the strongest of all passions, turn on pain and danger, "they are simply painful when their causes immediately affect us," but "delightful when we have an idea of pain and danger, without being actually in such circumstances." Such delight is not pleasure, because it turns on pain, and it is the source of the sublime.[26]

Second, there are social passions, which are of two sorts. There is "the society of the *sexes*," for the sake of propagation, and there is "the more *general society*," which men share with themselves, with other animals, and even with the inanimate world.[27]

Sexual pleasure, e.g., lust or love for the sake of propagation, is "of a lively character, rapturous and violent, and confessedly the highest pleasure of sense." Intense while felt, the absence of sexual pleasure is scarcely felt—the exception being the imaginary pains of the scorned lover. Thus, the pleasure here is positive, while the pain is not.[28]

The passions of general society comprise love and more general social passions. Love, as the "*beauty* of the *sex*," is a mixed passion. "Men are carried to the sex in general ... and by the common law of nature." Love attracts people to others and even to other animals that "inspire us with sentiments of tenderness and affection." Of the more general social passions, Burke writes, "Good company, lively conversations, and the endearments of friendship, fill the mind with great pleasure." While a temporary solitude is agreeable, a wholly solitary lifestyle is inconsistent with the aim of living, and "the total and perpetual exclusion from all society, is as great a positive pain as can almost be conceived."[29]

The more general social passions are sympathy, imitation, and ambition. The three together allow for moral improvement, and thus require fuller treatment.

Sympathy occurs when "we are put into the place of another man, and affected in a good measure as he is affected." When pain is shared, it can be a source of the sublime; when pleasure is shared, it can be a source of beauty, as in the cases of poetry, painting, and other affecting arts. Objects which shock are commonly seen as pleasant. "Our delight in cases of this kind, is very greatly heightened, if the sufferer be some excellent person who sinks under an unworthy fortune." Why? Terror always produces delight when it is not so close, and pity is pleasant when it arises from love and social affection.[30]

While sympathy is shared feeling, imitation "prompts us to copy whatever they do," and imitation incites pleasure, without reason. Therein lies the power of poetry and painting, which are essentially imitative arts. "When the object represented in poetry or painting is such as we could have no desire of seeing in reality; then I may be sure that it's power in poetry or painting is owing to the power of imitation, and to no cause operating in the thing itself."[31]

Imitation alone makes impossible improvement of the human condition. Thus, deity has implanted in men "a satisfaction arising from the contemplation of his excelling his fellows in something deemed valuable amongst them."[32] That satisfaction is ambition.

Burke then distinguishes between the sublime and the beautiful in an exposition that certainly influenced Jefferson.

"The sublime," Burke says, "is an idea belonging to self-preservation." It is the strongest passion and conducive of no positive pleasure, only positive pain.[33] Acting through terror or fear, the sublime "robs the mind of all its powers of acting and reasoning." Its characteristics are obscurity, which disenables us to sense true extent of danger, and that is why night and despotic governments frighten; privation (vacuity, darkness, solitude, and silence); vastitude; infinity as a sort of vastitude; succession and uniformity qua artificial infinite; magnitude qua infinity; difficulty, as in the building of Stonehenge; magnificence; light as a cause productive of color and darkness; sad and fuscous colors, such as black, brown, or deep purple; loud sounds, such as thunder or artillery; suddenness; low tremulous intermitting; animal cries, as they are instinctively grasped by us; tastes and smells, such bitters and stenches; and any feeling of great pain.[34]

The sublime, Burke states, is connected to fear, which is physically "an unnatural tension of the nerves" and mentally "an apprehension of pain or death." Fear, productive of terror, is "always the cause of the sublime." He writes, "If a certain mode of pain is of such a nature as to act upon the eye or the ear, as they are the most delicate organs, it approaches more nearly to that which has a mental cause." The pain and terror are mollified so that they produce, neither pleasure nor terror, but a "sort of delightful horror, a sort of tranquility tinged with terror; which as it belongs to self-preservation is one of the strongest of all the passions."[35]

"By beauty," begins Burke, "I mean, that quality or those qualities in bodies by which they cause love, or some passion familiar to it." Beauty, arises in us just as heat and cold do when hot or cold objects are present. Doubtless following Hogarth, it is not to be found in proportion, fitness, perfection, or in the virtues. Beauty is not in proportion, as roses, acknowledged to be beautiful, are large flowers in proportion to their shrub, while orange blossoms are small in proportion to their tree, yet just as beautiful.[36] Beauty is not in fitness, as "if beauty in our own species, was annexed to use, men would be much more lovely than women; and strength and utility would be considered as the only utilities."[37] Beauty is not in perfection, as the greatest beauty in women "always carries with it an idea of weakness and imperfection."[38] Finally, beauty is not to be found in virtue, as the stronger virtues—e.g., fortitude, justice, and wisdom—produce terror, and thus, are linked with the sublime, while the "softer virtues"—e.g., amiability, compassion, kindness, and liberality—"impress us with a sense of loveliness," but are "of less immediate and momentous concern to society."[39]

Burke turns to the nature of beauty. "Beauty is, for the greater part, some merely sensible quality, acting mechanically upon the human mind by the intervention of the senses."[40] Beauty is characterized by smallness; smoothness; gradual variation; delicacy; and clean, fair, mild, and diversified colors.[41]

Burke ends with a contrast of the sublime ("the great") and the beautiful.

> For sublime objects are vast in their dimensions, beautiful ones comparatively small; beauty should be smooth, and polished; the great, rugged and negligent; beauty should shun the right line, yet deviate from it insensibly; the great in many cases loves the right line, and when it deviates, it often makes a strong deviation; beauty should not be obscure; the great ought to be dark and gloomy; beauty should be light and delicate; the great ought to be solid, and even massive. They are indeed ideas of a very different nature, one being founded on pain, the other on pleasure; and however they may vary afterwards from the direct nature of their causes, yet these causes keep up an eternal distinction between them, a distinction never to be forgotten by any whose business it is to affect the passions.[42]

Overall, there is a clear link between aesthetic appreciation and morality for Burke. The sublime, causing terror, is linked with, though not reducible to, the stronger virtues; the beautiful, causing a sense of loveliness, is linked with, though not reducible to, the softer virtues. Thus, we are, in today's language, hard-wired such that aesthetic appreciation works in some measure to promote morally correct action and discourage vice.

Lord Kames: "An additional motive to virtue"

Lord Kames (a.k.a. Henry Home) begins *The Elements of Criticism* (1762) with an account of aesthetical pleasures. The pleasures of the ear and eye, Kames says, rise above those of the other senses, but do not rival intellectual pleasures. "Their mixt nature and middle place between organic and intellectual pleasures, qualify them to associate with both: beauty heightens all the organic feelings, as well as the intellectual: harmony, though it aspires to inflame devotion, disdains not to improve the relish of a banquet."[43] He continues, "The pleasures of the eye and the ear, … sweet and moderately exhilarating, … are in their tone equally distant from the turbulence of passion, and the languor of indolence; and by that tone are perfectly well qualified, not only to revive the spirits when sunk by sensual gratification, but also to relax them when overstrained in any violent pursuit." Aesthetic pleasures, then, are a sort of middle: They allow for reprieve of the turbulence of organic passion as well as the languor of indolence.

They are also a sort of middle to organic pleasures and intellectual pleasures. Organic pleasures are by nature transitory, and artificial attempts to extend such pleasures results in "satiety and disgust." Here the pleasures of the eye and ear are ideally suited to "restore a proper tone of mind." Intellectual pleasures, though not transitory, can too be overstrained. Overuse of intellectual powers overstrains the mind from which cessation offers no quick relief. The spirits need gentle relaxation, and organic pleasures, which relish only while the spirits are in vigor, are poorly suited for that task, while the fine pleasures of the eye and ear are ideally suited.[44]

Kames then waxes genealogically. Humans' first attachments are to external objects, hence organic pleasures are humans' first pleasures. As the mind ripens, it comes to relish increasingly the pleasures of the eye and ear. Such pleasures, almost entirely mental, do not exhaust the body, as do sensual exertions. "The author of nature, by qualifying the human mind for a succession of enjoyments from low to high, leads it by gentle steps from the most groveling corporeal pleasures, for which only it is fitted in the beginning of life, to those refined and sublime pleasures that are suited to its maturity."[45] There is no natural necessity in the enjoyment of aesthetical pleasures as there is with organic pleasures. Deity merely has made humans of such a nature that they are capable of enjoying the pleasures of the eye and ear, if they so choose.[46]

The key to aesthetical refinement is enculturation. "We stand ... to second the purposes of nature, by cultivating the pleasures of the eye and ear, those especially that require extraordinary culture, such as arise from poetry, painting, sculpture, music, gardening, and architecture." He adds: "A taste for these arts is a plant that grows naturally in many soils; but, without culture, scarce to perfection in any soil: it is susceptible of much refinement; and is, by proper care, greatly improved."[47]

What is said of taste is applicable neatly as well to the moral sense. "A taste in the fine arts goes hand in hand with the moral sense, to which indeed it is nearly allied: both of them discover what is right and what is wrong: fashion, temper, and education, have an influence to vitiate both, or to preserve them pure and untainted: neither of them are arbitrary nor local; being rooted in human nature, and governed by principles common to all men."[48] Thus, through cultivation, aesthetic enjoyment finds a link with morally correct action. The transition from "corporeal pleasures" to "the more refined sensual pleasures" and then to the "exalted pleasures of morality and religion" is "sweet and easy."[49]

We sense at once a difficulty. Enculturation is essential for aesthetical refinement, and all persons are capable of aesthetical refinement. However, enculturation seems possible only for the opulent, for the resources of wealth and leisure are critical for aesthetical refinement. What is true of aesthetical refinement seems true as well for moral sensitivity. So, contrary to Hogarth, only the coarsest pleasures—the organic pleasures—are accessible to the *hoi polloi*.

Aesthetic appreciation is rationally grounded. There are "genuine principles of the fine arts," and disclosure of such principles is the first step toward aesthetic refinement. "Hence a foundation for reasoning upon the taste of any individual, and for passing sentence upon it: where it is conformable to principles, we can pronounce with certainty that it is correct; otherwise, that it is incorrect, and perhaps whimsical. Thus the fine arts, like morals, become a rational science; and, like morals, may be cultivated to a high degree of refinement."[50]

Refinement takes us to the art of criticism, which thrived in Jefferson's day. The critic "must pierce still deeper" than one merely interested in aesthetic refinement, for his perception of the lofty and low, the proper or improper, and the manly and unmanly, among other things must be perspicacious.

Kames adds, "To those who deal in criticism as a regular science, governed by just principles and giving scope to judgement as well as to fancy, the fine arts are a favourite entertainment; and in old age maintain that relish which they produce in the morning of life."[51] The critic, thus, is one with the most refined aesthetic sense.

Thus, the science of rational criticism moderates the selfish passions "by sweetening and harmonizing the temper." With temper harmonized, a youth will forefend such bathetic and vacuous pursuits such as hunting, gaming, and drinking—such things that Jefferson himself came to disavow early in manhood. In full maturity, a man is not tempted by ambition, pride, or envy. In old age, a man eschews avarice. With the selfish passions moderated through taste, one "delights in the virtuous dispositions and actions of others," and neglects their faults and failings. One void of taste, in contrast, is inclined to all such passions, envy and pride especially, that the temperate avoid.[52]

Moreover, rational criticism improves the heart by invigorating the social affections. Delicacy of taste, Kames writes, heightens human feelings not only of pain and pleasure, but also of human sympathy—"the capital branch of every social passion." Sympathy allows for communication of joys, sorrows, hopes, and fears. "Such exercise, soothing and satisfactory in itself, is necessarily productive of mutual good-will and affection."[53] Thus, aesthetic appreciation inclines persons to morally correct action.

Moreover, cultivation of what is beautiful, proper, elegant, and ornamental fixes persons to moral duty.

> No occupation attaches a man more to his duty, than that of cultivating a taste in the fine arts: a just relish of what is beautiful, proper, elegant, and ornamental, in writing or painting, in architecture or gardening, is a fine preparation for the same just relish of these qualities in character and behaviour. To the man who has acquired a taste so acute and accomplished, every action wrong or improper must be highly disgustful: if, in any instance, the overbearing power of passion sway him from his duty, he returns to it with redoubled resolution never to be swayed a second time: he has now an additional motive to virtue, a conviction derived from experience, that happiness depends on regularity and order, and that disregard to justice or propriety never fails to be punished with shame and remorse.[54]

The argument therein contained—the just-relish argument—might be fleshed out as follows:

1. To a man who has acquired an acute and accomplished taste of what is beautiful, proper, elegant, and ornamental in, for instance, writing, painting, architecture, or gardening, every action improper must be highly disgustful.

2. So, such a man has an additional, experience-driven motive to virtue—*viz.*, the notion that happiness depends on regularity and order and that disregard to justice or propriety never fails to be punished with shame and remorse [1].
3. So, a just relish of what is beautiful, proper, elegant, and ornamental in the fine arts is a fine preparation for the same just relish of the qualities in character and behavior [2].

Acquiring a taste for doing what is right, a person flees from authority, the monitor of "Rude ages," and answers to his own internal monitor, rationally grounded and "in agreement with human nature," of what is right and what is wrong.[55] Rational criticism moderates selfish passions. It invigorates social passions. Taste for what is beautiful, proper, elegant, and ornamental in painting, writing, gardening, or architecture helps to fix one to morally correct action by engendering notice of such qualities in right action. Repugnance of the opposite qualities in such arts fixes similarly repugnance of vice.

Jefferson on Aesthetic Sensibility

Jefferson and the Beautiful

Since Jefferson never makes "beauty" the focus of any writing. The closest he comes is a brief discussion of beauty in a letter to Thomas Law (13 June 1814), in which he says that beauty cannot be a branch of morality, as it "is founded in a different faculty." He continues: "We have indeed an innate sense of what we call beautiful: but that is exercised chiefly on subjects addressed to the fancy, whether thro' the eye, in visible forms, as landscape, animal figure, dress drapery, architecture, the composition of colours &c. or to the imagination directly, as imagery, style, or measure in prose or poetry, or whatever else constitutes the domain of criticism or taste, a faculty entirely distinct from the moral one."

So, we are told that the aesthetic sense is "entirely distinct" from the moral sense, but as with Kames that does not mean that the two distinct faculties do not often work intimately together in moral "judgments." And so, the best we can do to grasp Jefferson's meaning of the term is analyze his usage of the term and its derivatives in his writings and see if there is consistency of usage and if that usage conforms to the aestheticians he recommends to Skipwith. Analysis of other writings shows that smallness, variety, and economy are three defining subcategories.

First, there is smallness. In an address to the Virginia House of Delegates,

Jefferson says that the beauty of statuary consists in its minutiae and that requires that statues be of a certain size. "As far as I have seen, the smaller [statues] are, the more agreeable.... A statue is not made, like a mountain, to be seen at a great distance. To perceive those minuter circumstances which constitute its *beauty* you must be near it, and, in that case, it should be so little above the size of the life, as to appear actually of that size from your point of view."[56] Moreover, he tells dear friend George Wythe (13 Aug. 1786), "The *beauty* of a motto is to condense much matter in as few words as possible." In both instances, smallness allows for economy of expression. To Madame de Tessé (8 Dec. 1813), Jefferson describes a "snowberry bush," whose beauty consists in its smallness and a mild prolificity of small, white berries. "I have growing, which I destine for you, a very handsome little shrub of the size of a currant bush. Its *beauty* consists in a great produce of berries of the size of currants, and literally as white as snow, which remain on the bush through the winter, after its leaves have fallen, and make it an object as singular as it is beautiful."

A second key feature of beauty, in keeping with Hogarth, is variety. In an address on the capital, Jefferson objects to the notion that all houses on a given street are to be built the same distance from it. "I doubt much whether the obligation to build the houses at a given distance from the street, contributes to its *beauty*. It produces a disgusting monotony."[57] To Charles Thomson (9 Jan. 1816), Jefferson writes of non-uniformity of thought as beautiful. "It is a singular anxiety which some people have that we should all think alike. Would the world be more *beautiful* were all our faces alike? Were our tempers, our talents, our tastes, our forms, our wishes, aversions and pursuits cast exactly in the same mould? If no varieties existed in the animal, vegetable or mineral creation, but all move strictly uniform, catholic & orthodox, what a world of physical and moral monotony it would be!" To his daughter Martha (31 May 1791), Jefferson states that Lake George is, without exception, "the most *beautiful* water." Thirty-five miles long and two to four miles broad, it is nestled in a contour of mountains and finely interspersed with islands. The water is limpid and crystal, and contains "an abundance of speckled trout, salmon trout, bass, and other fish." The mountains at its side are teeming with "rich groves of thuja, silver fir, white pine, aspen, and paper birch down to the water-edge." He adds, "Here and there precipices of rock to checker the scene and save it from monotony." The passage indicates purchase of variety as well as tranquility, purity, and mild and accommodating prolificity—accommodating the fish and not the trees because, Jefferson adds, the abundancy of fish offer sport to man.

2. "Art appears too much"

A third key feature of beauty for Jefferson is economy. Jefferson, to Edward Rutledge (18 July 1788), writes of the American Revolution empowering the people to correct governmental abuses. "We can surely boast of having set the world a *beautiful* example of a government reformed by reason alone without bloodshed."" The revolution, he adds, marks improvement in government toward what is economical. In a letter to James Thompson (18 Aug. 1814), Jefferson lauds Janes's improved loom, "the most *beautiful* machine I have ever seen"—beautiful, because economical. To Charles Thomson (11 Nov. 1784), Jefferson writes of new cylindrical lamps, giving off the light of "six to eight candles" and using olive oil. "They are a *beautiful* discovery and very useful.... The convenience of lighting a candle without getting out of bed, sealing letters without calling a servant, of kindling a fire without flint, steel, punk, &c., are of value." To Peregrine Fitzhugh (23 Feb. 1798), Jefferson writes analogically of the equilibrium upon which the Constitution is built as beautiful. "In time all these [ward, county, and state governments] as well as their central [national] government, like the planets revolving round their common sun, acting & acted upon according to their respective weights & distances, will produce that *beautiful* equilibrium on which our Constitution is founded, and which I believe it will exhibit to the world in a degree of perfection, unexampled but in the planetary system itself. The enlightened statesman, therefore, will endeavor to preserve the weight and influence of every part, as too much given to any member of it would destroy the general equilibrium." Here the general economy of the system is represented, if only ideally, as a general equilibrium. Finally, to Charles Thomson (9 Jan. 1816), Jefferson says of his "fountain of pure morals," *The Philosophy of Jesus* (c. 1804)—a "paradigma" of Jesus's teachings made by excision of the unreasonable and supernatural from the New Testament: "A more *beautiful* or precious morsel of ethics I have never seen." The idea in all such instances is similar to Hogarth's notion of fitness. It would have been difficult for Jefferson, given his disposition toward economy, not to link beauty and fitness.

Jefferson also refers to "beauty" or "beautiful" in *Notes on the State of Virginia*. In Query II, he calls the Ohio River "the most beautiful river on earth." He adds, "Its current gentle, waters clear, and bosom smooth and unbroken by rocks and rapids, a single instance only excepted."[58]

In Query XIV, Jefferson limns the physical features of Blacks in manner that today would be considered racist. Concerning skin color, he says: "Is it not the foundation of a greater or less share of *beauty* in the two races? Are not the fine mixtures of red and white, the expressions of every passion by greater or less suffusions of colour in the one, preferable to that eternal monotony, which reigns in the countenances, that immovable veil of black which covers all the emotions of the other race?"[59] Blacks also lack the beautiful flowing hair of non-blacks. The influence of Hogarth and Burke is apparent. Recall Hogarth's assessment that white, "nearest to light," is most beautiful, whereas all colors "absolutely lose their beauty by degrees as they approach nearer to black," which represents darkness. Burke states darkness is more sublime than light and productive of terror.[60] "Black will always have something melancholy in it, because the sensory will always find the change to it from other colours too violent; or if it occupy the whole compass of the fight, it will then be darkness and what was said of darkness, will be applicable here." Concerning hair, Hogarth states, "The most amiable [form] in itself is the flowing curl; and the many waving and contrasted turns of naturally intermingling locks ravish the eye with the pleasure of the pursuit, especially when they are put in motion by a gentle breeze."[61]

Jefferson and the Sublime

Apropos of natural phenomena, in Query IV of *Notes on the State of Virginia*, Jefferson writes of the magnificence of the passage of the Potomac River through the Blue Ridge Mountains. Here he illustrates best his distinction between the beautiful and the sublime. I quote *en bloc* this extraordinary, spellbinding passage.

> The passage of the Patowmac through the Blue ridge is perhaps one of the most stupendous scenes in nature. You stand on a very high point of land. On your right comes up the Shenandoah, having ranged along the foot of the mountain an hundred miles to seek a vent. On your left approaches the Patowmac, in quest of a passage also. In the moment of their junction they rush together against the mountain, rend it asunder, and pass off to the sea. The first glance of this scene hurries our senses into the opinion that this earth has been created in time, that the mountains were formed first, that the rivers began to flow afterwards, that in this place particularly they have been dammed up by the Blue ridge of mountains, and have formed an ocean which filled the whole valley; that continuing to rise they have at length broken over at this spot, and have torn the mountain down from its summit to its base. The piles of rock on each hand, but particularly on the Shenandoah, the evident marks of their disrupture and avulsion from their beds by the most powerful agents of nature, corroborate the impression. But the distant finishing which nature has given to the picture, is of a very different character. It is a true contrast to the foreground. It is as placid and delightful as that is wild and tremendous. For the mountain being cloven asunder, she presents to your eye, through the cleft, a small catch of smooth blue horizon, at an infinite distance in the plain country, inviting you, as it were, from the riot and tumult roaring around, to pass through the breach and participate of the calm below. Here the eye ultimately composes itself; and that way too the road happens actually to lead.[62]

The sublime is the first-glance impression, which occurs involuntarily. The senses, overwhelmed, are forced to conclude the earth was forged in time—first, the mountains, and then, the rivers. The mountains initially constrained the rivers so an "ocean," which flooded the entire valley, was formed. The rise of the ocean tore down the mountain "from its summit to its base," and the waters broke free, as evidenced from the piles of rocks on each hand—"the evident marks of their disrupture and avulsion from their beds by the most powerful agents of nature." The description features "ocean" (vastness); "disrupture" and "avulsion" (forced separation and tearing away); "most powerful" (power in superlative form); "wild," "riot," "tumult," and "roaring" (untamable ferocity); "tremendous" (awesomeness, massiveness, and frightfulness), "infinite" (unbound by time); "foreground" (immediacy of impression); and "height" (exaltedness).

The beautiful is the distant-finishing impression, which comes once a viewer has ceased to be overwhelmed. One gathers oneself and sees that what is wild and tremendous is also placid and delightful. Through the cleft in the mountain, there is a "small catch of smooth blue horizon" that literally sucks in a viewer and invites him to participate visually in the calm-below-the-storm impressions on high. This description features "background" (here implied), "placid" (peacefulness), "delightful" (enjoyableness), "small," "smooth," "blue" (tranquil color), "plain" (contrasts with tumult, etc.), "participate" (suggesting habitability), "calm," "below" (accessibility to humans), and "composes" (restoration of ocular fitness). Note also that the breach takes one away from the exalted riotousness of nature and to a man-made road, presumably leading from riotousness to tranquility—i.e., nature tamed.

In Query V, Jefferson introduces readers to another extraordinary passage. Again I quote *en bloc*.

> The Natural bridge, the most sublime of Nature's works, though not comprehended under the present head, must not be pretermitted. It is on the ascent of a hill, which seems to have been cloven through its length by some great convulsion. The fissure, just at the bridge, is, by some admeasurements, 270 feet deep, by others only 205. It is about 45 feet wide at the bottom and 90 feet at the top; this of course determines the length of the bridge, and its height from the water. Its breadth in the middle is about 60 feet, but more at the ends, and the thickness of the mass at the summit of the arch, about 40 feet. A part of this thickness is constituted by a coat of earth, which gives growth to many large trees. The residue, with the hill on both sides, is one solid rock of limestone. The arch approaches the Semi-elliptical form; but the larger axis of the ellipsis, which would be the cord of the arch, is many times longer than the transverse.[63]

Though Jefferson begins mildly, with the descriptive dispassion of a geologist, dispassion quickly dissolves. The sublime enters. He continues.

"Though the sides of this bridge are provided in some parts with a parapet of fixed rocks, yet few men have resolution to walk to them, and look over into the abyss. You involuntarily fall on your hands and feet, creep to the parapet, and peep over it. Looking down from this height about a minute, gave me a violent head ach." The three sentences express panic, which exacerbates as he continues to recollect. Each successive sentence is shorter than the one before it. Words cannot capture his fear. The recollection itself might be bringing on another "head ach." The sublime is disobliging, unaccommodating. Jefferson quickly leaves the subject.

Deserting what is "painful and intolerable," Jefferson turns to a tamer, more obliging and accommodating notion—recollection of the beautiful "below" the sublime.

> If the view from the top be painful and intolerable, that from below is delightful in an equal extreme. It is impossible for the emotions arising from the sublime to be felt beyond what they are here; so beautiful an arch, so elevated, so light, and springing as it were up to heaven, the rapturer of the spectator is really indescribable! The fissure continuing narrow, deep, and streight for a considerable distance above and below the bridge, opens a short but very pleasing view of the North mountain on one side, and the Blue ridge on the other, at the distance each of them of about five miles. This bridge is in the county of Rockbridge, to which it has given name, and affords a public and commodious passage over a valley which cannot be crossed elsewhere for a considerable distance. The stream passing under it is called Cedar creek. It is a water of James river, and sufficient in the driest seasons to turn a grist mill, though its fountain is not more than two miles above.[64]

Jefferson writes similarly of the sublime, as we have seen in Chapter 1, in his love letter to Maria Cosway (12 Oct. 1786). Here he essays to entice his beloved to visit America. American landscapes are especially inviting to brilliant artists such as her. "She wants only subjects worthy of immortality to render her pencil immortal." Jefferson cites the Falling Spring, Niagara Falls, the passage of the Potomac through the Blue Mountains, and of course his own Natural Bridge. He then turns to Monticello. "And our own dear Monticello, where has nature spread so rich a mantle under the eye? mountains, forests, rocks, rivers. With what majesty do we there ride above the storms! How sublime to look down into the workhouse of nature, to see her clouds, hail, snow, rain, thunder, all fabricated at our feet! and the glorious sun when rising as if out of a distant water, just gilding the tops of the mountains, & giving life to all nature!"

Moreover, Monticello is an Epicurean retreat from the bustle of human society. Such lofty retirement allows for pursuit of intellectual pleasures, befitting deities and noble humans. "Ever in our power, always leading us to something new, never cloying, [through contemplation] we ride serene &

sublime above the concerns of this mortal world, contemplating truth & nature, matter & motion, the laws which bind up their existence, & that eternal being who made & bound them up by those laws. Let this be our employ. Leave the bustle & tumult of society to those who have not talents to occupy themselves without them." The description invites, with some hubris, a comparison with Mount Olympus, abode of the Olympian deities. Monticello affords persons a deiform perch from which Nature itself is no longer threatening.

The first two passages are in keeping with Burke's "sublime" as something to be feared or threatening, but Jefferson's letter to Cosway is different. The beautiful seems to have soft-pedaled or tamed the sublime. Jefferson, in love with Cosway at the time, perhaps employs a divine conception of the sublime—i.e., the sublime qua beautiful—to entice Cosway to come to America and join the skyward abode of the gods at Monticello.

Jefferson's view of what is sublime in nature is ultimately not quite Burkean. The sublime in nature is often fearsome, but not always fearsome. Moreover, howsoever fearsome it might seem to be, it is always compliant—i.e., it never forbids human appropriation, so long as appropriation is not exploitation. Nature—in its roughest, wildest, and most magnificent guises—never disallows human intervention. Instead it invites human intervention, though its sublimity enjoins human ingenuity and respect. However forbidding the land might be in its heights or depths, its hotness or coldness, its ruggedness or softness, or its wetness or dryness, one can always throw a Cartesian grid over it and work the land to accommodate human needs in pursuance of the capacities of the land.[65] Hilly lands can be planed for improved farming; dry lands can be moistened through irrigation; heat can be mitigated by foliage; and so on. The numerous innovations and inventions in the science of his day—e.g., innovations for agriculture (threshing machines, improved mold boards for plowing, drill plows, and seed boxes for seeding evenly), travel (hot-air balloons, submarines, and odometers), and manufacture (steam power and carding and spinning machines)—were proof that nature was compliant, if man was innovative.

Concerning the fine arts, the Burkean notion of fear or dread is inessential.

First, there is the sublime in poetry. To Charles McPherson (25 Feb. 1773), brother of the James McPherson, Jefferson says of the ancient Gaelic poet Ossian's epics (most likely a sham creation of James McPherson)[66]: "The tender and the *sublime* emotions of the mind were never before so wrought up by the human hand. I am not ashamed to own that I think this rude bard of the north the greatest poet that has ever existed." The contrast of "sublime" with "tender," clearly is a contrast of "sublime" and "beauty," and the sense of "sublime" here is, given the epithet "rude" is roughness—perhaps even violence. Decades later, he writes to John D. Burke (21 June 1801) of his lack of appreciation for the muse of poets. "As age and cares advanced the powers of fancy have declined. Every year seems to have plucked a feather from her wings till she can no longer waft one to those *sublime* heights to which it is necessary to accompany the poet. So much has my relish for poetry deserted me that at present I cannot read even Virgil with pleasure."[67]

Second, there is the sublime in oratory. In Query XIV of *Notes on the State of Virginia*, Jefferson writes of the sublimity of the oratory of Native Americans. "They astonish you with strokes of the most *sublime* oratory; such as prove their reason and sentiment strong, their imagination glowing and elevated."[68] Reason and sentiment, each strong, are masculine. Imagination, glowing and elevated, is healthy (i.e., vast) and godlike. Moreover, Jefferson writes of the "*sublime* eloquence" of Patrick Henry's orations. Jefferson says to William Wirt (12 Apr. 1812). "[Henry's] imagination was copious, poetical, *sublime*, but vague also. He said the strongest things in the finest language, but without logic, without arrangement, desultorily." To James Monroe (8 Jan. 1825), he writes of Henry's "impressive and sublime" eloquence in a descriptively accurate, but pejorative manner. The so-called eloquence of Henry, "a man of very little knowledge of any sort," was "impressive and sublime." He continues:

> Although it was difficult when he had spoken to tell what he had said, yet, while he was speaking, it always seemed directly to the point. When he had spoken in opposition to my opinion, had produced a great effect, and I myself been [*sic*] highly delighted and moved, I have asked myself when he ceased: "What the devil has he said?" I could never answer the inquiry. His person was of full size, and his manner and voice free and manly. His utterance neither very fast nor very slow. His speeches generally short, from a quarter to a half an hour. His pronunciation was vulgar and vicious, but it was forgotten while he was speaking.

The sublime here is comparable to the sublime in nature. Henry has an oratorical style that is rough and barbaric (vulgar and vicious pronunciation), but powerful and persuasive (great in effect, full in size, breviloquent, and free and manly in manner and voice). The effect of being overwhelmed by Henry's speaking is immediate, non-volitional. Yet once one gets beyond the immediate impression of awe through skill in presenting,[69] one recognizes that the presentation is excerebrose. The words are vacuous; there is no beauty beneath the sublime, as there always seems to be in nature. Thus, Henry's sublimity is mere frontage.

Third, there is the sublime in writing. To grandson Francis Eppes (19 Jan. 1825), Jefferson, upon request, contrasts the writing styles of Thomas Paine and Lord Bolingbroke. "These two persons differed remarkably in the style of their writing, each leaving a model of what is most perfect in both extremes of the simple [Paine] and the *sublime [Bolingbroke]*." The comparison is in neither case pejorative and suggests the contrast of plainness and directness with loftiness.

Fourth, there is also the sublime in architecture. To Dr. James Currie (18 Jan. 1786), Jefferson writes of his designs for Virginia's State Capitol building.[70] "They are simple & *sublime*, more cannot be said, they are not the brat of a whimsical conception never before brought to light, but copied from the most precious, the most perfect model of antient architecture remaining on earth; one which has received the approbation of near 2000 years, and which is sufficiently remarkable to have been visited by all travellers." The sentiment here is reverence through approximation to human perfection.

Fifth and most significantly, there is the sublime in morality. Jefferson writes to Dr. Joseph Priestley (21 Mar. 1801) of the teachings of Jesus as "the most *sublime* & benevolent," but because mutilated, the "most perverted system that ever shone on man." Some two years later (9 Apr. 1803), he says: "Such are the fragments remaining as to show a master workman, and that his system of morality was the most benevolent & *sublime* probably that has been ever taught." He adds that Jesus was "the most innocent, the most benevolent, the most eloquent and *sublime* character that ever has been exhibited to man." Weeks later, he writes to Dr. Benjamin Rush (21 Apr. 1803), "Notwithstanding these disadvantages, a system of morals is presented to us, which, if filled up in the true style and spirit of the rich fragments he left us, would be the most perfect and *sublime* that has ever been taught by man."[71] The passages are consistent with a Burkean rending, though epithets like "benevolent," "innocent," "perfect," and "eloquent" make it difficult to see the sublime in terms of awe and terror. Choice of "sublime" in preference to "beauty" suggests a distancing from the teachings of Jesus. yet only on account of their superiority to other moral works, for the true superiority of Jesus's teachings relates to their democratic nature.

Finally, Jefferson often refers to "sublime delights," "sublime luxury," or "sublime pleasure." To John Adams (28 Dec. 1796), he speaks of the enjoyment of politicians. "I leave to others the *sublime* delights of riding in the storm, better pleased with sound sleep and a warm birth below, with the society of neighbors, friends & fellow-laborers of the earth, than of spies & sycophants." To Joseph Priestley (27 Jan. 1800), he says, "To read the Latin & Greek authors in their original, is a *sublime* luxury; and I deem luxury in science to be at least as justifiable as in architecture, painting, gardening, or the other arts." Jefferson's *billet doux* to Cosway also suggests that the "sublime delights" of Head and Heart differ substantially. Heart says: "What more *sublime* delight than to mingle tears with one whom the hand of heaven hath smitten! to watch over the bed of sickness, & to beguile it's tedious & it's painful moments! to share our bread with one to whom misfortune has left none! This world abounds indeed with misery: to lighten it's burthen we must divide it with one another." Heart then turns to Head: "Fill papers as you please with triangles & squares: try how many ways you can hang & combine them together. I shall never envy nor controul your *sublime* delights." Jefferson writes to Albert Gallatin (12 Oct. 1806) of his sublime pleasure on leaving the first office in a manner that advanced the wellbeing of the nation. "Our administration now drawing towards a close, I have a *sublime* pleasure in believing it will be distinguished as much by having placed itself above all the passions which could disturb its harmony, as by the great operations by which it will have advanced the well-being of the nation."

A Prudential Approach to Aesthetic Appreciation

Investigation into Jefferson's conceptions of the beautiful and the sublime show one key feature. Linkage of beauty to economy shows respect for the Hogarthian and Burkean notion that beauty is foremost a sort of fitness. Yet Jefferson's use of sublime also shows the sublime too is a sort of fitness. It is an ultra-fitness or extreme fitness—compare the French maxim *Je me sublime* (I exceed myself), where exceeding is not superfluity, but working to fullest potential. Overall, the fitness to which Hogarth and Burke refer is Aristotelian and hearkens back to Aristotle's formal and final causes. Thus, it might prove profitable to investigate Aristotle's notions of the formal and final causes as they relate to *technē* (craft, art, or science).

Technē, Aristotle believes, in the productive sense, is important only insofar as the end at which one aims is successfully achieved. The agent, in a sense, contributes nothing to the excellence of the product. The excellence of the product lies in the product itself, not the producer, and that is how its excellence is to be assessed. That is because, for Aristotle, the excellence (*aretē*) of the producer is of the physical, not ethical, sort. Thus, the formal cause—the essence of what is produced (its definition or function)—is superior to the productive or efficient cause—the actions of the craftsman in producing the object. Moreover, the final cause (*telos*) is superior to the formal cause, insofar as the final cause is the actualization of the essence of a thing. For instance, a double axe, by essence a chopping thing, is more of a double axe when it is actualized—i.e., when it is chopping and when both sides of the axe are used—than when it is just sitting in a shed. For Aristotle, to be, in the fullest sense, is to do. In aesthetical language, we might say that for Aristotle there is nothing beautiful about a double axe, however well-constructed, that does no chopping. Thus, we see in Aristotle's metaphysical scheme, art as we today think of it was of limited value.

Jefferson certainly was no Aristotelian, as he regarded such metaphysical analysis as tarradiddle. Yet he agreed with Aristotle on one thing: The true beauty of a thing crafted is not so much mere recognition of the essence of the thing—mere talk of essences was nonsense for Jefferson—but the actualization of the thing crafted—the use to which it could be put. We might go further and say for Jefferson there can be no real beauty without functionality. Utility, for Jefferson, is the test of beauty. Writes Horace Kallen: "Jefferson wanted beauty to come to some use, and aesthetic experiences to work out in moral consequences. Otherwise they are 'a luxury.'"[72] The sentiment is echoed by Merrill Peterson. "Jefferson prized beauty for what it could do, for its place in the future scheme of things, which he contemplated with the same fervor as the metaphysician contemplates the cosmos or the sentimental dreamer the picturesque past."[73] Thus, beauty that does not help shelter, clothe, feed, or protect is a needless luxury—a sign of an overindulgent, dissipative society. Consequently, Jefferson's approach to beauty is prudential.

For Aristotle, the *technai* (plural of *technē*) are three and axiologically ranked. From lowest to highest, there are productive science (knowledge for the sake of some produced end), political science (knowledge for the sake of political, ethics included, fulfillment), and theoretical science (knowledge for its own sake). Productive science (*poiētikē technē*)—the lowest, but the closest thing Aristotle has to the fine arts—is not without an important function. Concerning Poetics, categorized as a productive science, Aristotle writes, "Poetry is an imitation (*mimēsis*) with the media of rhythm, words, and melody that represents characters who are better than, equal to, or inferior to most and that uses narration or dramatic action in the manner of imitation" (47a14–18). Imitation is educative. We learn through imitation. A good poet uses the right guidelines to bring about catharsis—i.e., a purging that is morally instructive. In tragedy, one expurgates through pity and terror; in comedy, through laughter. Here intellect and emotion merge as we learn. A good poet knows the human condition.

Aristotle offers us a glimpse in *Poetics* of a child's early learning.

Catharsis is not expurgation in the Freudian sense of release of dammed up drive energy. Catharsis through imitation of characters on stage (*ta ēthē*) is expurgation through identification. Through pity, terror, or laughter, children identify emotionally with an actor and learn to deal similarly with their own emotions in similar contexts. Potentially magnanimous children learn most by tragedy; ordinary children find delight in pasquinade. The learning is moral training, as right action for Aristotle involves not just right thinking and choice, but also allows for proper display of emotional impulses. Note that "characters" is the translation for Aristotle's *ta ēthē*—from which we derive "ethics"—which has to do with the character or moral state in which the actors are perceived to be while on stage. It is certainly in this spirit that one is to take Kames's linkage of aesthetic sensibility and moral sensibility.

It is in the Aristotelian spirit too that it is best to take Jefferson. *Sine qua non* for proper moral cultivation is aesthetic cultivation. Consider Jefferson's 1771 letter to Skipwith, to which I refer in the beginning of this chapter. Acts of charity and gratitude, through recognition of their beauty, Jefferson begins, incite emulation; acts of atrocity, being deformed, invite repulsion. He writes: "Now every emotion of this kind is an exercise of our virtuous dispositions, and dispositions of the mind, like limbs of the body acquire strength by exercise. But exercise produces habit, and in the instance of which we speak the exercise being of the moral feelings produces a habit of thinking and acting virtuously."

Virtue-enhancing stories do not invite us to consider their truth or untruth. "If the painting be lively, and a tolerable picture of nature, we are thrown into a reverie," from which we wake as a better person. Jefferson appeals to Shakespeare, Ravaillac, Marmontel, and Sterne. Thus, fiction is preferable to history. He continues to Skipwith: "Considering history as a moral exercise, her lessons would be too infrequent if confined to real life. Of those recorded by historians few incidents have been attended with such circumstances as to excite in any high degree this sympathetic emotion of virtue. We are therefore wisely framed to be as warmly interested for a fictitious as for a real personage. The field of imagination is thus laid open to our use and lessons may be formed to illustrate and carry home to the heart every moral rule of life."

The letter to Skipwith gives an iteration of the just-relish argument— the beauty of right action is itself sufficient prompt for emulation—as well as an argument from exercise.

1. Every aesthetical emotion linked to virtuous action is an exercise of our virtuous dispositions.

2. Virtuous dispositions of the mind, like limbs of the body, acquire strength by exercise.
3. So, exercise of aesthetical emotion linked to virtuous action strengthens virtuous dispositions (1 & 2).
4. Exercise produces habit.
5. So exercise of virtuous dispositions produces a habit of thinking and acting virtuously (3 & 4).
6. So, exercise of aesthetical emotion linked to virtuous action produces a habit of thinking and acting virtuously (5).

The letter also contains an argument from fiction, which might be condensed in the following manner.

1. Aesthetical emotion linked with virtuous action even in fictive creations exercises virtuous dispositions, so long as the creation is "lively" and a "tolerable picture of nature."
2. Aesthetical emotion linked with virtuous action in historical accounts and texts on ethics exercises virtuous dispositions.
3. Historical accounts only too infrequently excite much high aesthetical emotion linked with virtue; dry texts on ethics, even less.
4. So, fiction teaches moral lessons better than history (1, 2 & 3).

Thus, the letter to Skipwith offers early and compelling evidence of a significant link between the aesthetic and moral senses—the substratal principles of each, discoverable through empirical investigation of the nature of man. It shows especial debt to the Kamesian notion that aesthetic sensitivity ought to be engendered chiefly for moral sensitivity. Also, it strongly suggests that the aesthetic sense is at day's end answerable to the moral sense.

Upshot

Given Jefferson's relative silence concerning the aesthetic sense in his writings—he never directly turns formally to expatiation of the topic in any of his writings—it is difficult to say just what he thought. I have therefore approached the subject somewhat elliptically and with due caution.

Though Jefferson expresses appreciation for William Hogarth in his letter to Skipwith, his writings show scant integration of him. He likely was attracted to Hogarth's notion of beauty being democratic—*viz.*, accessible to all, not merely the well-to-do. He also certainly was attracted to

Hogarth's observation that nature often couples beauty and utility. "In nature's machines how wonderfully do we see beauty and use go hand in hand."[74] Moreover, he certainly had Hogarth in mind in constructing the famous serpentine brick walls of the University of Virginia.

Hogarth's great discovery—that the waving line (the "line of beauty") and the serpentine line ("the line of grace") are the keys to what is aesthetic—does not, however, surface explicitly anywhere in Jefferson's writings. In his tour of the gardens of England, Jefferson is critical of the straight walkway at the gardens of Caversham—"the straight walk has an ill effect"—and the straight avenue at Stowe—"the straight approach is very ill."[75] Such criticism, however, does not entail that he was endorsing a preference for waving or serpentine pathways. Only in a letter to Charles W. Peale (17 Apr. 1813) is it clear that Jefferson implicitly refers to Hogarth when he speaks of the beauty of waving lines apropos of his use of contour

The serpentine walls of UVA. The walled gardens of each of the ten pavilions of Jefferson's original design of the University of Virginia were serpentine. The sinusoidal pattern combines beauty with functionality in that it allows a one-brick-thick wall to have the strength and durability it would not have had had it been straight (photograph by the author).

plowing. "We now plough horizontally, following the curvatures of the hills and hollows, on the dead level, however crooked the lines may be. Every furrow thus acts as a reservoir to receive and retain the waters, all of which go to the benefit of the growing plant, instead of running off into the streams. In a farm horizontally and deeply ploughed, scarcely an ounce of soil is now carried off from it. In point of beauty nothing can exceed that of the waving lines & rows winding along the face of the hills & vallies."

The influence of Edmund Burke on Jefferson aesthetic thinking appears not to be prodigious. He followed Burke, as we saw in his *Notes on the State of Virginia*, in treating separately the beautiful and the sublime. Yet he did not follow Burke in treating the sublime as something necessarily to be feared. Also Jefferson was attracted to the notion of aesthetic sensibility being something non-rational. Nonetheless, Burke has nothing to say about cultivating aesthetic sensibility.

His letter to Skipwith—through what I have dubbed the just-relish argument, the argument from exercise, and the argument from fiction—leaves no doubt of considerable influence of Kames on Jefferson's thinking on aesthetic sensibility. The aesthetic sense is naturally suited to work in concert with the moral sense such that refinement of aesthetic sensitivity is at once refinement of moral sensitivity.

There is one stark difference however. For Kames, aesthetic cultivation requires a considerable amount of leisure, and so aesthetic cultivation is chiefly the province of the opulent, who have fullest opportunity to develop aesthetic appreciation. The common people presumably will be moral laggards. For Jefferson, a plowman's moral discernment is at least equal to that of a professor, who is bogged down in moral rules. Jefferson, thus, offers a democratic account of aesthetic appreciation.[76]

Moreover, "art appears too much," was a complaint ingeminated by Jefferson concerning his visit to various famous gardens in England, so there are limits to aesthetic appreciation. When aesthetic appreciation is under-refined, moral sensitivity is unfledged. The beauty of virtuous action and the deformity of vicious actions are natural enticements to pursue virtue and eschew vice. When aesthetic appreciation is over-refined, moral sensitivity is enfeebled through neglect. One obsessed with aesthetic refinement can easily mistake beauty as the end of life, not happiness.

More must be said apropos of over-refinement. Jefferson's thoughts on extravagance of the Britain and France are aidful—excess and lavishness in art being a consequence. In England, the distance between the aristocracy and commoners is considerable, and the system is established so that the aristocracy feeds off the commoners.[77] Referring to British "pleasure gardens" and architecture in a letter to John Page (4 May 1786), Jefferson calls the "extravagance which has seized them" a "baneful evil." The difference between haves and have-nots is even greater in France, where "every man … must be either the hammer or the anvil," Jefferson writes to Charles Bellini (30 Sept. 1785). The lavish lifestyle of the wealthy "dazzle[s] the bulk of spectators." He does, however, express great enjoyment of the fine arts in France. "Were I to proceed to tell you how much I enjoy their architecture, sculpture, painting, music, I should want words." Yet enjoyment does not necessitate a desire to transplant French arts to America. Furthermore, he was not overwhelmed by all French art. In architecture, for instance, he was neoclassical, as evidenced by his attachment to the Hotel de Salm, which he used as a model for Monticello, and the Maison Carrée, which was his model for his design of the state capitol of Virginia. French rococo in architecture, inordinately lavish, was symptomatic of the sharp and exaggerated line between the wealthy and wellborn and all others. Thus, it was an architecture *hors de propos* for a country, defending the equality and rights of its citizenry.[78] Aesthetic indulgence was, thus, inconsistent with Jeffersonian participatory republicanism.

3

"Expediency can never contend with virtue"
Jefferson's Ancient Philosophy Sources

"That old age is wretched which must defend itself through speech."
—Cicero, *De senectute*

Given that Jefferson never wrote formally on any philosophical topic, there are obvious limitations to an approach to fleshing out his views on morality by appeal merely to his letters and sundry other writings over time. Thus, as a supplement to the findings of the first two chapters, it is profitable to include discussion of the varied ethical works that Jefferson read and ingested.

Immediately, there is an imbroglio. The number of books under "ethics" or "natural religion"—the two terms he tended to equate—in Jefferson's libraries was considerable. We cannot presume that Jefferson valued equally each book. How do we know which books Jefferson valued most—which books had the largest influence on Jefferson's own thinking on morality?

Throughout his life, Jefferson sent to select correspondents suggestions for reading. Correspondents included Robert Skipwith (1771), Bernard Moore (ca. 1773), Walker Maury (1785), Samuel Henley (1785), nephew Peter Carr (1785 and 1787), Archibald Stuart (1795), William G. Munford (1798), Joseph C. Cabell (1800), Richard Mentor Johnson (10 Mar. 1808), John Wyche (1809), Samuel R. Demarre (1809), John Minor (1814), and William Hilliard (1824). The earliest list is Skipwith's and the most extensive,[1] as it contains a large list of books and detailed instructions concerning their reading, is Minor's. We can assume that the books listed under

"Religion," "Ethics," or "Natural Religion" are books more valued, because they were recommended to friends, whose influence on Jefferson was large.

The letter to Jefferson's friend Skipwith, just one year after he lost his library in the Shadwell fire (3 Aug. 1771), lists 148 books in reply to Skipwith's letter (17 July 1771) for a catalog of books "suited to the capacity of a common reader who understands but little of the classicks and who has not leisure for any intricate or tedious study."[2] Skipwith's qualifications are significant, because they assign limits to Jefferson's recommendations: They must be educatively poignant, but easily accessible tests.

Under the category of "Religion," Jefferson recommends in his reply to Skipwith the following books.

> Locke's *Conduct of the Mind in Search of Truth*
> Xenophon's *Memoirs of Socrates*
> Carter's Epictetus
> Collin's Antoninus
> L'Éstange's Seneca
> Guthrie's Cicero's *Offices*
> Cicero's *Tusculan Questions*
> Lord Bolingbroke's *Philosophical Works*
> Hume's *Essays*
> Lord Kames's *Natural Religion, Philosophical Survey of Nature,* and *Economy of Human Life*
> Sterne's *Sermons*
> Sherlock's *On Death* and *On a Future State*

All of the books listed are as much ethical as they are religious treatises. In keeping with Skipwith's unfamiliarity with ancient material and his aversion to intricate or tedious study, the Latin and Greek works are in English translation and Jefferson includes no French authors.

Another list of books Jefferson gives decades later to General John Minor (30 Aug. 1814). The list, intended for Minor's son,[3] is a modified version of a list Jefferson gave to Bernard Moore many years prior.[4] The list of books here is prodigious and the course of study accompanying it, suited for one wishing to practice law, is brutal, and could only have been sent to a close friend or one with an insatiable appetence for learning. Under "Ethics and Natural Religion," Jefferson lists:

> Locke's *Essay* and *Conduct of the Mind in Search after Truth*
> Stewart's *Elements of the Philosophy of the Human Mind*
> Enfield's *History of Philosophy*

3. "Expediency can never contend with virtue"   65

Condorcet's *Progrès de l'esprit humain*
Cicero's *De officiis, Tusculana, De senectute*, and *Somnium Scipionis*
Seneca's *Philosophica*
Hutcheson's *Introduction to Moral Philosophy*
Paradis de Raymondis's *Traité élémentaire de morale et du Bonheur*
Charron's *La sagesse*

Under "Sectarian Religion," Jefferson lists:

Bible and New Testament
Middleton's commentaries on both
Priestley's *History of the Corruptions of Christianity, Christianity*, and *Early Opinions of Christ*
Volney's *Les ruins*
Sterne's *Sermons*
Massillon's *Sermons*
Bourdaloue's *Sermons*

In the list to Minor, Jefferson separates "Sectarian Religion" from "Ethics and Natural Religion," though no such separation exists in his letter to Skipwith, which lists Laurence Sterne's *Sermons* and Thomas Sherlock's *Discourses on Death, Judgment, and a Future State* with other works that are straightforwardly ethical. Such separation makes sense given Jefferson's execration of the political nature and political squabbles of sectarian religions. In the two letters, Jefferson recommends from the ancient moralists Xenophon's *Memoirs of Socrates*, Epictetus, Seneca's *Philosophical Essays*, Antoninus's *Meditations*, and a heavy dose of Cicero—*On Duties, On Old Age, Tusculan Disputations*, and *the Dream of Scipio*.

Some things are worth noting concerning the two letters.

First, the content from the reading list is heavily Stoical. Epictetus, Seneca, and Antoninus (i.e., Emperor Marcus Aurelius) were Stoics, and much of the content in the recommended works of Cicero, avowedly an Academic Skeptic and an eclectic, is Stoical. That is astonishing, given Jefferson's expressed disavowal of Stoic ethical thinking in his letter to William Short (31 Oct. 1819). Jefferson's prodigious uptake of Stoic ethical thought is the subject of Chapter 9.

Second, no works of the greatest Greek thinkers, Plato and Aristotle, are listed. That Plato should be overpassed is not surprising, as Jefferson thought Plato, "dealing out mysticisms incomprehensible to the human mind,"[5] was an unoriginal compiler, and following Priestley in *History of the Corruptions of Christianity*, he blamed Plato for Neoplatonist corruptions in the New Testament—e.g., exaggerations, sophistries, and enumeration of events inconsistent with the laws of nature.[6] That Aristotle's ethical works are pretermitted is surprising, given certain affinities between Jefferson's and Aristotle's ethical views.[7]

Third, it is astounding that Epicurus is omitted from both lists, for Jefferson says in the same letter to Short, "I consider the genuine (not the imputed) doctrines of Epicurus as containing everything rational in moral philosophy which Greece and Rome have left us." Even if Jefferson's ethical thinking was not much influenced by Epicurus, as I argue throughout this book and elsewhere,[8] one would at least expect, given his avowed regard for Epicurus, a reference to the philosopher's "genuine doctrines" in a recommended reading list.

In this chapter and the next, I aim to familiarize readers with Jefferson the moralist and to situate Jefferson's moral man in society and in the cosmos by familiarizing readers with moral works he thought significant enough to recommend to favored correspondents. In this chapter, I examine Xenophon's Socrates; the recommended writings of Cicero—*On Duties, On Old Age,* and *Tusculan Disputations*—the works of the Stoics Epictetus, Seneca, and Antoninus; and Jefferson's own version of the New Testament, *The Jefferson Bible*.

"The teacher of misery": Xenophon's Memoirs of Socrates

Xenophon's *Memoirs of Socrates* aims to give readers a portrait of Socrates through the eyes of its author, a disciple.

The work contains four books, each roughly the same length. It begins with a well-intended introduction to Socrates by an apologia, prior to his death. It ends with some thoughts on a good life as the best preparation for death.

Though peppered with philosophical insights, Xenophon's portrait of Socrates in *Memoirs* is mostly historical, not philosophical. Xenophon aims to acquaint readers with the historical Socrates through acquainting them with his philosophical thinking. Xenophon's manner of exposition throughout is anecdotal and episodic. He chooses vignettes, not narrative. Dialectic is his preferred method of acquaintance with Socrates's thinking.

For Xenophon, the historical Socrates was "the most self-disciplined of men"—"the most tolerant of … hardships of all kinds" and "very easily satisfied with very few possessions" (I.ii.1–2). He eschewed sexual relations with beautiful people—though he was surrounded by promising, handsome youths who were attracted to him (III.xvi)—involvement with them could readily lead to loss of self-control (I.iii.8 and II.i.4). "He took only so much food as he could eat with pleasure, and he was so ready for a meal when he came to it that his appetite was sauce enough. Any drink was agreeable to him, because he drank only when he was thirsty" (I.iii.5–8). He was "not foppish or ostentatious ... in his clothing or in his footwear or in the rest of his daily life" (I.ii.5). He lived Spartan-like, was in control of all pleasures, and he could best anyone, if he so chose, in argument (I.ii.15). So self-restrained and so neglectful of the conveniences of everyday life was he that Antiphon the Sophist dubbed him "the teacher of misery" (I.vi.3).

Socrates practiced daily dialectic (IV.viii.8), but accepted no fees for his "instruction." First, being paid for companionship required one to be a constant companion—in effect, a catamite (I.vi.12)—which would have encumbered his independency. Moreover, he regarded the reward for teaching goodness to be a foursquare friend, for which there could be no monetary compensation (I.ii.7–8).

Xenophon's Socrates does not philosophically concern himself with the nature of the physical cosmos, but with the affairs of men. His chief concern is virtue and how it is to be had, for physical knowledge is of no benefit to oneself or to others (I.i.11–6). Xenophon's Socrates affirms the centrality of virtue, which is knowledge. He asserts, "Not only justice, but all the other moral virtues [are aspects of] wisdom" (III.ix.4–5 and IV.vi.7). He also has much to say concerning the particular virtues. He affirms that self-control is needed for anyone who wishes to act effectively (IV.v.1), that a pious man knows how to act toward the gods (IV.vi.3–7), and that courage is beautiful and useful for "dreadful and dangerous situations" (IV.vi.8–13).

Xenophon's Socrates also states that "refraining from what is wrong is right" and that "what is lawful is right" (IV.iv.12–3). Weak will (*akrasia*)—knowing an action to be wrong and still doing it—is impossible. "I presume that everyone acts by choosing from the course open to him the one which he supposes to be most expedient. So I think that those who act wrongly are neither wise nor prudent" (III.ix). Vice, then, is ignorance.

Dialectic or elenchus—question-and-answer dialog in which Socrates customarily begins with brief, but penetrating questions, and proceeds to cross-examine interlocutors with the hopes of answers that might lead to knowledge of a particular virtue, and axial to Plato's early dialogs[9]—is a feature of Xenophon's vignettes, though the puzzlement (*aporia*) that ensues when an interlocutor engages with Socrates in elenchus rarely occurs in *Memoirs*.

Unlike Plato's Socrates who habitually confesses ethical agnosticism, Xenophon's Socrates holds fast to many principles: that right moral action is a matter of benefiting one's friends and harming one's enemies (II.i.18, II.i.28 ff., II.iii.14, II.vi.35, II.xi.35, and IV.ii.15); that one should consider one's value to a friend before considering the value of a friend to oneself (II.v); that the gods most favor those persons who do their work effectively (III.ix.15); that that sculptor is best whose works correspond to the moral character of the person being sculpted (III.x.9); and that industry and assiduity are key in a virtuous life (II.viii.6). Thus, Xenophon's Socrates is no agnostic. He embraces many ethical principles and also essays to convince his friends to accept them.

Many of the Socrates's principles are expressed through parable, metaphor, or other literary devices. Socrates explains Athens's deterioration through a comparison with athletes that have become enfeebled through lack of constant and adequate challenge (III.v.13). Socrates illustrates the principle that one should never undertake tasks for which one's capacities are unsuited by suggesting Glaucon ought to learn how to manage a household before managing a polis (III.vi.15). He mocks Pistias the armorer because of his reputation for fitting his armor to the irregularities of each soldier, but failing to grasp that in doing so, there is no ideal toward which each soldier has to work (III.x). To one angered because another did not return a greeting, Socrates replies that no one is angered by one physically debilitated, so one ought not to be angered by one psychically debilitated (III.xiii.1).

Xenophon's Socrates urges exercise of both body and soul. He says, "Just as those who do not exercise their bodies cannot carry out their physical duties, so those who do not exercise their characters cannot carry out their moral duties: they can neither do what they ought to do nor avoid what they ought to avoid" (I.ii.19–20). Physical exercise's benefits, he adds, outweigh its labor (III.xii).

Finally, Xenophon's Socrates is concerned with praxis, not theory. He, cynosural, and thus teaches by example (I.ii.3–4 and IV.vii). "If I don't reveal my views in a formal account, I do so by my conduct. Don't you think that actions are more reliable evidence than words?'" (IV.iv.11). He encourages the study of geometry, astronomy, arithmetic, and divination only insofar as are practicable. In all, he is zetetic, law-obeying, and ingenuous (IV.iv.1–4).

Why did Jefferson, who refers to Socrates so infrequently in his numerous writings, include Xenophon's *Memoirs* in his letter to Skipwith? Like Xenophon's Socrates, Jefferson wished to be judged by his deeds and not merely his words,[10] thought that study ought to be undertaken for usefulness of knowledge,[11] and believed that moral exemplars were better teachers of morality than were principles.[12] For both Socrates and Jefferson, friendship, industry, efficiency of action, self-knowing, fitness of mind and of body, and equanimity were important characteristics of moral living.

Why, then, did Jefferson not include the *Memoirs* in his letter to Moore? It is likely because he thought Xenophon's work was suitable reading for a philosophical novice, for whom enticement to further reading was perhaps more important than philosophical marrow, but not for one already committed to developing himself as fully as possible—the intendment of the list in the letter to Moore.

"Opportuneness of times for suitable actions": Cicero's Moral Writings

Marcus Tullius Cicero (106–43 BC) was one of the most prominent Romans of his time, which spanned roughly the decay and fall of the Roman Republic. A politician of great renown, and a great Roman orator and philosopher, he was an invaluable source for the history of the republic during his life. In political turmoil on account of his political refusal to abet Caesar, Pompey, and Crassus when they became the government, he was exiled and debarred from political participation. From 55 to 51 BC, he gainfully spent his time on three significant political treatises. When civil strife ensued and Caesar eventually become the first Roman emperor, Cicero was pardoned but still disallowed any political participation. He spent such forced retirement in the study and writing of philosophy till his murder in 43 BC.

Cicero was highly esteemed as a philosopher by Jefferson and numerous others of Jefferson's day. That reputation does not withstand critical analysis. Scrutiny of his many philosophical treatises reveals that Cicero was more of an unoriginal compiler than a philosopher of originality. His philosophical writings, in substance, tend not to go beyond the Greeks from whom he drew, and most of the arguments he employs are readily found in the works of Plato, Aristotelians, Epicureans, Academic Skeptics, and especially the Stoics.[13] In style, his philosophical works aim at a less erudite audience, and given that, they are unquestionably effective.[14]

Cicero's interest in philosophy was in ethics, the most fruitful of all arts,[15] and here, as Harry Hubbell writes, "Cicero was always a Stoic,"[16] in spite of frequent claims of eclecticism or Academic Skepticism.[17] His usefulness as a philosopher derives from Romanizing Greek philosophy and neoterizing the Latin language to accommodate Greek concepts. His significance for scholars today concerns not originality, but preservation of much of what we know today about Academic Skepticism, Peripateticism, Stoicism, and Epicureanism.

Jefferson thought Cicero was in the main a remarkable orator—in effect, not style, the Roman equivalent of the Greek Demosthenes. "Cicero did not wield the dense logic of Demosthenes, yet he was able, learned, laborious, practiced in the business of the world, and honest."[18] Yet Jefferson recognized that the chief merit of Cicero was his philosophical prose—specifically its style. "the merit of his philosophy is in the beauties of his style. diffuse rapid, rhetorical, but enchanting," he writes to William Short (31 Oct. 1819). As such, his philosophical works, combining Cicero's training as an orator with his analytic abilities as a philosopher, proved easily accessible digests of ancient ethical thinking. As Jefferson states to Jason Chamberlain (1 July 1814), Cicero—like Xenophon, Epictetus, Seneca, and Antoninus—makes *de trop* an ethical instructor. Thus, Jefferson often read Cicero's philosophical works and recommended them to numerous correspondents.[19]

On Duties

Cicero considered his *On Duties* to be the capstone of his ethical works. It was a work that was much read in Roman antiquity and thereafter, and Jefferson found it to be one of the most significant ethical works ever composed. In every non-supplemental recommended reading list that includes an entry for "ethics" or "religion," *On Duties* is named or Cicero's "philosophical works" is included. I suspect that it influenced Jefferson unlike any other formal ethical work.

Of the three books, Books I and II of *On Duties*[20] are the most significant, and they draw heavily from the first three books of the Stoic Panaetius's *On Appropriate Action*. Book III, sometimes unclear and often discursive, is Cicero's own construction.[21]

The work is straightforwardly ordered. Book I is an analysis of moral goodness or virtue (*honestum*). Book II concerns moral expediency (*utile*). Finally, Book III is an attempt to show that moral goodness is moral expediency, and conversely that moral expediency is moral goodness.

Cicero begins the first book by analysis of human impulses. Every animal has a self-preservative impulse and a procreative impulse. Yet humans are endowed with reason (*ratio*), which links men with men

3. "Expediency can never contend with virtue"   71

through language and life, which propels them to pursue truth. Men have feelings for orderliness (*ordo*) and propriety (*modus*) in word and deed, and they sense beauty, loveliness, and harmony. Thus, nature and reason bid that men strive for beauty, consistency, and order in their lives (I.11–14).

Cicero limns the face of virtue (*honestum*[22]), whose merit lies in study, not action. Virtue comprises wisdom (knowledge of truth; I.18–19), justice (preventing men from harming each other, enabling them to employ most efficiently what is common to them, and preserving for each what is his own, as well as generosity and benefitting; I.20–60), courage ("that virtue championing the cause of fairness"; I.61–92), and temperance (doing "what is fitting" or what in accord with nature; I.93–107).[23]

Between the extremes of self-love—recall the impulse toward self-preservation—and obligation to all other humans—the essence of Stoic cosmopolitanism—Cicero notes that there are nested layers of obligations. There is first a large circle that delimits the obligations of fellowship to all humans (1)—i.e., cosmic citizenship. Within that frame, each has obligations to the people of similar tribe and tongue (2) and to those of the same polis (3). There is also the small and narrow circle that defines the connection and the fellowship of kindred (*propinquorum*) (4)—i.e., kinship. One-home and between-home domestic relations involve first and second cousins (5), brothers and sisters (6), marital connections (7), connections shaped by marriages (8), parents and children (9), and husband and wife (10; I.53–56). Yet human obligations are foremost to the gods. Thus, "the primary [human] obligation is to the immortal gods, second, to our country, third, to parents, and so on to the rest in descending scale [of worth]" (I.160).

Pertaining to virtuous actions, Cicero distinguishes, following the Stoic Panaetius, between a middle or common obligation (*medium officium* or *commune officium*) and perfect or right obligation (*perfectum officium* or *rectum officium*). Both are visually indistinguishable, but only the latter is virtuous, as it is performed by a virtuous person (I.108). In addition, not all obligations have the same weight, and the same obligation in one scenario might not have the same weight in another (I.159). Furthermore, the obligations that attend to good living vary with age and with political duties (I.122–23).

Cicero also discusses Panaetius's four personae. Each person has two personae by nature: one is a rational persona, which each shares with every other; the other is conferred on men personally. What is fitting, he states, is uniformity with life as a whole (*universae vitae*) and with all its particular activities. It is a matter of knowing oneself as a rational being and knowing one's idiosyncrasies, properly regulating them, and not wishing to be anyone else but oneself. There are two other personae: the persona imposed by circumstances and the persona that is the result of deliberate choosing. Each persona affects human behavior, though each person is free to decide his own path (I.107–120).

From section I.141 to I.144, Cicero appropriates and Romanizes the Stoic conception *eutaxia* (good order, discipline) with his discussion of orderliness. Orderliness, as correctness of conduct (*modestia*), is systematic conduct in all actions. The Stoics, says Cicero, offer the following definition. "Correctness of conduct is the science of putting into order all such things that are done or said." So right-ordering (*collocatio*), which is "the arrangement of things according to appropriate and suitable places," is synonymous with orderliness. "Place of action is said to be opportune time; however, the opportune time of an action, called *eukairia* in Greek, is called *occasio* in Latin." Cicero sums, "Thus it is that in this sense correct conduct ... is the science of opportuneness of times for suitable actions."[24] Thus orderliness of action ought to govern all human conduct. Moreover, for orderly action, all circumstances must be considered. That requires great natural capacities (*ingenii*) to anticipate both the future through cognition and possible courses of action (I.81).

Again, cynosures and exemplary conduct are crucial for right action.

> We, if we are willing to be keen and careful observers of faults, often learn great things from small. From the glance of the eyes, from the expansion or contraction of the brows, from depression, from cheerfulness, from laughter, from the tone of the voice, from silence, from a higher or lower key of utterance, and other similar tokens, we may easily determine which of the greater things that they typify are fittingly done and which of them are at variance with duty and nature. Nor is it unsuitable in matters of this sort to judge of the character of our actions by looking at others, so that we may ourselves avoid whatever is unbecoming in them; for it is the case ... that we perceive any delinquency more readily in others than in ourselves.

He also advocates appeal to "men of superior natural intelligence"—e.g., Socrates or Aristippus—in difficult scenarios (I.146–49).

Book II concerns expediency (*utile*). Nothing is more scrofulous than something being expedient without being morally right and something being morally right without being expedient (II.9).

Many things are expedient for men—minerals, fruits, domesticated animals, other men, and gods; many things inexpedient—hurricanes, storms, shipwrecks, conflagrations, and assaults from wild beasts. Men, says Cicero, are the cause of the greatest aid and the greatest harm to themselves. Yet men are inclined to overcome misfortune by assisting each other through goodwill, esteem for another, confidence in another, fear, hope for a benefit, and even bribery through money. Service to others by means of benevolence, friendship, liberty, generosity, and even eloquence are critical (II.11–24 and 52–68).

Service to others must consider others' conduct (*mores*) and situation (*fortuna*). First, in every benefit, one ought never to oppose the right or to defend the wrong. Second, the statesman must ensure that every citizen has what belongs to him and that the state does not encroach on the rights of property of any citizen. Finally, state-sanctioned acts of kindness ought to favor as many of those suffering misfortune as possible (II.65–75).

Book III concerns reconciliation of virtue and expediency. "It cannot be doubted," Cicero begins, "that expediency can never contend with virtue." Whatever is virtuous is expedient, and whatever is not virtuous is not expedient (III.11). That point is iterated and reiterated throughout the book.

There are two hefty difficulties. First, there are those persons who aspire to moral goodness and refuse any place for expediency in assessment of progress to wisdom, and others who weigh everything by profits and personal advantage, and refuse any place for moral goodness. Second, one often finds that what was deemed morally good is not, and that what was deemed morally expedient is not. So, there is need of a rule (III.15–20).

The key principle that straightforwardly settles the latter, and indirectly the former, is that one ought never to gain by profiting on the loss of another. That is contrary to nature, nations, and the gods (*lex divina*), as the interest of each citizen is the interest of the whole, and that is a matter of following nature (III.21–27).

Cicero considers two scenarios: a starving wise man considering stealing bread from someone worthless and a freezing good man who might consider stealing clothing from the cruel tyrant Phalaris. In each case, the interests of society decide the issue. To take from another to render "great usefulness to the state and to human society" is no matter for moral reproach; to take for another reason is obliquitous. The wellbeing of a good man, one of service to the state, is always preferred to the wellbeing of a malingerer. Pertaining to Phalaris, since a tyrant is an enemy of humanity, there is nothing wicked about robbing "one whom it is morally right to kill." Likewise, other problems, he states, can be determined similarly, with the proviso that obligation is determined from circumstances, not principles. In that regard, morally right is equivalent to morally expedient, and no greater harm can be done than to separate the two principles. It follows that all conflicts between the two are apparent, not real—as when what seems morally expedient is taken to be morally expedient or what seems morally right is taken to be morally right (III.50–53).

Cicero illustrates with an assumed famine at Rhodes. A grain ship arrives, and several other ships, which have yet to sail, will shortly arrive. The Rhodian purchasers, not knowing of the other ships, are willing to pay a high price for the grain. Ought the captain of the grain ship tell the Rhodians of the other ships? According to Diogenes the Stoic, the seller has merely the obligation to speak truthfully about his grain. To dissemble (*celare*) is not to conceal (*tacere*). There are numerous other things that the seller might know—e.g., the nature of the gods or the greatest good—but he is under no obligation to reveal them to the purchasers, when making a purchase. He acts pursuant to expediency and in such a manner that is not morally wrong. According to Antipater the Stoic, the seller has the additional obligation to tell of the other ships bound for Rhodes. Dissembling is concealing. He acts pursuant to what is morally right. Cicero sides with Antipater. Diogenes has merely the apparent expedient, *viz.*, maximizing his own interest at the expense of the Rhodians, in mind (III.50–58).

Taking on board the key principle for deciding difficult cases—never to gain by profiting on the loss of another—does not imply self-sacrifice of one's own needs and interests. Following the great early Stoic, Chrysippus, when a competitor enters a footrace, he essays ingenuously to win. While competing, he does not use his feet or hands to trip or foul opponents. It is in life as it is in the footrace. Each can seek what he needs for his own advantage so long as in doing so he does not disadvantage his neighbor (III.42).

On Old Age

Cicero's *On Old Age* is a discussion between Marcus Porcius Cato (234 BC–149 BC), one of the most prominent Roman soldiers, politicians, and orators of his time; Publius Scipio Africanus Minor (ca. 185 BC–129 BC), who was adopted son of Publius Cornelius Scipio, the son of Publius Scipio Africanus Major; and the prominent soldier and orator Gaius Laelius Sapiens (186 BC–98 BC).

Reminiscent of Book I of Plato's *Republic*, the dialog begins with a conversation between Cato, as an old man, and the much younger Laelius and Scipio, who wish to know how Cato bears so well what should be his dotage. Cato begins by stating that old age (*senectus*) differs nowise from any other age for a person who seeks within to find good; for all others, old age is merely something that is "brought about of necessity by nature" (I.ii.4).[25] He adds that his wisdom is due to obedience to nature, and aging is a part of nature's plan for living things (I.5). Thus, old age "must be endured softly by the wise," for otherwise one fights against nature (II.5).

The tack of Cato is to address the four chief reasons why old age appears miserable to most: it inclines persons to passivity; it enervates the body; it disallows sensual pleasure; and it brings persons nearer to death (V.15). Cicero aims to show each is a no reason for distress. The arguments throughout are characteristically Stoical.

First, even if the body is incapable of numerous physical activities, the mind can remain active in significant ways. An older man is like a ship's captain, who can no longer do the work of the physical crew, but who does "what is much greater and better." Cato adds that great deeds (*res magnae*) are not performed by strength, speed, or swiftness, but by planning, respected authority, and purposive decision (VI.17).

Second, loss of physical strength is often the result of dissipative living as much as natural degeneration. Moreover, if an old man fits the strength he has to tasks relative to his age, he will find he has strength ample. The course of life is for each fixed. Nature's path for each is unique, and to be run only once. Every stage of life has its proper time (*tempestivitas*). Thus the feebleness of childhood, the impetuosity of youth, the seriousness of mid-life, and the ripeness of old age have something natural, which "must be harvested in its proper time (*suo tempore*)" (X.29–33).

Third, loss of sensual pleasures (*voluptates*) is more to be praised than reproached. Insignificant (*parvulis*[26]) are the pleasures of youth (XIV.48). "Old age lacks the banquets, the bounteous courses, and the frequent draughts. Therefore, it also lacks drunkenness, indigestion, and sleeplessness" (XIII.44). Moreover, old age has other sensual pleasures—e.g., those of agriculture, which "are best suited to the life of the wise man." The earth "at no time disobeys an order, and never makes a return on what it receives without interest (*usura*)" (XIV.51). Cato sums, "I am inclined to think that no life can be happier than that of the farmer." His labor benefits the whole human race, and has its delight (*delectatione*), richness (*saturitate*), and abundancy (*copia*). It pertains to the nutriment of men and the "cultivation" of the gods. "Nothing can be more fruitful in use and comely in appearance than a well-cultivated farm" (XVI.56–57).

Finally, the nearness of death, especially troublesome for most persons, is not to be feared. Following Plato in *Apology*,[27] death either conducts the soul to an afterlife, where it is to live forever, or it annihilates the soul, in which case no one can be unhappy. Moreover, any span of life is sufficient that allows one to live well and virtuously. Furthermore, nothing in pursuance of the dictates of nature—and death is just that—ought to be seen as bad (XIX.66–71). Even if another life should be granted by a god, it is vain for one who has run his course to wish to return to the starting line. Though not all lives are fraught with troubles, every life either has a standard time (*modum*) or is surfeit. Thus, one ought to leave life as if one were leaving an inn, not a home (XXIII.83–84).

It is reasonable to think that Jefferson returned to Cicero's *On Old Age* numerous times in his retirement. In a letter to John Adams (8 Apr. 1816), he acknowledges in Stoic fashion that the world as a whole is good and benevolently framed and that there is more pleasure in living than there is pain. Years later to Adams (18 Dec. 1825), he states that he would live again his life, if there could be an opportunity. Jefferson disdains idleness at any stage of life,[28] so he certainly relished the arguments against passivity and enervation. If sensually inclined, he spent most of his life in sublimation of such sensuality[29] and put his "libido" to use in more useful pursuits, such as statesmanship, writing bills and letters, and farming. Also, he appropriated fully the ancient notion of timeliness (Gr., *kairos*), or as Cicero states, each thing having a proper season (*tempestivitas*). Finally, he seemed not to have any fear of death.

Tusculan Disputations

Cicero's *Tusculan Disputations* is another work addressed to a general audience. The topics are, in order of the five books, five psychical concerns: fear of death, mitigation of pain, elimination of distress, alleviation of other psychical disorders, and the sufficiency of virtue for a happy life.

The range of topics, breadth of discussion, and conclusions drawn again exhibit Cicero's allegiance to the eclectic approach of Academic Skepticism (Book I especially), but they also betray sizeable debt to Stoicism.

Book I begins with Cicero's statement of the neglect of philosophy in Rome. He wishes to aid his countrymen by discussion of ethical topics (I.5–7).

The topic of Book I, despisal of death, is treated eclectically. "The man who is without fear of death," he begins, "not simply because it is unavoidable but also because it has no terrors for him, has secured a valuable aid towards rendering life happy" (II.1). He offers a fusillade of syllogisms to show that death is not to be feared (I.8–27). From I.27 to 36, he appeals to mythology, apparitions at night, *consensus gentium*, nature, patriotism, poets and artisans, and the best of men. From I.38 to 79, he appeals to the authority of philosophers: Pherecydes of Syros, Pythagoreans, Plato, Aristotle, Dicaearchus, Aristoxenus, and Panaetius and other Stoics. He ends

3. "Expediency can never contend with virtue" 77

Book I (I.117) thus. If death is merely change of place, our greatest wish is fulfilled. If death is total annihilation, it will prove a peaceful sleep. Consequently, death is a great good or a lesser good. So, death is not to be feared.[30]

Book II critically investigates what, if anything, humans can to do endure pain. Philosophy is a sort of salve of the soul. "Now the cultivation of the soul is philosophy; this pulls out vices by the roots and makes souls fit for the reception of seed, and commits to the soul and ... sows in it seed of a kind to bear the richest fruit when fully grown" (II.9–14).

Many philosophers—e.g., Aristippus, Epicurus, and Hieronymous—have argued that pain is the greatest evil; pleasure, the greatest good (II.14–17). If so, why then would anyone willfully undergo pain for the sake of glory, duty, reputation? For the Stoic Zeno, for whom virtue is the sole good and vice the sole ill, pain cannot be an evil, for "there is nothing evil except what is base and wicked." Nonetheless, pain is to be shunned, as "it is unpleasant, against nature, hard to endure, melancholy, cruel." Cicero then mocks Stoic arguments concerning pain. "Whether ... the sense of pain is an evil or no, let the Stoics settle in their attempt to prove that pain is not an evil by a string of involved and pettifogging syllogisms (*minutis conclusiunculis*), which fail to make any impression on the mind" (II.42). Yet after all plausible arguments have been investigated, he grants that the pettifogging syllogisms of the Stoics are the best philosophical unguent for enduring pain (II.64).

Book III concern the mitigation of distress (*aegritudo*). No sooner than men come into the world than they find themselves "in a world of iniquity amid a medley of wrong beliefs, so that it seems as if we drank in deception with our nurse's milk." As people age, they become "infected with deceptions so varied that truth gives place to unreality and the voice of nature itself to fixed prepossessions" (II.1).

Distresses, like other psychical disorders, are considered by Cicero, following the Stoics, as diseases of the soul (*morbi animi*). As a decadent soul always desires, such diseases are worse than those of the body. Philosophy again is the cure (III.5).

The collocutors agree to deal not only with distress, but all forms of psychic perturbations. Following the Stoics, remedy consists in employment of syllogisms (*argumenta*), aimed to show virtue is the cure for perturbation (III.13–31). At III.36–37, Cicero limns the four cardinal virtues—moderation (*moderatio*), courage (*fortitudino*), justice (*iustitia*), and prudence (*prudentia*), all of which "are mutually linked and bound together."

Cicero discusses other psychical perturbations in Book IV (65)—"all disorders are within our control, are all acts of judgment, are all voluntary"—and the Stoic sufficiency thesis—"Virtue is self-sufficing for living happily (*ad beate vivendum*)"—which he avows in Book V.

Jefferson refers often to Cicero's *Tusculan Disputations* in recommended reading lists for moral improvement.[31] He likely found the work a needed unguent for distressful times—e.g., the deaths of his wife and daughter Maria. Given the full amount of distress meted out to each person in a life, it comes as no surprise that he regularly recommended it to select correspondents.

"I rise to do a man's work": Late Stoics Ethical Works

Jefferson's lists to Skipwith and Minor have a fair amount of Stoic authors. The recommended reading to Skipwith includes Seneca, Antoninus, and Epictetus. Moreover, as I mention apropos of the philosophical works of Cicero, his eclecticism turns disproportionately to Stoic solutions to life's most pressing moral issues.

Stoicism began with Zeno of Citium (c. 334–262 BC), who was under the spell of Plato and several philosophers of Plato's Academy—Xenocrates, Polemo, Stilpo, and Crantor—from whom he learned the notions that that no good other than virtue exists and that morally appropriate acts must agree with nature. Around 300 BC, Zeno founded a school in Athens and his pupils eventually came to be called "Stoics" because of the "Painted Porch" (*Poikilē Stoa*) at which they met. The school, cosmopolitan, attracted some significant pupils: Cleanthes of Assos (c. 331–c. 232 BC), the successor of Zeno, and Chrysippus of Cilicia (282–206 BC), a prodigious scholar and the successor of Cleanthes.[32]

Philosophy, for Zeno and Chrysippus, had three interdependent parts: logic, physics, and ethics.[33] They posited that the soul was completely rational, and thus, that living rationally was living in accordance with nature. Vice was due to mistakes of reasoning.

Middle or Platonic Stoicism began in the second century BC with Diogenes of Babylon (c. 240–152 BC) or with his pupil Antipater of Tarsus (fl. 145 BC). The two most famous middle Stoics were the Panaetius of Rhodes (185–c. 110 BC) and his pupil the Posidonius of Apamea (135 BC–c. 151 BC). The works of neither survive, but we know of their teachings through, among others, Cicero and the physician Galen (129–200 AD). These writers show that those Stoics admixed Platonism and Aristotelianism to early Stoicism.

"Roman Stoicism," a third wave of Stoicism, began around the birth of Christ. Its main philosophers were Seneca the Younger, Epictetus, and Marcus Aurelius, whose writings, having survived through the centuries, Jefferson often recommends to favored correspondents for their moral content. Seneca (1 BC–65 AD), tutor and advisor to a young Nero, wrote numerous moral essays and letters on a great variety of ethical issues—*viz.*, consolation, tranquility, the shortness of life, providence, anger, benefits, leisure, suicide, and anger. Epictetus (c. 50–c. 130 AD), a slave from Phrygia, set up a Stoic school in Nicopolis, where his ethical teachings were preserved by his pupil Arrian in his *Discourses*, comprising four books,[34] and a short ethical manual called *Handbook*. Aurelius or Antoninus (121–180 AD), the Roman emperor from 161–180 AD, left behind his Stoic manual, *Meditations*.

That Stoic ethics was assimilated and taught in antiquity by an emperor and a slave speaks volumes to the democratic nature of Stoicism and its widespread appeal. As Seneca writes, "Virtue closes the door to no man. It is open to all, admits all, invites all, the freeborn and the freedman, the slave and the king, and the exile; neither family nor fortune determines its choice. It is satisfied with a naked human being."[35] As such, it was a perfect philosophical fit for Jeffersonian republicanism.

Seneca's *Philosophica*

The *Philosophica* that Jefferson recommends to his friend Skipwith and to many others is a collection of philosophical essays traditionally called "dialogues," though there is little that is dialogical in them. They read like informal treatises on specific ethical subjects. Seneca's style is often blunt and redundant, typically expository, and his points characteristically and in Stoic fashion are bolstered by syllogisms.

His dialog *On Providence* is addressed to his younger friend Lucilius, the addressee of over 100 letters. The topic is the existence of evil, given a providential cosmos.[36] An issue of special concern is why good men suffer. The answer is that for a man to know himself, he must be tested (IV.3), and deity tests good men (I.6). Written more economically, "Virtue withers without an adversary" (II.4). A good man also suffers hardship (*dura*) to be an exemplar for other men (VI.3). Accepting his fate, he becomes a follower of deity (V.6).

On Steadiness addresses the constancy of character of the wise man (*sapiens*). While other philosophers use softer and enticing means, the Stoics prefer the heroic or manly course (*virile* viam) (I.1).[37] A *sapiens* can receive neither injury nor insult (III.2). Injury is innocuous, as he can only be injured by loss of virtue, which is entirely within his control (V.2–5). Insult is innocuous, as he can only be insulted through anger, which is entirely within his control. (X.1). Consequently, a *sapiens* endures injury and insults in the manner that he submits to harsh winters, inclement weather, fevers, disease, and all other accidents of fortune (VIII.9). His victory is one of endurance, just as the finest athletes often win victories in sacred contests through stubborn endurance (IX.5).

Seneca considers anger (*ira*), "brief insanity" (I.i.2), to be the foulest and most furious of all emotions (*adfectus*), hence, he gives a sustained analysis of it in three books composing *On Anger*.[38] No amount of anger, regardless of circumstances, is ever warranted. First, it is easier to eschew wickedness than to master it. Second, reason becomes corrupt when it admixes with passion (II.xvi.2). Third, nothing bad, like anger, can be a good, if taken in small amounts (I.xiii.2). Fourth, anger cannot act without consent of the will to rouse one to action (II.iii.4). Overall, giving into anger is like leaping off a precipice. Having leapt, one might thereafter repent of one's action, but one is no longer in position to take back one's leap (I.vii.2–3).

There are three promptings (*motus*; lit., "movements") of anger, Seneca says. The first is involuntary, like winking when someone unexpectedly thrusts fingers before one's eyes. The second, not unruly, has the auspices of volition and judges it is right for one to seek revenge. The third quashes reason and is beyond control, for it seeks vengeance at all costs (II.iv.1–2). A wise person always gains control at the second prompting through delay (II.xxviii.8).

Thus, a wise person's wisdom keeps anger from gaining an upper hand. Unstirred by the enormity that surrounds him, he acts like "a great wild beast that hears with untroubled soul the baying of little dogs" (II.xxxii.3).[39]

Seneca addresses the issue of consolation in three dialogs, two of which concern grieving. In the dialogs on grieving, the argument is this: Each life is infested with varied calamities, of which death is one; yet death is inevitable; what is inevitable is due to nature and cannot be evil; so it is otiose to judge what is not evil as a calamity.

In *To Marcia*,[40] dedicated to a friend who was grieving the loss of her son Metilius, Seneca offers a *modus operandi*, applicable to all dialogs concerning admonition: Begin with precepts and end with examples (II.1). He writes that is natural to grieve for those departed, but unnatural to grieve greatly. Women, savages, and the uneducated grieve more than men, the civilized, and the educated. Thus, presumption adds to grief (VII–VIII).

In *To Polybius*,[41] Seneca says of grieving that the deceased either does not wish you to suffer, if extant in an afterlife, or knows not that you suffer, if he has perished. So, grieving either displeases the deceased or it is useless (V.1). Finally, bearing grief bravely is as an example for others close to the deceased to follow (V.4–5).

In *To Helvia*,[42] an essay addressed to Seneca's mother on account of his exile, he writes, "Constant unhappiness offers one good: whomever it always vexes, it hardens to the extreme" (II.3). Later, he adds: "We were born under good conditions if only we have not abandon those conditions. Nature intended that we would need no great equipment to live well. Each person can make himself happy" (V.1–2). Furthermore, it is up to each not to be inflated by good fortune so that one does not collapse when fortune is changed (V.5). His exile, thus, is nothing to be reviled. It is merely a "change of place" (*loci commutation*) (VI.1), since for a wise person, "every place is his country" (IX.7).

The good life, Seneca writes in his dialog of the same name,[43] must come about through a sound mind, courage, energy, and nobility, and it must use advantageously the gifts of fortune. It is a mind neither inflated nor crushed by fate, unmindful of fortune, free, lofty, fearless, and steadfast (III.3–IV.5). A wise person's perceptions are clear; his judgments, correct (V.3–VI.2). He follows god. "To obey deity is freedom," and deity bids us to live virtuously, as virtue is sufficient for happiness (XV.7 and XVI.3). Still a *wise person* will wish for conveniences—e.g., wealth, tallness, and strength of body—for though not goods, they "contribute something to the perpetual joy (*perpetuam laetitiam*) ... borne of virtue," have some value (*pretii*) in themselves, and are choice-worthy. Not goods, however, they add nothing to human happiness (XXII.1–4).

Seneca's dialog *On Leisure*[44] argues for a deedy lifestyle. The Stoics advocate public service until one is hindered from it. Being "hindered" includes having lack of influence, having services unaccepted, being in ill-health, having an unsuitable office, and refusing to serve, if the state is corrupt. "Public service" entails service to many; to a few, if service to many is impossible; to those nearest, if service to a few is impossible; or to oneself, if service to those nearest is impossible. Yet there is also service to deity. For there are two commonwealths—that of gods and men (cosmic obligations) and that to which the accident of birth has assigned each (parochial obligations)—and nature has assigned each for citizenship in both. Thus, contemplation of the goodness and beauty of the cosmos and general actions toward other humans comprise obligations to gods and men. Actions benefitting family, friends, demesmen, and the state comprise parochial obligations. Consequently, leisure or retirement is not withdrawal (III.2–V.).

On Mental Tranquility[45] is a dialog on how one can always pursue a steady and favorable course, be well-disposed to oneself, and view oneself with uninterrupted joy. The fickle and bored, the lolling and yawning, the restive and twitchy, and the Oblomovian and unambitious suffer mental disquiet, and are unable to withdraw within themselves and find happiness in quietude (II.3–10). Such men, incapable of contemplation, suffer the worst of ills: leaving the living before death, which they fear (V.5). A wise person, in contrast, does not fear death, for he who fears death "will never do anything worthy of a man who is alive" (X.1–6); labors without regret and for utility (XII.1); prefers laughter to tears when considering the follies of others, for laughter allows for good hope (XV.4); and is authentic and unpretentious (XVII.1–2).

In *On Shortness of Life*,[46] Seneca maintains that men ought to be miserly with their time. A wise person's time is his own, and thus, his life is long because "he has devoted wholly to himself whatever time he has had" (VII.5). In contrast, no man should be considered long-lived who has merely lived for many years. He is like a ship, trapped by storms upon leaving harbor and tossed here and there by raging winds from all directions, that gyres, though it is away from port for much time (VII.10). One living well ignores expectancy, for expectancy wastes the present in ever-preparation for the future (IX.1). He also uses well his leisure, as good leisure is neither attending a barbershop each day to trim down any hair that might have overgrown from the previous day nor is it preoccupation with pleasure (XII.3 and XIII.1).

Finally, there is Seneca's *On Benefits*[47]—a dialog on the giving and receiving of favors. The dialog, in seven books, is drawn principally from the Rhodian Stoic Hecaton, pupil of Panaetius. The work is unduly lengthy and mostly unstructured, with numerous redundancies and many points digressive, but it also contains many fine insights into the Stoic view of the giving, receiving, and returning benefits.[48]

Seneca states, "A benevolent action is the act of a well-wisher who bestows joy and derives joy from the bestowal of it, and who is inclined to do what he does from the prompting of his own will." It consists not in the action or thing given, but in the intention of the giver (I.vi.1), and the intentions of a wise person are always intemerate. "A good man cannot not give what he gives; for he would not be good, if he did not do what he did; and so neither does a good man give a benefit because he is doing what ought to do, nor can he do other than what he ought to do" (VI.xxi.2).

A benefit (*beneficium*) is to be weighed not by bulk, but in the spirit in which and goodwill by which it is given, and that spirit and goodwill is humane and generous. It is to be measured by the character of the giver, and is thus a virtuous act and an end itself (I.ix.1 and IV.i.1–3). The best gifts are those that endure, and so money is generally of no or little benefit (I.xii.1 and I.xv.6). Timeliness too is a key consideration (III.viii.3). A benefit is not to be given arbitrarily, but to one who is worthy, thus a giver must consider fully the character of the receiver as well as his own character, for "every obligation, involving two persons, makes an equal demand on both" (I.xiv.1, I.xv.3, and II.xv.3–xvii.2). The obligation to give to all of humanity, for Seneca, outweighs any obligation to a single person (VII.xix.9).

On receiving a benefit, Seneca writes, "He who receives a benefit with gratitude repays the first installment on his debt" (II.xx). A recipient ought not to receive from any giver whatsoever, but from whom he could have given a benefit (II.xviii.3 and 7). Concerning publicity, a recipient should invite the whole world to praise the giver, while the giver ought to add only such publicity with his gift that would do honor to the recipient (II.xx.ii.1).

"To return," Seneca writes of repayment of benefit with benefit, "is to give something, because you ought to give it, to the person of whom the return is owed, when he wishes it to be returned" (VII.xix.2), In repaying a benefit, a wise person will consider all circumstances: the quantity of the benefit, and when, where, how, and from whom he has received it. It must not be returned carelessly, tardily, insultingly (I.i.8). He who fails to return a benefit commits a greater evil that he who fails to give one (I.i.13). To accept a benefit freely and with complete gratitude is full repayment (II.xxxi.1).

The reasons Jefferson recommended Seneca's *Philosophica* to several correspondents for moral reading are the accessibility of the writings and assimilability of the moral lessons. Like Seneca, Jefferson believed that the cosmos was framed by a benevolent deity, and thus it is probable that he thought what appears wicked to humans is merely so because of the limited human perspective on cosmic affairs.[49] It is unclear whether he, like Aristotle, thought anger was unavoidable but controllable or he, like the Stoics, thought it was a disease of the soul, capable of eradication through moral training. What clear is that he thought anger, even if inescapable, was manageable.[50] Jefferson likely found Seneca's consolatory essays, like Cicero's *Tusculan Disputations*, valuable during taxing times. He plainly agreed with Seneca on self-sufficiency, as Monticello itself was designed to be as self-sufficient as possible, as his political philosophy is founded on self-sufficiency and many letters preach the gospel of self-sufficiency.⁵¹ He bought into self-knowing, as he tells his physician Dr. Vine Utley (21 Mar. 1819) that he seldom goes to sleep without reading something that is morally uplifting. Finally, the pattern of his life—decades of public service in his salad years, dutiful epistolizing, drafting of numerous bills, participation in science as scientist and patron, availability of his library to other scholars and promising youths, and establishment of the University of Virginia in his later years—shows utmost regard for economy of living and use of leisure to benefit others, without concern for a return on his benefitting.

Epictetus's *Discourses* and *Handbook*

Writing nothing but teaching abundantly, Epictetus's thoughts are preserved by historian Flavius Arrian in four surviving books titled *Discourses* (*Diatribai*) and a compendium of the *Discourses* for general consumption titled *Handbook* (*Encheiridion*). They are the "words of an extraordinarily gifted teacher"—a "character of extraordinary strength, elevation, and sweetness"—who converses with, reproves, exhorts, and encourages pupils, and enlivens formal instruction with "the red stripe of a conscious moral character in preparation for the problem of right living."⁵² Nonetheless the style has been called "rigid didacticism and spiritual dogmatism."⁵³

The lessons of the *Discourses* bear the mark of Epictetus's former slavery. W.A. Oldfather notes that the words "free" (*eleutheros* [m.], *eleuthera* [f.], or *eleutheron* [n.]) and "freedom" (*eleutheria*) occur with abundancy in *Discourses*. "Throughout his life he was obsessed with the fear of restraint, and tended to regard mere liberty, even in its negative aspect alone, as almost the highest conceivable good."⁵⁴ Epictetus finds in Stoicism a suitable salve for the wounds of his former thralldom, nonetheless his message is constantly framed in terms of endurance, acceptance of suffering, yielding, and renunciation, which are aptly summed in his utterance "bear and endure" (*anechou kai apechou*).

The sections of the four books are not systematically arranged. Arrian writes: "I have not composed these words of Epictetus as one might be said to compose books of this sort, and I have not voluntarily published them to the world. I have not composed them at all. Whatever I heard him say I used to jot down, word for word, in an effort to preserve his manner of thinking and his frankness of speech as a memorial for my future use" (I.1–3).⁵⁵

3. "Expediency can never contend with virtue"

Moral character (*prohairesis*) is the fundamental concept of Epictetean ethics. Man's good and evil, he says, lies solely in moral choice (I.xxv.1). Only moral character is capable of corrupting itself, since only it can be responsible for its corruption through bad choosing. So, "moral character is the only vice or the only virtue" (II.xxiii.19). Moreover, only moral character is one's own. Each man ought to know that no man is master of another's moral character, thus no one can make another good or evil (IV.xii.7–8).

Of things, some are good, others are evil, and still others are things indifferent. Good things are virtues and everything that participates in the virtues; evil things are the opposite; things indifferent (*adiophora*) are wealth, health, reputation (II.ix.15), which are independent of moral character, but are materials for moral character (I.xxix.1–3).

To have a free-flowing life one must yield to all things that fall outside of the sphere of moral character, to regard nothing as one's own but one's moral character, and to surrender up all things to deity (IV.iv.39–40). Overall, a wise man acts concerning things indifferent like one who plays at dice. He cannot control what will fall, but he makes a careful and skillful use of what has fallen (II.v.3–5).

Moral character can become right moral character only through exercise (II.xxiii.27). For Stoics, invincibility is the aim, and that person is invincible (*aēttētos*) whom nothing, outside of moral character, can dismay (I.xviii.21). "A good man (*spoudaios*) is invincible, as he never contests where he is not superior." He wins by letting go. One can take his office, property, and even his life, but one will never make him seek out what he ought to avoid or avoid what he ought to seek out (III.vi.5–7).

For Epictetus, prior to forming any judgment concerning all that one sees, one must ask whether what one sees is outside the province of moral character. A toothsome woman, the death of a child, an engagement with a consul? All such things are outside of moral character. Away with them (III.iii.14–15).

The functions of the soul, says Epictetus, are the exercise of choice, refusal, desire, aversion, preparation, purpose, and assent. Thus, only wrong decision can make feculent the soul. Its purification consists in making it suitable for right judgments (IV.xi.5–8). The aim is equanimity so that a soul can receive impressions true to their source. The unperturbed soul, like a ray of light that passes through water undisturbed in a bowl, receives impressions undisturbed and uncorrupted (III.iii.20–22).

Thus, moral character develops over time through mental training comparable to physical training. "Every habit and faculty is confirmed and strengthened by corresponding actions"—e.g., walking by walking, running by running, reading by reading, writing by writing. "In general, thus, if you wish to do something, practice it; if you do not wish to do something, refrain from it" (II.xviii.1–5).

What makes one deiform or godlike is the capacity for reason. So, men must know and model their character after deity through exercise of rationality (II.xiv.11–13). "Argument and persuasive reasoning have great power, especially if they should enjoy much exercise and receive some ornament through words" (I.viii.7).

The first principle of living rationally is self-knowing—"perception of the state of one's own governing principle" (I.xxvi.15). Self-knowing essentially involves knowing what is one's own and what is not—*oikeiōsis* (I.i.21–25). What is one's own for Epictetus is one's moral character—*viz.*, what cannot be taken from oneself. True freedom is desiring what is one's own and being antipathetic toward what is not one's own. Desiring more than what is one's own is acting like a child who puts his hand in a narrow-neck jar for figs and nuts. Grabbing for a full hand, he cannot release his hand from the jar. It is only by grabbing an appropriate amount that he can remove his hand from the jar (III.ix.22).

Rationality requires a veridical approach to the external world. The first and greatest task of a philosopher is to test and discriminate between impressions, and to apply only those that have been tested (I.xx.7–8). "Concerning actions, there is obligation and what is contrary to obligation, what is expedient and what is not expedient, what is my own and what is not my own." As with Panaetius, expediency and right action are equivalent. No one can think something to be expedient and not choose it (I.xxviii.5–7). The good or right action is profitable (*sumpheron*) and choice-worthy (*haireton*; I.xxii.1 and IV.i.44).

Sensory impressions (*phantasiai*) are as follows: what is and seems to be so; what is not and does not seem to be so; what is and does not seem to be so; and what is not and seems to be so. A knowledgeable man must judge aright in all such cases. The key for moral progress is to discriminate between what merely appears to be true and what really is true (I.xxvii.1–2). The aim is right action through proper use of impressions (III.xx.iv.50).

Study of philosophy is essential for appropriate action and true freedom (II.i.23). Instruction concerns learning "to desire each thing as it occurs"—as deity has ordained it. The aim is not to change the nature of things, but to accommodate one's understanding to the nature of things (I.xii.15–16).

To be educated amounts to "learning how to apply natural preconceptions (*prolēpseis*) to particular cases," in conformance with nature, and to learn that some things—e.g., moral character—are under our control, while others—e.g., the body and its parts, possessions, parents, brothers children, and country—are not (I.xxii.9–11).

Right action is action "in agreement with nature" (I.xxvi.2). A philosopher ought to align his will (*boulēsin*) with what comes to be. In such a way, he is never disappointed in desire; never pursues what he ought to avoid; is freed of pain, fear, and perturbation; and sustains the natural and acquired relations of son, father, brother, wife, neighbor, citizen, traveler, ruler, and subject (II.xiv.8 and I.xxi.2).

Thus, nature is a discriminating principle for right action. As every soul inclines to assent to the true, dissent to the false, and withhold judgment concerning what is unclear, so too does nature move desire to the good, aversion to the bad, and complete indifference to what is neither good nor bad (III.iii.1–3).

One who wishes to be a follower of nature must be capable of complete self-sufficiency and freedom. "It is foolish and superfluous to get something from another that one can get for oneself" (I.x.31–32). One self-sufficient must be capable of entertaining appropriate ideas, self-conversation, study of divine governance, understanding his place in the cosmos, and continued moral progress (III.xiii.6). Free, noble, and self-respecting men dutifully engage in citizenship, marriage, begetting children, love of god, and care of parents. They desire, avoid, choose, and refuse what ought to be desired, avoided, chosen, and refused, and act appropriately in every action (III.vii.26–27). They never grow attached to anything (III.xxiv.84), are equally themselves regardless of the place or of the time (III.xxiv.108–9), and die cheerfully (IV.i.30).

Without rules for appropriate action, exemplars are needed. "We seek out for every subject matter how the fine and good man can discover the appropriate outlet and mode of life" (I.vii.2). Epictetus appeals often to Socrates, who knew that he ought never to blame anyone—deity or man—except himself, and ought always to keep the same countenance under varied circumstances (III.v.16–19).

The aim of philosophy is cosmic citizenship—i.e., cosmopolitanism (I.ix.1). As a foot, not part of a body, is no longer a foot, a man, not part of a polis of men or of gods, is no longer a man (II.v.26). The calling of such a citizen is to treat nothing as a matter of private profit, but all things as cosmic concerns (I.ix.1).

Jefferson expressed fondness of Epictetus—"Epictetus indeed has given us what was good of the Stoics," he writes to William Short (31 Oct. 1819), "all beyond, of their dogmas, being hypocrisy and grimace." Yet in spite of hypocrisy and grimace, Jefferson, as I have been arguing throughout, was a Stoic through and through.[56] Epictetus reinforced the lessons of freedom and self-sufficiency, the need to exercise of morality and rationality, responsibility for moral choices, the equivalency of expediency and right action, the necessity of exemplars for moral guidance, the use of nature as a guide for moral action, and the notion of acceptance of one's station in life.

Marcus Aurelius's *Meditations*

The *Meditations* is more of a philosophical diary than a book. Its title in Greek is *Ta Eis Heauton*, which can be translated as *Thoughts to Himself*. In it, Aurelius or Antoninus does not order his thoughts—which are sometimes cryptic or ambiguous, often discursive—and there is considerable redundancy as one might expect in a diary. Some entries are exhortatory, as if he were talking to a son, others seem to be mere notes to himself.[57]

Aurelius's *Meditations* betrays the Stoicized preoccupations of an emperor: regard for order, connectedness, and social utility; the need of courage; and, as one might expect because of the numerous Roman cabals, concern for death, at the time. "In the midst of war, pestilence, conspiracy, general corruption, and with the weight of so unwieldy an empire upon him, we may easily comprehend that Antoninus often had need of all his fortitude to support him."[58]

Cosmopolitanism is a large concern for Aurelius. The early Stoics—who maintained the cosmos was *logos*, deity, or Zeus—were pure physicalists, and the cosmos was a sort of divine fire, and its elements were held together by *pneuma* through cosmic tension.[59] In the cosmos, all events were causally linked and fated by deity. It is the same for Aurelius. All things in the cosmos are interwoven and related to each other. What now happens is intimately conjoined to what went prior to it. Events do not occur in mere succession, but display and incredible affinity, a sacred bond, with each other (VII.9 and IV.45). There is a tension and a common spirit that breathes through them (VI.38). The cosmos is one, the god who pervades it is one, being is one, the law is one, the reason of all thinking beings is one, and truth is one (IV.23).

As with Epictetus, fate is critical. One must welcome whatever happens. Why? First, it was spun by fate. Second, what happens to any individual is for the wellbeing of the whole (V.8). "Be like the rock against which the waves ceaselessly break," advises Aurelius. "It stands unmoved, and the feverish waters around it are stilled." Endure happily all that happens,

3. *"Expediency can never contend with virtue"*

as what has happened to you could have happened to anyone (IV.49). Avoid disrelish, which disrupts the order of the cosmos (II.6).

Self-knowing, having an ineluctable cosmic dimension, is critical. One ought to examine methodically and truthfully all things. Observe all things in order to understand the nature of the cosmos, the usefulness of each of its parts, and the value of each thing in relation to the whole (III.11). Will things as they must come to pass (X.28). Moreover, recognize that discordancy exists only in thinking (IX.32). He advises: Get sober, summon yourself, wake yourself, and recognize that you were merely troubled by dreams. Examine reality as you then examined those dreams (VI.31).

The wise man aims at virtue. His only concerns are equanimity, actions for the common good, truthfulness, and a disposition of acceptance of all that occurs in the cosmos (IV.33). The good life requires acting according to nature—*viz.*, in pursuance of justice, temperance, bravery, and freedom (VIII.1). When benefitting others, expect no return, for the eyes expect no return for seeing (IX.42).

Toward things that do not relate to virtue, one ought to be pococurante. Every action is significant, though the circumstances in which it occurs is not (VII.58). Embrace of conveniences as goods burkes virtue. The more one does without them, the better the man he is (V.12–15). Fame, for example, is profitless once one looks at the infinite expanses of time prior to birth and after death. "The entire earth is just a point in the cosmos, and the part in which each lives is just a miniscule portion" (V.3). Pageantry, stage dramas, flocks and herds, sham battles, a bone thrown to puppies, scraps dropped into fish tanks, the calamities and burdens of ants, the scurrying of excited mice, and puppets jerked by strings are all empty pursuits (VII.3).

Despisal keeps one from seeing conveniences as goods. When conveniences appear enticing, strip them of their façade. Think of roasted meats as the carrion of a bird or pig; of wine, as clustered grapes; of a purple robe as sheep's wool dyed with the blood of a shellfish; and of sexual intercourse as internal rubbing followed by a spasmodic ejaculation of mucus (VI.13). Elsewhere he states that pleasant music, dances, wrestling, and boxing are despicable, when taken in their parts. Thus, analyze everything but virtue and the results of virtue, and apply that to the whole of life (XI.2). Enjoy simplicity, self-respect, and indifference to anything adiaphorous (VII.31).

One must aim to do what one can. "To pursue things impossible (*ta adunata*) is madness" (V.17). Yet never consider something impossible just because it is difficult. Painful labor (*ponos*), in keeping with the function of a man, is no ill (VI.33). One ought to act like a vine producing grapes. It seeks nothing beyond yielding its proper fruit.

Aurelius advocates Herculean hardihood and eschewal of faineancy. "I rise to do a man's work. Am I still resentful as I go to do the task for which I was born and for the sake of which I was brought into the world? Was I made to warm myself under the blankets? … Do you not see plants, sparrows, ants, spider and bees perform their proper task and contribute, as far as in them lies, to the order of the universe?" (V.1) A healthy eye does not see only soft colors, but what it must see. So too ought it to be the case with human action (X.35).

Look not at obstacles or losses as hindrances, but as change. "Observe continually all that is born through change, and accustom yourself to reflect that the nature of the Whole loves nothing so much as to change existing things and to make similar new things" (IV.36 and X.35).

Finally, Aurelius has numerous references to death, to which we ought to be indifferent. "The longest lived and the shortest lived shed the same thing at death." When the time is right, it is time to quit life. "There is smoke [in a room], and I go away." That rule can be applied to life (II.14). As a citizen of this great polis, the cosmos, what matter can it be to live five or 50 years? As an actor in a play, each must act well his role in life and disregard the length of his role (XII.36).

Aurelius, in keeping with the Stoic dictum concerning self-understanding, had an emperor's approach to Stoicism. In addition to canonical Stoic notions such as endurance, self-knowing, action in accordance with nature and one's capacities, and acting for the common good of men and the gods, he embraced hardihood and eschewal of stolidity, viewing inconveniencies as mere changes, and calmness, even cheer, in the face of death.

Jefferson clearly was not stolid, but ever active in affairs to better himself, his family and friends, and humanity. Though he often complained in letters about the inconveniencies attached to public service,[60] he accepted political offices when the time was right out of a sense of obligation to his country. As he writes to George Washington (15 Dec. 1789), when Washington asked Jefferson to be his Secretary of State: "It is not for an individual to choose his post. You are to marshal us as may best be for the public good." The sentiment bespeaks Stoic resignation as well as Stoic benefaction. Finally, Jefferson had a Stoic's approach to living and dying. He writes to Dr. Benjamin Rush (17 Aug. 1811), "There is a fulness of time when men should go, and not occupy too long the ground to which others have a right to advance."

3. *"Expediency can never contend with virtue"* 91

Thomas Jefferson's Bible

Among the recommended works under "Sectarian Religion," Jefferson lists the Bible. Given that he, on separate occasions, saw fit to make his own versions of the New Testament—*The Philosophy of Jesus of Nazareth* (1804; hereafter *PJ*) and *The Life and Morals of Jesus of Nazareth* (c. 1820; hereafter, *LMJ*)—it is meet to use his own reconstruction of the New Testament. Since *LMJ* is the latest reconstruction and the only one that survives, I draw from that work in this final section.

Jefferson in his mature writings consistently claimed that Jesus's teachings were superior to those of ancient moralists.[61] In his "A Syllabus of an Estimate of the Merit of the Doctrines of Jesus," included in a letter to Dr. Benjamin Rush (21 Apr. 1803), Jefferson states of Jesus and his moral message. I include *in toto*:

> [Jesus's] parentage was obscure; his condition poor; his education null; his natural endowments great; his life correct and innocent: he was meek, benevolent, patient, firm, disinterested, & of the sublimest eloquence.
> The disadvantages under which his doctrines appear are remarkable. 1. Like Socrates & Epictetus, he wrote nothing himself. 2. But he had not, like them, a Xenophon or an Arrian to write for him. On the contrary, all the learned of his country, entrenched in its power and riches, were opposed to him, lest his labors should undermine their advantages; and the committing to writing his life & doctrines fell on the most unlettered & ignorant men; who wrote, too, from memory, & not till long after the transactions had passed. 3. According to the ordinary fate of those who attempt to enlighten and reform mankind, he fell an early victim to the jealousy & combination of the altar and the throne, at about 33. years of age, his reason having not yet attained the *maximum* of its energy, nor the course of his preaching, which was but of 3. years at most, presented occasions for developing a complete system of morals. 4. Hence the doctrines which he really delivered were defective as a whole, and fragments only of what he did deliver have come to us mutilated, misstated, & often unintelligible. 5. They have been still more disfigured by the corruptions of schismatising followers, who have found an interest in sophisticating & perverting the simple doctrines he taught by engrafting on them the mysticisms of a Grecian sophist, frittering them into subtleties, & obscuring them with jargon, until they have caused good men to reject the whole in disgust, & to view Jesus himself as an impostor.
> Notwithstanding these disadvantages, a system of morals is presented to us, which, if filled up in the true style and spirit of the rich fragments he left us, would be the most perfect and sublime that has ever been taught by man.
> The question of his being a member of the God-head, or in direct communication with it, claimed for him by some of his followers, and denied by others is foreign to the present view, which is merely an estimate of the intrinsic merit of his doctrines. 1. He corrected the Deism of the Jews, confirming them in their belief of one only God, and giving them juster notions of his attributes and government. 2. His moral doctrines, relating to kindred & friends, were more pure & perfect than those of the most correct of the philosophers, and greatly more so than those of the Jews; and they went

far beyond both in inculcating universal philanthropy, not only to kindred and friends, to neighbors and countrymen, but to all mankind, gathering all into one family, under the bonds of love, charity, peace, common wants and common aids. A development of this head will evince the peculiar superiority of the system of Jesus over all others. 3. The precepts of philosophy, & of the Hebrew code, laid hold of actions only. He pushed his scrutinies into the heart of man; erected his tribunal in the region of his thoughts, and purified the waters at the fountain head. 4. He taught, emphatically, the doctrines of a future state, which was either doubted, or disbelieved by the Jews; and wielded it with efficacy, as an important incentive, supplementary to the other motives to moral conduct.

Jefferson lists several reasons for the corruptions of Jesus's teachings: Jesus wrote nothing; his life and teachings were left behind by ignorant, unlettered men; he was put to death prior to ascending to the heights of his moral powers; we possess only mutilated, misstated, and often unintelligible fragments; and the fragments have been further debased by schismatizing followers. In spite of such "disadvantages," Jefferson avers, "a system of morals is presented to us, which, if filled up in the true style and spirit of the rich fragments he left us, would be the most perfect and sublime that has ever been taught by man."

Jefferson's *PJ* and *LMJ* were attempts to locate the gemlike teachings of Jesus in the mass of "feculence" that the New Testament comprises. The process, he writes to John Adams (12 Oct. 1813), is easily performed "by cutting verse by verse out of the printed book, and arranging, the matter which is evidently his, and which is as easily distinguishable as diamonds in a dunghill."[62] Ferreting out the diamonds, he tells William Short (4 Aug. 1820), is a matter of "free exercise of reason"—*viz.*, of applying the same historical standards one uses when reading ancient authors. "When Livy or Siculus … tell us thing which coincide with our experience of the order of nature, we credit them on their word, and place their narrations among the records of credible history. But when they tell us of calves speaking, of statues sweating blood, and other things against the course of nature, we reject these as fables, not belonging to history." It is the same with a "character well known and established on satisfactory testimony." Thus, free exercise of reason disallows "evidence" that contradicts both known laws of nature and well-established testimonies.

Once the incredible, hyperbolic, and supernatural are excised, we have then fragments of the doctrines and life of Jesus inasmuch as the unlettered and ignorant writers have faithfully chronicled them. Concerning the doctrines of Jesus, we have a précis of our duties to other men and to deity. Those, he tells the Rev. James Fishback (27 Sept. 1809), are the moral precepts "in which all religions agree (for all forbid us to steal, murder, plunder,

3. *"Expediency can never contend with virtue"*

Thomas Jefferson's Bible. Jefferson constructed his bible by cutting out select verses from Greek, Latin, French, and English versions of the Bible (Alderman Library, Special Collections, University of Virginia).

or bear false witness)." For Jefferson, such duties do not entail belief in Jesus's divinity or even belief in an afterlife (see Chapter 7).

Embracing Christian benevolence and recognizing Christ as the greatest moral cynosure, Jefferson was in disposition more a Stoic more than a Christian. Yet Christ's teachings trumped Stoicism in one critical aspect: intentionality. What the Stoics and ancients got wrong, he says in his "Syllabus," was duty to others. In that, they were "short and defective." They taught justice towards neighbors and countrymen, but "scarcely viewed them as within the circle of benevolence." In short, the ancient ethicians, unlike Christ, did not teach unconditioned benevolence. For them, there was always a personal gain to benevolent action—equanimity. In that regard, the ancient virtue ethics of Plato, Aristotle, and the Stoics was for Jefferson axially egoistic and inferior to Jesus's teachings.

Why Jefferson thought purely altruistic beneficence was preferable to beneficence that promised the return of equanimity he never says. Virtuous action, as Plato says in *Republic*,[63] is both valuable in itself and for the sake of what comes from it (357b-c). Perhaps it is merely a matter of theoretical elegance, since for Jefferson and unlike the ancients whom his upbraids, the rational soul is only tangentially involved in moral decision-making. Morality is strictly a matter of the heart.

Upshot

In this chapter, I have argued that one might expect to find ethical works that Jefferson returned to time and time again in the reading lists he recommended to friends. Perusal of recommended ethical works shows a decided preference for Stoic authors and Stoic thinking for moral guidance and inspiration. In that, Jefferson was like Cicero, who disavowed Stoicism, but continually turned to the Stoics in preference to others for moral instruction—especially in times of distress.

Yet Jefferson's moral outlook and daily life were also significantly, but to a lesser extent, shaped by coeval ethicians, especially Scottish empiricists, whose thoughts also were significantly shaped by the Stoics, as well as poignant contemporary works of fiction and sermonizers. Those contemporary sources are the topic of the next chapter.

4

"The law of nature ... cannot be stationary"

Jefferson's Curious Immixture of Modern Moralists

> "Ah! When the dream of life is over, what will then avail all its agitations, if not one trace of utility remains behind?"
> —Volney, *The Ruins*

This chapter is an effort to show the influence of contemporary moralists on Jefferson's thinking. To do that, we have only to reconsider his recommended reading list for John Minor.

In that list, Jefferson, we saw, distinguishes between "Ethics and Natural Religion" and "Sectarian Religion." Under "Ethics and Natural Religion," he lists these contemporary authors:

Locke's *Essay* and *Conduct of the Mind in Search after Truth*
Stewart's *Elements of the Philosophy of the Human Mind*
Enfield's *History of Philosophy*
Condorcet's *Progrès de l'esprit humain*
Hutcheson's *Introduction to Moral Philosophy*
Paradis de Raymondis's *Traité élémentaire de morale et du bonheur*
Charron's *La sagesse*

Under "Sectarian Religion," Jefferson lists the following:

Bible and New Testament
Middleton's commentaries on both
Priestley's *History of the Corruptions of Christianity, Christianity,* and *Early Opinions of Christ*

95

Volney's *Les ruins*
Sterne's *Sermons*
Massillon's *Sermons*
Bourdaloue's *Sermons*

Unlike the recommended readings of ancient authors, these lists are a curious immixture, about which several things are worth noting. First, Jefferson values equally informal works—such as Volney's *Les ruins* and the sermons of Sterne, Massillon, and Bourdaloue—as he does formal works such as Kames's *Essays* and Charron's *La sagesse*. Second, some works—e.g., Locke's *Conduct of the Mind*, Stewart's *Philosophy of the Human Mind*, Enfield's *History of Philosophy*, Volney's *Ruins*, and Condorcet's *Progrès de l'esprit humain*—seem out of place, as they seem to be only tangentially moral writings. Third, all the religious readings recommended by Jefferson have marked ethical content—Middleton's and Priestley's works being detergencies of the Bible—which suggests that religion for Jefferson is superfluous if it does not serve ethical ends and if it is not in keeping with what is currently known through science. Fourth, Jefferson treats ethical fiction—e.g., Volney's *Ruins*—on par with history of ethics—e.g., Enfield's *History of Philosophy*.

This chapter is a selective examination of the coetaneous authors of Jefferson's recommended-reading list to Minor. I focus on the Scottish/British ethicians Hutcheson, Kames, and Enfield; the French moralists Condorcet, Charron, and Volney; and the sermonizers Sterne, Massillon, and Bourdaloue. The list appears to be a farrago only because Jefferson did not think an educated reader would need formal instruction on the working of the moral sense to act rightly any more than an educated reader would need formal instruction apropos of the working of the eyes to see rightly. Formal instruction might help for refinement—e.g., teaching someone how to discriminate among types of flowers) but it can also easily lead one astray if reason oversteps its bounds. For Jefferson, each person of sufficient maturity immediately "senses" the right thing to do, so education can only act as a goad for one to continue to strive for moral improvement both in self and in species. Thus, moral inquiry requires a thorough grasp of nature and its capacities, the human mind and its capacities, the history of philosophy (i.e., morality and religion), and even some amount of inspiration and reinforcement through pastorals or exposure to cynosures in fiction.

Overall, my aim in this chapter, like the chapter prior, is not so much speculation on the development of Jefferson's moral thinking over time,

4. *"The law of nature ... cannot be stationary"*   97

Books. Jefferson had perhaps the most extensive library in the young republic and books and reading shaped his daily activities throughout his life (courtesy Pixabay).

but rather to situate Jefferson's moral man in society and in the cosmos by familiarizing readers with moral works by contemporaries he thought significant enough to recommend to favored correspondents. Under "Ethics and Natural Religion," I look at Charron's *La sagesse*, Hutcheson's *Introduction to Moral Philosophy*, Kames's *Principles of Morality and Natural Religion*, Enfield's *History of Philosophy*, and Condorcet's *Progres de l'esprit humain*. Under "Religion," I look at Volney's *Ruins*, Priestley's *History of Early Opinions concerning Jesus Christ*, and selected sermons from Sterne, Massillon, and Bourdaloue. The influence of Stoic thinking on these writers will be readily apparent.

Ethics and Natural Religion

Pierre Charron: The "Two-edg'd Sword" of Reason

Pierre Charron's *De la sagesse* (*On Wisdom*, 1601) is a massive work, heavily influenced by Academic Skepticism and Stoicism, on self-knowing.

The human soul is corporeal, moveable, and divisible. Only deity, "so excellent a Substance," is incorporeal, incapable of motion, and indivisible. The soul's corporeality is neither "meer Matter," like the souls of brutes, nor an immortal spirit, corporeal, though without body and matter. Though the soul is one and corporeal, the intellective soul might not perish with it. "A body, tho' at present it be made use of an its Instrument [of the intellective soul] is not yet so necessary and essential to that, that it should not be able to subsist and act without it."[1]

The restive soul ever searches for truth, but is readily led to folly, even madness, when it takes appearance for truth. "*Reason* ... invents or entertains Arguments for the widest and most distant Contrarieties." He sums, "Absolute Certainty is not a Prize allotted to us." Thus, injustice and vice in one country is justice and vice in another. Charron sums: "You may observe, how many different Faces *Reason* puts on, and what a *Two-edg'd Sword* it is, which with dextrous Management will cut both ways." The mind is a weathercock that shifts with every wind. The greatest understanding is a grasp of one's ignorance and personal defects.[2]

Because of the mind's tendency to roam, the soul ought not to be allowed to roam freely. "There is greater need of a Clog than of Wings; and of a streight Rein, than of a Spur." Moreover, the mind, like the body, is subject to diseases. They are due, among other things, to faulty composition by nature or accident, infection of popular opinion, and the combination of disobedient will and strong passions.[3]

Given the divagations of the intellective soul, what are the advantages of learning? The sciences for Charron are several. Speculative sciences entertain the intellect. Nominal sciences—such as languages, elocution, and logic—concern discourse. Practical sciences aim at human action and are "the most excellent," for they aim at human happiness and teach us to live and die well. Next to practical sciences in significance are natural sciences, which entertain the intellect and are serviceable to human action. The rest "contribute nothing at all towards the making us one whit better Men."[4]

Will—the "seat of virtue," and "the only Faculty which Nature hath put in our own Power"—fixes our character and distinguishes good men from bad men. Will finishes an action and "determines the whole matter." In that, will is superior to Understanding. While understanding is receptive, will is agentive. Impressions operate on the mind and the understanding forms judgments consonant with the "Disposition and Capacity of the Person"; will reaches out to objects, even transforms itself into its object, and is deemed virtuous or vicious in pursuance of the object of its desire.[5]

The soul is ultimately driven by the passions—violent psychic motions toward some object, caused by the perception that something is good, or away from some object, caused by the perception that something is evil. Passion is moved equally by real or imaginary appearances. Judging through speculation something good that appears good results in love. If the good is perceived present, there is pleasure or joy. If the good is perceived distant, there is desire. Judging through speculation something ill that appears ill results is hatred. If the ill is perceived present, there is pain. If the ill is perceived distant, there is fear. If these first impressions qua motions are judged in the irascible part of the soul, they are given an additional push and become like a wheel in motion—*viz.*, much harder to control.[6] The account is essentially Stoical.

If living in agreement with nature is the standard of happiness, beasts—living a life of greater freedom, ease, security, moderation, and contentedness—are much happier. The crane, stork, swallow, serpent, dove, ox, and ass are "recommended as Teachers to us," and "Kindness, and Beneficence, and Mercy must needs be due to all Creatures whatsoever, that are in any condition of receiving Benefit by us." Thus, reason, whose evils are "infinite and insuportable," is a mere millstone.[7]

Does not will separate men from beasts? "Freedom does not consist in a Power of choosing Evil as well as Good (which is a Power, indeed, that never was, nor can be, strictly speaking) but in being Self-moved, and Self-acted; so as to be the Disposer of one's own Will, without any Compulsion or necessary Determination, from a Foreign or External Principle; and only acting, as one is acted upon." If brutes lack such self-determination, he concedes, they lack an excellence.[8]

Charron next turns to the value of living. Most men overvalue life. Taking it as the supreme good, they live for the sake of living. Others undervalue life. It is a burden or trifle, "worth nothing, or worse than nothing," and it is no matter to them, if they had never existed. "Wise Men ... consider that [life] was a Bargain made without their Knowledge or Consent." So, they are obliged to keep the bargain and make "*Virtue of Necessity*"—to "comply with their circumstances as well as they can."[9]

What is the proper length of a good life? Charron, following the Stoics, argues against esuriency. "When they have fixed themselves in this Method, then to live as long as is fit for them," in keeping with duty and decency, not as long as they can. "There is a Season proper for Dying, as well as one for Living; and a Virtuous Honourable Death is a thousand times rather to be chosen, than a Wicked and Infamous Life." A wise man lives only so long as living is preferable to dying.[10]

The shortness of life is a common complaint of both the vulgar and wise. Life does seem short, Charron concedes, especially because of numerous "void Spaces"—e.g., infancy, old age, time spent asleep, and time with illness. Yet Charron says, "What Advantage would a longer Life be to us?"

Do we need further sleep, food, drink, repose, or sight-seeing? We have sufficiently done each of them. "'Tis but a spinning of the same Web; and that which may serve a Child to play with, but can never be a fit Entertainment for grown men."[11]

In a longer life, cannot we aspire to higher degrees of virtue? What we now have is neglected; the greatest part we allow "to slip thro' our Fingers." Even if the time would be spent in pursuit of greater virtue, the day will soon come when the soul is dislodged. If the soul sinks into oblivion with death, what is the difference in the length of life? If it goes to a better state, why then should we tarry?[12]

Few men suffer to learn how to live, though all study other subjects. Some contemplate good living only when they can no longer live. "'Tis directly as if a Man should set his Cask to running, and let out all the best and sprightly Liquor, that he may reserve the Dregs for his own Drinking." Many persons "go off the Stage without considering why they were brought on, or what Part they were to act."[13]

Is retirement or solitude preferable to a life of company or business? Solitary living, writes Charron, is a buffer from the hurry and troubles of the world and a "very proper and effectual Defence against the Vices and Extravagances of a profligate Age." Still, solitude is no safe shelter from vice. There are "Spiritual and Internal Difficulties, Domestick and peculiar Evils" for the solitudinarian. "A Man had need be very Wise, to know how to make the best Use of Privacy; watchful and well fortify'd, before he is fit to be trusted with Himself." Charron says that no one with a capacity for public good and usefulness ought to neglect that capacity. Thus, the able solitudinarian is to be severely censured. Yet men are destined to live both public and private lifestyles, and a virtuous person, drawing no line between private and public living, acts as one in each.[14]

Charron next turns to critical examination of urban and rural living. Which is preferable for the lover of wisdom? "A Country Life is infinitely more plain, and innocent, and disposed to Purity and Virtue." He adds, "Great Towns are but a larger sort of Prisons to the Soul, like Cages to Birds, or Pounds to Beasts."[15]

There are without question numerous aspects of Charron's book that Jefferson found appealing. Jefferson, like Charron, had a distrust of reason apropos of human agency.[16] Jefferson too agreed that the practical sciences, concerned with human happiness, were preeminent.[17] Moreover, Jefferson saw war as a bootless human activity.[18] Furthermore, he believed that it is not life or its length, but a good life, which is the object of living.[19] Again, though he often repined for the solitude of retirement because of the hecticness of the political world, Jefferson never opted for solitudianism, as he chastised his daughter Maria for social disengagement and the unhappiness it brings (3 Mar. 1802). His actions in retirement show him to be no fenced-off Epicurean, but a person actively and utmost involved in his own and others' affairs—e.g., epistolizing and establishing of the University of Virginia. Finally, Jefferson's writings show plainly a decided preference for agrestic living.[20]

Francis Hutcheson: "A continued course of steddy virtue"

Francis Hutcheson's *An Inquiry into the Original of our Ideas of Beauty and Virtue* (1725) was a work largely influenced by the thought of Lord Shaftesbury and Richard Cumberland and a reaction to the cynical moral teaching of Mandeville's *Fable of the Bees*. Three years later, he published *An Essay on the Nature and Conduct of the Passions and Affections, With Illustrations on the Moral Sense*, as a response to critics. Hutcheson considered the two inquiries on beauty and virtue, the essay on passions, and the appended illustrations to be complementary and referred to them as "the four treatises" which constituted his moral teaching. In 1742, he published *Philosophiae Moralis Institutio Compendiaria*. A revised second edition came out in 1745. It was translated into English with the title *A Short Introduction to Moral Philosophy, in Three Books; Containing the Elements of Ethicks and the Law of Nature* in 1747. A second edition came out in 1753. I draw throughout from that edition.

The powers of the human soul are fundamentally two: understanding, aiming at knowledge, and will, aiming at happiness.[21]

Sensation, occurring externally and internally, is one of the operations of understanding, whose sole business is discovery of truth.[22] Through external sensation, humans acquire the first conceptions of good (pleasant sensations) and evil (painful sensations). Happiness is the excitation of pleasant sensations and the absence of painful sensations. Perceptions of primary qualities of things—e.g., magnitude, figure, situation, motion, or rest—are of a middle nature and incite neither pleasure nor pain, and are of greatest use in acting, knowing, and practicing the arts of life. There is also internal sensation, consciousness or reflection, by which the mind through reason perceives itself and ascertains the relations and connection of mental operations.[23]

Conceptions of good and evil, scrutinized by reason, incite motions of Will, "distinct from all sensation." Will has a "stable essential propensity to desire its own happiness"—i.e., to pursue pleasure and eschew pain. Desire occurs when good is in view; aversion, when ill is in view; joy, when good is had and evil avoided; sorrow, when ill is had and good is missed.[24] Will interacts with understanding to enable understanding to consider all evidence for a claim, and in times of ambiguous evidence, to suspend assent. When superior probability occurs for one side, assent to what is probable occurs.[25] The account draws much from Stoicism and Greek Skepticism.

There are also turbulent passions, which fall under four main groups. Cupidity or lust is pursuit of some apparent good; anger or fear is avoidance of some apparent evil; turbulent joys or delight obtain when an apparent good is had or an apparent evil is escaped; and sorrows or distress obtain when an apparent good is missed or an apparent evil is had.[26]

Moreover, there are many things *per se* that give no pleasure or pain, but are seen à la the Stoics as vehicles of pleasure or pain. Such things—e.g., society, riches, and power, and their contraries—are themselves to be desired or avoided.[27]

The pleasures are several. First, there are "reflex" or "subtiler pleasures" of sight and hearing: the gracefulness, beauty, and proportion of sight, and the concord and harmony of sound. Second, there are intellectual pleasures, aligned with discovery of truth and enhancement of knowledge, which are "joyful and pleasant in proportion to the dignity of the subject." Third, there is sympathy, "by which the state and fortunes of others affect us exceedingly, so that by the very power of nature, previous to any reasoning or meditation, we rejoice in the prosperity of others, and sorrow with them in their misfortunes." Fourth, there is virtue, "a steddy propensity or impulse toward its own highest happiness," which through "frequent impartial mediation," can govern all the selfish passions, for the sake of the "happiness of the whole system." Hutcheson sums, "By the wise contrivance of God, our senses and appetites are so constituted for our happiness, that what they immediately make grateful is generally on other accounts also useful, either to ourselves or to mankind."[28]

How is pleasure regulated? "The soul naturally desires action," says Hutcheson, and so "nature hath … constituted a certain *sense* or natural *taste*, to attend and regulate each active power, approving that exercise of it which is most agreeable to nature and conduce to the general interest." That is the moral sense, by which we "discern what is graceful, becoming, beautiful and honourable in the affections of the soul, in our conduct of life, our words and actions." He adds, "What is approved by this sense we count *right* and *beautiful*, and call it *virtue;* what is condemned, we count *base* and *deformed* and *vicious*." This moral sense is diffuse through "all conditions of life," and "insinuates itself into all the more humane amusements and entertainments of mankind," such as poetry, rhetoric, painting, sculpture, and even play.[29]

The moral sense, confirmed by "inward reflection and examining the feelings of our hearts," tells us that human dignity is in virtuous action and in what is beautiful and honorable in manners. It "prefers the most diffusive goodness to all other affections of soul" and "abundantly compensates" each loss of pleasure in pursuit of virtue, "since all these losses sustained increase the moral dignity and beauty of virtuous offices, and recommend them the more to our inward sense." It that regard, the moral sense, as a "diviner faculty," rules over the senses and "can be properly called *agreeable* or *suited to our nature*."[30] The naturalistic language again is clearly Stoical.

Though the moral sense is a relatively faultless adjudicator, enculturation can throw off its judgments. Different conceptions of divine laws can readily lead to one to condemn what another approves, though both will concede that all have a duty to obey God. "On these accounts they may have the most opposite approbations and condemnations, tho' the moral sense of them all were uniform, approving the same immediate object, to wit, the same tempers and affections." Hutcheson adds, "Hence arises the importance of this sense or disposition, in refining the manners of mankind, and correcting their faults."[31] Jefferson echoes the sentiment in letters to Thomas Law (13 June 1814) and John Adams (14 Oct. 1816).

What are the goods of which the moral sense approves? Following Aristotle, Hutcheson defines three categories of "good": goods of body, external goods or goods of fortune, and goods of soul. Goods of body are perfect sensory organs, strength, good health, swiftness, agility, and beauty. External goods are liberty, honors, power, and wealth. Goods of the soul, having the greatest axiological claim to be goods, are ingenuity, acuteness, tenacity of memory, arts and sciences, prudence, and good dispositions of will (desire, aversion, joy, and sorrow). Of the last, Hutcheson says, "'Tis manifest that there's some natural sense of right and wrong, something in the temper and affections we naturally approve for it self, and count honourable and good; since 'tis from some such moral species or forms that many of the most natural passions arise; and opposite moral characters upon like external events raise the most opposite affections, without any regard to the private interests of the observer." Goods of soul, Hutcheson says, are sufficient for happiness; but complete happiness, following Aristotle, requires some degree of external prosperity.[32]

With such a variety of goods, humans express themselves in a "wonderful variety of tempers." Some men are sensualists; others find pleasure in what is humane and elegant. Some pursue knowledge; others are moved by ambition or avarice. Some are benevolent; others are angry and envious. Such variety of tempers—increased by customs, education, habit, and even bodily constitution—makes human nature appear to be "a strange chaos." It is the function of moral philosophy to find order among the chaos, to disclose the regulative principles of human action.[33]

Such principles are to be found in the human heart, in the moral sense, which shows that actions toward general prosperity conduce toward personal happiness and that the "wisest and best Providence" governs the world. "All these practical truths discovered from reflection on our own constitution and that of Nature, have the nature and force of divine Laws pointing out what God requires of us, what is pleasing to him, and by what conduct we may obtain his approbation and favour." Thus, humans' social and selfish affections recommend themselves to the "same course of life and conduct"—a virtuous life.[34] "Virtue in the largest acceptation, may denote any power or quality which is subservient to the happiness of any sensitive being. In its stricter acceptation it denotes any habit or disposition which perfects the powers of the soul."

Virtue can also be broken down more naturally by reference to its three objects: Piety, good-will, and self-concern. First, piety concerns just opinions and sentiments about God and affections and worship suited to them. Humans must constantly keep in mind God's goodness, wisdom, and power. Thus, God, more than virtue, is the "supreme objective good"—the ruler, father, and rewarder, who governs the cosmos and regulates human affairs for the best to promote human happiness. Knowing deity, humans will wish to love, contemplate, and imitate deity.[35] Second, good-will is dictated by humans' moral sense, their "natural sense of right and wrong," and virtuous activity concerning others in keeping with it. Virtuous activity occurs through moral virtues, which are "perfections of the *will* and *affections*." The cardinal moral virtues, following the Stoics and "rooted in our hearts from our childhood," are prudence, justice, temperance, and courage, without which one can have "no notion of an happy course of life."[36] Third, self-concern relates to "forming just opinions about our duty" and "in procuring a large store of valuable knowledge about the most important subjects"—*viz.*, intellectual virtues. Intellectual virtues, "all improvements of the mind by ingenious arts and sciences" and *"purifications of the soul,"* aid the moral virtues through inquiry into nature and the cosmos, contemplation of the perfections of God, and recognition of human frailty and imperfections. Hutcheson adds, "All branches of knowledge have some use, and contribute in some measure to happiness, either by the immediate pleasure, or by discovering more fully to us the divine perfections, or enabling us better to know and discharge our Duty."

Finally, again following the Stoics, Hutcheson states that living is not the end of life, but living happily is. Thus, a life is to be preserved only if there are ample opportunities for virtuous action. When the opportunities for living virtuously are limited, death is not to be feared, but welcome.[37]

Jefferson's views of virtue and the moral sense are consonant with those of Hutcheson. Like Hutcheson, he believes that virtue is not sufficient for happiness; other goods are in some measure needed.[38] He also believes that useful knowledge is needed for moral action,[39] that right knowledge of deity is a part of good living,[40] and that it is not living, but living well, that matters.[41]

Lord Kames: The "voice of God within us"

Lord Kames's *Essays on the Principles of Morality and Natural Religion*[42] (1751) is a blow-by-blow reply to the stultifying skepticism of David Hume.

The way out of the metaphysical labyrinth of Humean skepticism is to disregard reason and follow a method "entirely suited to the nature of man": intuitive perception. Intuitive perception is "the faculty of perception, working silently, and without effort"—*viz.*, a sort of immediate grasp of some truth or conveniency that is guided by sensory data. By intuitive perception, not reason, we come immediately to see our moral duties, our continued identical existence over time, the self-existence and benevolence of deity, and the uniformity and causal framework of the cosmos.[43]

Men by nature are drawn to some emotions and averse to others. At birth, affection and aversion relate only to self-love or self-preservation. Upon maturity, humans are affectively drawn to others. "Nature, which designed us for society, has linked us together in an intimate manner, by the sympathetic principle, which communicates the joys and sorrow of one to many." Mutual sympathy is the "great cement of human society," as misfortune abounds and sympathy greatly excites the security and happiness of mankind."[44]

Sympathy occurs because of humans' moral sense, which functions intimately with aesthetic appreciation. Objects of perception are naturally deemed beautiful or ugly, or neither. Perception of beauty—e.g., seeing some object fitted to some use or related to some end—gives pleasure and is *approbation*. The perception of ugliness—e.g., seeing a beautiful-looking object that is ill-suited for its end—gives pain and is *disapprobation*. There is also beauty and ugliness of actions that relate to intention, deliberation, and choice. Some are "*fit, right,* and *meet* to be done"; others "*unfit, unmeet,* and *wrong* not to be done." Fitness applies to the means; rightness to the end; and meetness to the intention of the agent. Those perceptions are simple—i.e., incapable of definition. Hence, there are moral beauty and moral deformity, and the "power or faculty by which we perceive this difference among actions, passeth under the name of the *moral sense.*"[45]

The moral sense is not a principle of human action, as are passions, but a "guide and director"—"the voice of God within us which commands our strictest obedience." A second mover, it naturally regulates our appetites and passions by approving or disapproving human actions. It is an instinctual or appetitive faculty, not a rational faculty, though it is not entirely independent of reason.[46]

The moral sense is a natural faculty. It was with humans even in the brutish, pre-social state of nature, which engendered men's fears, not their virtues. The security provided by regular society expunged men's fears and the social virtues, through fit use of the moral sense, developed. "Their defect ... lies in the weakness of their general principles of action ... directed upon objects too complex for savages readily to comprehend." Mired in their perception of particular objects and in selfish passions, savages cannot easily forge general, complex ideas like the public good, usefulness to others, and love of country. Yet desuetude of the moral sense is remediable by enculturation.[47]

Thus, improvements in social settings toward sympathetic interactions allow for moral progress in the species of men, a sentiment consonant with many Enlightenment thinkers. "The law of nature, which is the law of our nature, cannot be stationary. It must vary with the nature of man, and consequently refine gradually as human nature refines." And so, practices given the consent of the moral sense centuries ago, like putting to death an enemy in cold blood or fighting with poisonous weapons, are presently condemned as vicious acts.[48] The refinement is toward a human ideal, divinely established.

There are primary and secondary virtues. The primary virtues—e.g., justice (restraint from harming others and keeping promises and covenants), veracity, trust, fidelity, gratitude, and honesty—are essential for the subsistence of society and more universal. "Entirely withdrawn from our election and choice," we are duty-bound and indispensably obliged to follow them. Transgression of primary virtues is attended by "severe and never-failing punishment" and pain, while obedience conduces to mild pleasure.[49] The secondary virtues—e.g., generosity, heroism, benevolence, friendship, and mildness of manners—contribute to the improvement of society, but are not necessary for social stability. Hence, they are within our choice and supererogatory: We have no duty to follow them. Failure to act in accordance with secondary virtues effects no guilt, but acting on them conduces to great pleasure. Though not the first in order of utility, the secondary virtues are "objects of the strongest perceptions of moral beauty" and excite greatest praise.

Of the virtues, two deserve especial attention: benevolence and justice. Benevolence, Kames asserts, is not a primary virtue. There can be no duty to be benevolent, as no person is naturally generally fond of all men.[50] Thus, advocacy of equal benevolence to all humans is advocacy of "a principle, which, in truth, has no place in our nature." Yet we can and do show affection to groups—our religion, our country, and even mankind. In that sense, every man "is endued with a principle of universal benevolence," which works most efficiently when each person, as a particular moral being, does his own duty, not that of another. Still there are instances—e.g., relief of another's distress—when benevolence can be a duty.[51] Justice, in contrast, is not only a primary virtue, but also the most significant one. Justice, abstaining from harming others and performing certain positive engagements, is natural to man because, *pace* Hume, property is natural to man. "A relation is formed betwixt every man and the fruits of his own labour, the very thing we call property.... *Yours* and *mine* are terms in all languages, familiar among savages, and understood even by children." Each has a peculiar affection for what he calls his own—a hoarding instinct. When one's property is taken by force, there is a sense not only of pain, but of wrong and injustice.[52]

In a chapter titled "Liberty and Necessity," Kames tackles the bristly issue of free will. "Nothing can happen without a cause" is a principle intuitively perceived to be true. Every event is linked with every other event in a colossal, inscrutable tangle of causes and effects. Yet many things—e.g., future events and human actions—seem loose, fortuitous, and uncertain, and the contingency does not seem to be a matter of mere uncertainty about causes.[53] Though humans ascribe motives to a person that determine every action, they also recognize that that person could have done otherwise in many cases. We are led to a distinction between the material world, where all things proceed in a fixed and unalterable train of causes and effects, and the moral world, where man, guided by will and choice, determines his own path.[54]

The two worlds are reconcilable, because liberty, rightly grasped, is reconcilable with necessity. Humans recognize, upon examination, that every action, however arbitrary, is determined by a motive. Even a person, indecisive in a course of action, eventually acts in pursuance of his strongest motive, whether rational or passionate in nature. Even a person who claims to act inconsistently with motives, say by choosing the most unfit woman as a wife, is motivated by the motive of controverting motives. Thus, though we act by will and choice, motive determines will and will determines choice.[55]

All motives are rooted in desire. We desire some end and then act to bring about that end. Yet desire is "not under our own power," thus "neither can our actions be under our power." Yet liberty "must signify a power to act in contradiction to desire." Such a conception, though, is absurd. Humans act not according to liberty, but according to moral necessity. They will and choose what they desire, though desire is not up to them.[56]

Moral necessity, Kames contrasts with liberty of indifference—a power to act against or without motives, an impossible state of affairs. True liberty, then, is not liberty of indifference, but liberty to act without constraint—i.e., to act unimpeded and in accord with one's will.[57]

Unlike liberty of indifference, moral necessity is congruent with physical necessity. As with Calvin, foreordination follows. "The Divine Being decrees all future events for he who gave such a nature to his creatures … must have foreseen the consequences [and] did certainly resolve or decree, that events should fall out, and men should act as they do."[58]

What, then, of praise and blame, if humans' desires are not up to them? Kames says: "If virtue ought to be rewarded, that man hath the best claim, who is virtuous by the constitution of his nature, and upon whom a vitious motive never hath the smallest influence. On the other hand, no man is more guilty, or more deserving of punishment, than he who, by his nature, hath the strongest propensity to vice, and upon whom virtuous motive have little or no effect." In sum, praise or blame is merited by the "constitution of [man's] nature," even if man's nature is ultimately not up to him.[59]

What of the strong sense of contingency vis-à-vis human actions? Deity, Kames states, formed humans not that they could readily grasp the nature of things *per se*, but that their impressions and the notions of them are of utmost use. The senses are not so much for "discovery of the intimate nature and essences of things," but more for "the uses and conveniences of life." Humans perceive color in objects, but learn that color is not a property of objects, but of light. They believe the precise moment of their death is unfixed, though it is strictly determined. Hence, "contingency in this view may justly be considered as a secondary quality, which hath no real existence in things; but, like other secondary qualities, is made to appear as an attribute of events, in order to serve the purposes of human life." Thus, liberty and necessity are reconciled. Though humans are determined animals, they perceive themselves to be free.[60]

Jefferson plainly agreed with Kames's notions of naturalism, a moral-sense faculty, moral progress in the species over time, and property. Jefferson too was a staunch empiricism and had great distrust of metempirical arguing[61] and approached issues of morality and religion from an empirical examination of the nature of man.[62] He too made purchase of moral progress[63] and recognized the need for equal distribution of property to ensure true liberty.[64] Yet though it is unquestionable that Jefferson's notion of a moral sense, in general sketch, owed much to Kames, it seems unlikely that Jefferson made purchase of Kames's "intuitive perception" to solve with a sweep of the hand numerous thorny metaphysical matters, since Jefferson shows a preference for the writings of Locke, Tracy, and Stewart on such Byzantine issues.[65] Furthermore, Jefferson gives no evidence in writings of every having thought through the necessity/free will argument as did Kames. His disrelish in varied writings of key tenets of Calvinism—e.g., trinitarianism, divine foreordination and predestination, and the unlawfulness of reason in religion[66]—and Kames's express embrace of Calvinism in an appendix to "Liberty and Necessity"[67] show that Jefferson probably would have found Kames's reconciliation of liberty with necessity unacceptable, though such a view would have fit neatly with Jefferson's own materialist cosmology.[68]

William Enfield: "A useful lesson of modesty and diffidence"

William Enfield (1741–1797) was a Unitarian minister, who established himself through his ministry, tutorials, and varied writings, including literary criticism, sermons, and history of philosophy. As a religionist, he was foremost a moralist. Biographer John Aikin says that Enfield was mostly interested in religion as "*a rule of life*." He writes: "Despising superstition, and fearing enthusiasm, he held as of inferior value every thing in religion which could not ally itself with morality, and condescend to human uses. His theological system was purged of every mysterious or unintelligible proposition; it included nothing which appeared to him irreconcileable [*sic*] with sound philosophy, and the most rational opinions concerning the divine nature and perfections." He was "much more comfortable with moral topics than doctrinal topics, and he had a knack for addressing minutiae and unobvious moral points with delicacy."[69]

The history of philosophy, Enfield begins, as a "register of experiments to ascertain the strength of the human understanding," is invaluable. Yet, there are Gordian issues—such as the origin of all things, the nature of deity, the existence and duration of the human soul, and the foundation of morals—that have been treated thetically, though without resolution, by dogmatists of every sect for millennia. Still there are incontestable advantages to a comparative study of history of philosophy. Usefulness here is key. For one, "it will lead to the full discovery of the origin of many notions and practices, which have no other support than their antiquity, and consequently to much important reformation and improvement." Moreover, a comparative study of ancient wisdom will reform modern practices. In religion, for instance, pagan doctrines transplanted to Christianity, such as the unity of the Divine Nature, have undergone corruptions. Thus, reform in religion will "free its public institutions from the incumbrance of scholastic subtleties, and … render religion itself more interesting and efficacious, by making its forms more simple and intelligible."[70]

The most prominent stumbling block, Enfield acknowledges, is the ambiguity of "philosophy." He continues. "Philosophy may be defined, [as] that love of wisdom, which incites to the pursuit of important and useful science. Philosophy discovers and teaches those principles by means of which happiness may be acquired, preserved, and increased: wisdom applies these principles to the benefit of individuals and society." Knowledge without application is not wisdom.[71]

Philosophy differs from theology as reason differs from revelation. Philosophy aims to (1) cultivate and refine the understanding, (2) to guide the will and affections to lead to actions "most productive of happiness," (3) to inquire into the causes of natural appearances to arrive at the knowledge of deity, (4) to acquaint men with the properties and actions of natural bodies to be used to their conveniency, and (5) to lead men to the principles guiding proper human conduct.[72]

The history of philosophy, as a history of doctrines, "lays open the origin of opinions, the changes which they have undergone, the distinct characters of different systems, and the leading points in which they agree or differ." As a history of men, "it relates the principal incidents in the lives of the more eminent philosophers; remarks particularly, these circumstances in their character or situation, which may be supposed to have influenced their opinions; takes notice of their followers and their opponents, and describes the origin, progress, and decline of their respective sects."[73] As a history of men, it is also a history of human error. It shows the folly of opinions based on weak misconceptions, blind respect for authority, and self-interest. Detection of error allows for the likelihood of truths, long overpassed, being disclosed.[74]

In such a prodigious undertaking, there in evasibly are numerous hurdles, two of which are anachronism and polysemy/vagueness. Enfield explains, "We have been particularly careful, not to ascribe modern ideas and opinions to the ancients,[75] nor to torture their expressions into a meaning which probably never entered into their thoughts, in order to accommodate them to a modern hypothesis or system." It is better to leave the "veil of obscurity" on any system than to clarify what is unclear and risk misinterpretation.[76]

Enfield's history comprises three periods. The first, ancient period traces the rise of philosophy and its progress to the establishment of the Roman Empire. The second, middle period covers some 1200 years—from the period of the Roman Empire to the revival of letters. The third, modern period comprises the time of the revival of letters, the "resurrection of literature and science," to the present. The progress of the modern period, he notes, has been staggering.[77]

There is much about Enfield's *The History of Philosophy* that Jefferson must have found attractive. First, the work was thorough, without being dense and prolix. Useless knowledge to prevent "farther waste of precious time" was pretermitted. Second the history of philosophy offered, as a "register of experiments," aimed to advance learning by acquiring, preserving, and increasing human happiness. Third, it was exact, as Enfield realized one cannot give an account of philosophy without first precisely defining the slippery term.[78] Fourth, it was honest, for it aimed to preserve the vagueness and ambiguity of the ancient and to evaluate them on their own terms. It also treated weighty metaphysical matters with solemnity and due agnosticism.[79] Finally, it was meticulous, because Enfield approached the history of philosophy with a cheerful appreciation for minutiae—a trait dear to Jefferson.[80]

Marquis de Condorcet: "Nature has fixed no limits to our hopes"

"Philosophy has no longer any thing to guess," says Marie-Jean-Antoine-Nicholas Caritat, a.k.a. the Marquis de Condorcet's in his posthumously published *History of the Progress of the Human Mind* (1795). "All it has to do is to collect and arrange facts, and exhibit the useful truths which arise from them as a whole, and from the different bearings of their several parts." Condorcet then sketches 10 epochs of human development, which aim to capture in gist human progress throughout history.[81]

The parts of progress are three: first, the growth of human faculties to allow for language, morality, and social order; second, the attainment of language; and last, the triumph of truth over prejudice and the linkage of knowledge with liberty, virtue, and respect for the natural rights of man.[82]

In the first epoch, families were natural, and hunting-and-gathering hordes formed with the union of several families. Circumstances created a unity of purpose, and unity of purpose led to enmity to anyone who would harm the horde. There thus were the first seeds of the "sentiment of justice and a reciprocal affection between the members of the society"—the beginning of morality and political associations. The errors of this epoch were the vengeance and cruelty shown toward enemies, enthrallment of females, command in war to a single family, and the "dawn of various kinds of superstition."[83]

The second epoch marked the transition from hunting and gathering to agriculture. Men learned to domesticate animals and work the soil. Superfluity gave rise to commerce, which created a need for money, and led to leisure. Men cultivated the arts, though crudely. Language became less figurative. Differences in possessions led to differences in wealth. The wealthier, sympathizing with the destitute, exhibited beneficence. Disputes were decided by chiefs and jurisprudence was formed to determine property and rights. Errors of the epoch included aversion to novelty, bodily and mental indulgence, embrace of superstition through religion, and the avarice, cruelty, and corruption of "polished nations."[84]

In the third epoch, men learned to work the land without their own labor, hence class division began. Language went from hieroglyphs to the alphabet, which allowed for heightened communication. Children of the wealthy received a common education. Commerce increased. Hereditary succession of chiefs or kings led to tyrannies. During war, cessation of land, ransoms, and tribute replaced killing prisoners of war. Conquests extended the arts. Science, progressing slowly, served the perpetuation of political power. Practical, agriculture-based virtues formed, but were misused by priests as impostures to augment their powers through metaphysical deceptions.[85]

The fourth epoch, the progress of the human mind from early Greece to the age of Alexander, gave rise to all political systems. A spirit of independence gave rise to philosophers, who speculated on the natures of man and the gods, and on the origins of man and the cosmos. They endeavored to reduce nature to one principle and disclose "the secret of true happiness." The death of Socrates, who abjured metaphysics and advised men to search rationally after things "placed within their reach," was the "first crime in the war between philosophy and superstition." Geometry and astronomy

4. "The law of nature ... cannot be stationary" 113

prospered. Hippocratic medicine began. The fine arts—e.g., comedy, tragedy, oratory, painting, and sculpture—flourished to a degree hitherto unknown. Morality advanced, for "the progress of virtue has ever accompanied that of knowledge, as the progress of corruption has always followed or announced its decline."[86]

The fifth epoch began with the age of Alexander and ended with the decline of science. Four schools—Plato's Academy (turned Skeptical), Aristotle's Lyceum, the Stoics' Portico, and Epicurus's Garden—made significant contributions to learning. Archimedes flourished in Alexandria. With the advance of the Roman republic, liberty and philosophy were burked, Greek poleis were swallowed up, and political science ceased to be taught. Tyranny ensued. Yet the Roman Republic's armies were destroyed and it citizens were corrupted. Christianity took root and strengthened in proportion to the decline of the empire. "The triumph of Christianity was thus the signal of the entire decline both of the science and of philosophy." With "expiring liberty," moral science could not be refined.[87]

The sixth epoch continued the decline of learning and ended with the Crusades and the resuscitation of learning. Theological reveries and superstitious delusion thrived. Religion was interweaved into all transactions of daily living. Kings and warriors served the church. Christian armies laid waste to the provinces. Claims were substantiated not by observation, but supernaturally, and truth or untruth was decided by superstitious experiment or combat. Western nations conquered eastern territories to claim "places rendered holy" by the miracles and death of Christ. Authority subrogated reason. "The morality of this period, which it was the province of the priests alone to inculcate, comprehended those universal principles which no sect has overlooked; but it gave birth to a multitude of duties purely religious, and of imaginary sins."[88]

The revivification of science began the seventh epoch, which ended with the printing press. Learning was resuscitated and advanced, but did not flourish. The sciences comprehended "a few anatomical researches; some obscure productions of chymistry, employed in the discovery of the grand secret alone [alchemy]; a slight application to geometry and algebra, that fell short of the discoveries of the Arabians, and did not even extend to a complete understanding of the works of the ancients; and lastly, some astronomical studies and calculations, consined to the formation and improvement of tables, and depraved by an absurd mixture of astrology." Horology was perfected. Windmills and paper-mills were established. Firearms rendered war less murderous and less brutal.[89]

The eighth epoch started with the art of printing and closed with the challenge of philosophy to authority. Printing educated the masses, and the spread of learning suffocated tyranny. The art of criticism was discovered, and everywhere reason grappled with authority for mastery. Science thrived through men such as Copernicus and Bacon. Exploration of the globe and commerce between East and West extended knowledge of other peoples. Yet the regnant morality of princes and pontiffs—"to support the morality of the people by false pretences"—was Machiavellianism. "The science of morals … could not at that time have being, since priests alone enjoyed the privilege of being its interpreters and judges."[90]

The ninth epoch, the current epoch, began with the time of Descartes. Free presses led to free thinking and free writing. Machiavellianism was discarded. Political philosophers arrived at a significant advance—"knowledge of the true rights of man"—deducible from the principle that "*he is a being endowed with sensation, capable of reasoning upon and understanding his interests, and of acquiring moral ideals.*" The will of the majority, embodied in a constitution, became the political standard. Philosophers made morality a science by disclosing its axioms through examination of human Jurisprudence flourished. Penality was overhauled with the aim of reform, not punishment. Truth was pursued with zeal, on assumption of "the infinite perfectibility of the human mind." Sciences and arts began to prosper, and points of contact formed between many—e.g., mathematics and physics. History was reformed to be the history of the "mass of men," not merely of great men.[91]

The tenth and final epoch concerns the future progress of mankind. If the experience of the past enables man to predict the future with probability, then delineation of the future destiny of mankind with some degree of truth is no chimerical undertaking. Progress must be made toward equality in three areas: international affairs, domestic affairs, and the improvement of man. "Will not men be continually verging towards that state, in which all will possess the requisite knowledge for conducting themselves in the common affairs of life by their own reason, and of maintaining that reason uncontaminated by prejudices; in which they will understand their rights, and exercise them according to their opinion and their conscience; in which all will be able, by the development of their faculties, to procure the certain means of providing for their wants; lastly, in which folly and wretchedness will be accidents, happening only now and then, and not the habitual lot of a considerable portion of society?" Condorcet adds, "Nature has fixed no limits to our hopes."

Much still needs to be done. There remains great inequality of wealth. Disproportion exists only because laws exist that allow for amassing and perpetuating wealth. A needed step for enjoyed rights is equality in education to make self-sufficient the citizenry. Equality in instruction, thus, leads to equality in industry.[92]

Is there a limit to progress? "The absolute perfection of the human species" is the true limit. When reason walks with science, men will aim for "the general welfare of the human species [and] not the puerile idea of encumbering the earth with useless and wretched mortals." Men will come to regard war as the "most dreadful of all calamities, the most terrible of all crimes." Men too must cultivate morality. Like other sciences, the "moral goodness of man" is "susceptible of an indefinite improvement."[93]

A large number of the sentiments in Condorcet's *History* are found in Jefferson's writings: equality of all citizens through securing their rights; the relative equal distribution of property; the will of the majority as the only viable procedural rule of a political body; the need of a constitution to embody that will; illimitable political, scientific, and moral progress; constitutional reform to ensure political progress; reform and simplification of laws; eradication of religious hypocrisy; self-determination of citizens, free and equal; education to enforce the rights of citizens; and education to enable the self-determination of citizens; *inter alia*. So great is the agreement on so many points that it would be fair to assert that Jefferson was largely in concord with Condorcet's basic schema of human progress over epochs.

Religion

Joseph Priestley: "A prince and a conquerer"

Joseph Priestley's *An History of Early Opinions concerning Jesus Christ, Compiled from Original Writers; Proving that the Christian Church was at First Unitarian* (1786)[94] focuses on two related issues: common acceptance of the divinity of Christ and of the trinity. Was Christ man or god? Nothing in the Old Testament refers to the coming of a second person in a trinity, but to a prophet (e.g., Deut. 18.18). Priestley says, "The Jews of his time expected that their Messiah would be a *prince* and a *conquerer*, like David, from whom he was to be descended."[95] Moreover, nothing in the New Testament speaks unambiguously of Christ as God. "There is nothing that can be called an account of the divine, or even the super-angelic nature of Christ in the gospels of Matthew, Mark, or Luke; and allowing that there may be some colour for it in the introduction to the gospel of John, it is remarkable that there are many passages in his gospel which are decisively in favour of his simple humanity." The tenor of the work—e.g., Mark 12.29; John 5.19, 14.10, and 20.17; Acts 2.22; Tim. 2.5; and Heb. 2.9—is monotheistic. There are many passages where the unity of God is plainly expressed "in the clearest and strongest manner." Why, then, is there not at least one such unambiguous passage on the trinity. Passages that pose problems for monotheism are rare.[96]

In a later section, Priestley offers the materiality of man as another argument against the divinity of Christ. "There is just as much connexion between the principles of *sensation* and *thought* and the brain of a man," he asserts, "as between the powers of a magnet and the iron of which it is made, or between the principle of gravitation and the matter of which the earth and the sun are made; and whenever we shall be able to deduce the powers of a magnet from the other properties of iron, we may perhaps be able to deduce the powers of sensation and thought from the other properties of the brain." The argument, Priestley adds, "is conclusive against the doctrine of *a soul*, and consequently against the whole system of pre-existence."[97] Jefferson uses the analogy of the powers of a magnet in a letter to John Adams (14 Mar. 1820) to show that the soul might be no more than certain dispositions of matter, and references the three ablest metaphysicians of his day—Tracy, Stuart, and Cabanis—in support of the claim.

Given the several arguments above, Priestley asserts, "no reasonable doubt can remain of the *general tenor of Scripture* being in favour of the doctrine of the *divine unity*, in opposition to that of the *trinity*, and even to that of the *pre-existence*, as well as the *divinity of Christ*."[98]

Priestley later turns to the Arian hypothesis—i.e., that Christ was creator and sustainer of the world and forsook that role when he became man. If God superintended the world while Christ was on earth, why did not God superintend all the while? Moreover, there is no mention of the hypothesis in Scripture.[99]

The Arian hypothesis and the notion of the trinity were the result of Platonist corruptions to the Scriptures. "Had there been no *Platonic nous*, or *logos*, christians would never have got a *divine logos*, or *second God*, the creator of the world under the supreme God, and the medium of all the divine communications to the patriarchs."[100] Priestley draws from Plato's *Timaeus*. The Platonic *nous* is the divine intellect (*demiourgos* or *idea*), and the trinity is derived from Plato's use of the divine intellect as father, the matter as mother, and the visible world as offspring.[101] Such notions underwent further development in the "strange confusion of ideas"[102] of later Platonists—e.g., Philo, Maximus Tyrius, Proclus, Numenius, Julian, Plotinus,

Porphyry, and Iamblichus. The word "trinity," Priestley asserts, first appears in Proclus, who speaks of a "trinity of trinities" and of "all trinity [as] wholeness," and adds that "in every trinity there is an end, an infinite, and a mixed," that "every thing divine is fair, wise, and powerful," and trinity belongs to "all the gods."[103]

Finally, Priestley examines the shaky Unitarian hypothesis concerning the status of Jesus. Unitarians essay to escape the charge of idolatry by asserting that Christ is maker and superintendent of the cosmos, but a lesser being than God—*viz.*, there is only one God.[104] Yet making and superintending the cosmos, Priestley states, show "greatness of power," and if "God" means anything, it means greatness of power. So, Christ too, on the Unitarian hypothesis, must be a god. To assert in addition a god apart from Christ is to assert the existence of two infinite beings, and that is superfluous.[105]

There is no question that Priestley's *An History of Early Opinions concerning Jesus Christ* as well as his *The History of the Corruptions of Christianity* and other writings made a sizeable impression on Jefferson. That is clear through the correspondence between the two. Moreover, Jefferson's "Syllabus of an Estimate of the Merit of the Doctrines of Jesus" testifies to a strong impression. In it, he argues strenuously for monotheism and gives a picture of Jesus as a great moral reformist. Though he skirts there the issue of Jesus's divinity, Jefferson clearly believed with Priestley in Jesus's mortality, though Priestley, *pace* Jefferson, thought Jesus was rewarded with a life after death by God to make his living and dying a lesson concerning the hereafter for men. The Jesus depicted in Jefferson's writings and in his *The Life and Morals of Jesus of Nazareth* or what is today commonly called *The Jefferson Bible* is that of a great moralist and reformer, not a god. In Jefferson's bible, all references to supernature (miracles, divine inspiration, and the like), the trinity, and Jesus's divinity are expunged, when not through the mouth of Jesus.[106]

François Volney: "The testimony of monuments"

Les Ruins of Constantin-François de Chasseboeuf, Comte de Volney, was published in French in 1791. Visiting the United States from 1795–1798, Volney met with then Vice President Jefferson and Jefferson agreed to translate the book into English, so long as he could remain anonymous. He presumably translated the Invocation and at least the first 19 chapters, after which Joel Barlow translated the rest.[107]

The book is not an ethical work in any straightforward sense, but is illustrative of man's moral progress over time and the ruinous effects of politicized religion and empleomanic priests.

Les Ruins begins by Volney limning his travels through Egypt and Syria. "My whole attention bent on whatever concerns the happiness of man in a social state, I visited cities, and studied the manners of their inhabitants; entered palaces, and observed the conduct of those who govern; wandered over fields, and examined the condition of those who cultivated them: and nowhere perceiving aught but robbery and devastation, tyranny and wretchedness, my heart was oppressed with sorrow and indignation."

The ruins at Hems overwhelmed Volney, so he decided to spend some days contemplating them. The solitude, tranquility, and majesty of the scene led to a "religious pensiveness" and elevated his mind to "high contemplations."[108]

A phantom, a "Genius," appeared, and they began a conversation on the fate of humankind. Volney became dejected, yet the Genius was guardedly sanguine. "The sun shall change his course, before folly shall prevail over wisdom and knowledge, or ignorance surpass prudence, in the noble and sublime art of procuring to man his true enjoyments, and of building his happiness on an enduring foundation." The Genius added that man must study his own past and learn from his mistakes, for "man is made the architect of his own destiny."[109]

In the state of nature, there was "original equality"—freedom of person, security of property, good manners, and order. Yet survival was tenuous, so humans formed societies. Guided by "experience of various and repeated accidents, the fatigues of a wandering life, by the distress of frequent scarcity," they herded and domesticated animals for their own "repose and comfort." They then began to farm. They next build houses, villages, and towns, and formed societies and nations.[110]

The ancient states were formed, and were prosperous and powerful. "Self-love multiplied talents and civic virtues." Each citizen contributed freely according to his talents and person." Property was distributed evenly. There was abundancy of produce, rapid growth of population, public wealth, and commerce between states. "Wherever a people is powerful, or an empire prosperous," the Genius sums, "there the conventional laws are conformable with the laws of nature—the government there procures for its citizens a free use of their faculties, equal security for their persons and property. If, on the contrary, an empire goes to ruin, or dissolves, it is because its laws have been vicious, or imperfect, or trodden under foot by a corrupt government."[111]

The ancient states came to ruin because of breach of social compact, appropriation of powers by administrators that once guarded such powers, and priests that preyed on the credulity of the ignorant. States subdued other states. Empires were formed. Tyrants ruled. Farmers increased their labor without compensation; merchants were despoiled; the multitude, in perpetual poverty, labored only for the barest necessities. "All productive industry vanished." There was a "false equilibrium" between the wealthy few and the penurious many. "Fatal doctrines" and "gloomy and misanthropic" religions, serving the needs of tyrants, thrived.[112]

Yet the people were responsible for their own misery. The Genius spoke: "People! Know that those who govern are your chiefs, not your masters; your agents, not your owners; that they have no authority over you, but by you, and for you; that your wealth is yours and they accountable for it; that, kings or subjects, God has made all men equal, and no mortal has the right to oppress his fellow-creatures." Heaven remorselessly speaks, "You have caused your own misfortunes; cure them yourselves."[113]

Volney, disgusted with life at this point, is chided by the Genius. There are the "testimony of monuments" and the "voice of the tombs" to be heard. Knowledge has increased and civilization has prospered over the last three centuries. Governments, though more concentrated, are more systemic and harmonious. Wars, though more extensive, are less sanguinary.[114]

Experience, the catholicon of ignorance, will teach "private happiness is allied to public good." The ambitions of nations will be restrained by "respect due to [citizens'] reciprocal rights." In time, humanity will become monolithic. The Genius turns westward and hears "a cry for liberty ... on the ancient continent"—"a secret murmur against oppression ... in a powerful nation."[115]

There is a pother between two factions in "the west": the governors (the civil military and religious agents of government) and the governed ("all professions useful to society," e.g., farmers, artificers, and merchants). First the people engage the ruling privileged class, who argue that they are paid for governing the people. The people reply: "We toil and you enjoy! We produce and you dissipate! Wealth proceeds from us, and you absorb it." Second the people engage the nobles, who appeal to the deeds of their ancestors as conquerors to justify their wealth and leisure. The people reply that nobility was bought with money. Third, the people engage the civil governors, who state that the law enjoins submissiveness. The people reply, "The law is the general will." Fourth, the people engage the military governors, who say that the people, timorous, will submit to force. The people reply that the soldiers are of the people. Last, the people engage the priests, who claim divine privilege for governing and argue that the people need priests to function as mediators between men and God. The people reply, "Your services are too expensive." The people, thus, have become enlightened.[116]

Liberty acquired needs to be preserved, so laws must be put into place to prevent the return of the tyrants and their parasites. The people now choose their own representatives and say to them: "We raise you to-day above us ... but remember that you are our fellow-citizens; that the power we confer on you is our own; that we deposit it with you, but not as a property or a heritage; that you must be the first to obey the laws you make; that to-morrow you redescend among us, and that you will have acquired no other right but that of our esteem and gratitude."[117]

The representatives are asked to search for "the true principles of morals and of reason." Equality and liberty are promulgated as fundamental principles of morality and reason.[118]

A global religious congress is formed—under the banners of nature, reason, justice, and union—to "banish all tyranny and all discord." Each religious faction is invited to argue in open discussion for the truth of its doctrines. The congress proves bootless and each religious faction is shown to be fraudulent.[119]

At that point, a new group, comprising "men from various standards," comes forth to examine the "origin and filiation of religious ideas." They disclose eight systems of religious filiation. The religions of the day, however, have shown themselves to have lost all notions of their "filiation of ideas," and so religion has become nothing more than a "political engine to conduct the credulous vulgar."[120] The Genius sums:

> The whole history of the spirit of religion is only the history of errors of the human mind, which, placed in a world that it does not comprehend, endeavors nevertheless to solve the enigma; and which, beholding with astonishment this mysterious and visible prodigy, imagines causes, supposes reasons, builds systems; then, finding the one defective, destroys it for another not less so; hates the error that it abandons, misconceives the one that it embraces, rejects the truth that it is seeking, composes chimeras of discordant beings; and thus, while always dreaming of wisdom and happiness, wanders blindly in a labyrinth of illusion and doubt.[121]

It is the metaphysical status of religious belief that results in the amaranthine argufying among religionists and proves it unneeded. When people argue about matters of sensation, the arguing ceases by appeal to sensation. When matters are beyond the reach of the senses, no appeal to sensation can stop the arguing. Moreover, much of religious belief has no bearing on human action. "What is believing, if believing influences no action?"[122]

The second part of the book, "The Law of Nature," comprises a question-and-answer session among the delegates. The law of nature is defined as "the constant and regular order of events, by which God governs the universe; an order which his wisdom presents to the senses and reason of men, as an equal and common rule for their actions, to guide them, without distinction of country or sect, towards perfection and happiness." One axial precept of the law of nature related to man exists: self-preservation related to the strong, involuntary sensations of pleasure and pain.[123]

Through the law of nature, men can become virtuous. Virtue is the practice of actions useful to individuals and to society; vice, actions prejudicial to the individual and to society. In keeping with other thinkers of the day, the categories of virtue are three: individual virtues, having the preservation of individual men as its object (science, temperance, courage, activity, and cleanliness); domestic virtues, having the preservation of man as its object (economy, the "proper administration of every thing that concerns the existence of the family or house"; paternal love, the care of parents to inculcate habits in children so that they are useful to themselves and others; filial love, the practice of children's actions useful to themselves and their parents; conjugal love, the love between a married couple; fraternal love, the concord and union of brothers as it stabilizes the family; and the duties of master and slave); and social virtues, having the utility of men in society as its object (charity, humanity, probity, love of country, sincerity, generosity, simplicity of manners, and modesty—all of which are subsumable under justice, which entails three equality, liberty and property).[124]

The delegates conclude: "Preserve thyself; Instruct thyself; Moderate thyself; Live for thy fellow citizens, that they may live for thee." Strive for simplicity of manners by "restricting our wants and desire to what is truly useful to the existence of the citizen and his family," for "the man of simple manners has but few wants, and lives content with little."[125]

Many of the lessons of Volney's *The Ruins* certainly resonated greatly with Jefferson: equal and free participation of citizens, the distribution of property, and the need of good laws. Jefferson too embraced the notion of humans, not deity, being responsible for human own woes; the stultifying effects of sectarian religion; the inevitability and importance of scientific, political, and moral progress; and claim that virtue ought to be cultivated at all levels through simple living. That he consented to translate the work speaks volumes.

Laurence Sterne: "Moral delight [and] the conscience of well-doing"

Jefferson's fondness of the Rev. Laurence Sterne (1713–1768) is undisputed. He writes his nephew Peter Carr that the writings of Sterne form the "best course of morality ever written."[126] It is probable that he has in mind here Sterne's novels—*The Life and Opinions of Tristram Shandy, Gentleman,* and *A Sentimental Journey,* each infused with moral insight—but it is noteworthy that he recommends Sterne's sermons to Moore (and Minor), not his fiction. I draw merely from two sermons that would have especial appeal to Jefferson.

In "The Parable of the Rich Man and Lazarus," Sterne argues that the station in which God has placed us at birth is our lot and we need to conduct ourselves accordingly.[127]

One day, Lazarus, a beggar full of sores, was laid at the gate of a rich man, clothed in purple. Wishing only to feed on the crumbs of the rich man's table, Lazarus was given none. The beggar died and was carried away. Soon the rich man died, and in Hades he was judged severely by Abraham. The severity of Abraham's judgment was not on account of the wealth of the man. "That he had received his good things,—'twas from heaven, and could be no reproach: with what severity soever the scripture speaks against riches, it does not appear, that the living or faring sumptuously every day, was the crime objected to the rich man." The rich man, having "passed through this world with all the blessings and advantages of it," lacked an idea of want and felt no compassion for the poor. He was a friend, protector, and benefactor to no one.[128]

Riches, though dangerous, are useful. On the one hand, they furnish us with ease, nonsense, flattery, and false friends. They decuple our faults and conceal them from us. On the other hand, God has a use for riches. "Let [the rich man] comfort the captive, or cover the naked with a garment, and he will feel what is meant by that moral delight arising in the mind from the conscience of a human action."[129]

In his sermon "The Temporal Advantages of Religion," Sterne tackles the issue of the worth of religion, independent of its promise of a future life. That worth is cashed out in terms of the liberty of a religious, virtuous life.

First, there is the false perception that the vicious life is free, pleasureful, and happy, while the religious life is servile and uncomfortable. Happiness and freedom lie in "always following [one's] own humour." Yet the scriptures tell us that "service to God is true liberty" and that any other manner of living is yoked. "Let any one try the experiment"—let him aid the needy, comfort the broken-hearted, check an appetite, or receive an affront with meekness—"and he will see what is meant by that moral delight, arising from the conscience of well-doing."[130]

True liberty is virtuous living—e.g., living without corruption, doing

4. *"The law of nature ... cannot be stationary"*

what is right, speaking without deceit, and doing no ill to neighbors. First, justice and honesty prevent dark and warped machinations as well as grief and melancholy, and they regulate the passions, and enable cheerfulness, activity, and diligence. Second, a virtuous person is unlikely to fall into disappointments and calamities, for honesty buffers him from the dangers of deceit. Third, a virtuous man "believes he has God on his side [and] acts with another sort of life and courage." Fourth, a virtuous man, loved and trusted more the better he is known, is never friendless in times of need. Finally, all the paths of virtue lead to peace and equanimity. So well does religion secure secular wellbeing, states Sterne in Kantian fashion, that if we could expostulate with God and choose our own moral laws, "it would be impossible for the wit of man to frame any other proposals, which upon all accounts would be more advantageous to our own interests than those very conditions to which we are obliged by the rules of religion and virtue."[131]

Jefferson found irresistible the "sermonizing" in Sterne's novels, so it is not strange that he should also recommend his sermons as ethically enriching. Like Sterne and the Stoics, Jefferson did not think riches themselves were evil. His attitude was Stoic: They were adiaphorous, and a good man could put them to good use. Wealth like political power, in the hands of the right persons, could be an aidful tool for moral advance and human happiness. Similarly, Jefferson's ambitious pursuit of knowledge was not due to pride or lack of humility.[132] Knowledge was needed for self- and other-betterment. Knowledge in the hands of the right persons was wisdom. Only through wise living does one find freedom, which for Jefferson is not a matter of doing what one wants when one wants, but entails levels of responsibility to others.

Lewis Bourdaloue: "Death speaks to us"

The Rev. Lewis Bourdaloue (1632–1704) was a second sermonist whom Jefferson recommended to Moore. His sermons are more cerebral, though not coldly so, than orectic. Moreover, they are peppered with profound psychological insights.[133] I illustrate through a sermon on death.

In "The Thought of Death," Bourdaloue maintains that "death is the mirror which represents without disguise the general instability, the constant fluctuation, the daily decay of all earthly things." Human passions, "impetuous for superfluity and excess," are by nature larrikin. Yet even the thought of death extinguishes the passions.[134]

Bourdaloue bids a wealthy man to see himself dead. He was wealthy, but now he is naked, impoverished, and without revenues. "Six feet of earth; a shroud to wind him up in, but which will not keep him from rotting and becoming the food of worms." He bids also an ambitious man, a man of rank, and a vain woman to do the same. Death puts an end to the projects of ambition, rank, and vanity.[135]

Death is the same for the learned and the ignorant, the nobleman and the tradesman, and the conqueror and the slave. "When we make these reflections, the thought of death assuages the swellings of our heart, brings down all its ferment, and preserves it in humility and sage moderation; death speaks to us of the equality God has ordained between us and the rest of mankind, an equality we so willingly consign to oblivion but the prospect of which is so salutary to us."[136]

Jefferson, I believe, seems never to have been driven by acquisition of wealth, vanity, or ambition. That he yearned for knowledge is clear, but his appetence for learning was not self-conceit, but a part of his depiction of a virtuous life, for knowledge was needed for self-betterment as well as domestic, social, and global progress. Jefferson was also well-apprised of the moral equality of all persons, and recognition of moral equality led to belief, expressed explicitly in several letters, of there being no need to live beyond one's days—e.g., to know when to bow out of the public scene and leave matters to younger, more capable hands and when to leave the stage due to utter inutility.[137] "I forget for a while the hoary winter of age," he writes to John Adams (12 Oct. 1812), "when we can think of nothing but how to keep ourselves warm, and how to get rid of our heavy hours until the friendly hand of death shall rid us of all at once." Moreover, Jefferson was too intimately acquainted with the leveling tendency of death—e.g., he experienced the deaths of his father, his wife, his daughter Maria, four children in infancy, and close friend Dabney Carr—to see himself as a Triton among minnows.

Jean Baptiste Massillon: "Fidelity to duty"

The Rev. Jean Baptiste Massillon (1663–1742), a later contemporary of Bourdaloue, is the third sermonizer recommended by Jefferson. Inspired by Seneca and Cicero, he sermonizes with smoothness and a "rich, polished, chaste and harmonious" eloquence.[138]

It is only through God's earthly works, ponderous but finite, Massillon says in "Sanctity and Duty," that we know Him, so we can admire Him only through those works. Yet so infinitely great is God that it is impossible for men to give Him His due. How then can we form an estimable idea of our duty to God?[139]

4. *"The law of nature ... cannot be stationary"*

Through sanctity men know their duty to God. The saints show that sanctity—"which consists in doing our duty, and doing it always as in the sight of God; in being thoroughly all that we ought to be and that God would have us to be; in fashioning our whole life and conduct in a manner worthy of the state to which God has called us"—is within our reach. The saints, "without any entanglement of precepts," are cynosures.[140]

Yet the saints are not saints because of their extraordinary deeds. That however confuses cause with effect. "They did these things ... because they were Saints; but in no instance were they Saints because they did them."[141] Massillon adds, "The foundation of [the Saints'] glory and their blessedness was fidelity to duty, zeal in discharging it, the giving up of all things that hindered the prefect fulfillment of that duty." Doing their duty, the saints brought their state of life in harmony with their religion. They honored persons worthy of honor, obeyed persons worthy of obedience, and were just and charitable to all. In all things, obeying conscience and not self-interest, they sacrificed ease, health, and even life to the claims of their calling. They were sincere in word, frank in dealings, just in judgments, upright in commercial transactions, indifferent to restive strivings, content in lot, without envy, faithful to friends, generous to enemies, grateful for benefits, patient under ills, forgiving of injury, and kind to the weak.[142]

"Religion and Morality" is a sermon that aims to show that true religion and true morality are mutually entailing. There is no morality without religion and there is no religion without morality.[143]

First, religion is needed for morality. Only religion can be a universal principle and solid foundation for the duties of morality. Only religion provides motive against certain temptations to which morality is continually exposed. "Let the principle of religion, that primary spring of action, be destroyed or even distorted in the soul, and there ceases to exist in that soul any rule of guidance, any honesty of purpose and conduct" other than perhaps a fitful and spasmodic force. Without religion, every temptation will overcome a man, for reason can be corrupted by sin or passion. Through reason, each judges merely his personal interest.[144]

Second, morality is needed for religion. Religion without morality is apocryphal. "As grace supplants nature and as faith is ... grafted upon reason, so also religion has for its basis morality." Massillon adds that justice, faith, and disinterest compose the "invariable order of things to which religion is bound to conform." Without such order, God will not have human worship. Moreover, religion without morality exposes religion to contempt and censure.[145]

The two sermons I have selected Jefferson doubtless found inspiring.

First, sanctity was important to Jefferson as a guide for human happiness in this world. Exemplars were indispensable for ethical instruction, since for Jefferson, morally correct action was not a matter of rationally embracing and following inflexible rules. There were no inviolable moral rules. Social settings provided varied and numberless trappings for depravity. To avoid such trappings, reflecting on what someone of unimpeachable moral fiber would do was aidful.[146] Thus, doing the right thing would come easily by knowing those persons Jefferson most loved and respected—e.g., Wythe and Small—would had done the same thing in similar situations.

Second, Jefferson had a similar view of the close relation of religion and morality (see Chapter 7). To Thomas Leiper (21 Jan. 1809), Jefferson says: "My religious reading has long been confined to the moral branch of religion, which is the same in all religions; while in that branch which consists of dogmas, all differ, all have a different set. The former instructs us how to live well and worthily in society; the latter are made to interest our minds in the support of the teachers who inculcate them." Here and in other letters,[147] Jefferson is clear that sectarian religions are of interest only insofar as they give us a common core of "precepts" which aid human action. To other correspondents, Jefferson seems clear that there is a personal dimension to religion: It involves a relationship between deity and each person.[148] Deity is responsible for giving each person a moral sense,[149] and no one can be perfectly happy, without acknowledging the existence of deity and deity's gift of awareness of right action.[150] Thus, an atheist can behave virtuously, but he cannot be virtuous.

Upshot

"I never go to bed without an hour, or half hour's previous reading of something moral, whereon to ruminate in the intervals of sleep," Jefferson writes to his physician, Dr. Vine Utley (21 Mar. 1819). Though he had a colossal library, Jefferson was a selective reader. He read history that was educative and inspirational. He avoided political writings that encouraged coercive political principles and practices. He was chary of indulgence in fiction. He avoided dogmatic writers. Later in life, he eschewed most poetry. Yet he did read morally rousing works, and he did so often.

As I have shown in this chapter, Jefferson drew from a multiplicity of modern sources for moral instruction. Formal treatises were of limited application, for each person, equipped with an inborn sense of wrong and right, intuitively knew right and wrong action. Thus, ethical reading was not so much for instruction, but more for inspiration. That fully explains why his recommended reading list for Minor appears to be a gallimaufry.

Yet the gallimaufry tells us much about Jefferson's vision of moral man. Moreover, it also tells us much about Jefferson—about the significance of moral goodness in Jefferson's life. Working on the reasonable assumption that a man is in some sense what he reads, it makes it difficult to take seriously so much of today's literature that paints Jefferson a hypocrite and a rogue, a prevaricator and racist—a man whose deeds were far removed from the writings he cherished and to whom he continually turned.

5

Ethicizing Through Truth and Untruth
The Lessons of History and Useful Fiction

> "Will not men be continually verging towards that state, in which all will possess the requisite knowledge for conducting themselves in the common affairs of life by their own reason, and of maintaining that reason uncontaminated by prejudices? ... Nature has fixed no limits to our hopes."
> —Marquis de Condorcet, *Progress of the Human Mind*

Men naturally, observes Lord Kames, have a strong desire to be acquainted with the history of others. We approvingly or disapprovingly judge others and take particular delight in judging. "This turn of mind makes history, novels, and plays, the most universal and favourite entertainments." Yet such entertainments are not abortive indulgences. They offer each person the possibility of invaluable moral lessons.[1]

"The advantages found in history," writes David Hume, "seem to be of three kinds, as it amuses the fancy, as it improves the understanding, and as it strengthens virtue."[2] Concerning the last, he adds, "The historians have been, almost without exception, the true friends of virtue, and have always represented it in its proper colours, however they may have erred in their judgments of particular persons."[3]

Jefferson concurs with Kames and Hume on the value of history and with Kames on the value of useful fiction. Reading history and the right sort of fiction in youth instills in the young the first lessons of morality. Reading history and fiction are inspirational goads to moral activity in later life. Seeing the beauty of virtue and the ugliness of vice in written works incites the mind to emulation.

History

Jefferson was a practicalist when it came to education, which was to be maximally useful and efficient.[4] He was also a practicalist about good living, which too was to be maximally useful and efficient, and education was for the sake of useful and efficient living.

History was one of the most important subjects of a person's education. It was chiefly to be studied in one's formative years. Its aim was to instill in young minds the sorts of character-enriching moral lessons that were needed for responsible, participatory citizenship.

"Everything must be remembered": Tacitus on History

"The more corrupt the republic, the greater number of its laws," wrote Tacitus in *Annals*.[5] Jefferson in gist makes the same point in a letter to John Norvell (14 June 1807). "History, in general, only informs us what bad government is." Thus, when a government is just, history is closemouthed. He iterates the sentiment months earlier in a letter to Comte Diodati (29 Mar. 1807). "Wars and contentions, indeed, fill the pages of history with more matter. But more blessed is that nation whose silent course of happiness furnishes nothing for history to say." In his "Bill for the More General Diffusion of Knowledge," Jefferson writes of the merits of the study of history. "The most effectual means of preventing the perversion of power into tyranny are to illuminate, as far as practicable, the minds of the people at large, and more especially to give them knowledge of those facts, which history exhibits, that possessed thereby of the experience of other ages and countries, they may be enabled to know ambition under all its shapes, and prompt to exert their natural powers to defeat its purposes."[6] Those sentiments show that it is the role of historians to reproduce faithfully the political sentiments of the day in an effort to provide later human generations with a depiction of the political climate of the day, subject to moral evaluation.

Publius Cornelius Tacitus was Jefferson's favorite historian. We can thus learn much about the importance of the study of history for Jefferson by examination of Tacitus's approach to history.

Tacitus was a Roman Senator and historian, who chronicled time of a time of violence, unchecked political corruption, widespread fear and panic, hypocrisy, and sycophantism in the Roman republic, through his *Annals* and *Histories*,[7] and other writings. Tacitus believed in chronicling events and the motives behind them without literary bias for the benefit of futurity.

Tacticus's manner of writing was laconic. Stylistically he resorts frequently to paradox, ellipsis, parataxis, and grammatical irregularity—a point which certainly endeared Jefferson to him. Addenda were frequent and such addenda were often discursive and of moral content. Consider Tacitus's account of Agricola's enticements to British states, with which the Roman Republic was at war, toward peace, luxury, and repose in Book I.21 of *Agricola*.

> The following winter [in the British states] passed without disturbance, and was employed in salutary measures. For, to accustom to rest and repose through the charms of luxury a population scattered and barbarous and therefore inclined to war, Agricola gave private encouragement and public aid to the building of temples, courts of justice and dwelling-houses, praising the energetic, and reproving the indolent. Thus an honourable rivalry took the place of compulsion. He likewise provided a liberal education for the sons of the chiefs, and showed such a preference for the natural powers of the Britons over the industry of the Gauls that they who lately disdained the tongue of Rome now coveted its eloquence. Hence, too, a liking sprang up for our style of dress, and the "toga" became fashionable. Step by step they were led to things which disposed to vice, the lounge, the bath, the elegant banquet. All this in their ignorance, they called civilization, when it was but a part of their servitude.[8]

In short, the enticements of Agricola were a means of Romanizing the Britons and placing them in the servitude that the Roman citizens of the day were suffering.

Much of the drama of Tacitus's history comes through sharply and smartly constructed personages of varied shades of moral character. Consider his depiction of Agricola's measuredness and authenticity in Book I.22 of *Agricola*. "Never did Agricola in a greedy spirit appropriate the achievements of others; the centurion and the prefect both found in him an impartial witness of their every action. Some persons used to say that he was too harsh in his reproofs, and that he was as severe to the bad as he was gentle to the good. But his displeasure left nothing behind it; reserve and silence in him were not to be dreaded. He thought it better to show anger than to cherish hatred."

Characters come alive, even in translation, through constructed speeches in keeping with their character. Marcus Lepidus, a man of principles in a time of obsequiousness and a man that steered clear of defiant independence and debasing servility, offers a striking illustration that one could rise above the obloquy of the time. "[Tacitus's] Lepidus," writes Irene Coltman Brown, "showed that there was a meaning to moral choice even when Romans lay at the mercy of a ruler like Tiberius. There was a pattern

5. Ethicizing Through Truth and Untruth   131

of behaviour available to every Roman, which was neither the futile resistance of conspiracy and barbarism, nor the dehumanize submission of the Senate, or the active complicity of the tools of despotism."[9] Consider this speech in *Annals* III.50 by Lepidus to the Roman Senate on behalf of leniency for Caius Lutorius Priscus, who had been sentenced to death for presumably writing and reciting a political poem for personal profit.

> Senators, if we look to the single fact of the infamous utterance with which Lutorius has polluted his own mind and the ears of the public, neither dungeon nor halter nor tortures fit for a slave would be punishment enough for him. But though vice and wicked deeds have no limit, penalties and correctives are moderated by the clemency of the sovereign and by the precedents of your ancestors and yourselves. Folly differs from wickedness; evil words from evil deeds, and thus there is room for a sentence by which this offence may not go unpunished, while we shall have no cause to regret either leniency or severity. Often have I heard our emperor complain when any one has anticipated his mercy by a self-inflicted death. Lutorius's life is still safe; if spared, he will be no danger to the State; if put to death, he will be no warning to others. His productions are as empty and ephemeral as they are replete with folly. Nothing serious or alarming is to be apprehended from the man who is the betrayer of his own shame and works on the imaginations not of men but of silly women. However, let him leave Rome, lose his property, and be outlawed. That is my proposal, just as though he were convicted under the law of treason.[10]

The epoch about which Tacitus wrote was a time of enslavement of Roman citizens through great fear. Yet citizens gladly accepted the check on their freedom for the exchange of security. Brown, who labels Tacitus a "political realist," states, "A generation that took part in the atrocities of Imperial Rome was eager to forget them, but Tacitus insisted that everything must be remembered."[11]

Tacitus wrote of a rather inglorious time for the Roman Empire. Nonetheless, his insistence, in Brown's words, that everything must be remembered must have resonated much with Jefferson, who did much to preserve our knowledge both of the laws of early Virginian and of the course of debate by the American revolutionists.

Writing History

"Tacitus I consider as the first writer in the world without a single exception," Jefferson says of Tacitus's *Histories* to granddaughter Anne Randolph Bankhead (8 Dec. 1808). "His book is a compound of history and morality of which we have no other example."

Jefferson was a philologist in the literal sense of the word—a lover of words and languages. He enjoyed and preferred to read Greek and Latin authors in their original languages, not in translation. He spoke French and Italian and he could read Spanish to some degree.[12] In his "Bill for Establishing a System of Public Education" (1817), he urged not only that the ancient languages be taught at grammar schools, but also French, Italian, Spanish, and German.[13] He also showed especial interest in Anglo-Saxon and the various Indian "tongues." Moreover, given his purchase of progress in science, politics, and morality, he was a staunch advocate of neoterism in language, which needed to have the flexibility to accommodate discoveries in the different branches of learning.[14] In "Thoughts on English Prosody," he shows more than a dilettante's appreciation for sonority, meter, rhyme, and verse.

In the manner of Tacitus, Jefferson appreciated laconic history. To William Short (8 Jan. 1825), Jefferson writes: "It is impossible to read thoroughly such writings as those of Harper and Otis, who take a page to say what requires but a sentence, or rather, who give you whole pages of what is nothing to the purpose. A cursory race over the ground is as much as they can claim." Jefferson's preference was for *ad rem*, concise, and factual history.

Perhaps the best illustration of his appreciation for laconic history, use of addenda or discursions, and grammatical "stretchiness," as it were, is Jefferson's *Notes on the State of Virginia*. Although the work cannot be considered history—at least, not in Jefferson's sense of history—there are multitudinous scattered historical anecdotes. Query XIV, one of the longest of the book, aims to catalog the "administration of justice and description of the laws" of Virginia. The varied accounts he gives are usually laconic. Jefferson gives a description of magistrates; superior courts; the board of auditors; the extant laws pertaining to payment of debts, marriages, naturalization, land conveyances, land acquisition, slavery, bills of exchange, preservation and improvement of useful animals, *inter alia*; and the revisal of the laws, undertaken by him, George Wythe, and Thomas L. Lee, etc. Under the rubric "A Description of the Laws," Jefferson gives a short sketch of the laws of England, adopted by Virginians. Next, turning to an account of how the poor are supported, he takes up beggary and notes as an discursive addendum, "I never yet saw a native American begging in the streets or highways."[15] While discussing the revision of Virginia's laws, Jefferson mentions the emancipation of all slaves "born after the passing of the act" and begins a lengthy digression on the nature of Blacks. He also offers a précis of his scale for proportioning crimes and punishments and then ends with another digression, here on the general diffusion of knowledge.

Moreover, grammatical pliancy is evident throughout the book. I offer merely two illustrations, apropos of educational reform at the end of Query

XIV. Jefferson says, "The general objects of this law are to provide an education adapted to the years, to the capacity, and [to] the condition of every one, and directed to their freedom and happiness." In stating the first object of the law, "years" and "capacity" are introduced with the preposition "to," while "condition" has no preposition. When he turns to pretermission of religious instruction in ward schools, he mentions education through "Grecian, Roman, European and American history." In the next sentence, he states that history also gives moral lessons by showing happiness is not due to chance, but is "always the result of good conscience, good health, occupation, and freedom in all just pursuits."[16] Note inclusion of a comma after "occupation" in the second sentence and omission of a comma after "European" in the first.

Neoterism was also an indispensable tool for historians, for history in large part was a measure of human progress in learning over time. To Joseph Milligan (6 Apr. 1816), he says, "Nothing is more evident than that as we advance in the knowledge of new things, and of new combinations of old ones, we must have new words to express them."[17] Moreover, to John Waldo (16 Aug. 1813), Jefferson advocates hybridity—*viz.*, the formation of a word by combining one part from one language and another part from another language. He lists several examples of new words by combination of English, Greek, and Latin. For illustration, three words with the same meaning *over-place* (English), *hyper-thesis* (Greek), and *super-location* (Latin) can be expressed by the combinations *over-thesis* (English with Greek), *hyper-location* (Greek with Latin), and *super-place* (Latin with English). In such a manner, "the language would become, in strength, beauty, variety, and every circumstance which gives perfection to language, were it permitted freely to draw from all its legitimate sources."[18] Hybridity gives historians a greater array of words with which to express themselves.

Like Tacitus as well as Livy, Sallust, and Plutarch in antiquity and Kames and Hume in his time, history was mostly a character-enriching enterprise for Jefferson. Writes Plutarch, for illustration, in his "The Life of Pericles" of each person's natural fondness of seeing, learning, and virtue[19]: "It is meet ... that he pursue what is best, to the end that he may not merely regard it, but also be edified by regarding it. A colour is suited to the eye if its freshness, and its pleasantness as well, stimulates and nourishes the vision; and so our intellectual vision must be applied to such objects as, by their very charm, invite it onward to its own proper good. Such objects are to be found in virtuous deeds; these implant in those who search them out a great and zealous eagerness which leads to imitation."

To William Duane (4 Apr. 1813), Jefferson writes straightforwardly of his disrelish of modern history. "The total banishment of all moral principle from the code which governs the intercourse of nations ... sicken[s] my soul unto death. I ... take refuge in the histories of other times, where ... their stories are handed to us under the brand of a Livy, a Sallust and a Tacitus, and we are comforted with the reflection that the condemnation of all succeeding generations has confirmed the sentence of the historian, and consigned their memories to everlasting infamy, a solace we cannot have with the Georges and Napoleons but by anticipation."

Finally, like Tacitus, Jefferson is not just a political realist, but a moral realist. Truth, not fabulation, is the aim of history. To Josephus B. Stuart's plea (10 May 1817) that Jefferson give an account of early American history, Jefferson replies: "While in public life I had not time, and now that I am retired, I am past the time. To write history requires a whole life of observation, of inquiry, of labor and correction. Its materials are not to be found among the ruins of a decayed memory." To James Madison (20 Feb. 1784), Jefferson speaks highly of Chastellux's *Travels to North America*. "He has visited all the principal fields of battle, enquired minutely into the detail of the actions, & has given what are probably the best accounts extant of them." Jefferson also likes Chastellux's Tacitus-like regard for character. For instance, Chastellux writes elliptically of the great humanity of Gen. George Washington, "Thus we see that the great events of war are not always great battles, and humanity may receive some consolation from this sole reflection, that the art of war is not necessarily a sanguinary art, that the talents of the commanders spare the lives of the soldiers, and that ignorance alone is prodigal of blood."[20]

Jefferson is highly critical of fabulists masquerading as historians. "You have certainly practiced vigorously [in *The Life of Patrick Henry*] the precept of 'de mortius nil nisi bonum,'"[21] Jefferson complains to William Wirt (12 Nov. 1816). "This presents a very difficult question,—whether one only or both sides of the medal shall be presented. It constitutes, perhaps, the distinction between panegyric and history."

Jefferson is also highly critical of historians with a political slant. He especially targets David Hume, who, he admits, writes judiciously and with charm and by whom he, as a youth, was bedeviled. "I remember well the enthusiasm with which I devoured it when young," he writes. Yet then there was "the length of time, the research and reflection which were necessary to eradicate the poison it had instilled into my mind." The chief difficulty, for Jefferson, is that Hume wrote unapologetically with a Toryist agenda.[22] "It is this book which has undermined the free principles of the English government, has persuaded readers of all classes that there were usurpations on the legitimate and salutary rights of the crown, and has spread universal toryism over the land."[23]

The Problem of Newspapers

Newspapers in Jefferson's day were anything but beacons of objectivity. Early in Virginia they were in the service of governing authorities, as presses needed government subsidy to stay afloat. With competition, fueled by the pressure of commerce, and with imposition of and opposition to the Stamp Act, which imposed a half-penny duty on every paper and a two-shilling tax on every advertisement, presses began to break free of governmental yoke. They were to become a venue for public sentiment.[24]

Through his life, Jefferson had an ambivalent attitude toward newspapers. In letters, he often openly expressed contempt for them.[25] They were often used, he told Peregrine Fitzhugh (23 Feb. 1798), as a "fair mark of every man's dirt," and Jefferson quietly endured denigrative dirt like few prominent politicians in the history of America. Yet Jefferson also realized that free presses were needed for dissemination of information to keep the citizenry apprised of the goings on, political and otherwise.[26] So important were they deemed for enlightened republicanism that when faced with the prospect of government without newspapers or newspapers without government, Jefferson expressed unequivocal preference for the latter.[27]

Jefferson's view of the indispensability of free presses in a large state was not shared by most. The received view was that freedom of the press in a large republic would lead to anarchy, not orderly government, for large states required stout, centralized government. Thus, like government for and by the people, free presses were a sort of experiment for Jefferson to show the falsity of the notion that "freedom of the press is incompatible with orderly government," Jefferson writes to Thomas Seymour (11 Feb. 1807). "The fact being once established, that the press is impotent when it abandons itself to falsehood, I leave to others to store it to its strength, by recalling it within the pale of truth. Within that it is a noble institution, equally the friend of science and of civil liberty." In sum, though free presses had a capacity to do great harm, Jefferson recognized their indispensability for republican government, which could not exist without informed people.

It is obvious that newspapers, obligingly embracing falsehoods, posed a problem for historians. Historians relied mightily on newspapers as sources of information. Yet accounts of events often varied pell-mell, and papers generally had a political slant, as is often today the case. With slanted accounts, evidence not vetted, and pretermission of truth, how could papers be regarded as reliable resources?

A late-life letter to William Short (8 Jan. 1825) suggests that they could not be reliable. The conflict of the two parties will never be truly known, Jefferson says, till "the death of the actors in it," when "the hoards of their letters shall be broken up and given to the world."

Preserving U.S. History

Jefferson believed that the American Revolution was a kairotic moment in world history. The confederation of American states was in position to show the world that republican government would mark an advance in politics and morality for other science-abiding, progress-minded nations to follow. He, thus, recognized that the revolution that led to republican government, being of utmost significance, needed to be chronicled with meticulous exactitude. Here Jefferson was fronted with another importunate difficulty. Who was in an advantageous position to chronicle the events of the American Revolution with meticulous exactitude?

Jefferson plainly expresses pessimism in a letter to John Adams (10 Aug. 1815). The councils, designs and discussions of the revolution were conducted by Congress with closed doors, and no members took notes. To William Wirt (14 Aug. 1814), Jefferson expresses dismay that the chief actors in political affairs seldom take notes. To Hugh P. Taylor (4 Oct. 1823), he states, "It is the duty of every good citizen to use all the opportunities which occur to him, for preserving documents relating to the history of our country."

There is also the issue of just what to preserve. Jefferson expresses his worry about inexactitude in a letter to editor of *Journal de Paris* (29 Aug. 1787). After expressing displeasure on the historical fabrications of d'Auberteuil, Longchamps, and Abbé Robin, he asks: "Will those rise from their graves to bear witness to the truth, who would not, while living, lift their voices against falsehood? If cotemporary histories are thus false, what will future compilations be? And what are all those of preceding times?" Jefferson latches on to a passage from a book, titled *Les ligues achéenne, suisse et hollandoise; et révolution des États Unis de l'Amérique* (Charles-Joseph Mayer), in which John Dickinson is credited not only with signing the Declaration of Independence, but also with being a singular mover of American independence. "Il (M. Mayer) assure qu'une seule voix, un seul homme, prononça l'independance des etats unis, ce fut John Dickinson.—

l'Amerique lui doit une reconnoissance eternelle; c'est Dickinson qui l'a affranchie." Dickinson, Jefferson asserts, was neither among the signers, nor was he a principle player.

In "Notes on Prof. Ebeling's Letter of July 30, 1795," Jefferson critiques Christoph Daniel Ebeling's sources of information for his upcoming book *Biography and History of North America*.[28] President Stiles, he says, is a man "of very great learning," but also of great credulity. Dr. Willard, Dr. Barton, Dr. Ramsay, and Mr. Barlow are "men of respectable characters worthy of confidence as to any facts they may state, and rendered, by their good sense, good judges of them." Mr. Morse and Mr. Webster are "good authorities for whatever relates to the Eastern states, & perhaps as far South as the Delaware," but that is where their credibility ends. Each took one trip to the South to merit a reputation as eye-witnesses. "To pass once along a public road thro' a country, & in one direction only, to put up at it's taverns, and get into conversation with the idle, drunken individuals who pass their time lounging in these taverns, is not the way to know a country, it's inhabitants, or manners." Thus, Ebeling's generalizations concerning the fledgling United States are parologistic, because his sources are too few and too mistemious.

Jefferson then critiques the Federalist newspapers from which Ebeling garners data—Ebeling in his letter to Jefferson mentions John Fenno's *Gazette of the United States* (New York), Noah Webster's *American Minerva* (New York), and Benjamin Russell's *Columbian Centinel* (Boston).[29] The critique requires a lengthy explanation of the advent of the American Revolutionary War.

Jefferson writes about pre-revolution assimilation of British political ideas, the forging of the "first federal confederation" or constitution intended as cement for the federation of states, and a convention to amend that constitution, which gave rise to anti-republican sentiments and led to an anti-republican majority in both houses. By the second election, two distinct parties—republicans, comprising all landholders throughout the United States and the body of non-landholding laborers; and anti-republicans, comprising old refugees and tories, alienigenate British merchants, American merchants trading on British capital, speculators and holders in the banks and public funds, many officers of the federal government, office-hunters willing to give up principles for places, and "nervous persons, whose languid fibres have more analogy with a passive than active state of things"—formed in Congress. By the third election, Jefferson writes with clear hyperbole, "The people in general became apprised of the game which was playing for drawing over them a kind of government which they never had in contemplation." By the fourth election, "the anti-republicans have become a weak minority" and the inevitability of a republican purging of all branches of government was begun.

Jefferson then returns to the subject of newspapers. "As in the commerce of human life, there are commodities adapted to every demand, so there are newspapers adapted to the Antirepublican palate, and others to the Republican." In addition to the *Columbian Centinel*, the *American Minerva*, the *Gazette of the U.S.*, Jefferson lists the *Connecticut Courant* (Hartford), and Augustine Davis's *Richmond Gazette* as illustrations of papers with a decided Federalist slant. He lists as illustrations of papers with a republican slant Samuel Adams's *Boston Gazette*, Thomas Greenleaf's *The New York Journal and Daily Patriotic Register*, Philip Freneau's *National Gazette* (New Jersey), Benjamin Franklin Bache's *Aurora General* (Philadelphia), Samuel Pleasants's *Virginia Gazette and Richmond and Manchester Advertizer*.

In a letter to John Norvell (14 June 1807), Jefferson writes of the importance of access to accurate accounts of British history. "As we have employed some of the best materials of the British constitution in the construction of our own government, a knowlege of British history becomes useful to the American politician." He adds, however, that there is no recommendable general history of England. He considers the estimable work of David Hume, whose *History of England*, howsoever bewitchingly written, he finds politically slanted and inconsistent with republican principles of governing. He recommends instead John Baxter's *A New and Impartial History of England*, an abridged and republicanized deterging of Hume's work. "Baxter has performed a good operation on it. He has taken the text of Hume as his ground work, abridging it by the omission of some details of little interest, and wherever he has found him endeavoring to mislead, by either the suppression of a truth or by giving it a false coloring, he has changed the text to what it should be, so that we may properly call it Hume's history republicanised." In a letter to Matthew Carey (22 Nov. 1818), Jefferson states that there are only two ways to counter the poison of Hume: first, to publish Hume's text in one column along with a running critique of "its disguises, its misrepresentations, its concealments, its sophisms, and ironies"; second, to absterge the work in the manner of Baxter.[30]

It comes as no surprise that Jefferson has been roundly criticized for his detestation of Hume's history and his championing of Baxter's greatly inferior abstergent. Yet Hume himself agrees with Jefferson apropos of Tory prejudices when it comes to history. "My views of *things* [e.g., politics] are more conformable to Whig principles; my representations of *persons* [e.g., history] to Tory prejudices."³¹ Douglas Wilson sums the scholarly uneasiness, "It has appeared [to critics] all the more unseemly that the great champion of freedom and education should protest so loudly about the dangers of reading a book." Wilson urges caution however. Behind the venom, there is profound admiration, for Jefferson's letter to Carey concedes that Hume's work would be "the most perfect sample of fine history which has ever flowed form the pen of man," were it not for its Toryish slant. Consequently, the issue is much more Gordian than most critics acknowledge.³² To Wilson's sound cautionary words, I add that Jefferson's axial aim was never political, but always moral. Hence, his patronage of Baxter's abstergence and condemnation of Hume's work expresses his concern for moral contamination. Hume is a masterful writer and it is easy, as it was for Jefferson, to be seduced by the "entrapments" of his subtle pen.³³

That Jefferson was aiming at truth, not political propaganda, is evident in his lifelong commitment to preserving materials of legal and political significance for later generations. To Ebenezer Hazard (18 Feb. 1791), he laments the loss of precious documents. "Time and accident are committing daily havoc on the originals deposited in our public offices. The late war has done the work of centuries in this business. The last cannot be recovered, but let us save what remains; not by vaults and locks which fence them from the public eye and use in consigning them to the waste of time, but by such a multiplication of copies, as shall place them beyond the reach of accident." To Judge William Johnson (12 June 1823), Jefferson pleads for public exposure to the "private hoards" of the "letters of the day": "History may distort truth, and will distort it for a time, by the superior efforts at justification of those who are conscious of needing it most. The opening scenes of our present government will not be seen in their true aspect until the letters of the day, now held in private hoards, shall be broken up and laid open to public view." Last, there are Jefferson's continued efforts to preserve the laws of Virginia and other important documents for historians,³⁴ to which Jefferson refers in his letters to George Wythe (16 Jan. 1796), William Waller Hening (14 Jan. 1807 and 1 Dec. 1809),³⁵ and to Hugh Paul Taylor (4 Oct. 1823). They comprise Jefferson's collection of the proceedings of the Virginia Company in England and the Records of the Council of Virginia from 1622 to 1700. Therein are Virginia's court cases, compilations of laws, business records, records of the General Assembly, and even a commonplace book for prospective students of law, among other things. They became part of Jefferson's library.

Teaching History

Not only is it important to write truthful history and to preserve it, it is important to disseminate it. History, Jefferson says in *Notes on the State of Virginia*, is the most important part of a boy's ward-school education, as it is capable of inculcating "the first elements of morality." Nonetheless, it is also to be a significant part of higher education, for when "their [moral] judgments advance in strength," students might come "to work out their own greatest happiness"—the result of "good conscience, good health, occupation, and freedom in all just pursuits" and recognition that circumstances are irrelevant to happiness.[36] Referring to his "Bill for the More General Diffusion of Knowledge," Jefferson writes that nothing is more important and legitimate than that of "rendering the people the safe, as they are the ultimate, guardians of their own liberty." He continues: "History, by apprising them of the past, will enable them to judge of the future; it will avail them of the experience of other times and other nations; it will qualify them as judges of the actions and designs of men; it will enable them to know ambition under every disguise it may assume; and knowing it, to defeat its views." Without the education of the general citizenry, the rulers, taking themselves to be above the people, will tend to govern in their own best interests and pretermit the people. "Every government degenerates when trusted to the rulers of the people alone. The people themselves, therefore, are its only safe depositories. And to render even them safe, their minds must be improved to a certain degree."[37]

With rationality still not sufficiently mature from ages roughly from 10 to 15, the educational focus at grammar schools is study of languages, but languages are to be taught while reading history. In that regard, while learning languages, youths "at the same time impress their minds with useful facts and good principles."[38] Finally, history also will be taught at universities.

Fiction

Jefferson's attitude toward literary fiction—novels, poetry, and the like—is more complex. Perusal of his catalogs of books and his literary and legal commonplace books are evidence of great enjoyment of fiction. The category "Fiction" from his library's catalog of books is represented by the label "Poetry," under which Jefferson subsumes "Epic"; "Romance, Tales, Fables"; "Pastorals, Odes, Elegies, &c."; "Didactic"; "Tragedy"; and "Comedy." I offer a listing of authors listed under "Poetry."

5. Ethicizing Through Truth and Untruth   141

Greek: Achilles Tatius, Aeschylus, Aesop, Anacreon, Apollonius, Aristophanes, Bion and Moschus, Chariton, Colluthus, Euripides, Hesiod, Homer, Longus, Lycophron, Menander, Phaedrus, Philemon, Pindar, Smyranaeus, Sophocles, Theocritus, Tyrtaeus, and Xenophon.

Roman: Publius Terentius Afer, Titus Petronius Arbiter, Decimus Magnus Ausonius, Titus Lucretius Carus, Catullus, Cicero, Caludius Claudianus, Aurelius Prudentus Clemens, Aulus Persius Flaccus, Quintus Horatius Flaccus, Horace, Silius Italicus, Juvenal, Lucanus, Manilius, Titus Maccius Plautus, Ovid, Sextus Propertius, Statius, Albius Tibullus, and Virgil.

American: Hugh Henry Brackenridge, Thomas Branagan, Timothy Dwight, Philip Freneau, David Humphreys, John Blair Linn, Judith Lomax, Robert Morris, James Philip Puglia, Joseph Story, John Trumbell, Mercy Otis Warren, George Watterston, and Phillis Wheatley.

Chinese: work titled *Hau Kiou Choaan* (*The Pleasing History*).

Dutch: Desiderius Erasmus and Jan Luzac.

English: Joseph Addison, Mark Akenside, Christopher Anstey, Joel Barlow, Francis Beaumont, Andrew Becket, Simon Berington, Vincent Bourne, Samuel Butler, Edward Capell, Susanna Centlivre, Geoffrey Chaucer, Colley Cibber, William Congreve, Charles Cotton, Abraham Cowley, Sir Herbert Croft, John Cutts, Erasmus Darwin, Daniel Defoe, William Dodd, Robert Dodsley, Michael Drayton, John Dryden, Elijah Fenton, John Fletcher, Philip Frowde, Sir Samuel Garth, Edmund Gayton, Thomas Gilbert, Richard Glover, Oliver Goldsmith, Eliza Haywood, John Hughes, Richard Paul Jodrell, Thomas Johnson, Ben Jonson, John Langhorne, William Langland, John Lilly, Mary de la Riviere Manley, William Mason, Thomas James Mathias, John McCreary, John Milton (cataloged as an epic poet), Edward Moore, Thomas Moore, Thomas Morell, Thomas Moss, Thomas Northmore, Teresa John Oldham, Thomas Otway, Thomas Percy, John Philips, Constantia Phillips, Alexander Pope, Joseph Reed, Thomas Clio Rickman, Nicholas Rowe, Sir Charles Sedley, William Shakespeare, John Sheffield, William Shenstone, Edmund Spenser, James Thomson, Sir John Vanbrugh, George Villiers, Ralph Winterton, William Wycherley, and Edward Young.

French: Pierre Augustin Caron de Beaumarchais, Alexandre Louis Bertrand Robineau Beaunoir, Pierre Jean Baptiste Choudard Desforges, Nicolas Boileau-Despréaux, Paul Philippe Gudin de la Brenellerie, Nicolas Edme Restif de la Bretonne, Étienne Morel de Chédeville, Denys Diderot, Charles Simon Favart, François de Salignac de la Motte Fénélon, Jean Pierre Claris de Florian, Nicolas Freret, Angelin Gazet, Anne Loiuise Germaine, François Toussaint Gros, Etienne François de Lantier, Jean François Marmontel, Louis Sebastien Mercier, Jean Baptiste Poquelin de Molière, Jacques Marie Boutet de Monvel, Pierre Nicole, Pierre Germain Parisau, François Rabelais, John Racine, Andrew Michael Ramsay, François-Louis Gand le Bland Bailli du Rollet, L'Abbé Nicolas Saboly, Alain René le Sage, Charles de Margotelle de St. Denys Saint-Evremond, Guillaume de Saluste, Lucius Annaeus Seneca, Jacques Vanière, and Marie Madeleine Pioche de la Vergne.

German: Johann Melchior von Birkenstock.

Indian: Cálidás (trans. from Sanscrit and Prácrit).

Irish: George Farquhar, Philip Francis, Francis Gentlemen, Charles Johnston, Morgan McNamara, Thomas Southerne, Sir Richard Steele, Laurence Sterne, and Jonathan Swift.

Italian: Dante Alighieri, Lodovico Ariosto, Giovanni Boccaccio, Giovanni Battista

Guarini, Miccolo Machiavelli, Marcus Manilius, Pietro Metastio, Lorenzo Pignotti, Torquato Tasso, and Marco Girolamo Vida.

Spaniard: Vincente Garcia de la Huerta, Marcus Valerius Martialis, Bernardino de Rebolledo, Miguel de Cervantes Saavedra, Gonzalez de Salas, Estevan Manuel de Villegas, and Alonzo de Ercilla y Zuñiga.

Scottish: John Armstrong, James Beattie, Thomas Campbell, Charles Hart, John Home, James MacPherson, David Mallet, John Ogilvie, Alexander Ross, Tobias George Smollett, and James Thomson.

Welsh: Elizabeth Griffith.

In the main, the authors are evidence of Jefferson's purchase of useful fiction. "The entertainments of fiction are useful as well as pleasant," Jefferson writes to Robert Skipwith (3 Aug. 1771). Their pleasantness is apparent to anyone who reads, but what of their utility? He, like Lord Kames, responds: "I answer, everything is useful which contributes to fix in the principles and practices of virtue."

Jefferson illustrates with an act of charity or gratitude, either observed or conjured up in imagination. Such an act's beauty forges a deep impression on persons and incites a powerful urge toward emulation. Thus, entertaining or observing charitable actions offers exercise to the moral sense, which, like a bodily limb, strengthens with exercise, and exercise leads to habits of thought and action. Again like Kames, we also see, through references to beauty that the aesthetic sense works intimately the moral sense.

Reading works of fiction, not void of moral content, functions to strengthen the moral sense via imagination. Jefferson continues: "We never reflect whether the story we read be truth or fiction. If the painting be lively, and a tolerable picture of nature, we are thrown into a reverie, from which if we awaken it is the fault of the writer." He exemplifies with references to the works of Shakespeare, Marmontel, and his beloved Laurence Sterne, whose writings, he tells nephew Peter Carr (10 Aug. 1787) "form the best course of morality that ever was written."[39] Thus, he says to Skipwith, it matters nowise whether Sterne in his *A Sentimental Journey* ever went to France.

Finally, there is a sense in which works of fiction are preferable to works of history. "Considering history as a moral exercise," he states to Skipwith, "her lessons would be too infrequent if confined to real life." He adds that few incidents of historians "excite in any high degree this sympathetic emotion of virtue." He continues: "We are therefore wisely framed to be as warmly interested for a fictitious as for a real personage. The field of imagination is thus laid open to our use and lessons may be formed to illustrate and carry home to the heart every moral rule of life." A "lively and lasting sense of filial duty" is better impressed on the mind by reading

"King Lear" than by "all the dry volumes of ethics, and divinity that ever were written."

The notion is again Kamesian. Fiction, as "feigned history," Kames says, "generally makes a stronger impression than what is real," because incidents are chosen to make deep moral impressions. Such impressions are not so frequent in history.[40] Hume, however, thinks otherwise. He writes that no study or occupation is "so unexceptionable as history" in acquainting humans morally with their own affairs.[41]

The moral sense can also indirectly be strengthened propensity to vice through repulsion to vice. To granddaughter Anne Randolph Bankhead (26 May 1811), Jefferson writes of Maria Edgeworth's novel *Modern Griselda*, which he intends to send it to his granddaughter, though he has a reservation—that the main character is more of an antiheroine than heroine. "The heroine," Jefferson writes, "presents herself certainly as a perfect model of ingenious perverseness, and of the art of making herself and others unhappy. If it can be made of use in inculcating the virtues and felicities of life, it must be by the rules of contraries."

The Blind Poet Homer. This statue of Homer sits on the southern part of the Lawn of University of Virginia before Old Cabell Hall (photograph by the author).

Jefferson's views on the merit of the fiction of poetry likely changed in later life. "In early life I was fond of [poetry]," he writes some 30 years after his letter to Skipwith to John D. Burk (21 June 1801), "and easily pleased. But as age and cares advances, the powers of fancy have declined.

Every year seems to have plucked a feather from her wing till she can no longer waft one to those sublime heights to which it is necessary to accompany a poet. So much has my relish for poetry deserted me that I cannot read even Virgil with pleasure."

A letter to Nathaniel Burwell years later (14 Mar. 1818), urges caution concerning novels. The "inordinate passion prevalent for novels" he calls "a great obstacle to good education." One reason is that the time spent reading such novels—"this mass of trash"—is time that could have been spent doing something more instructive. "When this poison infects the mind, it destroys its tone and revolts it against wholesome reading. Reason and fact, plain and unadorned, are rejected. Nothing can engage attention unless dressed in all the figments of fancy, and nothing so bedecked comes amiss. The result is a bloated imagination, sickly judgment, and disgust towards all the real businesses of life." Jefferson's verdict, however, is not categorical rejection. Some novelists model their fictive narratives on "the incidents of real life" so as to make them "interesting and useful vehicles of a sound morality." He lists as examples Marmontel's new moral tales, the writings of Edgeworth—presumably his caution has vanished—and some of works of Madame Genlis. What is said of novels applies equally to poetry, though the poetry of Pope, Dryden, Thompson, Shakespeare, Molière, Racine, and the Corneilles will not only improve character, but also improve style and taste.

Overall, Jefferson's verdict here is still consistent with his verdict in his letter to Skipwith. It is probable that he still believes works of fiction are more accessible tools for moral improvement. The difficulty is finding the diamond in the dunghill.

6

The Politics of Progress
The Lessons of Government by the Few

"There are cases wherein it is a duty to risk all against nothing."
—TJ to George Washington, 10 May 1789

Following current meanings of "science" as an empirical discipline and "philosophy" as a metempirical discipline, there is no doubt that Thomas Jefferson had more of a scientist's than a philosopher's curiosity concerning the world around him. In keeping with British and Scottish philosophers of his day—e.g., Bacon, Bolingbroke, Locke, Kames, Hume, and Smith—his writings, *Notes on the State of Virginia* especially, show him to be a hardshell empiricist. He was constantly in the business of framing hypotheses from scientific disciplines,[1] testing them against data, and essaying to subsume them, when confirmed, under more general and well-corroborated hypotheses. Ever-curious and empiricist-oriented, Jefferson was always engaged in varied scientific experiments of one sort or another—whether they concerned the viability of the American whaling industry, testing foreign crops in American soils, establishing an isochronic pendulum to be used as a measuring instrument, or assessing the moral and rational faculties of Native Americans and African Americans. "I am myself an empiric in natural philosophy, suffering my faith to go no further than the facts. I am pleased, however, to see the efforts of hypothetical speculation, because by the collisions of different hypotheses, truth may be elicited and science advances in the end."[2] Consistently forward-looking and sanguine, and perhaps obsessively attached to human intellectual progress, he was as much as any American citizen and perhaps more than any other eminent politician of his time a child of the Enlightenment.

Jefferson was severely rebuked in his day for his scientific outlook and his attachment to progress. Most of the rebuking was designed to show that a scientist was no fit politician, no friend to religion, and thus, no friend of the people. Government attached to the interests of science would, therefore, be government waggishly out of touch with the needs of its citizenry in spite of its express claims to be government for the people.

Against the animadversions of Federalists, Jefferson's republicanism was dependent on science for its success. For republicanism to thrive, the people would have to thrive. So too would science, whose chief task for Jefferson was to serve the needs of the people. And so Federalism was wrongheaded, he cognized, because it was indifferent to the forward movement of science, and thus, it was anti-republican and obscurantist.

Jefferson's advocacy of republicanism with its need of science had a built-in paradox. Government for and of the people, of course, had to be answerable to the people. Therefore, Jefferson advocated constitutional renewal in periodic constitutional conventions, in which the amendments or changes by representatives would be approved by the people. In that regard, constitutional renewal was to reflect the varied and kaleidoscopic interests of the people. Yet how could a government, answerable to and reflective of the interests of a temperamental citizenry, be progressive?

Many scholars eschew any hint of paradox merely by ignoring the progressivist element in Jefferson's republicanism. For them, Jefferson's advocacy of periodic constitutional renewal shows he was a relativist about constitutions.

In this chapter, I show that the relativists are wrong. Jefferson was intimately and irreversibly wedded to scientific progress, and he advocated constitutional renewal not to ensure representative leadership, but to ensure enlightened representative leadership—*viz.*, political progress in republican government for the sake of human happiness. The key was education of the general citizenry. Jefferson had greater faith in the integrity of the general citizenry, suitably educated, than he had in their political representatives.

Patron of the Sciences

Jefferson, while Secretary of State, speaks of a dinner engagement with Alexander Hamilton and John Adams in a letter to Benjamin Rush (16 Jan. 1811). After discussing certain differences of political opinion, Hamilton turned the conversation to identifying the men, depicted on three separate paintings. Incredulous, Jefferson told Hamilton that the men were Bacon, Locke, and Newton—"the three greatest men the world had ever produced." After a pause, Hamilton countered, with *sang froid*, "The greatest man that ever lived, was Julius Caesar."

That Jefferson's heroes were men of learning speaks volumes about him. Bacon's identification of four idols—tribe, cave, marketplace, and theater—marks him as an empirical philosopher, focused on breaking with the sophistries of the past and moving knowledge forward by investigating phenomena through etiological analysis. Locke—writing on topics such as religious tolerance, epistemology, property, liberty, value, money, natural law, political philosophy, and education—was an empiricist of unquestioned breadth and depth. Newton, of course, broke the Aristotelian teleological mold with his discovery of the three laws of bodily motion and the universal law of gravity. Consequently, by identifying Bacon, Locke, and Newton as the three greatest men ever to have lived, Jefferson shows his commitment to settling matters from politics to physics by an appeal to experience.

Jefferson was no Bacon, Locke, or Newton. He was, however, a devoted patron of the sciences and a practicing scientist of some distinction.[3] He is known to have made substantial contributions to architecture, paleontology, botany, geography, agriculture, and meteorology, and he had a knack for invention. His aim was improvement of the human condition. Writes Lucia Stanton:

> Jefferson pursued the improvement of the human condition as a passionate Baconian, gathering information with the aid of his watch, ruler, and scales. He applied his measuring mind to plantation projects in a search for economy and efficiency. He enveloped his unwieldy operations in the consoling security of mathematical truths.... His many monumental earth-moving projects, in particular, led to a lifetime of time-and-motion calculations.... At the same time that Jefferson applied a geometric grid of field boundaries to the irregular features of his mountain, he imposed Enlightenment ideals of economy and order on the people who lived there.[4]

As a politician and patron of the sciences, the enemy was not Federalism or autocracy, but obscurantism. Jefferson writes to Elbridge Gerry (26 Jan 1799): "I am for the encouraging the progress of science in all its branches; and not for raising a hue and cry against the sacred name of philosophy; for awing the human mind by stories of raw-head and bloody bones to a distrust of its own vision, and to repose implicitly on that of others; to go backward instead of forward to look for improvement; to believe that government, religion, morality, and every other science were in the highest perfection in the ages of the darkest ignorance, and that nothing can ever be devised more perfect than what was established by our forefathers."

A true disciple of Enlightenment thinking, he was irrevocably wedded to human progress.

In a letter to Dr. Joseph Willard (24 Mar. 1789), president of Harvard, Jefferson writes of his generation of patriots, having lain the substructure for intellectual advance by procuring liberty for future generations. Now it is the task of the younger generation to prove that liberty is the "great parent of science and of virtue" by advancing science and morality. "A nation will be great in both, always in proportion as it is free."[5]

Since "the main objects of all science are the freedom and happiness of man," politics is in the service of science.[6] To David Rittenhouse (19 July 1778), Jefferson says that genius must be employed most efficiently. All men, as part of a republican government, have a duty to serve their fellow citizens in some capacity, so all men are able politicians at some level. Men of genius serve at the highest levels of governing. Men of greatest genius are scientists, in the service of humanity.

High-Federalist Obscurantism

Throughout his life, Jefferson was animadverted on what were deemed his heterodox views. Yet during the presidential campaigns of 1800 and 1804, he was abundantly blistered by political opponents for his avowed Francophilism and his political liberalism, agrarianism, and irreligiosity. His purchase of science and love of gadgetry and invention were equally targets.

To be a philosopher in Jefferson's day was to be committed to the advance of knowledge (L., *scientia*) in all its varied—i.e., empirical and metempirical—guises. It also meant in many Federalist circles that one was an insidious interloper. Writes Edward T. Martin:

> "Philosophy"—or science—could ... signify an unwholesome prying into the secrets of nature for the purpose of discrediting the Bible, promoting atheism, encouraging a harmful nationalism, a deistic naturalism, materialism, the wildest ideas of the Enlightenment, chaotic and uncontrolled speculation, impracticality, confused and fuzzy thinking, tedious, trivial, and indiscriminate discussion, a modernism which would destroy the finest values of the past, Jacobism ..., political anarchy, blind and servile love of France (home of rationalism, the philosophes and godlessness)—and any other evil that come to a Federalist's mind.[7]

Jefferson's interests in experimentation and invention, sky-travel through balloons, and sea-travel through submarines were fodder for condemnation in Federalist David Daggett's *Sun-Beams May Be Extracted from Cucumbers, but the Process Is Tedious*. Daggett even found Jefferson's mold-board for improved plowing, an invention that received considerable acclaim, as a subject for pasquinade. With Jefferson, "the plow, harrow, spade, hoe, and sickle and scythe have undergone a thorough change, on mathematical principles, and the speculative husbandman has yearly expected to see the fields covered with grass, and the hills and vallies with corn and wheat, without the clownish exercise of labour."[8]

Asbury Dickins in "The Claims of Thomas Jefferson to the Presidency, Examined at the Bar of Christianity" writes: "Science and government are two different paths. He that walks in one, becomes, at every step, less qualified to walk with steadfastness or vigour in the other. The most lamentable prelude, the worst preparation possible for a ruler of men, was a life passed like that of Newton." The author adds: "O that his friends were aware, that to him the only honourable station is a private one—that mankind would suffer his talents and energies to be harmlessly exhausted in adjusting the bones of a *non-descript* animal, or tracing the pedigree of savage tribes who no longer exist, and forbear to bring them forth into a scene untried—a scene in which his most ardent worshippers may tremble for his magnanimity, and those who hold his opinions in abhorrence may be certain of his failure!"[9]

Washington Irving makes sport of Jefferson's love of invention in Book IV of his *Kickerbocker's History of New York*. Jefferson is portrayed by the character Governor William Kieft—a.k.a., "William the Testy."

> He had ... skirmished smartly on the frontiers of several of the sciences, was fond of experimental philosophy, and prided himself upon inventions of all kinds. His abode, which he had fixed at a bowery, or country seat, at a short distance from the city, just at what is now called Dutch Street, soon abounded with proofs of his ingenuity; patent smoke jacks that required a horse to work them; Dutch ovens that roasted meat without fire; carts that went before the horses; weathercocks that turned against the wind; and other wrong-headed contrivances that astonished and confounded all beholders. The house, too, was beset with paralytic cats and dogs, the subjects of his experimental philosophy; and the yelling and yelping of the latter unhappy victims of science, while aiding in the pursuit of knowledge, soon gained for the place the name of "Dog's Misery," by which it continues to be known even at the present day.[10]

Fearing Yankees assailing the city of New Amsterdam, it occurred to the governor that he could protect the city not by the dint of arms, but by the wind of windmills. In an effort to eradicate crime, he invented "a gibbet, of a very strange, uncouth, and unmatchable construction ... for the punishment of poverty." Criminals were to be "hoisted by the waistband, and kept dangling and sprawling between heaven and earth for an hour or two at a time, to the infinite entertainment and edification of the respectable citizens who usually attend exhibitions of the kind."[11]

There was also the link of science with irreligiosity. Federalists played up Jefferson's patronage of science as espousal of atheism. New Englanders were said to have hidden their Bibles for fear that Jefferson's first official act as president would be "a ukase ordering all copies of the sacred volume to be seized and burned." Reverend William Linn castigated Jefferson for not believing in the Flood and for having insufficient faith to believe in miracles. Clement Clarke Moore, having recently read Jefferson's *Notes on the State of Virginia*, reproached the politician for looking downward, not upward, through nature and seeing nature's demon, not nature's deity. The countless religious subversions are nothing but "French philosophy."[12]

The Problem of the Will of the People

Much to his credit, Jefferson, aware that the animadversions were fueled both by above-board obscurantism and political bombast, was undaunted. He had faith in the judgment of the American citizenry. To William Findley (24 Mar. 1801), he states, "It is rare that the public sentiment decides immorally or unwisely, and the individual who differs from it ought to distrust and examine well his own opinion." He also recognized that the charge of "possessing some science" did little to discredit him in the minds of the American public.[13]

The problem, for Jefferson, was more than one of partisan politics. It was "tyranny over the mind of man"—i.e., coercive government.[14] Adds Dumas Malone: "What Jefferson regarded as the worst of evils was the coercion of opinion. To him this was a question that went beyond party or state or even the Union: it bore directly on the future progress and happiness of mankind. Along with his distrust of all rulers and fear of governmental power in any form went a profound faith in the limitless potentialities of unfettered intelligence."[15]

Republican government, Jefferson was clear, was a "great experiment," a term commonly employed, whose success or failure would be confirmed or disconfirmed in time.[16] He writes in his "Draft Declaration and Protest of the Commonwealth of Virginia, on the Principles of the Constitution of the United States of America, and on the Violations of Them" that "man is capable of living in society, governing itself by laws self-imposed, and securing to its members the enjoyment of life, liberty, property, and peace."[17]

Jefferson gave every indication that he thought the experiment was bearing fruit. After ascending to the presidency, he writes to Joseph Priestley (31 Mar. 1801) of the triumph of republicanism over heavy-handed federalism. "As the storm is now subsiding, and the horizon becoming serene ... we can no longer say there is nothing new under the sun. For

The Jefferson Memorial. Pantheon-like and erected by a suggestion of Franklin Roosevelt in 1934, and officially dedicated by Roosevelt on the 200th anniversary of the death of Jefferson (13 Apr. 1943) (courtesy Pixabay).

this whole chapter in the history of man is new. The great experiment of our Republic is new. Its sparse habitation is new. The mighty wave of public opinion which has rolled over it is new." Jefferson's relief concerns the people's avowal of the principles of republican government by disavowal of the tyranny of Federalist government—a sentiment to which he would later refer as the "revolution of 1800," a return to the principles behind the revolution of 1776.[18] He iterates the sentiment again metaphorically in a late-life letter to John Adams (12 Sept. 1821): "The flames kindled on the 4th. of July 1776 have spread over too much of the globe to be extinguished by the feeble engines of despotism. On the contrary they will consume those engines, and all who work for them." The implications, here unmistakably global, are that political science is advancing every bit as much as astronomy, physics, geology, and other sciences and that political science is also in the general service of human betterment.

That republican government is described often as an experiment by Jefferson is telling, for there is a special relationship, he asserts, between republican government and science. He writes to an unknown correspondent (28 Sept. 1821). "Science is more important in a republican than in any other government." It preserves republicanism and protects it from foreign powers.

Yet republican governments must appeal to the will of the people and constitutions must reflect that will. So, there must be continual constitutional renewal every so often—19 years he says to James Madison (6 Sept. 1789)—in keeping with the will of the people. Citizens have a right to overthrow governments that either fail to secure their rights and independency or refuse to keep pace with the evolving interests of the citizenry.

Because Jefferson embraces the notions that each generation of humans has the right to choose its own constitution, that government's principle function is to secure for its citizens their independency and natural rights, and that citizens have a natural right to revolt against their government, when a government fails to secure for its citizens their independence and natural rights,[19] he is often painted as a political relativist apropos of constitutions.

Richard Matthews[20] maintains that Jefferson was committed to a right to revolution that would leave open the possibility for each generation to draw up for itself its own constitution, and along with it, its own form of government, whatever form that might take. On Matthews's view, being rational and free entails for Jefferson that humans are essentially and merely choosing animals: What they choose is of little consequence. Citizens of future generations have the right to determine for themselves their own constitution whatever form it may take.

That too is a view that Dumas Malone, Henry May, and Gilbert Chinard share. "There can be no doubt about [Jefferson's] adherence to [political relativism] throughout the rest of his life," after his years abroad, writes Malone, for reasons similar to those of Matthew.[21] "[Jefferson's] belief in unalienable, natural rights may have sat a bit uneasily with his historical relativism: rights endure but everything else must change," writes May.[22] Gilbert Chinard states Jefferson's seeming utopian commitment to agrarianism was mere mouth honor to an ideal, incapable of realization. Behind the façade, he was a political relativist.[23]

There is an imbroglio. To paint Jefferson as a political relativist implies that the will of the people is injudicious and discretionary. What is worse, it shows Jefferson to be committed to inconsistent principles—political progress and discretionary government by the people. How does Jefferson reconcile the special relationship of republican government and science with constitutional renewal in keeping with the changing, capricious interests of the people?

A Rightful, Reasonable Will

Ascription of political relativism to Jefferson fits him into a Montesquieuian frame, where there are not better or worse constitutions, but where constitutions are fitted merely to particular peoples, like jackets to persons—a view Philipp Ziesche[24] correctly rejects. Jefferson was no political relativist in that subjectivist sense. Adrienne Koch makes a similar point. "Jefferson sincerely believed that there is a 'best' form of government, a limiting ideal toward which legislators, statesmen, and educators may look for inspiration and guidance." She adds that he knew no political ideal could be instantiated before its time.[25] Otto Vossler makes the point more strongly. He posits that Jefferson was an imperialist that believed one particular form of government was superior to others.[26]

Jefferson was anything but a political relativist in the discretionary sense, but he was probably no imperialist, as Vossler asserts. Jefferson's republicanism is not advocacy of any particular form of government—i.e., any particular constitution. It is merely a political schema for any just, moral system of government, not any one instantiation of that schema.[27] He advocated a specific schema of government, harmlessly elitist, where virtue and talent were rewarded over wealth and birth, and that harmless elitism was put into place precisely to ensure progress.[28]

As such, Jefferson's "republicanism" allows for a multiplicity of constitutions, but it also rules out numerous others—e.g., those where those governing are not elected by and representative of the people, those where birth and money determine who governs, and those where natural rights are violated for personal gain. Jefferson's political aim is a moral aim: He wishes government to be responsible to the general citizenry. His schema, thus, is fundamentally medianistic: It is government by the true *aristoi*, whose actions are aligned with the interests of the people, suitably educated.

In short, Jefferson's republicanism was neither discretionarily relativistic about constitutions nor was it autocratically elitist. Jefferson's republicanism was not substratally about constitutions, but instead about setting up a basic schema of government for any political system that is liberal, responsive to the needs of its people, and progressive. His schema was established empirically as an experiment, and it had broad implications. Thus, Jefferson's republicanism, as a synthesis of republican sentiments of his time,[29] posed a challenge for the Federalists of his day and poses a challenge for Machiavellians, Hobbesians, and Hamiltonians of any day.

So swept away by Enlightenment thinking was Jefferson—and here again we focus on his triumvirate of Bacon, Locke, and Newton—that one could say that "rational" and "free" entailed "progressive." From Bacon, Jefferson learned that knowledge is not for its own sake, but for the sake of utility. He writes to Sheldon Clark (5 Dec. 1825): "The business of life is with matter that gives us tangible results. Handling that, we arrive at knowledge of the axe, the plough, the steam-boat, and everything useful in life." From Locke, Jefferson learned the basic principles of liberal government, in the service of progressive human interests. "Nothing is more evident," writes Locke on human equality, "that Creatures of the same species and rank promiscuously born to all the same advantages of Nature, and the use of the same faculties, should also be equal one amongst another without Subordination or Subjection."[30] From Newton, Jefferson gained empirical succor for his materialism.[31] He learned about the physical, atomistic framework for every physical body in the universe. From all, Jefferson acquired some degree of irreverence for the past. He became disabused of anthropocentric-based teleological thinking, which dominated cosmological thinking for some 2,000 years. From all, Jefferson acquired his forward-looking, sanguine disposition. He became a deep-dyed progressivist that was convinced that independency, truth, and rationality were indispensable for progress and that progress was indispensable for human happiness.

Jefferson's republicanism was not Montesquieuian. He followed Montesquieu only insofar as he noted that republican governments needed to be fitted to particular peoples and that those peoples agreed to a basic liberal schema that guaranteed human rights, allowed for individual choice, and granted periodic constitutional reform or upheaval. Constitutional reform or upheaval, for Jefferson and against Montesquieu, was framed within the parameters of progress.

Because of his purchase of progressivism, Jefferson emphasized that people should not be democratized before they were ready to be democratized. As he wrote in a letter to Madame La Comtesse de Tessé (20 Mar. 1787), "Should they attempt more than the established habits of the people are ripe for, they may lose all, and retard indefinitely the ultimate object of their aim." Jefferson also emphasized that for the will of the people to be rightful, it must be an educated, morality-sensitive will. "Though the will of the majority is in all cases to prevail, that will, to be rightful, must be reasonable; that the minority possess their equal rights, which equal laws must protect, and to violate would be oppression."[32]

In sum, Jefferson's republicanism was an attachment to his "mother principle"—government for and of the people through elected representatives. In asserting that all persons' natural rights needed to be preserved, he was asserting that no government could intrude in the happiness of its citizens, free and rational. That, in conjunction with his mother principle, allowed for the fullest active participation in the affairs of government as well as the fullest amount of independency.

For Jefferson, independency and political participation were mutually entailing. Thus, he was neither a political atomist, committed to citizens' volitional independency through fullest instantiation of governmental non-interference, nor a communitarian, committed to citizens' volitional dependency through fullest instantiation of contractual ties to facilitate common purpose. He was instead a political medianist. Citizens were free to act as they wished, because of regard for human autonomy; yet citizens, suitably educated, would adhere to certain reasonable contractual ties, because of their moral ties. Science, in service of morality, was the glue.

A Rubric for Progress

Jefferson's medianism is progressive, not conservative or discretionary, for "laws and institutions must go hand in hand with the progress of the human mind."[33] The "Gothic idea" that people ought to look backward for human improvement, he writes to Joseph Priestley (27 Jan. 1800), is absurd. That is a bigoted, filiopietistic idea that serves the purpose of political conservatives that would have the ideals of one era serve as the ideals of every era.[34] In "Thoughts on Lotteries," he speaks of the "ineffable joy" of those in retirement on seeing "a grade of science beyond their own ken."[35] In a letter to Pierre Samuel Dupont de Nemours (24 Apr. 1816), he grants that the human condition might never advance to such a state of perfection that all pain and vice will be eradicated, but concedes "it susceptible of much improvement, and most of all in matters of government and religion [i.e., morality]."

Thus, constitutional renewal and the right of the citizenry to revolt are put into place to ensure political advance at pace with moral and intellectual advance. Jeffersonian republicanism is wedded to general and higher education to ensure that there will be scientific progress and that that progress will be accessible to and meet the needs of the general citizenry. In consequence, higher education and lower education are to be in place with the aim of employing science to promote fully human flourishing.

Jefferson recognizes that his purchase of intellectual and moral advance has made him an enemy to political conservatives. "It suffices for a man to be a philosopher, and to believe that human affairs are susceptible of improvement, and to look forward, rather than backward to the Gothic ages, for perfection, to mark him as an anarchist, disorganizer, atheist and enemy of the government."[36]

Though committed to progress, Jefferson was too much of a realist to be a radical revolutionist, as he is often taken to be by scholars today.[37] One could not instantiate a plan for which the nation was not ready. Though he was convinced that the general citizenry was republican in spirit, many citizens, taking science to be a *bête noire* and embracing conservatism, were still under the sway of federalist newspeak. Thus, when it came time to consider a constitution for Virginia pursuant to republican aims in 1776, Jefferson did not propose complete effacement and wholesale reconstruction, but a substantial revision of the old laws. As John Howe states: "Virginia's republican order would be new, but it would emerge organically from what had existed before.... At no time did he reject Virginia's established social and political orders."[38] When Jefferson took office as president in 1801, he proposed conciliation with the past Federalist administration, which had been hostile to Republican interests, as "every difference of opinion is not a difference of principle." He added, "We are all Republicans, we are all Federalists."[39]

In short, though he might have appeared to be a radicalist in selected letters to some, he was a moderate in praxis. The right idea, pushed forward too hastily and too early, could do more to retard than accelerate intellectual and moral advance. Thus, for every progressive idea, there was need of a rubric for instantiation. Not all cultures possessed knowledge to the same degree and not all cultures had the same level of moral refinement. The American Indians, for him, were a shining example. That is why Jefferson emphasized that people should not be democratized before they were ready to be democratized.

The rubric for instantiation was the "diffusion of knowledge among the people."[40] Education is the key to steady improvement. "I look to the diffusion of light and education," he writes to Cornelius Blatchly (21 Oct. 1822), "as the resource most to be relied on for ameliorating the human condition, promoting virtue, and advancing the happiness of man."[41] Education, at the lower levels, equips all citizens with the requisite intellectual tools to be self-sufficient. It readies each person for some level of political participation, if only at the level of wards. Education, at the higher levels, equips the natural aristocrats for morally sensitive participation in the highest levels of governmental affairs and in other disciplines, deemed essential for the progress of the state.

Thus, happiness and liberty can be secured only through continued intellectual and moral advancement. Such advancement, however, requires constitutional renewal in keeping with intellectual and moral advances and educational reform in the direction of general, practical education.[42] Jefferson, as is well known, had a schema for that too.

Jefferson's purchase of progressivism and his impassioned yen for moving his state and country forward made him ill-disposed as governor and as president to rush his state or country into wars. As Alf Mapp notes, his was the "battle for the human mind." He wished to build up, not break down. When the British were set to overrun Virginia, his thoughts were not only on establishing military posts in the West for defense of the frontier and future volumes of commerce but also on Wythe's School of Law at William and Mary. "Jefferson was looking confidently above and beyond the smoke of battle to more distant fields of national conquest."[43]

Impious Presumption of False Religions

A product of Enlightenment liberalism, Jefferson was a freethinker. Yet unlike many of the freethinkers of his day, he was unobtrusive and restrained in his freethinking. "He made no parade of his own free thinking," writes Dumas Malone. "He neither flouted nor derided conventional observances; and he was a scrupulously moral man."[44] Pertaining to difficult matters on which men could reasonably disagree, he thought the result of one's deliberations of little consequence in contrast to the integrity with which those deliberations were conducted. "Your own reason is the only oracle given you by heaven," he writes to nephew Peter Carr (10 Aug. 1787), "and you are answerable not for the rightness but uprightness of the decision."

In Query XVII of his *Notes on the State of Virginia*, Jefferson acknowledges that heresy, according to the common law of Virginian and interpreted by the ecclesiastical judges prior to revision of the laws, was punishable by burning. By a 1705 act of assembly, any Christian who denied deity or the Trinity, assented to the existence of more than one deity, or disavowed the Christian religion or the divine origin of the scriptures was, on first offense, disallowed ecclesiastical, civil, or military employment; on second offense, disallowed ability to sue and to take a gift or legacy, debarred form guardianship, executorship, and administration, and imprisoned, without bail, for three years. "This is a summary view of that religious slavery, under which a people have been willing to remain, who have lavished their lives and fortunes for the establishment of their civil freedom."

Yet rulers have authority over only such natural rights to which the people willfully submit to their governors, Jefferson continues, and rights of conscience, for which people are answerable only to deity, were never submitted to the rulers, because they could never be submitted to them. Government is in the business of preventing citizens from harm and no citizen was ever harmed by positing no deity or more than one deity.[45]

Jefferson's "A Bill for Establishing Religious Freedom"—Bill 82 of 126 bills drafted by him, George Wythe, and Edmund Pendleton in 1779, and Jefferson's own project—was a watershed in political and moral reform. In it, pursuant to his training as lawyer, he begins by listing a large number of "thats."[46] He states

- *that* the opinions of men do not depend on their will, but "follow involuntarily the evidence proposed to their minds,"
- *that* god has made the mind free and insusceptible of restraint,
- *that* attempts to corral or burke reason by punishment, burdens, or civil incapacitations produce "hypocrisy and meanness,"
- *that* the "impious presumption of [civil and religious] legislators and rulers," being "fallible and uninspired," has led to a "false religions over the greatest part of the world and through all time,"
- *that* it is "sinful and tyrannical" to force a person to contribute money toward propagation of religious opinions he "disbelieves and abhors,"
- *that* it is even wrong to force a person to contribute to a teacher of his own religious persuasion,
- *that* "our civil rights have no dependance [sic] on our religious opinions,"
- *that* it is unjust to keep a person from public office because of his religious opinions,
- *that* rewarding public office to a person because of religious opinions undermines the principles of that religion,
- *that* civil government ought not to concern itself with the opinions of men,
- *that* any civil magistrate who makes his opinions the rule of judgment sets a dangerous, autocratic precedent,
- *that* governmental officials should intervene when principles conduce to "overt acts against peace and good order," and
- *that* "truth is great and will prevail if left to herself; that she is the proper and sufficient antagonist to error, and has nothing to fear from the conflict unless by human interposition disarmed of her natural weapons, free argument and debate; errors ceasing to be dangerous when it is permitted freely to contradict them."

The "thats" of Bill 82, forming the entirety of Section I, are premises for the conclusions, succinctly stated in Sections II and III. Section II comprises two conclusions: *All persons will be free to opine and profess their own religious beliefs and worship as they deem appropriate* and *No person will be punished in any manner—including debarment from public office—because of his religious beliefs.*[47] Section III comprises two conclusions: *The "rights hereby asserted [the that's] are of the natural rights of mankind"* and *Any attempt to repeal the bill or narrow its compass is "an infringement of natural right."*[48]

Jefferson's bill, aimed at a separation of matters of religious belief and the affairs of government, was one of the most important pieces of legislation in American history. Though he was not the first to champion that stance, he likely did as much, if not more, than any other of his day to see it through to completion. It passed at the bidding of James Madison on January 16, 1786, while Jefferson was in Paris. It was, in Jefferson's eyes, a needed step for progressive, republican government.

Upshot

There was nothing, in spite of Jefferson's unwavering optimism, inevasible about political progress, as there was nothing inevasible about scientific progress, generally construed. What fueled Jefferson's optimism were the observations that science was making rapid technological and theoretical advances, that morality was progressing slowly and surely, and that republicanism seemed secure in America and was being tested in varying degrees in other nations across the globe. Through his eyes, only an incredulist could believe that these advances were independent phenomena. Only an obscurantist could turn a blind eye to them.

Still, there were aplenty incredulists and obscurantists in Jefferson's day, as there are in our day. Few today, I suspect, would maintain that there is anything essentially "progressive" about the changes in political systems over time. Much of the skepticism vis-à-vis political progress is the result of the slow emasculation of human reason since Enlightenment times. Science, which was once construed as a method of disclosure of the secrets of the cosmos, is now often seen as just another way of thinking that has no claim to priority over, say, revelation or intuition. It is, to my thinking, a sad state of affairs.

Scientific advances exist abundantly today before our eyes. So too do scientific pragmatists, subjectivists, and perspectivists, who deny that the advances of science are the result of some degree of knowledge of reality. Realism, the view that we are at least in some degree capable of gleaning reliable information about the world in which we live, is *passé*. What is left, if not smoke and mirrors?

Were he alive today, Jefferson would have been astonished both by the rapid-pace progress of the sciences and by our modern skepticism apropos of rationality and scientific method. It also obvious that he would have considered the large-scale corporate capitalism of America and like-minded nations inconsistent with true "Christian" benevolence and government by and for the people.

7

Duty to God and Duty to Man
Jefferson on Religion, Natural and Sectarian

> "Now whoever does Good to another, does after some sort exist in that Person; and he who gives Being, manifestly lives and acts in that Being which is propagated by him."
> —Pierre Charron, *De la sagesse*

Jefferson's interest in religion extends only so far as it relates to morality. That suggests his interest in religion is confined to a person's other-related duties, accessible to him through his moral sense. It also suggests dearth of interest in the numerous metaphysical squabbles in which the prelates of various particular religions engage. Yet Jefferson also expresses a keen interest in what appear to be certain metempirical concerns—e.g., the nature of deity and the existence of an afterlife—which seem more in the province of religious concerns, void of morality.

This chapter is a critical investigation of Jefferson's view of religion. In it, I answer the following questions. What exactly is religion for Jefferson and how does it relate to morality? Why was he adamant that there be a strict separation of church and state? Finally, why did he believe that religion ought not to be studied until a person's rational faculties reached some degree of maturation?

"The moral branch of religion": On Religious Belief

"The care of every man's soul belongs to himself," writes a young Thomas Jefferson to John Hancock (11 Oct. 1776). "Laws provide against injury from others; but not from ourselves." Four decades later (6 Aug. 1816), Jefferson writes to Margaret Bayard Smith: "I have ever thought religion a concern purely between our God and our consciences, for which we are accountable to Him, and not to the priests. God himself will not save men against their wills." In gist, consistent over a lifetime, religion is a personal, not a political matter. Government has no right to encroach on concerns of the soul—religion being chief among them. Government can, if it decides, coerce religious uniformity in behavior, but it cannot effect uniformity of will.

Religion, for Jefferson, is a personal matter. He continues in the same 1816 letter to Margaret Bayard Smith, "I have ever thought religion a concern purely between our god and our consciences, for which we were accountable to him, and not to the priests."[1] Thus, saying "I am of a sect by myself,"[2] he was wedded to no form of sectarian religion. He writes to Thomas Parker (15 May 1819) that if he were to found his own sect, he would call them "Apriarians" [sic] "after the example of the bee." Again, "I have never permitted myself to mediate a specified creed," he writes to the Rev. Thomas Whittemore. "If by religion we are to understand sectarian dogmas, in which no two of them agree," Jefferson writes John Adams (5 May 1817), "then your exclamation on them is just, that this would be the best of all possible worldn, if there were no religion in it." Finally, "he who steadily observes those moral precepts in which all religions concur," he tells William Canby (18 Sept. 1813), "will never be questioned, at the gates of heaven."

He writes to James Madison (16 Dec. 1786) of the human mind held in vassalage by kings, priests, and nobles for numerous ages, and of his pride of the legislature of Virginia for having "the courage to declare that the reason of man may be trusted with the formation of his own opinions." He says to Miles King (26 Sept. 1814) that deity has so authorized matters that each tree must be judged "by it's fruit." Thus, any religion is "substantially good which produces an honest life," and for that, each is accountable solely to deity. As expressed by one scholar, "Jefferson eliminated all intermediate authorities between God and man as the source of religious truth, such as exclusive revelation or scripture, church or tradition, and most of all, the clergy."[3]

Being a personal matter, religion cannot be politicized. When empleomatic clergy engraft themselves into the "machine of government," he tells Jeremiah Moor (14 Aug. 1800), they become a "very formidable engine against the civil and religious rights of man." Jefferson says to Elbridge Gerry (29 Mar. 1801) that "the mild and simple principles of the Christian philosophy" have been corrupted by the priesthood, who "sophisticate it, ramify it, split it into hairs, and twist its texts" just so they are then needed to explain it. Years later, Jefferson states to John Adams (22 Aug. 1813) that all people should follow the Quakers: live without priests, follow their internal monitor of right and wrong, and eschew matters inaccessible to common sense, for belief can only rightly be shaped by "the assent of the mind to an intelligible proposition." Jefferson tells George Logan (12 Nov. 1816), "The sum of all religion as expressed by it's best preacher, 'fear god and love thy neighbor' contains no mystery, needs no explanation."

As the letter to Gerry suggests, the "mild and simple principles of the Christian philosophy" are the principles common to all right-intended religions. That is a sentiment he iterates in numerous other letters.[4] His letter to James Fishback (27 Sept. 1809) is an especially stirring expression of the relation of true religion and morality. "Reading, reflection and time have convinced me that the interests of society require the observation of those moral precepts only in which all religions agree (for all forbid us to steal, murder, plunder, or bear false witness), and that we should not intermeddle with the particular dogmas in which all religions differ, and which are totally unconnected with morality."

Two common threads exist in all such passages. First, religion is a personal matter. What one believes might bring harm to a believer, but if that harm in the main extends to no others, the believer ought not to be coerced to think otherwise. Thus, government has no right to intervene in such concerns and impose a uniform religious standard. Second, the principles common to all religions are few, exoteric, simple, and the true principles of morality. The numerous and esoteric principles that are topics of rigorous religious disputation are metaphysical twaddle, beyond the comprehension of any rational being. Esoteric religious principles are created to muddle common understanding and to allow for religious imposition in political matters at expense of others' civil and religious rights.[5] "A man must be very clear-sighted who can see the impression of the finger of God on any particular one of them."[6]

Religion and Morality

For Jefferson, religion, rightly apprehended, is equivalent to morality. In gist, that is in accord with David Hume, an older contemporary of Jefferson, who says through the mouth of Cleanthes in *Dialogues concerning Natural Religion*. "The proper office of religion is to regulate the hearts of men, humanize their conduct, infuse the spirit of temperance, order, and obedience; and, as its operation is silent and only enforces the motives of morality and justice, it is in danger of being overlooked and confounded with these other motives. When it distinguishes itself, and acts as a separate principle over men, it has departed from its proper sphere and has become only a cover to faction and ambition."[7]

The interlocutor Philo agrees, "It is certain, from experience, that the smallest grain of natural honesty and benevolence has more effect on men's conduct than the most pompous views suggested by theological theories and systems."[8]

Essentially social beings, people are adequately equipped with a moral sense to guide them in social situations, as a benevolent deity would not make humans social beings and also create them to be morally deficient.[9]

The Doctrines of Jesus

"Jefferson," writes Charles Sanford, "was among the few great men in history who not only studied and wrote about the meaning of the words and example of Jesus Christ for the human condition, but also used his beliefs about Jesus as a guide to accomplish needed social reforms."[10]

Christianity, notwithstanding all its abuses over the centuries, had special status for Jefferson. He stated unambiguously that the teachings of Jesus were the greatest moral system ever put together and that "the greatest of all the reformers of the depraved religion of his own country, was Jesus of Nazareth."[11] He writes to Samuel Greenhow (31 Jan. 1814), "There never was a more pure & sublime system of morality delivered to man than is to be found in the four evangelists." Year later, he writes to TJ to Jarred Sparks (4 Nov. 1822), "I hold the precepts of Jesus, as delivered by Himself, to be the most pure, benevolent, and sublime which have ever been preached to man." So intemerate and sublime are Jesus's teachings that "had the doctrines of Jesus been preached always as pure as they came from his lips, the whole civilized world would now have been Christian."[12] Thus, inspection of Jefferson's view of the teachings of Jesus too sheds additional light on Jefferson's views on religion and morality.

What are the doctrines of Jesus? It is clear—since Jefferson on two separate occasions, constructed his own Bible by cutting and pasting numerous passages from the four Evangelists and leaving out numerous other passages—that he thought much in the Bible was redundant, hyperbolic, bathetic, absurd, and beyond the bounds of physical possibility. That is confirmed by inspection of his second reconstruction, *The Life and Morals of Jesus of Nazareth* (c. 1820).

To Dr. Benjamin Waterhouse (26 June 1822), Jefferson writes: "The doctrines of Jesus are simple, and tend all to the happiness of man. (1) That there is one only God, and he all perfect. (2) That there is a future state of rewards and punishments. (3) That to love God with all thy heart and thy neighbor as thyself, is the sum of religion."

To George Thatcher (26 Jan. 1824), Jefferson says Jesus was "the Herald of truths reformatory of the religions of mankind in general, but more immediately of that of his own countrymen, impressing them with more sublime and more worthy ideas of the Supreme being, teaching them the doctrine of a future state of rewards and punishments, and inculcating the love of mankind, instead of the anti-social spirit with which the Jews viewed all other nations."

In his "Syllabus," sent with a letter to Dr. Benjamin Rush (21 Apr. 1803), lists four of Jesus's reforms of Jewish religion:

(1) He corrected the Deism of the Jews, confirming them in their belief of one only God, and giving them juster notions of his attributes and government. (2) His moral doctrines, relating to kindred & friends, were more pure & perfect than those of the most correct of the philosophers, and greatly more so than those of the Jews; and they went far beyond both in inculcating universal philanthropy, not only to kindred and friends, to neighbors and countrymen, but to all mankind, gathering all into one family, under the bonds of love, charity, peace, common wants and common aids. A development of this head will evince the peculiar superiority of the system of Jesus over all others. (3) The precepts of philosophy, & of the Hebrew code, laid hold of actions only. He pushed his scrutinies into the heart of man; erected his tribunal in the region of his thoughts, and purified the waters at the fountain head. (4) He taught, emphatically, the doctrines of a future state, which was either doubted, or disbelieved by the Jews; and wielded it with efficacy, as an important incentive, supplementary to the other motives to moral conduct.

Consequently, Jesus's message, the "sum of religion" which "tend[s] all to the happiness of man," comprises love of god (who is one, not three), love of mankind, and belief in an afterlife of reward or punishment. If those are the doctrines of "natural religion" and if natural religion and morality are equivalent, then they must be also the fundamental doctrines of morality.

There is grit in the oil. Why should both belief in or love of deity and belief in an afterlife be subjects of morality? What have they to do with beneficence?

Here we run into the problem of moral atheists. To Thomas Law (13 June 1814), Jefferson says that love of God cannot be the "foundation of morality," because some of the most virtuous of men—Diderot, D'Alembert,

D'Holbach, and Condorcet—are atheists. "Their virtue, then, must have had some other foundation than the love of God."[13]

The letter has been misapprehended by scholars. Arthur Scherr makes too much of this letter as well as Jefferson's 1787 letter to Carr (Aug. 10), in which Jefferson advises his nephew to think through belief in deity—even the possibility of there being no deity. Scherr wishes to show that "upright atheist" is not oxymoronic for Jefferson. Jefferson believed that an atheist could be a moral-abiding person, but not a moral person. Belief in deity was *sine qua non*.

The passage, however, does not state that love of god is not *one* of the principles of morality, but that love of god is not the *foundation* of morality. Jefferson does say in the letter that love of god is a "branch of our moral duties," which he adds are "generally divided into duties to God and duties to man." By implication, moral atheists are morally deficient.

Neem too mistakenly argues that Jefferson dismisses love of God as the basis of morality, because an atheist can be moral. He quotes Jefferson, "If we did a good act merely form the love of God and a belief that it is pleasing to Him, whence arises the morality of the Atheist?" He adds, "The only conclusion was that atheists' 'virtue, then, must have some other foundation than the love of God,' namely the moral sense."[14]

Yet Jefferson does not state that an atheist can be virtuous, merely that an atheist can act in conformance with and from a sense of morality. That does not imply that an atheist thus acting is moral. Morality for Jefferson comprises duties to other men and duties to deity. That is why Jefferson says love of God is a part of morality.

Love of deity is part of morality because deity is the creative intelligence and power, responsible for the cosmos (see Chapter 9). A true moralist, as Jefferson says in a letter to John Adams (8 Apr. 1816), literally sees deity in the cosmos. "When the atheist descanted on the unceasing motion and circulation of matter through the animal, vegetable and mineral kingdoms, gifted with the power of reproduction, the theist, pointing 'to the heavens above, and to the earth beneath, and to the waters under the earth,' asked, if these did not proclaim a first cause possessing intelligence and power." Again to John Adams (11 Apr. 1823), he states, "When we take a view of the Universe, in it's parts general or particular, it is impossible for the human mind not to be percieve and feel a conviction of design, consummate skill, and indefinite power in every atom of it's composition." In both cases, there is no argument from analogy; Jefferson, consistent with Kamesian "intuitive perception,"[15] writes of direct perception of deity. What we can know of deity through perception is design, skill, and power.

Jefferson and the Afterlife

Jesus preached belief in an afterlife, yet there is no mention of belief in an afterlife as one of the branches of morality in the letter to Law. Jefferson mentions belief in an afterlife merely as one of the correctives to lack of a moral sense, along with self-interest, the approbation of others upon doing good, and the rewards and punishments of laws.

This leads to the problem of belief in an afterlife. To George Logan (12 Nov. 1816), Jefferson says the sum of all religion is "fear god and love thy neighbor." In his letter to Waterhouse too, Jefferson says nothing of an afterlife, "Be this the wisdom of Unitarians, this the holy mantle which shall cover within its charitable circumference all who believe in one God, and who love their neighbor!"

The tantalizing suggestion is that belief in an afterlife, one of the chief teachings of Jesus, is not an essential part of true religion or morality for Jefferson. True religion or morality merely comprises, as he says to Law, duties to God and duties to man.

Yet the scholarly consensus is that Jefferson did believe in an afterlife, given numerous references to the hereafter in letters, messages, and addresses. Evidence cited consists of the many writings in which Jefferson speaks approvingly of an afterlife. For instance, Charles B. Sanford, citing two of Jefferson's letters to Adams (9 Aug. 1816 and 8 Dec. 1818), maintains that Jefferson was "influenced by Adams' arguments about spirit to find room in belief in immortality among the wondrous attributes of certain forms of matter."[16] Elsewhere he says: "Matter had many mysterious properties, such as magnetism gravity, and the power of the brain to think. Why not immortality for human beings?"[17] E.S. Gaustad maintains that the immortality of the soul was for Jefferson a "guarantor of morality." He sums, "Justice and goodness must ultimately prevail, else this is not a moral universe."[18] Eugene R. Sheridan acknowledges that Jefferson entertained doubts concerning an afterlife, "but, on the whole, hope triumphed over despair."[19] Paul Conkin says that Jefferson "was always confident of life after death."[20] John Ragosta argues that Jefferson's insistence, *pace* Calvin, that one is to be judged by one's deeds "suggests some belief in an afterlife," though he admits the issue is far from settled.[21]

There is reason to be guarded here. All references to an afterlife in writings are terse. Even of deity, whose nature he considers too boundless for human cognizance, he does allow himself *some* discussion—e.g., he writes of deity as material and of such capacities to create and sustain the cosmos[22]—yet he never lapses into discussion of an afterlife in any writings, where he seems open to it as a possibility. Such references should not be taken as evidence of belief, for belief, as Jefferson wrote formally to Adams, is assent to a rationally intelligible proposition, and the notion of an afterlife seems not to be rationally intelligible—at least, not in the metempirical manner in which it had been historically discussed.

Consider for instance Jefferson's response to the Rev. Isaac Story (5 Dec. 1810), who writes of belief in the transmigration of souls. Jefferson replies that he has nothing to say on the subject. Revelation is silent on the issue and "the laws of nature have withheld from us the means of physical knowledge of the country of spirits." Thus, he has consigned himself to ignorance. To John Adams (5 July 1814), Jefferson states, "Plato … is peculiarly appealed to as an advocate of the immortality of the soul; and yet I will venture to say that were there no better arguments than his in proof of it, not a man in the world would believe it." Given the counterfactual expression, Jefferson commits himself to better arguments for the immortality of the soul than Plato's—arguments sufficient to elicit the consent of some persons—but nothing more can be said. Given his reply to Story, I suspect he does not hold such arguments in high regard.

We do know, as Sanford concedes, that Jefferson unequivocally commits himself to materialism, and there is no reason to believe, given the philosophical and scientific literature that Jefferson read, that he was ever anything but a full-fledged materialist.

> I can concieve *thought* to be an action of a particular organisation of matter, formed for that purpose by it's creator, as well as that *attraction* is an action of matter, or *magnetism* of loadstone. when he who denies to the Creator the power of endowing matter with the mode of action called *thinking* shall shew how he could endow the Sun with the mode of action called *attraction*, which reins the planets in the tract of their orbits, or how an absence of matter can have a will, and, by that will; put matter into motion, then the materialist may be lawfully required to explain the process by which matter exercises the faculty of thinking. when once we quit the basis of sensation all is in the wind. to talk of *immaterial* existences is to talk of *nothings*. to say that the human soul, angels, god, are immaterial, is to say they are *nothings*, or that there is no god, no angels, no soul. I cannot reason otherwise.[23]

Thus, mind or the soul is some sort of matter; so too is deity. So the question of an afterlife reduces to the question of whether psychic matter is indissoluble, or as Carl Richard thinks, whether for Jefferson there can be an instauration of matter, once decayed. Richard states that Jefferson believed in the dissolution of the soul upon dissolution of the body, but adds that Jefferson believed in resurrection of the body after death.[24]

Four important letters offer evidence that Jefferson has lifted his head from the soft pillow of ignorance, mentioned in his letter to Story, because the science in his day had begun to shed light on what Jefferson had earlier perceived to be wholly a metempirical concern. Such letters I take as evidence sufficient to show a shift from agnosticism to doubt.

The first is a very early letter, indicative of early skepticism apropos of the soul leaving the body "at the instant of death," to boyhood friend John Page (26 July 1764). Jefferson recounts a story from a magazine that concerns a man, drowned and submerged in water for some 24 hours. The man was brought back to life by a method such as "to give the vital warmth to the whole body by gentle degrees, and to put the blood in motion by inflating the lungs." We are taught, he continues, that when the bodily parts completely cease to function, the "soul leaves the body." He sums, "But does not this story contradict this opinion?"

To John Adams (14 Mar. 1820), Jefferson—referring to the works of Dugald Stewart, A.L.C. Destutt de Tracy, and Pierre Jean George Cabanis—offers an argument in two parts. First, he proceeds analogically. Thought is to the material organ of thought as is magnetism is to a needle or elasticity is to a spring—merely a product of the matter thus structured. Dissolve the matter and the magnetism and elasticity cease. It is likewise with thought. "On ignition of the needle or spring, their magnetism and elasticity cease. So on dissolution of the material organ by death, its action of thought may cease also, and that nobody supposes that the magnetism or elasticity retire to hold a substantive and distinct existence. These were qualities only of particular conformations of matter; change the conformation, and its qualities change also."[25]

The question now becomes whether matter can be so structured that thought can occur. Following Locke, Jefferson considers deity endowing matter with thought. He asserts, "When I meet with a proposition beyond finite comprehension, I abandon it as I do a weight which human strength cannot lift, and I think ignorance, in these cases, is truly the softest pillow on which I can lay my head." Immediately, he adds: "Were it necessary, however, to form an opinion, I confess I should, with Mr. Locke, prefer swallowing one incomprehensibility rather than two." In sum, matter endowed with thought is less incomprehensible than "an existence called spirit, of which we have neither evidence nor idea, and then ... how that spirit, which has neither extension nor solidity, can put material organs into motion."

In late-life letters to John Adams (8 Jan. 1825) and to Francis Adrian van der Kemp (11 Jan. 1825), Jefferson excitedly refers to experiments by Flourens and Cabanis on vertebrates. Writes Jefferson to Adams of Flourens, after removing cerebrum of some vertebrates, finding that "the animal loses all it's senses of hearing, seeing, feeling, smelling tasting, is totally deprived of will, intelligence, memory, perception," though it retains the power of locomotion, given external stimuli. After removing the cerebellum from vertebrates, "the animal retains all it's senses, faculties & understanding, but loses the power of regulated motion, and exhibits all the symptoms of drunkenness." Puncture of the medulla elonga results in instantaneous death. Jefferson adds: "I wish to see what the spiritualists will say to this. whether, in this state, the soul remains in the body deprived of it's essence of thought, or whether it leaves it as in death and where it goes?"

Three days later, Jefferson to Adrian van der Kemp again writes of Flourens's experiments, which demonstrate that the cerebrum is the "organ of thought" and "possesses alone the faculty of thinking." He wishes to know whether the soul remains in the body when the brain is deprived of thought, and if it does leave, where it goes, if the thoughtless body still lives.

The letters to Adams and van der Kemp offer abundant evidence of doubt concerning the soul's capacity to survive without the body. Given the cerebrum is the seat of sensation, perception, intelligence, memory, and thought, and given that the cerebellum is responsible for regulated motion, all the functions attributed to soul seem to be explicable by the brain. The conclusion seems plain that the soul just is the brain and the cerebrum is the intellective soul—a view that is consistent with much literature in contemporary philosophy of mind.

Finally, there is also the prose from Laurence Sterne's *Tristram Shandy* that Jefferson copies to a sheet of paper. "And every time I kiss thy hand to bid adieu, every absence which follows it, are preludes to that eternal separation which we are shortly to make."[26] This is the second half of a passage on the folded paper—the first half written in the writing of Jefferson's wife—which contained a lock of Martha Jefferson's hair. The term "eternal separation," copied by a man and his moribund wife, is revelatory.

When mulling over the issue of an afterlife, it is likely, given the common-placing of Lord Bolingbroke in Jefferson's *Literary Commonplace Book*, that he never seriously entertained thoughts of the possibility of an afterlife where reward and punishment was meted out. First, Bolingbroke considered human wickedness to be a defacement of god's work—the product of a "sovereignly good" and "almighty and alwise" creator. No such deity would create in such a manner to allow a greatly inferior being do deface what is perfectly constructed.[27] Moreover, Bolingbroke notes in gist that there is no possible deed whose wickedness warrants eternal damnation and no deed whose goodness warrants eternal reward.[28]

At day's end, I think it likely that Jefferson, given his purchase of materialism, never really took seriously belief in an afterlife—at least, not late in life. Thus, I think it is probable that the doctrines of morality or natural religion for Jefferson comprise only man's duties to god and man's duties to his fellow men.

Jefferson's Recommended Reading Lists

There are also extra-textual evidence that confirms the equivalency of morality and true religion: Jefferson's list of books in key letters and his catalog of books in his libraries.

Recall from Chapter 3 the 1771 letter to Skipwith where Jefferson lists 12 books under "Religion"—there is no category for morality in that letter—he lists the ancients Xenophon, Epictetus, Antoninus, Seneca, and Cicero as well as the moderns Locke, Bolingbroke, Hume, Kames, Sterne, and Sherlock. To Minor in 1814, he includes "Ethics and Natural Religion"—which lists works by Locke, Stewart, Enfield, Condorcet, Cicero, Seneca, Hutcheson, de Raymondis, and Charron—and "Sectarian Religion"—which lists the Bible and works by Middleton, Priestley, Volney, Sterne, Massillon, and Bourdaloue.

Some comments are required.

First, the books under "Ethics and Natural Religion," with exception of Stewart's and Enfield's books, are straightforwardly moral works. The listing of "Ethics and Natural Religion" suggests equivalency of the terms. That is further corroborated with the section "Sectarian Religion," in which Middleton's and Priestley's works and Volney's *Ruins* offer sustained criticisms of the politicized Christianity of Jefferson's day. Hence, we are warranted in distinguishing formally between "natural religion," which contains the basal principles of morality common to all religions, and "sectarian religion," a category under which the various religious sects can be subsumed.

Second, the sermons of Sterne, Massillon, and Bourdalou are ethically exhortatory though they are written within the frame of the Christianity of Jefferson's day. It is well known that Jefferson rejected both the divinity of Christ and miracles. Consequently, like Priestley and Middleton, he believed that one could not take the Bible at face value. The teachings of Jesus, he thought, could be known by stripping off supernature from nature—ridding the New Testament of its thaumaturgy[29]—and by removing historical inconsistencies, and he did just those things in *The Philosophy of Jesus* (1804), of which no known copy exists, and *The Life and Morals of Jesus of Nazareth*, compiled very likely in 1820.³⁰ He also indicated in a letter to William Short (13 Apr. 1820) that he did not embrace all of Jesus's doctrines. "I am a Materialist; he takes the side of Spiritualism; he preaches the efficacy of repentance towards forgiveness of sin; I require a counterpoise of good works to redeem it." Consequently, that he included sermons of Christian ministers indicates forthrightly that he did not believe, as it were, in throwing out the baby with the bathwater.

In sum, the cataloging of his list of books to Minor is additional evidence to take as equivalents true or natural religion and ethics.

Library Catalogs

It is generally accepted that Jefferson had four libraries: his library at Shadwell containing at first some 40 books and as many as 400 at the time of the Shadwell fire (1757–1770), his library at Monticello prior to selling it to create the Library of Congress (1770–1815), his library at Poplar Forest (1811–1826), and what has come to be known as his "Retirement Library" (1815-death).³¹

In 1783, Jefferson cataloged his books—following Bacon's tripartitioning of History (Memory), Philosophy (Reason), and the Fine Arts (Imagination). Numbering 2,640 books,³² the catalog contains the following breakdown of subtopics under the general rubric "Philosophy."³³ I follow only such lines that might shed light on the relationship of "religion" to "morality" or "ethics."

"Religion" and "Moral Philosophy" in Jefferson's 1783 Catalog of Books

Under "Moral," we find "Jurisprudence" and "Ethics." Ethics comprises "Moral Philosophy" and "Law of Nature & Nations"; Jurisprudence comprises "Religious," "Municipal," and "Oeconomical." Why Religion is not subsumable under Ethics is unclear. Douglas Wilson writes, "Jefferson's unusual designation of religion as belonging to jurisprudence shows that he approached religion less as theology, for which he provided no category, and more as a sphere of institutionalized moral suasion."³⁴ More can be said. Subsumption under Jurisprudence suggests Jefferson here approaches Religion as a man-made or political institution, not a natural institution. Hence, by "Religion" he likely means here "Sectarian Religion," as he says in his letter to Minor. The linkage of "Moral Philosophy" with "Law of Nature & Nations" suggests Moral Philosophy is a sort of natural religion.

Jefferson's Retirement Library Catalog begins with the same three main Baconian categories—History, Philosophy, and Fine Arts—yet he subtilizes the groupings, here less complex. Under Philosophy (Reason) he lists "Mathematics" and "Ethical." Under Ethical one finds "Morality," "Moral Supplements," and "Social Organization." "Ethics" is the sole subcategory of Morality; "Religion" and "Law" the sole subcategories of Moral Supplements. "Politics" falls under Social Organization.

"Religion" and "Ethics" in Jefferson's Retirement Library

In the 1783 catalog, "Religion" came under "Religious Jurisprudence." In the Retirement Library, it is linked again with "Law," under "Moral Supplements," and kept apart from "Ethics." Once again, the linking of Religion to Law suggests "Religion" likely means "Sectarian Religion."

In the 1783 catalog, "Moral Philosophy" is both a higher category than "Ethics" and subsumable under it. In the Retirement Library, "Ethical Philosophy" is a higher category than "Morality," though "Ethics" is placed under "Morality." I have found nothing in Jefferson's writings to suggest a distinction between "Ethics" and "Morality." The insouciant manner in which he uses the terms suggests in these catalogs (and elsewhere) that the two could be used interchangeably.

In sum, Jefferson's recommended reading lists and library catalogs give additional reason to believe the equivalency of "True Religion" or "Natural Religion" and "Morality" or "Ethics."

Jefferson's Unitarianism

Finally, Jefferson's espousal of Unitarianism has some bearing on the relationship between religion and morality.

The Trinitarianism of Calvin and Athanasius, Jefferson states in a letter to Benjamin Waterhouse (26 June 1822), asserts that (1) there are three gods, (2) benevolence and beneficence are nothing, (3) faith especially in what is unfathomable in religious matters is everything, (4) reason is unavailing in religious matters, and (5) we are saved or damned if predestined by deity to be saved or damned and not from our good or ill works. Yet such Trinitarianism, Jefferson says in keeping with Joseph Priestley in his *An History of Early Opinions concerning Jesus Christ*, was "nowhere expressly declared by any of the earliest fathers, & was never affirmed or taught by the Church before the Council of Nice."[35] Thus, it was a scabrous and senseless political embellishment to the teachings of Jesus the Nazarene.

Unitarianism, as a formal movement and response to Trinitarianism, was a relatively recent development in Jefferson's day. Its main teachings, according to Jefferson in the same letter, were (1) belief in one omni-perfect deity, (2) belief in a future state of rewards and punishments, and (3) complete love of deity and of one's neighbor as one loves oneself. Thus, Jefferson rejected each of Calvin's tenets.

Yet as we saw in Chapter 4, there were religious controversies endemic to Unitarianism that Priestley examines in his *Early Opinions* and of which Jefferson, having studied Priestley, was aware. Unitarians posited the existence of only one God, but some maintained that Christ, as a lesser being than God, created and superintended the cosmos. Hence, eschewing the difficulty of explaining how Father, Spirit, and Son could be unique and yet one, those Unitarians faced the difficulty of explicating how Christ could have such superordinary powers without being a god.[36]

Moreover and as Priestley acknowledged, the existence of Christ as creator and superintendent of the cosmos made God *de trop*. If cosmic design demands belief in an omnipotent and omnipresent Being—"He who *made all things*, and who *upholds all things by the word of his power*, must necessarily be present every where, and know all things, as well as be able to do all things"—then what need is there of another infinitely powered Being?[37]

Jefferson, I suspect, was inattentive to the imbroglios. Deity existed, the cosmos was evidence of that, and Jesus for Jefferson was simply mortal. He told William Short (4 Aug. 1820) that Jesus did not mean to impose himself on mankind as the son of God, though he might have believed himself to be inspired by God. For Jefferson, Jesus, though mere man, was the greatest moral reformer. Jefferson's embrace of Unitarianism, thus, was a sort of selective engagement with certain axial principles of the sectarian religion and disengagement with other axial principles. In effect, "Unitarianism" was a name he appropriated (or misappropriated) for his own religious views.[38]

What then did "Unitarianism" mean for Jefferson? Like Priestley, he finds the notion of three deities in one inscrutable, and therefore physically impossible. Here he falls back on his naturalism. He allows nothing inconsistent with the laws of nature, gleaned through experience. Yet there is more. The sort of Unitarianism Jefferson promotes is not a religious sect, but instead a manner of approaching religion.[39] Of his Unitarianism, Jefferson asserts to John Adams (22 Aug. 1813), "We should all then, like the Quakers, live without an order of priests, moralize for ourselves, follow the oracle of conscience, and say nothing about what no man can understand, nor therefore believe." To Dr. Thomas Cooper (2 Nov. 1822), Jefferson contrasts Unitarians with sectarian preachers, so Unitarians can be grasped as persons living fully in accordance with the dictates of their moral sense faculty. To Benjamin Waterhouse (8 Jan. 1825), Jefferson states that Unitarianism is "primitive Christianity, in all the simplicity in which it came from the lips of Jesus." Such letters show plainly that monotheism, incomplexity, and non-sectarianism are dependent issues. Jefferson made purchase of monotheism because it and benevolence were key tenets of Jesus's uncorrupted teachings. Those two tenets, he believed, were the framework of his Unitarianism, or of any right religion.[40]

Jefferson's God

There has been and continues to be overwhelming confusion apropos of Jefferson's religiosity. That is, in large part, due to Jefferson, whose behavior invites contradictory assessments of it. He attended worship and participated in prayers and hymns at churches of various denominations, though he railed against the empleomania of religious clerics. He wrote of god as privileging humans—"When the measure of [slaves] tears shall be full ... a God of justice will awaken to their distress ... by His exterminating thunder" (TJ to Jean Nicholas Démeunier, ca. 26 June 1786)—though he commonplaced Lord Bolingbroke concerning the cosmos or even the planet not being made for the sake of man. He had amicable relationships with many local ministers, many of whom were Calvinists, though he generally spoke ill of Calvinism—its trinitarianism being a "hocus-pocus phantasm of a god like another Cerberus, with one body and three heads" (e.g., TJ to James Smith, 8 Dec. 1822). Here, once again, his numerous critics grouse, there are clear instances of Jefferson's hypocrisy—his capacity to say anything to anyone to suit his purposes. Was Jefferson such a chameleon?

The confusion concerning Jefferson's conception of religion exists in large measure because of widespread confusion concerning his conception of deity.

Jefferson employed often "deity" and "god" in writings. "I pray to God" and "god bless you" occur with great frequency in writings, and he frequently ignored capitalizing the latter, when doing so would not prove offensive to a correspondent. That is not inconsequential.

Yet Jefferson seemed never to have had much to say on the nature of deity, and he habitually refused to speak of his religiosity. To John Adams (11 Jan. 1817), he gave his customary reply to anyone who would press him on religion: "Say nothing of my religion. It is known to my God and myself alone."

Jefferson, however, wrote enough on deity to enable us to piece together, with a great degree of accuracy, the nature of his god. One must appeal especially to his letters to intimates, his *Literary Commonplace Book*, and his version of the bible.

In his *Literary Commonplace Book*, Jefferson abundantly commonplaces Lord Bolingbroke's religious views from the latter's *Philosophical Works*. Bolingbroke's deity is "sovereignly good ... almighty and alwise" (§14), and has no difficulty enabling certain types of matter to think (§§11–13). Bolingbroke's god does not intervene in foreordained cosmic events—e.g., through Christ's miracles (§22 and §26), punishment for the fall of man (§15 and §42), or divine superintendency—but establishes once and for all cosmic harmony, as "nothing can be less reconcileable [*sic*] to the notion of an all-perfect being, than the imagination that he undoes by his power in particular cases what his wisdom ... once thought sufficient to be established for all case" (§49)—thus, deism, not theism. Moreover, Bolingbroke's deity has not made "man the final cause of the whole creation" (§16 and §46). Bolingbroke's deity does not communicate his existence through revelation or inspiration, or only to one type of people (§16, §§20–22, §24, §32). Bolingbroke's deity does not punish or reward humans in an eternal afterlife, for "justice requires that punishments ... and rewards ... [ought to] be measured [o]ut in various degrees and manners, according to the various [c]ircumstances of particular cases, and in due proportion to them" (§52)—i.e., justice ought to be meted out in this life. The religious law of Bolingbroke's deity—"the law of nature is the law of god" (§36)—is to be found in nature. "Natural religion represents an allperfect being to our adoration and to our live," and requires humans to "love the lord thy god with all thy heart" (§56).

Jefferson appropriated Bolingbroke's conception of god and largely kept that conception throughout his life.

Like Bolingbroke and others (e.g., Kames, Hume, Smith, and Tracy) whom Jefferson read and assimilated, Jefferson thought deity was visible in the cosmos. He writes to John Adams (11 Apr. 1823): "When we take a view of the Universe, in it's parts general or particular, it is impossible for the human mind not to be percieve [*sic*] and feel a conviction of design, consummate skill, and indefinite power in every atom of it's composition." Use of "see" and "feel" indicate appropriation of the epistemology of Destutt de Tracy and Lord Kames, each of whom stated deity was immediately visible in or felt through the cosmos. Neither invoked an argument from design. That sensual epistemic appropriation is also manifest in a letter to John Adams (15 Aug. 1820) to whom Jefferson states paranomastically in the manner of Descartes: "I feel: therefore I exist.... On the basis of sensation, of matter and motion, we may erect the fabric of all the certainties we can have or need." There is no appeal to reason.

Jefferson limns the attributes of deity in both letters to Adams. In the 1823 letter, he says that God is the designer and "fabricator of all things from matter and motion, their preserver and regulator while permitted to exist in their present forms, and their regenerator into new and other forms." God is a "superintending power" that "maintains the Universe in it's course and order." Regeneration and superintendency are attributed to deity because of new discoveries in astronomy—"Stars, well known, have disappeared, new ones have come into view"—and in biology—"certain races of animals are become extinct." In the 1820 letter, he states that all things—"the human soul, angels, god"—are matter, for if not, "they are *nothings*." He cites Locke, Tracy, and Stewart as authorities for his materialism.

The question redounds: Was Jefferson a deist, like Bolingbroke, or a theist? Some writings, especially early ones, offer evidence of deism. He writes to Dr. Benjamin Rush (23 Sept. 1800) concerning the yellow-fever epidemic in Philadelphia: "When great evils happen, I am in the habit of looking out for what good may arise from them as consolations to us, and Providence has in fact so established the order of things, as that most evils are the means of producing some good." Here the suggestion is that of a pre-established order, implying nonintervention and deism. Yet the 1823 letter to Adams speaks of god as a regenerator or superintendent—implying periodic intervention and theism.

Could it be, as others have claimed, that Jefferson began as a deist and was forced to accept theism because of species extinction, which he was early in life disinclined to accept, and supernovae, like that of 1572?

On settling that bristly issue, Jefferson's 1820 bible has a bearing. Reconstructing the works of the four evangelists in the New Testament, Jefferson was insistent on removing all thaumaturgy—"things against the course of nature" (TJ to William Short, 4 Aug. 1820). He cites "calves speaking" and "statues sweating blood" as illustrations. Hence, passages in which Jesus feeds a great crowd with two fish and five loaves of bread (Matthew 15:32–38) or brings back to life a dead young woman (Matthew 9:18–26) are excised. Insistence that all thaumaturgy be removed from his bible, believed to be the real life and words of Jesus, is another way of Jefferson, following Bolingbroke, saying that god, through Jesus's miracles, "undoes by his power in particular cases what his wisdom … once thought sufficient to be established for all case"—*viz.*, that he allows for periodic exceptions to the laws of nature—evidence of divine impotency, not divine omnipotency. Thus, divine superintendency is best explained for Jefferson by a deity that is either equivalent to the cosmos (a Stoic deity) or a deity that has built superintendency into the cosmos in the manner of a builder who fashions a thermostat for a house to regulate its temperature. Theism is unneeded.

Nonetheless, such a god, creator of an enormous cosmos, is not a being to whom a person would sing or pray. Such a god could take no notice of song or prayer by creatures, beautifully constructed and essential parts of the cosmos, but nonetheless relatively inconsequential. Such a god could care nowise of its name being spelled by humans with a lowercase "g."

Yet the existence of the cosmos is one miracle in which Jefferson, a disdainer of miracles, believes. And so he considers it to be a moral duty of sensual and rational creatures to pay homage to their creator, because of human awareness of the enormousness, beauty, and perfection of the cosmos. Perhaps the best ways of fulfilling that duty are through science—e.g., study of the cosmic "skeleton" through reading Newton's *Principia*, examining telescopic and microscopic phenomena, or even participating in scientific farming—or through art—e.g., replicating great figures of human history for future generations through sculpture or painting or innovating in architecture of the sort in the pavilions at UVa.

Why then did Jefferson periodically attended religious services and sing and pray at such services when his god was deaf to supplication and praise? Why did Jefferson befriend certain religious clerics of various denominations when he always believed that the principles that distinguished one religion from another were political or metaphysical twaddle? Given his god, are these not instances of his infamous hypocrisy?

Jefferson's god, for whatever reason, created humans in such a way that they would greatly debate religious (and political) matters through misuses of reason.[41] Thus, they would even form different conceptions of deity, and worship god in varied manners. Deity, it follows, must have deemed inhomogeneity vis-à-vis such concerns to be good, at least at this stage of human development, and humans ought not to question the ways of deity. In such matters, ignorance, as he is sometimes wont to say, is the softest pillow.

It follows that Jefferson's avowed hypocrisy is best explicated by his conception of deity and by his love of god and of the cosmos. Knowing that god has created humans to be religiously and politically diverse, it is not his task to challenge another's religious views—even those of an atheist. Reason, in time, will have its say. As he says famously: "Reason and free enquiry are the only effectual agents against error.... They are the natural enemies of error, and of error only."[42]

Freedom of Religion

Jefferson had antipathy toward politicized religion and the sorts of rituals and disputes that were essential to the political edifice. In travelling notes, while touring the south of France, he writes of the poor people of several villages and the foofaraw made of daily mass. "Few chateaux. No farm houses, all the people being gathered in villages. Are they thus collected by that dogma of their religion which makes them believe that, to keep the Creator in good humor with his own works, they must mumble a mass every day? Certain it is that they are less happy and less virtuous in villages than they would be insulated with their families on the grounds they cultivate."[43] In Query XVII of *Notes on the State of Virginia*, he writes succinctly but illy of metaphysical religious squabbling. "The way to silence religious disputes, is to take no notice of them."[44] The sentiment here is that if all religions are allowed expression and none is given political allegiance, their disputes will produce at best parochial turbulences, which will be swamped out catholically.

The two issues, however, are dependent. The rituals attending on politicized religions are put into place for the sake of political and moral oppression. "I think it will produce considerable good even in these countries where ignorance, superstition, poverty and oppression of body and mind in every form, are so firmly settled on the mass of the people, that their redemption from them can never be hoped," Jefferson writes, concerning the potential effect of the bill for religious freedom, to George Wythe (13 Aug. 1786). He continues, "If the almighty had begotten a thousand sons, instead of one, they would not have sufficed for this task. If all the sovereigns of Europe were to set themselves to work to emancipate the minds of their subjects from their present ignorance and prejudices, and that as zealously as they now endeavor the contrary, a thousand years would not place them on that high ground on which our common people are now setting out." Want of religious freedom and religious taint of politics are responsible for ignorance, superstition, poverty, and oppression. Republicanism demands religious freedom.

Query XVII of *Notes on the State of Virginia* also offers an expressive defense of religious freedom. Jefferson begins with an account of how the various religions of Virginia came into the state. Many fled England for reasons of religious persecution, but found similar intolerance in Virginia, as Anglicanism was the dominant, state-sanctioned religion for some 100 years. An act of assembly ratified in 1705, referred to in Chapter 6, exemplifies the insularity, and bigotry: "If a person brought up in the Christian religion denies the being of a God, or the Trinity, or asserts there are more Gods than one, or denies the Christian religion to be true, or the scriptures to be of divine authority, he is punishable on the first offense by incapacity to hold any office or employment ecclesiastical, civil, or military; on the second by disability to sue, to take any gift or legacy, to be guardian, executor, or administrator, and by three years imprisonment, without bail."[45] Soon other religions "began then to creep in" till Anglicans were not the majority. A convention in 1776 declared that free exercise of religion was "a truth, and a natural right."

Jefferson then turns squarely to the topic of religious freedom. Rulers have authority over the natural rights of citizen only insofar as citizens grant such authority. No citizen has or even could ever submit "rights of conscience." He continues in an oft-quoted passage: "The legitimate powers of government extend to such acts only as are injurious to others. It does me no injury for my neighbor to say there are twenty gods, or no god. It neither picks my pocket nor breaks my leg." Constraint might lead to conformity of actions, but it does not lead to truth. For truth, there must be reason and free inquiry. "Give a loose to them, they will support the true religion, by bringing every false one to their tribunal, to the test of their investigation."[46]

Jefferson gives several arguments for religious freedom vis-à-vis religious truth. First, only error needs governmental succor; truth can stand on its own. Coercion in religious matters is a sign of error. Second, coercion in religious matters occurs for the sake of uniformity.[47] Yet uniformity in religious inquiry is no more desirable than uniformity of face and stature. Third, uniformity through coercion is impossible. The reasons are twofold. On the one hand, uniformity through coercion has not worked. "Millions of innocent men, women, and children, since the introduction of Christianity, have been burnt, tortured, fined, imprisoned; yet we have not advanced

7. Duty to God and Duty to Man

The Rotunda at the University of Virginia. This is the original library of the university and was placed in the central-most position on the campus, where a church might have been placed (photograph by the author).

one inch towards uniformity.... What has been the effect of coercion? To make one half the world fools, and the other half hypocrites. To support roguery and error all over the earth." On the other hand, uniformity through coercion cannot work. Assume that the globe has on it some one billion people, that the number of religions is one thousand, and that one of those religions is the correct one. To effect uniformity through coercion, members of the one correct religion would have to coerce the numerous members of the 999 different sects, which is impossible. Only through reason and free inquiry is religious truth possible.[48]

Jefferson's most significant writing apropos of freedom of religion is his Bill for Religious Freedom, Bill 82 of the 126 bills proposed by him, Wythe, and Pendleton for the revisal of Virginia's code of laws. It was, he recognized, one of his greatest services to humankind—one of three services to humankind listed on his obelisk at the cemetery behind Monticello. Jefferson writes to James Madison (16 Dec. 1786) of its reception abroad, "The Virginia act for religious freedom has been received with infinite approbation in Europe & propagated with enthusiasm." He continues: "It is comfortable to see the standard of reason at length erected, after so many ages during which the human mind has been held in vassalage by kings, priests & nobles: and it is honorable for us to have produced the first legislature who had the courage to declare that the reason of man may be trusted with the formation of his own opinions."[49]

Alexis de Tocqueville in his travels through America, noted that religionists in America "all attributed the peaceful influence excercised by religion over their country principally to the separation of Church and State." He concludes, "I assert confidently that, during my stay in America, I did not meet a single man, priest or layman, who did not agree about that."[50]

Dumas Malone states, "Belief in the freedom of religion—which to him meant freedom of the mind—lay at the heart of his philosophy and he was always proud to be identified with it."[51] Merrill Peterson adds: "More than a statute, it was an eloquent manifesto of the sanctity of the human mind and spirit. It gave mature expression to convictions that, though they might have been reached wholly along the untroubled path of reason, were, in fact, tempered and formed in the crucible of religious controversy in Virginia. In denouncing the establishment and in advocating the fullest freedom in religious concerns, Jefferson drew on his experience as well as his philosophy."[52]

Malone and Peterson are right to note that the bill is substratally philosophical, not political. Jefferson begins in Section I with a complex and broad statement of the philosophy undergirding the politics. He starts with a statement of human rationality, turns to a statement of the freedom of the human mind, and follows with a statement of the futility of coercion concerning freedom of the human mind. It is plain "that Almighty God hath created the mind free, and manifested his supreme will that free it shall remain by making it altogether insusceptible of restraint; that all attempts to influence it by temporal punishments, or burthens, or by civil incapacitations, tend only to beget habits of hypocrisy and meanness."

Jefferson then turns to several other claims—some of which are political implications of his undergirding philosophy. First, ecclesiastical and civil rulers who have established their own opinions concerning religion as law have "established and maintained false religions over the greatest part of the world and through all time." Second, compelling anyone "to furnish contributions of money for the propagation of opinions which he disbelieves and abhors, is sinful and tyrannical." Third, compelling anyone to support a particular pastor of his own religion that is not of his own choosing is wrongful. Fourth, "our civil rights have no dependance on our religious opinions, any more than our opinions in physics or geometry." Fifth, prohibiting anyone from public office because of his religious convictions is wrongful and so is allowing that person to hold public office only on condition of disavowing such opinions is wrongful. Sixth, it is not the object of civil government to tell men how to think. "Truth is great and will prevail if left to herself," Jefferson sums. "She is the proper and sufficient antagonist to error, and has nothing to fear from the conflict unless by human interposition disarmed of her natural weapons, free argument and debate; errors ceasing to be dangerous when it is permitted freely to contradict them."

In Section II, Jefferson summarizes the political implications as a proposed code of law: "We the General Assembly of Virginia do enact that no man shall be compelled to frequent or support any religious worship, place, or ministry whatsoever, nor shall be enforced, restrained, molested, or burthened in his body or goods, or shall otherwise suffer, on account of his religious opinions or belief; but that all men shall be free to profess, and by argument to maintain, their opinions in matters of religion, and that the same shall in no wise diminish, enlarge, or affect their civil capacities."

The final statement of Section III grounds religious freedom in natural rights. "We are free to declare, and do declare, that the rights hereby asserted are of the natural rights of mankind, and that if any act shall be hereafter passed to repeal the present or to narrow its operations, such act will be an infringement of natural right."

Jefferson also argues for religious freedom in a letter, as president, to the Danbury Baptist Association. On October 7, 1801, members of the association—Nehh Dodge, Ephram Robbins, and Stephen S. Nelson including their names—drafted a letter to newly elected president, Thomas Jefferson. The letter states:

> Our Sentiments are uniformly on the side of Religious Liberty—That Religion is at all times and places a matter between God and individuals—That no man ought to suffer in name, person, or effects on account of his religious Opinions—That the legitimate Power of civil government extends no further than to punish the man who works *ill to his neighbor*. But Sir our constitution of government is not specific. Our ancient charter together with the Laws made coincident therewith, were adopted on the Basis of our government, at the time of our revolution; and such had been our Laws & usages, and such still are; that Religion is considered as the first object of Legislation; and therefore what religious privileges we enjoy (as a minor part of the State) we enjoy as favors granted, and not as inalienable rights: and these favors we receive at the expense of such degrading acknowledgements, as are inconsistent with the rights of freemen. It is not to be wondered at therefore; if those, who seek after power & gain under the pretense of *government & Religion* should reproach their fellow men—should reproach their chief Magistrate, as an enemy of religion Law & good order because he will not, dare not assume the prerogatives of Jehovah and make Laws to govern the Kingdom of Christ.

> Sir, we are sensible that the President of the United States, is not the national legislator, and also sensible that the national government cannot destroy the Laws of each State; but our hopes are strong that the sentiments of our beloved President, which have had such genial affect already, like the radiant beams of the Sun, will shine and prevail through all these States and all the world till Hierarchy and Tyranny be destroyed from the Earth. Sir, when we reflect on your past services, and see a glow of philanthropy and good will shining forth in a course of more than thirty years we have reason to believe that America's God has raised you up to fill the chair of State out of that good will which he bears to the Millions which you preside over. May God strengthen you for the arduous task which providence & the voice of the people have cald [*sic*] you to sustain and support you in your Administration against all the predetermined opposition of those who wish to rise to wealth & importance on the poverty and subjection of the people.

On January 1, 1802, Jefferson drafted a brief reply to the concerns of the Danbury Baptists. The letter contains his now-famous wall-of-separation metaphor—the subject of considerable debate in the secondary literature today. Acknowledging receipt of the letter of the Baptists, Jefferson writes of his duty as president to recognize and represent the interest of his constituents. "My duties dictate a faithful and zealous pursuit of the interests of my constituents, & in proportion as they are persuaded of my fidelity to those duties, the discharge of them becomes more and more pleasing." He then proceeds to a breviloquent expression of the freedom of religious practice, which introduces the famous metaphor of a wall of separation. "Believing with you that religion is a matter which lies solely between Man & his God, that he owes account to none other for his faith or his worship, that the legitimate powers of government reach actions only, & not opinions, I contemplate with sovereign reverence that act of the whole American people which declared that their legislature should 'make no law respecting an establishment of religion, or prohibiting the free exercise thereof,' thus building a wall of separation between Church & State."

The phrase "the whole American people which declared that their legislature should 'make no law respecting an establishment of religion, or prohibiting the free exercise thereof'" suggests to some that Jefferson's intendment was prohibition of government's intervention in matters of church. Derek Davis writes: "A fair examination of Thomas Jefferson's 1802 letter to the Danbury Baptist Association clearly shows that Jefferson understood the religion clauses to militate against religious institutions being government's guiding force or the beneficiaries of government benefits. His 'wall of separation between church and state' would be a permanent barrier to such practices." Consistent with abolition of entails and primogeniture and his Bill for Religious Freedom, Jefferson was attempting once again to redress the issue of an artificial aristocracy—the centuries-old notion that birth or wealth qualify one for public office and the topic of the next chapter. Nonetheless, he argues that the wall of separation is not unidirectional. It is meant to prohibit religious encroachment in political affairs as well as political encroachment in each person's religiosity.[53]

Robert Cord, appealing to several of Jefferson's actions as politician as well as Bills 84 and 85 of the *Revisal of the Laws of Virginia* (which he assumes were in the hand of Jefferson), argues that Jefferson was not averse at times to using sectarian institutions for secular ends, so long as in doing so he was not privileging any one religion to the detriment of others. Thus, the "wall of separation" metaphor employed by Jefferson in the Danbury-Baptist letter is "nonabsolutist": Particular religions can never use government to advance their aims, while government can sometimes use particular religions to advance secular aims.[54]

Daniel Driesbach, in keeping with Cord's thesis, argues that Bill 82 should not be taken independently of the four other companion bills—Bills 83 through 86, of which "Jefferson was the chief architect, if not the actual draftsman," even though "a couple of them were revisions of provisions that had long been on the statute books of Virginia." Those bills allow for "limited state cooperation with religious institutions ... if it advanced freedom of religious belief and expression" or if they advanced "the legitimate secular goals of the civil state." The wall-of-separation metaphor, then, was meant to apply strictly to the federal government and religious institutions or practices.[55]

Johann Neem says Jefferson's intent was more fundamental than a wall that protected church from state or state from church. Its implications went beyond political and religious concerns. Jefferson's intendment was free inquiry. "The wall of separation was not intended to banish religion from the public sphere of civil society. Instead, it was intended to prohibit an alliance between ministers and politicians that would limit free inquiry. Free inquiry would allow persons to question centuries of fabricated mysticism invented by ministers."[56]

Davis is correct to note freedom of religion was both for freedom from governmental intrusion in citizens' personal affairs—*viz.*, matters of conscience—and for freedom from religious intrusion in governmental affairs, which historically have been contaminated by religious prelates. Moreover, the conclusions of Cord and Dreisbach must not be given short shrift, if it is the case that Jefferson fully endorsed[57] the proposals of Bills 83 through 86.

However, I wish to follow up on the suggestion of Neem that Jefferson's real intent in setting up a wall of separation between church and state was free inquiry. That claim has, I believe, much in its favor. However, Neem does not go far enough, for free inquiry for Jefferson was not an end, but a means. As always, Jefferson's true aim was continued human advance—i.e., human thriving or happiness. For that to happen, the natural, not the artificial, aristocrats had to be governing, and the natural aristocrats for Jefferson comprised those persons preeminent in genius and virtue. Religiosity was irrelevant. Thus, there needed to be a wall of separation between church and state so that political affairs, at least at the federal level, were not decided by religious partialities.

There are numerous other articulations of freedom of religion. I give merely a few. Jefferson drafts a proposed constitution for Virginia in 1776. In it, he states, "All persons shall have full and free liberty of religious opinion; nor shall any be compelled to frequent or maintain any religious institution."[58] In a memorandum now titled "Services to My Country," believed "All persons shall have full and free liberty of religious opinion; nor shall any be compelled to frequent or maintain any religious institution." to be drafted around 1800, Jefferson lists "freedom of religion" and "demolition of the church establishment" of two elements of one of his services—11 are listed—and thereafter writes briefly of his efforts to write up and pass Bill 82.[59] In a 1781 proclamation, Jefferson invites British mercenaries to desert, and one of the reasons given for desertion is "the free exercise of their respective religions."[60] In Article 11 of a proposed treaty between the United States and Denmark and Norway, Jefferson writes, "The most perfect freedom of conscience and of worship is granted to the citizens or subjects of either party within the jurisdiction of the other without being liable to molestation in that respect for any cause other than an insult on the religion of others."[61]

When and How to Study Religion

Before closing, I turn to Jefferson's *avant-garde* views on study of religion.

Jefferson writes in Query XIV of *Notes on the State of Virginia* that in the first stages of education, "wherein the great mass of the people will receive their instruction," children should not be studying the Bible, for their "judgments are not sufficiently matured for religious inquiries." Instead, they can be "the most useful facts from Grecian, Roman, European and American history," through which "the first elements of morality … may be instilled into their minds."[62]

Jefferson's concerns here are principally two. First, ward-school education is critical, as it "lays the principal foundations of future order." Thus, such subjects need to be taught that will allow for future order—useful facts from history and the first elements of morality (and it is probable that the two are not exclusive). Second, cognizant that human rationality takes years to develop and mature, Jefferson insists that youths should not be exposed prematurely to subjects that require critical reflection. Religion is listed as the only example. The two concerns are not independent of each other. Premature exposure to religion can impede an underdeveloped rational faculty by disallowing its capacity for critical engagement with religious issues, thereby making one a slave for life to its precepts. Such uncritical acceptance of religious precepts is not voluntary acceptance of them, hence, it is not avowal of them. In contrast, useful facts from history that are not directly related to morality complement the first lessons of morality without taxing the burgeoning rational faculty. Eschewing religion and bolstered by the lessons of history, each person develops a strong sense of independency, and learns that being happy is not a matter of things outside of one's control, but the result of "good conscience, good health, occupation, and freedom in all just pursuits."

Jefferson also investigates the topic of the time for religious study in a letter to Peter Carr (19 Aug. 1787). Carr, born in 1770, is sufficiently mature at the time to undertake the subject of religion. Jefferson proffers counsel.

The letter gives a step-by-step recipe for how to study religion. He begins with mental preparation. First, one must approach the subject with "novelty and singularity of opinion," not bias. Second, one must approach the subject with courage, not "fears and servile prejudices." Third, one must allow reason full jurisdiction. "Question with boldness even the existence of a god; because, if there be one, he must more approve the homage of reason, than that of blindfolded fear." Fourth, one must entertain every relevant fact and opinion.

Jefferson then turns to critical engagement with religious materials. He advises Carr on how to read the Bible. "Read the bible then, as you would read Livy or Tacitus. The facts which are within the ordinary course of nature you will believe on the authority of the writer, as you do those of the same kind in Livy and Tacitus. The testimony of the writer weighs in their favor in one scale, and their not being against the laws of nature does not weigh against them. But those facts in the bible which contradict the laws of nature, must be examined with more care, and under a variety of faces."

How is one to assess a report of a miracle—an event in contravention with the laws of nature? Here Jefferson qua empiricist falls upon probabilistic assessment. "Here you must recur to the pretensions of the writer to inspiration from god. Examine upon what evidence his pretensions are founded, and whether that evidence is so strong as that it's falsehood would be more improbable than a change of the laws of nature in the case he relates."

He illustrates first with an example from Joshua (10: 12–13) in which the sun is said to have stood still for numerous hours to allow the Israelites more time to engage in battle with and defeat the Amorites—a passage made famous by Galileo in his "Letter to the Grand Duchess Christina."[63] Following Galileo, Jefferson notes that sudden stoppage of a body such as the earth, which turns on its axis would prostrate animals, trees, and buildings, and the same would occur on resumption of the earth's rotation. Yet the writer of Joshua was said to be inspired, and millions believe the account in spite of the obvious absurdities. Jefferson says, what evidence do we have of such inspiration?

Jefferson illustrates next what some believe of Jesus in the New Testament. Some say "he was begotten by god, born of a virgin, suspended and reversed the laws of nature at will, and ascended bodily into heaven." Others say "he was a man, of illegitimate birth, of a benevolent heart, enthusiastic mind, who set out without pretensions to divinity, ended in believing them, and was punished capitally for sedition by being gibbeted according to the Roman law which punished the first commission of that offence by whipping, and the second by exile or death *in furcâ*." Here too, Carr is invited to examine all accounts of the life of Jesus, while giving reason free expression.

Jefferson bids his nephew not to be frightened at the perceived consequences of putting Jesus's life and the existence of a deity to the test of reason. If disbelief in deity follows, "you will find incitements to virtue in the comfort and pleasantness you feel in it's exercise, and the love of others which it will procure you." If belief in deity follows, "a consciousness that you are acting under his eye, and that he approves you, will be a vast additional incitement." Moreover, inquiry might also bring about belief in a future state, thereby increasing "the appetite to deserve it" by promoting good deeds. Finally, inquiry might also bring about belief that Jesus was a god, thereby offering the believer added comfort.

Jefferson sums. "In fine, I repeat that you must lay aside all prejudice on both sides, and neither believe nor reject any thing because any other person, or description of persons have rejected or believed it. Your own reason is the only oracle given you by heaven, and you are answerable not for the rightness but uprightness of the decision." The final sentiment is critical. More important is the uprightness of the decision—the gravity, solemnity, and sincerity of the undertaking—than the correctness of one's decision. Obtaining the right answer through wrong or hasty reasoning or without reasoning is a crime unpardonable; obtaining the wrong answer through a right-intended, thorough, and unbiased process is not only pardonable, but also admirable.

That sentiment is corroborated in Henry Randall's biography of Jefferson. Grandson Thomas Jefferson Randolph wrote thus to Randall concerning his grandfather's views on religion. "It was a subject each was bound to study assiduously for himself, unbiased by the opinions of others—it was a matter solely of conscience; after thorough investigation, they were responsible for the righteousness, but not the rightfulness of their opinions; that the expression of his opinion might influences theirs, and he would not give it!"[64]

Upshot

Here I sum my findings by answering the three questions posed at the beginning of this essay: the first, concerning the relationship between religion and morality; the second, concerning the extent of his belief in a separation of the religious from the political; and the last, concerning his belief that children ought not to be exposed to religiosity.

Rightly grasped, religion, Jefferson consistently averred, was a personal matter, and a matter of living aright, not a matter of adoption of a particular religious creed. Thus, true religion was equivalent to morality, and sectarian religion, politicized, was at least potentially a toxin. He did, however, believe that there were principles salvageable from sectarian religions—those common to all (or most) of them. Those included, fundamentally, belief in and love of deity and benevolence toward all other humans. Because Jefferson thought that belief in and love of deity was foundational to morality, there cannot, strictly speaking, be a moral atheist, only a morality-abiding atheist.

Avowal of the political nature of sectarian religions naturally led Jefferson to formulate his "Bill for Religious Freedom," which allowed for free expression of all religions that did not threaten the existence of the republican nation and which debarred religious considerations from having influence on political affairs. To what extent Jefferson was endorsing a two-way wall of separation—preclusion of religious influence on political affairs at any level of governing and preclusion of political influence on individuals' right to religious expression—is still a matter of scholarly debate, as many believe Jefferson never meant to debar some amount of religious influence in political matters at some level, and that view seems reasonable.

Last, Jefferson asserted that religion and metaphysical religious controversies ought not to be studied prior to the maturation of the rational faculty. The worry was that the centuries-old practice of premature exposure to the dogmata of any religion would lead to involuntary and uncritical acceptance, and likely make the child exposed to them a prisoner of that religion for life.

8

Government by the Natural *Aristoi*

Education and the Problem of Virtuous Politicians

> "We are always happy when our duty coincides with our desires; nothing is then difficult, all things bear a pleasing aspect."
> —Louis-Sébastien Mercier, *L'An 2440*

Over the years, Jefferson's educational views have received and continue to receive ample attention by philosophers and educational theorists and practitioners. There is consensus that his was a substantial contribution to the philosophy and praxis of education, but there is no consensus on just what that contribution was and whether it was sustaining.

Jefferson was proposing wholesale, systemic educational reform consistent with his burgeoning vision of participatory republican governing. His aim was normative: human flourishing or happiness in a progressive political unit, people-governed. For that to happen, Jefferson recognized the citizenry as a whole would need to have readily access to general education to conduct their lives without the paternalistic interposition of government. Moreover a mechanism, higher education, would have to be in place to ensure that the best citizens, both the greatest genius and the most virtuous, would be in positions to assume the most important roles in governance. Between the bookends of elementary-level education and university-level education, Jefferson proposed a sufficient number of grammar schools as educative conduits.

Thus, higher education aims to promote talent and virtue for political stability and advance. Perusal of Jefferson's proposed systemic reforms in his two chief educational bills of 1779 and 1817 shows that his system is anything but wholly egalitarian—*viz.*, not all citizens of outstanding talent would be given equal opportunity for political ascendency. Nonetheless, the educational system does accommodate talent to a modest degree by offering a systemic approach to honing usefully intelligence in the service of political stability and advance. The educational system does accommodate virtue inasmuch as it essays to educate each according to his own needs in a political schema that is set up to allow, within limits, each person to chart his own path to happiness.

A System of Education

Systematicity for Political Stability

In Jefferson's day, there was no structure to education. First, there was no system in place for educating the general citizenry and little access to general education. Some families, with sufficient means, pooled resources to hire an itinerant teacher to allow some amount of education for their children. Rarer still was the scenario in which a wealthy man provided a "free school" for the children of his neighborhood in his will. Yet such "charity schools" were looked upon with derision by the gentry.[1] Second, there was no system in place to transport a student from an elementary school to, say, the College of William and Mary. Writes Roy Honeywell: "There was virtually no coordination between the elementary schools and the grammar schools and very little between these and the college. The elementary school did not prepare for the grammar school, nor did this prepare for the college as well as did private tutors." Moreover, one graduating from William and Mary was suitably readied for no profession other than perhaps the Church of England.[2] In short, while it was typically recognized that citizens needed education, and some at higher levels, there was no general plan to decide who needed what sort of education and to what level.

What Jefferson was proposing through his educational bills was educative structure that went hand-to-glove with wholesale political changes in keeping with the normative aim of republicanism—human flourishing. The educative system he was proposing was not a matter of alterations to an in-place schema, for there was no in-place schema. Moreover it was no mere mechanism for coupling the institutions that existed, for there was no sure way to do that, so incongruous was the instruction at each level in his day.

8. Government by the Natural Aristoi

Systematicity, for Jefferson, entailed uniformity of education at elementary and grammar schools, quality of instruction at each level through accountability, accessibility of schools to students, and instruction in pursuance of the needs of each citizen.

Overall, systemic reform of education is evident in Jefferson's "Bill for the More General Diffusion of Knowledge" (1779) in which a scheme is proposed for creating elementary schools and grammar schools and for revising the curriculum of William and Mary College. His focus, however, in light of the recency of the American Revolution, is to sustain American independency and regard for the rights of men. His concern is political retrogradation. For retrogradation to be forestalled there must be instantiated a twofold scheme: democratically, general education for the citizenry, and meritocratically, higher education for the best genius and most virtuous.

Jefferson begins the bill by noting that some governments are better at allowing the exercise of freedom and preventing degeneracy. Yet appeal to experience shows that those persons entrusted with power will degenerate into tyrants if no checks are in place. The best check, he adds, an education which enables the citizenry to recognize "ambition under all its shapes, and prompt to exert their natural powers to defeat its purposes." What allows for a happy citizenry, he continues, is good laws, and "laws will be wisely formed, and honestly administered, in proportion as those who form and administer them are wise and honest." Therefore, to best promote public happiness, "those persons ... with genius and virtue ... should be called to that charge [of political office] without regard to wealth, birth or other accidental condition or circumstance."[3]

The bill points to two needed levels of education. Those citizens of the best rank—the intelligent, capable, wise—must be incentivized to govern. Even then, the threat of corruption looms, so the general citizenry needs an education that minimally enables them to recognize ambition and corruption and remove unprincipled governors.

In stark contrast, Jefferson's "Bill for Establishing a System of Public Education" (1817) begins breviloquently, without concession. "For establishing schools at which the children of all the citizens of this Commonwealth may receive a primary grade of education at the common expense [b]e it enacted." Unlike his Bill 79 of 1779, there is no preamble, because there is no need of one. Political degeneracy of the sort that preoccupied him in 1779 is not a concern in 1817.

Thus, Darren Staloff warns against positing continuity of effort and aims in these two bills, separate by nearly 40 years, as the political circumstances behind the two bills were markedly different and there were significant changes in Jefferson's political thought and rhetoric over the years. In 1779, Jefferson "sought to secure the liberties of a newly established and potentially fragile republican order in his state." In 1817, with the unity of the nation at stake, his "campaign was against a perceived sectional threat."[4]

Staloff's guardedness notwithstanding, comparative scrutiny of the bills shows mostly cosmetic differences in basic structure, though the details of the plans differ significantly. In the main, both bills aim dead-center at political stability through educational systematicity by instantiation of elementary schools, grammar schools, and a state-level university. Both plans offer a précis of uniformity of education at elementary and grammar schools, quality of instruction, accessibility, and instruction according to the needs of each citizen. Both plans, aiming at reform of Virginia's educational system, allow for intra-national implementation. The bill of 1817 gives no evidence of concern for the North and South forming independent nations, though the tension was real at the time of the drafting of the bill. Nonetheless, the bill of 1817 like the bill of 1779 is a blueprint for political stability at any level through educational reform.

The Problem of Grammar Schools

Wholesale educational reform for Jefferson was undertaken as a necessary ingredient of his recipe for political reform. Given that republican government required that all people had to take an active role in political participation at some level, a political structure had to be put into place to allow for popular participation in government. That was Jefferson's ward system, modeled on the township system of New England. General education was needed for wards to thrive, for empowerment of the general citizenry without a certain base of knowledge would nowise enable citizens to exercise their powers wisely. Given that the great majority of citizens would not be capable of high-level participation—county-, state-, and federal-levels of participation—a political structure had to be put into place that allowed not only talent, but also virtue to govern the masses of men. That was the meritocratic aspect of Jeffersonian republicanism. University-level education was needed to assure the emergence of talent as well as virtue, for talent without virtue would invite disaster for his political system[5]—a salient point pretermitted by numerous scholars.

Thus, there was a bottom to Jefferson's thoughts on educational reform—the democratic, elementary-schools component in which all, males and females would be educated equally at public expense—and a top to educational reform—the meritocratic, university-level component in which the best geniuses and most virtuous would have access to a state-level institution such as the University of Virginia. There was also a gap in the system: General education was to end at roughly 10 years of age and university-level education was to begin at roughly 16 years of age. Those few that wished to and showed promise of matriculating and succeeding at, say, the University of Virginia had to do something *ad interim*. In that sense, Jefferson devised colleges or grammar schools to supply the education needed to take those scholars with greatest promise of virtue and talent from ward schools to a university. To Wilson C. Nicholas (2 Apr. 1816), Jefferson writes of his uncertainty of the curriculum at grammar schools: "The university must be intended for all useful sciences, and the [ward] schools [are] elementary ones, for the instruction of the people, answering to our present English schools; the middle term, colleges or academies, may be more conjectural. But we must understand from it some middle grade of education."

At this point, one might argue that Jefferson had a quasi-functionalist's focus on educational reform—a focus on inputs and outputs. Thus, grammar schools were defined not so much by their content, but their function, which was to funnel the best pupils from elementary schools to a university. He readily recognized what needed to be done basally for political and moral stability and progress—i.e., elementary education for all citizens. He readily recognized what needed to be done apically for political and moral stability and continued progress—i.e., a state-sponsored university for the best citizens. Grammar-school education was essential because it filled a gap in the system, without which there would be no system.

There is weight to the functionalist objection, at least early in Jefferson educational thinking. In his "Bill for the More General Diffusion of Knowledge," he gives Latin, Greek, English grammar, geography, and higher arithmetic as subjects. Nonetheless he adds it is the role of the counties' visitors to see to it that "any general plan of instruction recommended by the visiters of William and Mary College shall be observed."[6] In his "Bill for Establishing a System of Public Education" almost 40 years later, the curriculum is expanded to include French, Italian, Spanish, and German as well geography, but the Visitors again are empowered to "proscribe ... the course of education to be pursued."[7]

Recognizing that grammar schools are principally conduits for taking ward-level scholars and readying them for university-level education, Jefferson gives this defense in a letter to Gov. Wilson C. Nicholas (2 Apr. 1816) for a focus on ancient languages in such preparatory schools:

> Now, when we advert that the ancient classical languages are considered as the foundation preparatory for all the sciences; that we have always had schools scattered over the country for teaching these languages, which often were the ultimate term of education; that these languages are entered on at the age of nine or ten years, at which age parents would be unwilling to send their children from every part of the State to a central and distant university, and when we observe that the resolution supposes there are to be a plurality of them, we may well conclude that the Greek and Latin are the objects of these colleges.

The passage contains two main arguments. First, there is what might be called the groundwork argument: The ancient languages offer a preparatory foundation for all science. He fails to expatiate. Second, there is the argument from orthodoxy: The ancient languages are customarily taught at schools across the country to juvenescent students whose youth prohibits them from being sent to schools too far from home. Why not then merely systematize that orthodoxy?

The groundwork argument is fleshed out in a letter to John Brazier (24 Aug. 1819). Jefferson mentions that there are "stores of real science" in the ancient.[8] A moralist will find "highly and justly esteemed" ethical writings. Greek ethical thought contains the seed of modern thought. A lawyer will find Latin of inestimable use. The language of civil law is essentially Latin. A physician will find "as good a code of his art as has been given us to this day." The present store of medical knowledge builds on Hippocratic medicine. A statesman will find useful ancient accounts of history, politics, mathematics, and ethics. He will also be moved by ancient eloquence and philopatry. A merchant will not need ancient languages, but will find much useful content in ancient writings. Ethics, mathematics, geography, political economy, and history are likely the "immediate foundations of his calling." An agriculturist and a mechanic will need ethics, mathematics, chemistry, and natural philosophy. In short, there are numerous instances of men of uncommon capacities in all the businesses of life that have gotten where they have gotten with nothing but an education in the ancient languages. Finally, every science has the roots of its fundamental terms in the ancient languages. Jefferson sums, "The classical languages are a solid basis for most, and an ornament to all the sciences."

There is hyperbole, perhaps desperation, in Jefferson's apologia. One grants the relevance of ancient ethical thinking in shaping current moral behavior and for contemporary mathematics. Yet there are good reasons to be distrustful of the relevance of ancient literature appertaining to law, medicine, politics, and the business of merchants. Even the practiced classicist, the Rev. Maury, Jefferson's former teacher, questioned the usefulness of the ancient languages in America.

Republicanism as Democracy and as Meritocracy

Education and Equality

For republicanism to take root, there needed to be recognition of some basal level of equality of citizens, and general education was the means of providing that equality. Jefferson writes in Query XIV of *Notes on the State of Virginia*, "The first stage of this education being the schools of the hundreds, wherein the great mass of the people will receive their instruction, the principal foundations of future order will be laid here."[9] In his 1818 "Rockfish Gap Report," Jefferson, in an effort to illustrate how such order will come about, gives a list of the aims of general education—the democratic component of his proposed system of educational reform.[10] I condense what he says there to the following four criteria.

For political order to exist, there must be the fullest measure of political participation, for the affairs of each person in a thriving republic involve the affairs of others. For fullest political participation, each citizen's personal affairs must be conducted efficiently, for no one will concern himself with communal involvement if his own affairs are in disarray because, as Jefferson says in "Opinion on the French Treaties," "the law of self-preservation overrules the laws of obligation to others."[11] Thus, the first and perhaps most critical aim of general education, consonant with the general aim of each citizen being educated in pursuance of his own needs, is that all citizens—the laboring and the learned as well as males and females—are to be generally educated to give them a foundation for conducting their own affairs. Such affairs include the transaction of personal business, the preservation of one's ideas, and the calculation of contracts, accounts, and ideas.

Second, general education, both through the reading of history and fiction with discernible moral content, will strengthen each person's moral sense and enhance his intellect.[12] "The first elements of morality," he writes in *Notes on the State of Virginia*, can be learned through general education to show people, when their critical faculty has matured, that their happiness is not due to the circumstances of their situation, but is a consequence of "good conscience, good health, occupation, and freedom in all just pursuits."[13] Each person will be able to triumph over circumstances and seek an internal monitor of happiness. Each person will learn his duties to neighbor and country and discharge them with diligence, pride, and efficiency. Each person, upon detecting political ambition in himself through study of history, will be encouraged to act to expunge it.[14] In short, primary education aids the moral faculty, facilitates industry, reinforces social relations, and checks ambition. It involves memory, reason, and imagination.

Third, general education teaches citizens their natural rights and how to exercise them with order and justice—i.e., without encroaching on the rights of others. It is well known that Jefferson, when apprized of the drafted Constitution of the United States while he was in France, objected not only to the lack of term limits for the executive, but also to neglect of a bill of rights. "What I disapproved from the first moment," he writes James Madison (15 Mar. 1789), "was the want of a bill of rights to guard liberty against the legislative as well as the executive branches of the government; that is to say, to secure freedom in religion, freedom of the press, freedom from monopolies, freedom from unlawful imprisonment, freedom from a permanent military, and a trial by jury in all cases determinable by the laws of the land."[15] The worry here is not merely parochial. Jefferson aims at establishing a universal standard. "A bill of rights is what the people are entitled to against every government on earth, general or particular," he again writes to Madison (20 Dec. 1787) "& what no just government should refuse, or rest on inferences."[16]

Finally, education enables citizens to choose and oversee those who govern them. In a letter to Mann Paige (30 Aug. 1795), Jefferson says Rouchefoucauld and Montaigne were wrong to assert that 14 of every 15 men are scapegraces. Men, he thinks, are fundamentally honest. Those persons who insidiously "rise" to positions of governance are the scapegraces. "These rogues set out with stealing the people's good opinion, and then steal from them the right of withdrawing it, by contriving laws and associations against the power of the people themselves." Thus, governors are to be chosen by the people, overseen or even bird-dogged by the people, and, if needed, recalled by the people. When government turns coercive and vilipends the rights of its citizens, citizens have a right to rebel and even overthrow the government.[17]

Education and Merit

For republicanism to take root, there needed to be some recognition of inequality—i.e., that given rough equality of opportunity, not all men would rise to levels of political prominence. Yet as things stood in the early republic, the politically prominent were the wealthy and wellborn, not men of talent and virtue. Jefferson's republicanism was an effort to remedy that defect.

In an important letter to John Adams (28 Oct. 1813), Jefferson maintains that there exists a natural aristocracy, comprising the virtuous and talented, and an artificial aristocracy, comprising the wealthy and wellborn. Wealth and birth are sufficient to place one among the natural aristocracy. Lack of either is sufficient to exclude one. Lack of virtue or talent, coupled with wealth or birth, place one among the artificial aristocracy.[18] Birth and wealth, in sum, are irrelevant for governing. The wealthy and wellborn might have certain conveniences or resources that those non-wealthy and non-well-born do not have—*viz.*, they might be better enabled to pursue virtue and to develop their talent, if they should so choose—but those conveniences themselves nowise make them any better suited for good governing.

Jefferson continues: "The natural aristocracy I consider as the most precious gift of nature, for the instruction, the trusts, and government of society. And indeed, it would have been inconsistent in creation to have formed man for the social state, and not to have provided virtue and wisdom enough to manage the concerns of the society. May we not even say, that that form of government is the best, which provides the most effectually for a pure selection of these natural *aristoi* into the offices of government?" In contrast, the artificial aristocracy, "a mischievous ingredient in government," should be disallowed ascendency.[19]

Jefferson is proffering a definition of *aristoi* (Greek for "best men") in an effort to distance himself from Adams's political conservatism and advance a notion of "republicanism" idoneous for his progressivist political thinking. This notion of republicanism is, however, not a political agenda; it is a moral undertaking. He realizes that the people can govern themselves only to such an extent. As members of a county, state, and a federation of states, there are non-parochial concerns that influence them—one, of course, being securing their rights. For non-parochial concerns, they must have trustworthy and caring governors and officials. The best way to ensure that is to create a schema of government which guarantees only the true best, the natural *aristoi*, will be enabled to govern, if they so choose. Only the natural best, with an eye to the good of the whole, will prorogue their own interests to be responsive to the needs and concerns of the general citizenry.

The need of institutions of higher education was generally recognized in Jefferson's time—at least, by the gentry. Yet in Jefferson's day, institutions of higher learning were established for the sake and needs of the gentry. They were a means of keeping the wealthy and wellborn separate from the common people.

Jefferson's notion of republican government, an *avant-garde* idea for his day, was a radical attempt to redefine *aristoi*—to eliminate the "artificial *aristoi*." Jefferson rejected the notion of betterment through birth and aimed to mitigate differences in wealth.[20] Such mitigation allowed for differences in wealth, but those were to be determined through industry and intelligence, not rank, and those divisions were not to be such that they would create divisions among the people.

Key for Jefferson was that higher education for the true best was not to be viewed as something independent of primary education of the general citizenry. Higher education without general education would only perpetuate the centuries-old foolery of government by the self-aggrandizing and unfit.

In that regard, Jefferson's aims at educational reform were wholesale and methodical,[21] as educational reform was in the service of his republicanism. "[The people's] greatest good requires, that while they are instructed in general, competently to the common business of life," he writes to Joseph Cabell (28 Nov. 1820), "others should employ their genius with necessary information to the useful arts, to inventions for saving labor and increasing our comforts, to nourishing our health, to civil government, military science, &c." The contrast here is between general education and university-level education—the epitome of secondary education.

Jefferson tells Peter Carr (7 Sept. 1814) that higher education must aim to teach "every branch of science, deemed useful at this day" to it "highest degree." For utmost utility, it must have specific aims. In his "Rockfish Gap Report," Jefferson lists the specific aims of higher education—the meritocratic component of his system of educational reform—as follows.

First, higher education is responsible for forming statesmen, legislators, and judges for "public prosperity and individual happiness." The notion expressed here attends on what I have said earlier vis-à-vis the natural *aristoi*. Higher education is a sort of selection mechanism that ensures that the true best—the talented and virtuous, not the wealthy and wellborn—are readied for governing and willing to govern. Thus, it rewards not birth or wealth, but intelligence and moral uprightness. As we shall see later, the specific proposals that Jefferson countenanced for ensuring talent and virtue to surge to the political top through access to higher education were insufficient. Nonetheless, as is readily known, he did much to pave the way for access of future generations to higher education—e.g., riddance of entails and primogeniture as well as instantiation of freedom of religion.

Second, higher education is needed for well-structured government, instantiating sound principles of government, developing the laws of national and international government, and creating a "sound spirit of

8. Government by the Natural Aristoi

legislation" that leaves citizens "free to do whatever does not violate the equal rights of another." Though this is a structural point, it is not independent of the first aim. Here one might ask: How are the right sort of political leaders to lead well? It is by having a certain minimal schema for governing that prohibits governors from contravening the rights of citizens and keeps them in attendance of matters on which they ought to focus—issues of legislation that concern the nation and its interactions with other nations. That schema involves popular overseeing of elected officials. Jefferson writes to William Jarvis (28 Sept. 1820): "I know no safe depository of the ultimate powers of the society but the people themselves; and if we think them not enlightened enough to exercise their control with a wholesome discretion, the remedy is not to take it from them, but to inform their discretion by education. This is the true corrective of abuses of constitutional power."

Third, higher education should promote and harmonize agriculture, manufacture, and commerce. Here, Jefferson shows that his notion of liberalism is in today's terms not merely negative or atomistic—that is, negative liberty or freedom from political interference. Political leaders are responsible for the wellbeing of the citizenry through some degree of active intervention in their affairs, but only for the sake of promoting human flourishing by offering varied and more numerous opportunities for profitable and progressive human industry and expression—that is, positive liberty. Elected officials, especially at the state level, must be actively involved in overseeing agriculture, manufacture, and commerce by patronizing scientific inventions, creating roads and navigable waterways for commercial exchange, and seeing to it that agriculture, manufacture, and commerce work together for the sake of a thriving state and nation and a happy citizenry.

Fourth, higher education teaches mathematics and the physical sciences to young men for the sake of advancing the arts, and administering the health, subsistence, and comforts of life. This aim manifestly betrays Jefferson's preference for a practical education. One ought not to study chemistry or algebra for the sake of knowing chemistry or algebra, but for the sake of learning something that is applicable to and promotional of political and, especially, moral advance. "It either is, or ought to be the rule of every collegiate institution to teach to every particular student the branches of science which those who direct him think will be useful in the pursuits proposed for him, and to waste his time on nothing which they think will not be useful to him," Jefferson writes to grandson Francis Wayles Eppes (13 Dec. 1820). "This will certainly be the fundamental law of our

University to leave every one free to attend whatever branches of instruction he wants, and to decline what he does not want."[22] Such liberty at the University of Virginia, Jefferson thinks, will incline scholars to pursue an education in pursuance of their own needs.

Last, higher education will develop "reasoning faculties of our youth, enlarge their minds, cultivate their morals, and instill into them the precepts of virtue and order." It also forms "habits of reflection and correct action, rendering them examples of virtue to others, and of happiness within themselves." These aims are merely an iteration of the notion that education at both levels ought to be directed not only at the head, but also the heart; education ought to focus on advancing not only science, but also morality.[23] The relationship between the two, as I have argued all along, is not codependency. Jefferson's practicalism has a moral slant—a moral undergirding. The advances of science are for the sake of advances in morality—human happiness. In that sense, Jefferson might be dubbed a "liberal eudemonist."

These principles clearly demonstrate that higher education, for Jefferson, is not solely or even chiefly for the benefit of those persons educated. As is the case with Plato's guardians in *Republic*, higher education is for the sake of the state—for the wellbeing of the general citizenry. Overall, it exists to "provide for the good and ornament of their country, the gratification and happiness of their fellow-citizens, of the parent especially, and his progeny, on which all his affections are concentrated." For individuals, it makes application, order, and love of virtue habitual and controls any "innate obliquities" in human behavior.[24]

The Problem of Virtuous Politicians

Thus far, I take myself to have shown that Jefferson's educational reforms went hand in glove with his political reforms, each in service of the normative ideal of promotion of human happiness. I take myself also to have shown that the vehicle of his normative ideal, his republicanism, has both democratic and meritocratic elements.

The issue to which I now wish to attend is the extent to which Jefferson's system of education allows for a mechanism that ensures, or mostly so, that the true *aristoi*—viz., the natural *aristoi*—will be positioned to govern. It seems clear that the system behind his educational reforms is designed to do just that. Does it deliver?

The educational system sufficiently allows for talent to emerge, but it

Pavilion X of University of Virginia. Each of the ten pavilions was uniquely designed by using ancient and modern architectural techniques to create for students an architectural dialog between ancients and moderns (photograph by the author).

might not provide sufficient incentive for the talented to agree to rule, given the personal disadvantages of governing—i.e., lost time away from family and friends and negligence of private affairs, etc.—which Jefferson himself suffered. The solution, in effect, is morality. Given the high moral standing of those scholars completing their education at a state-level university, many will merely recognize political service to be their moral duty and agree to govern in spite of the drawbacks of political offices.[25]

Yet one might call into question that conclusion. Though Jefferson's system of education sufficiently allows for the emergence of talent, it is not obvious that it genuinely selects for morally superior persons. We have here a mare's nest, which I call the problem of virtuous politicians.

In Chapter 1, I show that, though reason is a faculty separate from and, in some sense, relatively independent of the moral sense, it is also answerable to the moral sense, insofar humans are for Jefferson foremost moral creatures and only secondarily rational ones. For Jefferson, reason is beholden to the moral sense, not in the manner of a first-order faculty to a second-order faculty, but in the manner of a weaker, less significant, and fluctuant faculty to a stronger, more significant, and more stable faculty. Reason is given as an aid to the moral faculty. Reason, given fully to too few, is not there to decide courses of action, but merely to assist the moral sense with information sufficient to complement its decisions and perhaps help the organism to do what it ought to do in labyrinthine scenarios.

Because morally correct action is not the result of rational deliberation on possible outcomes, right action is imprescriptible. There are no inviolable rules. One merely knows the right thing to do in circumstances.

If one knows the right thing to do and if learning is a matter of honing one's instincts—i.e., doing what in some sense what one already knows—then teaching is a matter of bolstering the developing moral sense and encouraging right action, or, as Jefferson says to Peter Carr (10 Aug. 1787), of encouraging and directing one's feelings. Ethical education, thus, is mostly a matter of ethical encouragement. It follows that moral education is principally to be had early in life, when moral encouragement can have greatest effect.[26] It is at such time that ethical encouragement is to occur and ethical encouragement is to come through study of history and reading of inspirational works of fiction. Jefferson is also clear that religious study should be eschewed, for the mind is too underdeveloped for critical reflection and religious study without critical reflection is parlous.

Again, the message of Jefferson's "Bill for the More General Diffusion of Knowledge" is that general education is the only means of preventing or curbing the enormities of ambitious politicians in a republican government.[27] The study of history will make students later in life fit judges of political corruption and its makebates. "History, by apprising them of the past, will enable them to judge of the future," he adds in *Notes on the State of Virginia*. "It will avail them of the experience of other times and other nations; it will qualify them as judges of the actions and designs of men; it will enable them to know ambition under every disguise it may assume; and knowing it, to defeat its views."[28] Thus, Jefferson suggests that history ought to be written in such a manner that it is an easily accessed account of the mistakes of the past—in short, a guarantor of future moral progress to which Jefferson was unquestionably wedded.

As we have seen in Chapter 5, the lessons of history, chiefly moral in content, are supplemented by reading useful fiction. In his letter to Robert Skipwith (3 Aug. 1771), Jefferson argues that works of fiction are potentially superior to works of history in that they allow more frequently and more plainly for moral lessons. In a word, moral instruction, not being a matter of reason but in a manner of speaking, of blandishing the moral sense, can be had early in life by exposure to good books and espial of moral exemplars.

Yet recall that Jefferson disadvises study of ethics at a university, and that seems inconsistent with his statement that the educational system churns out virtuous politicians. To Peter Carr, he writes: "I think it lost time to attend lectures in this branch [ethics]. He who made us would have been a pitiful bungler if he had made the rules of our moral conduct a matter of science" (10 Aug. 1787). To Dr. Thomas Cooper decades later (14 Aug. 1824), he states: "It would be a waste of time for [my grandson] to attend professors of ethics, metaphysics, logic. This first of these may be as well acquired in the closet as from living lecturers."

However, in numerous other writings, Jefferson speaks of the significance of education for morally correct action. In an advisory letter to Gen. John Minor (30 Aug. 1814), we have seen, he suggests an ethical course of study that seems to be a farrago, as it includes diverse writers such as Locke, Stewart, Enfield, Condorcet, Cicero, Seneca, Hutcheson, Kames, Charron, Sterne, Massillon, and Bourdaloue. In his bills of 1779 and 1817, he allows for a professorship of Ethics at William and Mary College and the University of Virginia.

Why is there such ambivalence?

In an effort to untie the knot, seemingly Gordian, let us return to the issue of what it is about the system that allows for the talented and virtuous to thrive. Returning to the problem of grammar schools, it seems that such schools are unavailing preparatory institutions for later political activity. On the one hand, the claim seems reasonable. Study of history and languages does little *prima facie* to ready straightforwardly a scholar for later political activity. On the other hand, the claim seems unreasonable. Study of history and languages, at least in Jefferson's eyes, does much to ready a scholar for later political activity. The principle aim of history is moral refinement and its lessons are indirect—e.g., "History, in general, only informs us what bad government is," Jefferson writes to John Norvell (14 June 1807), and that country is most blessed "whose silent course of happiness furnishes nothing for history to say," he says to Comte Diodati (29 Mar. 1807). Thus, grammar schools are first-rate preparatory institutions for moral refinement. Given that political activity is answerable to moral activity, it is, thus, naïve to assert grammar schools nowise prepare one for political activity. In effect, grammar schools turn out to be the most appropriate appurtenances of later political activity. Useful languages are acquired and the lessons of morality are hammered home.[29]

It follows that the problem of virtuous politicians is really for Jefferson a pseudo-problem. Those successfully completing grammar-school education, chockablock with moral lessons for later life, will be fully prepared to matriculate at a university, where they, having had their moral sense refined, can focus on the sorts of subjects that will mold them into first-rank politicians, if they so choose, or first-rank scientists.

9

The (Stoic) Sage of Monticello
"Truth [as] a branch of morality"

> "Endurance is something that spooks and blue devils respect. And they respect all the tricks that panicky people use to outlast and outwit their panic."
> —Tennessee Williams, "The Night of the Iguana"

Jefferson's letters are cryptic, it is sometimes claimed.[1] He panders to each correspondent and seldom, if ever, betrays the true self behind the quill. Personalia are always missing. He is masterfully, unavailingly, and most often intentionally uninformative.

Perusal of Jefferson's letters, however, shows a stylistic consistency and a personage behind them that is reserved, measured, contemplative, unadorned, and dispassionate. Letters with ethical content—and there are numerous such letters—and letters to his family of fellow scientists across the globe betray an ingenuous, sympathetic concern for others.[2] The person behind the quill reveals himself to be so imbued with Stoic thinking—especially in the realm of ethics—that he might indeed be said to be a living Stoic.

There are, of course, a number of objections one could put forth. The most telling objection is that, though he is well-read in the works of the Stoics Epictetus, Antoninus, and Seneca, and Cicero's works that concern the Stoics (e.g., *On Fate*, *On Duties*, and especially *Tusculan Disputations*), he never claims to be a Stoic or even to have Stoic leanings. In a letter to John Adams, he out-and-out repudiates Stoicism as an ethics that is too demanding.[3] Years later, he tells William Short (31 Oct. 1819) he is a disciple of Epicurus, as he claims Epicurus, not Epictetus or Seneca, to be his "master." Most scholars have settled on taking Jefferson at his word.[4]

We have an imbroglio. Jefferson is much more indebted to the Stoics than to Epicurus—chiefly, when it comes to cosmology, epistemology, and, especially, ethics—yet he disaffirms Stoicism and declares allegiance to the Greek Epicurus.

In this final chapter I shall show that, though he disavowed Stoic ethics and claimed Epicurean discipleship, Jefferson lived his life like a Stoic, not an Epicurean, and embraced an ethic that was greatly indebted to the Stoics and drew scant inspiration from Epicureanism.

Discipleship or Mouth Honor?

In a commonly cited letter to William Short, his former secretary, Jefferson writes: "As you say of yourself, I too am an Epicurian. I consider the genuine (not the imputed) doctrines of Epicurus as containing everything rational in moral philosophy which Greece and Rome have left us. Epictetus indeed, has given us what was good of the stoics; all beyond, of their dogmas, being hypocrisy and grimace."[5]

In a letter to John Adams (8 Apr. 1816), Jefferson repudiates outright Stoic ethics. "The perfection of the moral characters is, not in a Stoical apathy, so hypocritically vaunted, and so untruly too, because impossible, but in a just equilibrium of all the passions." Jefferson goes on to say that happiness is not in rejection of the passions, but in corralling them to make use of them.

Such passages are commonly cited in the secondary literature as evidence of Jefferson's purchase of Epicurean ethics and disavowal of Stoicism. That view is neatly summed by Gilbert Chinard, who notes, early in Jefferson's life, a heavy influence of Stoicism that gets "transferred [to] moral allegiance to Epicurus" in his later years.[6]

Karl Lehmann acknowledges the influence of the Stoics on Jefferson, but says "he could accept only [the ancient philosophical system] of Epicurus." He states, "In general, he adhered to the Epicurean ethical creed, and it is exactly this creed which Jefferson came to share consciously with him in his later years.... It is true, this philosophy aimed not only at achieving serenity and tranquillity [*sic*] of the human mind, as did all the other philosophies of antiquity. It also aimed a bodily ease. As the latter had to be achieved by good and healthy, enjoyable but not extravagant living, tranquillity of the mind the *summum bonum* of the Epicureans was only increased by it."[7]

Harold Hellenbrand also acknowledges Jefferson's interest in Stoic thinking, as he speaks of what Jefferson learned from Cicero's extreme stoicism."[8] Yet Jefferson was too much drawn to lavishness—e.g., bound books, fine wines, and inelegant home—to adopt Stoicism. "Jefferson did not write as a stoic who renounced all emotions and avoided social contact; instead, he sympathized with the epicureans who accepted the passions and then tried to moderate them."[9]

Andrew Burstein states that Jefferson, in his famous Head-and-Heart letter to Maria Cosway, is "a philosopher of friendship, somewhat Socratic, and even more Epicurean."[10] He fails unfortunately to amplify, so it is unclear precisely how Jefferson's view of friendship resembles Epicurus's.

Daryl Hale writes of Jefferson's neglect as a philosopher being due to his disesteem of and insouciance toward the "two giants of ancient Greece": Plato and Aristotle. Analysis of Jefferson's architecture, readings, and writings shows him to be a "genuine philosopher," who "advocated a modern scientific and moral version of Epicureanism."[11]

Finally, as we have seen in Chapter 1, Charles Miller, referring also to the Head-and-Heart letter, posits that Heart, in his view the winner of the debate with Head, represents Epicurus, and Head, Stoicism.[12]

Jefferson's Stoic Naturalism

For the Stoics, ethical theory is axially naturalistic. That too is true of Jefferson's view on morality and that was typical of Scottish empiricists who influenced mightily Jefferson as well as the views of many of the philosophes of Jefferson's day.

For the Stoics, what dictates how men ought to act in social settings are the laws of nature. Thus, the Stoics speak of "nature" both normatively and descriptively. They speak of "nature" normatively as cosmological and anthropological regulative forces. They speak of "nature" descriptively as the physical stuff to be investigated of which the cosmos and man is made.[13]

For the Stoics, the aim of life, virtue, is to live in agreement with nature.[14] Chronicler Diogenes Laertius says of the Stoics: "This is why the end [of life] may be defined as 'life, following nature' or, again, '[living] in agreement with our own human nature as well as that of the universe.' In such a life, we refrain from every action forbidden by the law common to all things—that is, by right reason that both pervades all things and is identical with Zeus, lord and ruler of all that is."[15]

What nature shows was that humans have a self-concern impulse and other-concern impulse.[16] The primary human impulse, dictated by nature and evident at birth, is self-preservation. "Impulses toward useful objects and revulsion from the opposite are according to nature. Without any reflection to prompt the idea and without any advice, whatever nature has prescribed is done."[17] Yet humans also have a social impulse. In such a manner, people are by nature fitted to form unions, societies, and states, as well as fitted to integrate with the cosmos.[18] "Our relations with one another are like a stone arch that would collapse," states Seneca, "if the stones did not mutually support each other."[19]

Nature guides moral progress by merging virtuous activity with knowing. For the Stoics, the universe, of which humans are a part, is itself a divine and rational animal (Gr., *zōon*), and the best human life is one that emulates divine activity, which acts always in the most rational, most efficient, and best manner. The aim of human activity is to emulate deity by optimizing rationality, efficiency, and goodness. Sagacity is *homologia*—acting in complete agreement with Nature or deity.

How is *homologia* achieved? Beginning with the instinct of self-preservation, humans soon come to value all such things that are in agreement with nature and disvalue all such things that are contrary to nature, and they pattern their actions, through choice, thus. Next, they learn to choose by considering what is appropriate. Continued choice becomes fixed habit to act appropriately. Appropriate action (G., *kathekon*; L., *officium*) does not imply that one's actions must have the right outcome, but only that one's actions must be properly motivated. Purity of intention is everything.[20] When habit harmonizes perfectly with reason and obligation, there is *homologia*—complete integration with divine or cosmic design. Human intention is perfectly in keeping with cosmic intention, action and outcome converge, and all of one's actions now, as it were, hit the mark, because all of one's intentions are perfectly virtuous. Appropriate action now becomes perfect appropriate action (G., *katorthoma*; L., *recte factum*) and sagacity is achieved.[21] Thus, *homologia* implies complete cosmic immersion or integration, and thus a sage is a citizen of the cosmos.

A Stoic bedfellow of cosmopolitanism is egalitarianism. Egalitarianism bars no one—slave or king—from aiming at sagacity. Each person comes to virtue, as it were, unclothed. Seneca states, "Virtue shuts out no one. It is open to all, admits all, invites all—the freeborn and the freedman, the slave and the king, and the exile. Neither family nor fortune determines its choice. It is satisfied with a naked human being."[22] It neither enjoins a wealthy man to give away his possessions and comforts; nor does it forbid a penurious woman to strive for possessions and comforts.

Jefferson's thinking is often seen as antipodal to Stoic naturalism, as it is mistakenly viewed as a form of liberal atomism that is normatively neutral, since his political thinking is often mistakenly viewed as a form of normatively neutral liberal atomism.[23]

That depiction is mistaken for two chief reasons.

First, liberal atomism is not normatively neutral, but has an on-the-quiet normative dimension. Liberal atomism, as a political code, champions autonomy as a value, and championing autonomy as a value is not normatively neutral.

Second and most significantly, Jefferson was not a liberal atomist. People for Jefferson are essentially social creatures, not political atoms. He writes to William Green Munford (18 June 1799), "I consider man as formed for society, and endowed by nature with those dispositions which fit him for society." Again, "Man was created for social intercourse," he writes to Francis Gilmer 18 year later (7 June 1817). "He was also born with a sense of justice to regulate his moral duties."

Like the Stoics, Jefferson believed that the cosmos was ordered and that order was manifestation of divine causation and superintendency.[24] Moreover, deity has given humans the capacity for moral perfectibility. "I have trust in him who made us what we are, and knows it was not his plan to make us always unerring. He has formed us moral agents…. We may promote the happiness of those which whom he has placed us in society, by acting honestly towards all, benevolently to those who fall within our way, respecting sacredly their rights bodily and mental, and cherishing especially their freedom conscience, as we value our own."[25] The sentiment is echoed by Adam Smith, greatly influenced by Stoicism, who maintains that all right intended human action ought to be guided by "the love of Deity, the desire of rendering ourselves agreeable to him, and of directing our conduct, in every respect, according to his will."[26]

Like many in his day, Jefferson made purchase of natural-law theory. "To Jefferson, any theory of society that ignored the fundamental character of man was doomed to failure," writes Caleb Perry Patterson. "Natural law was the source of our knowledge of the true character of man. Jefferson believed this so thoroughly that he considered the American theory of government to be the discovery man had been searching for and felt that it would remain a model for governments because of the permanency of the principles of natural law on which it was grounded."[27]

Jefferson's natural-law theory is Stoical, not Hobbesian or Rousseauian. It aims at reconciliation of the state of society with the state of nature. Unlike Rousseau and Hobbes, the laws of nature that obtain when man is in the state of nature are, for Jefferson, the self-same laws that obtain in civil society. "The moral duties which exist between individual and individual in the state of nature, accompany them into a state of society, and the aggregate of the duties of all the individuals composing the society constitutes the duties of that society towards any other; so that between society and society the same moral duties exist as did between individuals composing them, while in an unassociated state, and their maker not having released them from those duties on their forming themselves into a nation."[28]

The Stoics hold that the study of nature—both human nature and the nature of the cosmos—indicates through a discovery of its laws the proper course of human action. Proper action is always action in accordance with nature; inappropriate action is always action in discordance with nature. The same is true for Jefferson. The chief difference is that for Stoics right action is driven by reason, while for Jefferson it is determined non-rationally—by one's moral-sense faculty.

Thus, like the Stoics, Jefferson had a view of human nature, conceptually distinguishable from cosmic nature, but in alignment with it.

Obligation to Others

The view that Jefferson was a Stoic in early life and an Epicurean in later life is driven by Jefferson's express admiration of Stoic thinking in his *Literary Commonplace Book*, which contains several Latin quotes from Cicero's *Tusculan Disputations*, whose arguments are recognized as Stoical. Jefferson was fond of reading Stoic authors or reading about the Stoics. His library contained the complete works of Seneca, Antoninus, and Epictetus, and he often referenced Stoics like Seneca and Epictetus among the great ancient moralists.[29] Thus, in spite of his expressed disavowal of Stoic ethics, he greatly admired the Stoics.

Nonetheless, though he claims to be a disciple of Epicurus and disavows Stoicism, his ethical thinking shows scant appreciation of Epicureanism and a great debt to Stoicism.

Jefferson's avowed *bête noire* was Stoic apathy (*apatheia*). To John Adams (8 Apr. 1816), he writes of the quantity of pleasure and pain meted out on average to persons. Since the cosmos has been framed on a "principle of benevolence," one ought to be sanguine. "All our other passions, within proper bounds, have an useful object," and moral perfection a "just equilibrium of all the passions."

Jefferson's gripe with Stoicism is that its aim, Stoic apathy, is riddance of all passions, not merely a just equilibrium of them. Considering mastering the passions, Seneca says, "I do not grasp how any halfway disease can be wholesome or helpful."[30] For the Stoics, passions are swellings (pleasure and desire) and contractions (distress and fear) of the material soul apropos of present and future events, deemed good or bad, which were actually neither good nor bad. For instance, to fear the prospect of injury or death in saving a drowning man is to behave irrationally, to be under the spell of the passions, and to exhibit vice. In sum, passions for Stoics are misjudgments of reason—reason misaligned with reality—and the misjudgments, since Stoics were complete physicalists, are identical to bodily swellings and contractions.

Yet the Stoics did not countenance riddance of all passions. They embraced *eupatheiai*—literally "good passions" but better grasped as mild sensual enjoyments or mild sensual revulsions—which were slight swellings (joy and wishing) and slight contractions (caution) of the soul apropos of present and future events, deemed good or bad and being in reality good (virtues) or bad (vices). Illustrations are experiencing joy on seeing one's child excel in learning and experiencing caution before attending a dinner at which numerous profligates will be in attendance. Either for a Stoic is a legitimate—*viz.*, reason-founded—concern. And so Jefferson's disrelish of the Stoic notion of riddance of all passions was unfounded.

One large botheration was doubtless metaphysical—i.e., with the Stoic notion of a monolithic, rational soul as the source and warrant for morally correct action—because, for Jefferson, right action was neither rationally generated nor in any direct sense rationally sanctioned.

Another large botheration, characteristic of the "most esteemed sects of ancient philosophy" (see Chapter 3), was that in positing our "duties" to ourselves ancient ethicians neglected our duties to others. "Epictetus and Epicurus give [only] laws for governing ourselves," he writes to William Short.

The target of Jefferson's criticism manifestly includes the Stoics. His use of "circles" is reminiscent of the Stoic Hierocles[31]—fragments of his writings are contained in Stobaeus's *Anthology*, and 300 lines of his main work, *Elements of Ethics*, were discovered in 1901 at Hermopolis—and who writes analogically in *Elements of Ethics* of 10 concentric circles to illustrate each person's ethical duties. They are, in order of significance, these:

1. one's mind and body;
2. parents, siblings, wife, and children;
3. one's uncles and aunts, grandparents, nephews, nieces, and cousins;

4. other relatives;
5. local residents (i.e., neighbors);
6. fellow demesmen (a unit of a city-state);
7. fellow citizens of a city-state;
8. people of neighboring city-states;
9. fellow countrymen; and
10. the entire human race.

Hierocles adds that we ought to live in such a manner that the circles contract—viz., that the distance between the first and last circles increasingly diminishes.

If Jefferson had known Hierocles's circles, he likely would have objected that Hierocles's notion of obligation to others is motivated by justice, not by benevolence. Acts of justice are rationally (contractually) motivated. They are not acts of the heart—i.e., acts of peace, love, and charity that are "within the circle of benevolence."

Jefferson's "Stoicism"

Those objections are not major stumbling blocks. Jefferson admits to a fondness of reading the Stoics—Epictetus and Seneca especially—and about them, mostly in the works of Cicero. Moreover, as I show below, the commonalities between Jefferson's express ethical purchases and what elsewhere I call Stoic "ethical curatives"[32]—the Stoics deemed vice as a disease and Stoic philosophy as curative—are striking.

Veridical Lifestyle: Honesty and Authenticity

For the Stoics, being a good, virtuous person is the same as having a veridical approach to living. It is to be a "scientist" in the largest sense of the word—i.e., to be driven by pursuit of knowledge. The cosmos is a living, "ordered thing,"[33] and thus, is graspable by human reason.[34] Thus, the height of human virtue is to grasp the cosmos and know one's role in the awe-generative cosmic design. It follows that virtuous living is a matter both of assenting to those sensory experiences that nowise admit of doubt and of refraining from assenting to doubtful impressions. To do otherwise is to be vicious, as vice for Stoics is due to misjudgments of reason.

To attain equanimity, authenticity is required. Seneca writes: "Philosophy teaches us to act, not to speak. It requires every person to live according to his own standard (*legem suam*). It requires that his life should not be at odds with his words and that his inner life should be united and not out of harmony with all his actions. This, I say, is the greatest duty (*maximum ... officium*) and the greatest evidence of wisdom—that deed and words should be in agreement, that a man should be equal to himself and always be the same person under all conditions."³⁵

Epictetus considers a teacher who busies himself with arguments at school and yet leaves his words behind, when he leaves the school.³⁶ Aurelius bids us to shun persons who say, "Let me be frank," for frankness ought not to be qualified by speech. It ought to be part of one's being.³⁷

Statue of Jefferson. This statue is on the west side of the Lawn of the University of Virginia (photograph by the author).

Having a veridical approach to living is key for Jefferson as well. "Truth is certainly a branch of morality," he writes to Thomas Law (13 June 1814), "and a very important one to society." Five years later, he says to John Adams (10 Dec. 1819), "In all cases ... follow truth as the only safe guide, and ... eschew error which bewilders us in one false consequence after another. To Nathaniel Burwell (14 Mar. 1818), Jefferson speaks with disdain of people who spend an inordinate time reading novels—"the result [being] a bloated imagination, sickly judgment, and disgust toward all their real business of life." They live in cloud-cuckoo-land, not the world of the bodily senses.

Regard for veridicality has implications for one's dealings with others. First, one must be honest. He advises Peter Carr (19 Aug. 1785) to behave justly, honestly, and with integrity. Chicanery decuples difficulties and vice.[38] He writes to grandson Francis Eppes (21 May 1816), "Honesty, disinterestedness and good nature are indispensable to procure the esteem and confidence of those with whom we live, and on whose esteem our happiness depends." Questioning the moral motives of the generation currently governing affairs, he writes to Nathaniel Macon (12 Jan. 1819), "Whether the succeeding generation is to be more virtuous than their predecessors, I cannot say; but I am sure they will have more worldly wisdom and enough, I hope, to know that honesty is the first chapter in the book of wisdom." Second, one must be authentic. Jefferson does not allow for any divide between one's private and public lives. Jefferson tells Carr to act always and in all circumstances as if everyone in the world were looking at him.[39] Authenticity is also evident in his disgust of lengthy, flowery perorations, intended to persuade without regard for truth—i.e., sophistry[40]—as well as Jefferson's disdain of sensationalism in journalism.[41] Finally, authenticity is evident in Jefferson's contentedness with living the life into which he was born—e.g., putting his wealth and status to good use instead of riddance of them.[42]

Cosmopolitanism

The Stoic view of *apatheia* is not a matter of being indifferent. Epictetus says, "I ought not to be undisturbed (*apathes*) like a statue, but I ought to maintain my natural and acquired relations, as a duty-bound man as well as a son, brother, father and citizen." *Apatheia*, for Stoics, involves full, yet disinterested involvement in the affairs of human and gods. "A Stoic is not only a citizen of his community, but also a citizen of the cosmos—grasped as … a community of humans and gods." Thus, Stoics were duty-bound both to gods and humans.[43]

Jefferson consistently speaks of obligations to others and to god as critical components of morality (see Chapter 7).[44] Obligation to others, founded on genuine other-concern, is the reason why Jefferson delayed retirement time after time for some sort of political service to his fellow Americans. "In a virtuous government, and more especially in times like these," he writes to Richard Henry Lee (17 June 1799), "public offices are, what they should be, burthens to those appointed to them, which it would be wrong to decline, though foreseen to bring with them intense labour, and great private loss." In addition, asked by President Washington to be his Secretary of State, Jefferson unequivocally expressed a preference for staying in his present position, as Ambassador to France, but added: "It is not for an individual to choose his post. You are to marshal us as may best be for the public good; and it is only in the case of its being indifferent to you, that I would avail myself of the option you have so kindly offered in your letter."[45] Recognition of obligation to others is also the reason why he embraced what Greeks call *philioxenia* ("love of foreigners") and entertained all visitors at Monticello.[46]

Jefferson also speaks of obligations to deity. To Benjamin Waterhouse (26 June 1822), he states, "To love God with all thy heart and thy neighbor as thyself, is the sum of religion." He tells Thomas Law (13 June 1814) that love of deity is one of the branches of morality.[47] Finally, loving god is advice he gives namesakes in late-life letters.[48]

Obligations to love others and deity, done with willfulness, suggests mental alignment with Stoic sympathy (Gr., *sympatheia*)—a sort of cosmic connectedness and belonging. Moreover, for Jefferson, the same duties that regulate human morality in the state of nature are they, which regulate humans in social settings, and they, which regulate the behavior of one nation and all others.[49]

Jefferson's cosmopolitanism has not gone unnoticed by key Jeffersonian scholars. Julian Boyd adds that Jefferson was remarkably connected to the world around him.

> There was ... the astonishing range of the man. His view swept an arc of the intellectual horizon wider even than that of Franklin. From architecture to zoology Jefferson probed, reflected, and adapted his finding to the society in which he lived. His insatiable inquiries fathered versatility. Even before he drafted the Declaration of Independence at thirty-three he could "calculate an eclipse, survey an estate, tie an artery, plan an edifice, try a cause, break a horse, dance a minuet, and play the violin," to say nothing of being an informed parliamentarian, a collector of manuscript laws, an author of a revolutionary tract, a craftsman in metal, a creative pioneer in archeology, and an organizer of plans for improving the navigation of a river.[50]

Robert Dawidoff, mostly harshly critical of Jefferson, calls him a "citizen of several republics." He says of an instance where Jefferson made a simple request for seeds. "It is characteristic that Jefferson would place a request for seeds in this context of universal cooperation. His prose was meant to erect in his writing the republic of America, the republic of friendship, the republic of science. He writes as a citizen of the several republics, and the prose is fashioned as a means by which he can carry on his business."[51] Merrill Peterson notes a sense in which Jefferson's political view concerning the reciprocal rights of citizenship—e.g., a U.S. citizen in England would enjoy the exact privileges of a British citizen, and conversely—bespoke a notion of cosmopolitanism. "As the circle of friendship widened, men would truly become citizens of the world."[52]

Exemplars, Not Rules

Since principles, both generic and specific (L., *decreta* and *praecepta*), were not infallible guides of morally right action for Stoics, cynosures were *sine qua non*. Epictetus, who refers abundantly to Socrates, says that Socrates' renowned quest for self-understanding should be that of every person. "What does Socrates say? "As one man rejoices in improving his own farm and another his own horse," he says, "I rejoice every day in following the course of my own improvement.... Who among you, then, makes that purpose of Socrates the purpose of his own life? Why, if you did, you would have been glad even to be ill, to go hungry, and to die."[53] Later in *Discourses,* Epictetus sums the life of Socrates. Having a wife and children, Socrates regarded obedience to the law as his foremost obligation. When he was called to serve as a solider, "he was the first to leave home." When he had to defend his life before a jury of his peers, "he did not behave as one who had children or wife." When it was time to drink the hemlock, "he did not care ... to save his paltry body, but only what is increased and preserved by justice and what is decreased and destroyed by injustice," Epictetus sums, "It is impossible to save such a man by dishonor, but he is saved by death, not by fleeing from prison."[54] Because Socrates—putting divine affairs ahead of human ones—has treated everything other than the pursuit of knowledge as inferior to the pursuit of knowledge, he was in deeds the first Stoic. As Socrates showed by willingly going to his death, even life was answerable to virtue.[55]

As with the Stoics, for Jefferson, moral judgment was driven mainly by situations, not principles. "State a moral case to a plowman and a professor," Jefferson says to Peter Carr (10 Aug. 1787). "The former will decide it as well and often better than the latter, because he has not been led astray by artificial rules."[56] So, cynosures, as we saw in Chapter 1, were indispensable.

Right action, in cases in which the moral sense is perplexed, can be ascertained by appeal to moral exemplars. Recall Jefferson's advice to grandson Thomas Jefferson Randolph (24 Nov. 1808). He stated temptations would be overcome and difficulties would be resolved by appealing in imagination to William Small, George Wythe, or Peyton Randolph.[57]

Honestum et Utile

As we saw in Chapter 1, there is a utilitarian strain in Jefferson's mature ethical thinking, as evidenced by letters to Thomas Law (13 June 1814) and

John Adams (14 Oct. 1816). Those letters have convinced some scholars that Jefferson had a shift in thinking late in life such that right action was action with advantageous results; wrong action, with disadvantageous results.

A more economical option, defended in Chapter 1, is that Jefferson thought that both intention and outcome were significant for right action. That is a thesis, I suspect, that was adopted by most Stoics,[58] not only Panaetius. It is also a thesis that was common among Scottish empiricists of Jefferson's day.[59]

Use/Disuse

Epictetus gives use-disuse as a general strategy for strengthening desirable activities. The rational faculty, like bodily muscles, must be exercised to be strengthened for morally right action. "Every skill (Gr., *hexis*) and capacity (Gr., *dynamis*) are built up and strengthened by corresponding actions—walking by walking, running by running. ... The same thing holds true in the affairs of the mind as well."[60]

For Jefferson, the moral sense, though a "sensory" and not a rational faculty, also is strengthened with use. He tells Peter Carr (19 Aug. 1785) that the moral sense is as much a part of a person as his leg or arm, and like strength of limbs, it can be "atrophied" or "hypertrophied" through exercise or its neglect to encourage or discourage right action. Moral valetudinarianism or impotency is cupatory if it is due voluntary sluggardliness or disengagement.

Flee from Strong Impressions

A general, though not inviolable, rule for apprenticeship in Stoic philosophy early in one's apprenticeship is to shun temptations by fleeing from strong impressions. Trying to master temptations without being sufficiently habituated will probably lead to debacle. Epictetus says that one might learn in time to master strong impressions, but for a tyro, it is best to "flee far away from impressions that are too strong, [as] a pretty wench is not a fair match for a young beginner in philosophy."[61]

Jefferson was similarly disposed to eschew conflict. In a letter to grandson Thomas Jefferson Randolph (24 Nov. 1808), Jefferson writes that good humor preserves peace and tranquility. Politeness gives sop to Cerberus. "It is the practice of sacrificing to those whom we meet in society all the little conveniences and preferences which will gratify them, and deprive us of nothing worth a moment's consideration; it is the giving a pleasing and flattering turn to our expressions which will conciliate others, and make them pleased with us as well as themselves. How cheap a price for the goodwill of another!" He advises him to avoid both young students on the threshold of science and ill-tempered men with a passion for politics. "Get by them … as you would by an angry bull: it is not for a man of sense to dispute the road with such an animal."[62]

Jefferson today is often rebuked for his tendency to avoid confrontation—especially when it came to refusal to address slander. Some claim it is evidence that he was Janus-faced[63]; others, that he was craven.[64] Jefferson's tendency to avoid confrontation is explained simply by internalization of Stoicism. He aimed, following the approving voice of his conscience, to do what was right, and leave condemnation or approbation to the solid judgment of the people or deity, not his calumniators.[65]

Moral Progress

For Stoics, the aim of life is to advance toward virtue. The best life is a fully virtuous life, and the fully virtuous person is incapable of vicious activity. Yet complete virtue is a life of invincibility, not invulnerability. A virtuous person, like any other, gets wounds, but they nowise affect his happiness. "Who is the invincible person?" Epictetus asks. He is like an indomitable athlete that treats whatever is in his path to victory as something indifferent. He suffers blows and setbacks, but continually moves forward.[66]

Jefferson never speaks of a fully virtuous lifestyle, but he is committed to moral progress in individuals, and there is no reason to think he believed there were limits to moral progress—i.e., moral progress, for him as for Condorcet (see Chapter 4) was something like convergence toward a mathematical limit.[67] Yet for Jefferson, the human species too is capable of and has exhibited moral progress. Past moral codes are no longer acceptable, not because of a capricious shift of moral interests over time, but because an improvement in moral discernment of right actions. He writes to Patrick Henry (27 Mar. 1799) in the manner of Lord Kames: "But is an enemy [prisoner of war] so execrable that tho in captivity his wishes and comforts are to be disregarded and even crossed? I think not. It is for the benefit of mankind to mitigate the horrors of war as much as possible."

The moral (and intellectual) progress of the species is evident in microcosm in the North-American continent of Jefferson's day. A "philosophic observer" that commences a journey from the Rocky Mountains to the eastern seacoast would notice the changes. First, he would see savage Indians, clothing themselves with the flesh and skins of wild beasts, who live under only the law of nature. Next, he would see pastoral frontiersmen that domesticate animals for food. Third, he would see the "semi-barbarous citizens"—"pioneers of the advance of civilization." Finally, he would reach man in his most advanced state in the seaport town. "This ... is equivalent to a survey, in time, of the progress of man from the infancy of creation to the present day." He adds, "Barbarism has ... been receding before the steady step of amelioration; and will in time ... disappear from the earth."[68]

Jefferson's progressivism *prima facie* seems inconsistent with that of the Stoics. Moral improvement for Stoics is a matter of individuals realizing fully their human capacities, implanted by nature. A person, drawn toward virtue, progresses toward virtue by performing actions that are consistent with full virtue. At day's end, there is the potential for complete virtue and perfect living through right actions. Jefferson, however, has a broader view of moral improvement—what one might dub "moral advance"—as he speaks of the improvement of the human species over time, not just of its individuals.

Yet Jefferson's view of moral advance is not so dissimilar from that of the Stoics. For him, moral advance is not a matter of the species converging toward some as-yet unseen ideal. The moral ideal toward which humans are and ought to be converging is something like that of a Stoicized Jesus of Nazareth, who has preached the purest moral code, stripped off the falsities of corrupters, and who, qua mortal man, seems for Jefferson to have come as close to perfect human living as is possible. It follows, given the fixity of the human species and the limits of human abilities for both, there is a distinct end toward which each human ought to aim—for the Stoics, a completely veridical ideal in which knowledge is sufficient for virtue and happiness; for Jefferson, full integration of the benevolent teachings of a Stoicized Jesus, epitomized by loving oneself, others, and deity with all one's heart and unconditionally—a notion captured as well by Francis Hutcheson, Adam Smith, and Laurence Sterne.

Prepare for the Future

Good fortune is it, without warning, might not only cease, but also suffer a *volte-face*. In times of reversal of fortune, perceived goods reveal themselves to be bagatelles—even impedances. What use is a plethora of fine things, when disaster strikes suddenly? "No man can swim ashore and take his baggage with him," Seneca reminds us.[69] That is why a Stoic prepares for harsher days, when things are going well. When food is abundant, he readies for scarcity. When there is peace, he hardens himself for war. In times of wealth, he prepares for poverty. "That," Seneca says, "is anticipating (*praeoccupare*[70]) the arrows of Fortune."[71]

Ill-fortune anticipated is a blow that is softened. Thus, a Stoic is no more surprised by a reversal of good fortune than he is when a fig tree produces figs, when a doctor has ill patients, or when a helmsman has a wind that blows against him.[72] "Nothing ought to be unexpected by us. Our minds should be sent forward in advance to meet all problems, and we should consider, not merely what is likely to happen, but what can happen."[73]

Stoicism prepares a person for life by asking him to begin without delay what is worth doing. Delay in matters that are imminently worth pursuing may prove costly, for no one is guaranteed another day of life.[74] Virtuous living is, thus, efficient living, because no one is guaranteed another day. Seneca sums, "Let us order our minds as if we had come to the very end. Let us postpone nothing. Let us balance life's account every day…. One who puts the finishing touches to his life every day is never in want of time."[75]

Jefferson's scheme for preparing for the future is twofold and Stoical: morally correct action and knowledge.

A person who aims at a life of morally correct action has nothing to fear apropos of the future. He advises Peter Carr (19 Aug. 1785) that Byzantine difficulties can be overcome by "doing what is right." He adds, "Though you cannot see, when you take one step, what will be your next, you follow truth, justice, and plain dealing, and never fear their leading you out of the labyrinth, in the easiest possible manner." He tells his daughter Martha (11 Dec. 1783) that the finest preparation for death or the world's end is to follow with strictest obedience her moral sense.

Moreover, Jefferson believes that knowledge is a surefire guide for the vagaries of the future. He tells his daughter Martha (21 May 1787) that virtue and goodness are not only valuable in themselves, but they make one "valuable to others." He adds that she ought to acquire "those talents and that degree of science" which will keep her from ennui—"the most dangerous poison of life." He commends study of the "useful sciences"[76] to William Green Munford (18 June 1799) as well as some knowledge of astronomy, botany, chemistry, natural philosophy, natural history, and anatomy, because "some knowledge of them is necessary for our character as well as comfort." Education, thus, is the handmaiden of virtue. To grandson Francis Wayles Eppes (6 Oct. 1820), Jefferson advises that no time be wasted in education. Efficiency is critical. That is evidence that the good life for Jefferson is Stoical with respect to efficiency—i.e., virtue is maximally efficient living.

Taking Daily Inventory

For Stoics, right moral action is a private as well as a public concern. Entertaining vicious thoughts without acting on them is a sign of human vice. Aurelius states, "The things that you often think about determine the quality of your mind. Your soul takes on the color of your thoughts." Color the soul, Aurelius adds, with thoughts that elevate the mind, not those thoughts that disgrace it.[77]

Jefferson too believes that the nature of one's thoughts determine the quality of one's mind. In a letter to his physician Vine Utley (21 Mar. 1819), Jefferson writes, "I never go to bed without an hour, or half hour's previous reading of something moral, whereon to ruminate in the intervals of sleep." To Peter Carr (10 Aug. 1787), he says, "In [morality] … read good books because they will encourage as well as direct your feelings." His daughter Martha Jefferson (28 Mar. 1787) he enjoins to obey his experience-driven "precepts" so that she can be "more qualified than common." The sentiment in such letters is that reason encourages the habituation of right action.

Again, Jefferson's habit of taking inventory on his character is evident in his memorandum "Services to My Country."[78]

Counsel for a Namesake

Jefferson's Stoicism is perhaps best summed advice to and in a list of his 10 principles for a good life in a letter to a namesake Thomas Jefferson Smith (21 Feb. 1825). Assuming he will have given up the ghost at the time the boy first reads his words, Jefferson writes: "Adore God, reverence and cherish your parents. Love your neighbor more than yourself. Be just. Be true. Murmur not at the ways of Providence." He ends with the following list of 10 principles, each of which is in keeping with Stoic sagacity.

1. Never put off till tomorrow what you can do to-day.
2. Never trouble another for what you can do yourself.
3. Never spend your money before you have it.
4. Never buy what you do not want, because it is cheap; it will [not?] be dear to you.
5. Pride costs us more than hunger, thirst and cold.

6. We never repent of having eaten too little.
7. Nothing is troublesome that we do willingly.
8. How much pain have cost us the evils which have never happened.
9. Take things always by their smooth handle.[79]
10. When angry, count ten, before you speak; if very angry, an hundred.

Jefferson the Man

Even if Jefferson's "heart" is not expressly with the Stoics, his ethical thinking and demeanor are from soup to nuts Stoical.

Jefferson writes to John Adams (8 Apr. 1816) about the goodness of the world: "I think ... that it is a good world on the whole, that it has been framed on a principle of benevolence, and more pleasure than pain dealt out to us. There are indeed ... gloomy and hypochondriac minds, inhabitants of diseased bodies, disgusted with the present, and despairing of the future; always counting that the worst will happen, because it may happen. To these I say How much pain have cost us the evils which have never happened?" Again, he writes Maria Cosway (12 Oct. 1786) that there is "no rose without it's thorn; no pleasure without alloy. It is the law of our existence; & we must acquiesce."

Moreover, Jefferson's disposition is sanguine. He admits that his hopes sometimes fail, but they fail no more often than "the forebodings of the gloomy." The sentiment is in keeping with the Stoic views that the cosmos is entirely good and that perception of ill is failure to see things as a whole.

Coupled with sanguineness is Stoic resignation. To Abigail Adams (11 Jan. 1817), he says: "Perhaps ... one of the elements of future felicity is to be a constant and unimpassioned view[er] of what is passing here. ... On the whole however, perhaps it is wise and well to be contented with the good things which the master of the feast places before us, and to be thankful for what we have, rather than thoughtful about what we have not." The sentiment is likely drawn from the *Handbook*, where Epictetus writes of a banqueter not reaching out for food, but merely taking food from what is handed to him, when it is handed to him.[80] Monticello overseer Edmund Bacon states: "His countenance was always mild and pleasant. You never saw it ruffled. No odds what happened [*sic*], it always maintained the same expression."[81]

Finally, there was Jefferson's commitment to gainful occupation. "Mr.

Jefferson was the most industrious person I ever saw in my life," writes Edmund Bacon. Having permission to enter his study at any time when there was pressing business, Bacon "never went into it but twice in the whole twenty years I was with him that I did not find him employed."[82]

Many scholars have recognized in Jefferson a Stoic demeanor. William Gould states: "His experience had taught him that the only way to overcome one's difficulties, and find contentment was to resign oneself completely to the divine will. One's calamities are only increased by trying to escape from them. But by conforming one's will to the will of God, one finds that peace of mind which enables one to patiently bear the burdens of life."[83] Herbert Schneider writes: "Throughout his life he was by temperament a stoic. He was a necessitarian about both public and private affairs, and his love of liberty did not imply for him any belief in metaphysical freedom."[84]

If Jefferson was such an outright Stoic in thought and demeanor, why did he disaffirm Stoicism? Jefferson was theoretically committed to disaffirm Stoicism. His moral faculty was guided by sense, not by reason. In that regard, the two ethical systems were theoretically miles apart. Nonetheless, in practice, that difference was negligible. For Stoics, ethically correct action was only loosely guided by principles (doctrines and precepts). It rested on rational intuition, based on well-formed habits and deliberation on circumstances. The result, for one fully virtuous, was spontaneous activity, guided by infallible intuition. That was much the same result with Jefferson's non-rational moral-sense faculty.

If Jefferson was an outright Stoic in thought and demeanor, was he an ingenuous Stoic? Henry May gives reason for doubt. Jefferson's optimism, resolve, dispassion, and commitment to virtue, says May, were manifestations of strenuousness and desperation. "Jefferson was above all and always serious.... A man of lofty virtue and carefully disciplined passion, he could not tolerate frivolity, moral skepticism, pessimism, undisciplined emotion, or unresolved paradox." He was always optimistic, but his personal life was sad and political experiences were too "broad and deep" for his optimism to be Panglossian. "To believe in the moral sense and the enlightened future was absolutely essential to his equilibrium: his was a strenuous, at times almost a desperate optimism."[85]

There is merit to May's verdict. Jefferson's optimism, at least in later life when the nation was clearly moving away from the perhaps oversimple georgic model he had of republican thriving and when his hopes for domestic stability were dashed by lumbering debt, does seem strained.

Yet Jefferson consistently maintained that the world "on the whole" was good and that his life on the whole sufficiently pleasant to be worth reliving, were reliving possible.[86] Thus, it is much preferable to claim that Jefferson's "desperate optimism" was merely ethical consistency under strained circumstances, and if there is one thing Jefferson surely learned from the Stoics, it is that "life is full and beset with various tragedies." He also learned that it is possible to endure them and that, if victory lay in endurance, then victory is had through mere voluntary engagement in battle, not in its end.[87]

Chapter Notes

Preface

1. Epictetus, *The Encheiridion*, trans. W.A. Oldfather (Cambridge: Harvard University Press, [1928] 2000), §43.
2. William Cohen, "Thomas Jefferson and the Problem of Slavery," *Journal of American History* 56, No. 3 (1969): 506–25.
3. Howard Temperly, "Jefferson and Slavery: A Study in Moral Philosophy," *Reason and Republicanism: Thomas Jefferson's Legacy of Liberty*, ed. Gary L. McDowell and Sharon L. Noble (Lanham, MD: Rowman & Littlefield, 1997), 86.
4. E.g., Howard Temperly, "Jefferson and Slavery," 86.
5. http://www.en.utexas.edu/amlit/amlitprivate/texts/patterson.html, accessed 15 Jan. 2014.
6. Peter Onuf, *The Mind of Thomas Jefferson* (Charlottesville: University of Virginia Press, 2007), 38.
7. Robert Dawidoff, "The Jefferson Option," *Political Theory*, Vol., 21, No. 3, 1993, 438.
8. Winthrop D. Jordan, *White over Black: American Attitudes toward the Negro, 1550–1812* (Baltimore: Penguin Books, 1969), 429–31.
9. Conor Cruise O'Brien, *The Long Affair: Thomas Jefferson and the French Revolution, 1785–1800* (Chicago: University of Chicago Press, 1996), 316–18.
10. Joseph Ellis, *American Sphinx: The Character of Thomas Jefferson* (New York: Alfred A. Knopf, 1997).
11. Peter Onuf, *The Mind of Thomas Jefferson*.
12. Merrill D. Peterson, *The Jefferson Image in the American Mind* (Charlottesville: University of Virginia Press, 1998), 9.
13. Merrill D. Peterson, *The Jefferson Image in the American Mind*, 278.
14. Merrill D. Peterson, *The Jefferson Image in the American Mind*, x.
15. There are several major compilations of Jefferson's writings, the most widely used are the following: *The Writings of Thomas Jefferson: Being his Autobiography, Correspondence, Reports, Messages, Addresses, and Other Writings, Official and Private: Published by the Order of the Joint Committee of Congress on the Library, from the Original Manuscripts, Deposited in the Department of State*, 9 Vols., ed. Henry Augustine Washington (Washington: Taylor & Maury, 1853–4); *The Works of Thomas Jefferson*, ed. Paul Leicester Ford, 12 Vols. (New York: Putnam, 1902); *The Writings of Thomas Jefferson, Definitive Edition*, 20 Vols., ed. Andrew Adgate Lipscomb and Albert Ellery Bergh (Washington: Thomas Jefferson Memorial Association, 1907); and *The Papers of Thomas Jefferson*, 42 Vols. (to date), ed. Julian Boyd et al. (Princeton: Princeton University Press, 1950-). There are also several one-volume compilations of Jefferson's writings—the best of which is Merrill D. Peterson's *Thomas Jefferson: Writings* (New York: The Library of America, 1984). Moreover, many of Jefferson's writing are readily available online—e.g., Hathi Trust Digital Library, The Online Library of Liberty, and Founders Online.

Chapter 1

1. Dumas Malone, *Jefferson and the Rights of Man* (Boston: Little, Brown and Company, 1951), 76–77.
2. Douglas L. Wilson, "Jefferson and the Republic of Letters," *Jeffersonian Legacies*, ed. Peter S. Onuf (Charlottesville: University Press of Virginia, 1991), 50–76.

3. Norman K. Risjord, *Thomas Jefferson* (Lanham, MD: Rowman & Littlefield Publishers, Inc., 2002), 62–63.
4. R.B. Bernstein, *Thomas Jefferson* (New York: Oxford University Press, 2003), 63.
5. Alf Mapp, Jr., *Thomas Jefferson: America's Paradoxical Patriot* (Lanham, MD: Rowman & Littlefield, 1987), 242–44.
6. Joseph Ellis, *American Sphinx: The Character of Thomas Jefferson* (New York: Alfred A. Knopf, 1998), 95.
7. Andrew Burstein, *The Inner Jefferson* (Charlottesville: University of Virginia Press, 1995), 94–96.
8. Robert Dawidoff, "Man of Letters," *Thomas Jefferson: A Reference Biography*, ed. Merrill D. Peterson (New York: Charles Scribner's Sons, 1986), 193.
9. Thomas Jefferson, *The Papers of Thomas Jefferson, Vol. X*, ed. Julian Boyd (Princeton: Princeton University Press, 1954), 453.
10. Daryl Hale, "Thomas Jefferson; Sublime or Sublimated Philosopher?" *International Social Science Review*, Vol. 72, Nos. 3 & 4, 2001, 81–82.
11. Lee Quinby, "Thomas Jefferson: The Virtue of Aesthetics and the Aesthetics of Virtue," *The American Historical Review*, Vol. 87, No. 2, 1982, 338.
12. Disparagement of the climate of the Americas and its effect on the biota, both indigenous and imported, of the two continents was commonplace by European intellectuals, such as Buffon, Raynal, DePauw, Robertson, and Volney.
13. The issue of friendship for Epicurus is a sticky wicket. His philosophical views seem to commit him to the view that friendship is justifiable only insofar as it conduces to pleasure—i.e., avoidance of pain. Yet Epicurus seems to award it a status that is inconsistent with his egoistic hedonism. For more, see M. Andrew Holowchak, *Happiness and Greek Ethical Thought*, 86–88.
14. TJ to William Short, 31 Oct. 1819. Jefferson's Epicurus comes from Gassendi, who gives us a Stoicized and Christianized Epicurus. Jefferson did own three volumes of Diogenes Laertius's *Lives of Eminent Philosophers*, which contain key writings of Epicurus, but his references to Epicurus give little indication of assimilation of those writings.
15. Cf. Laurence Sterne, *The Life and Opinions of Tristram Shandy, Gentleman* (New York: Penguin Books, [1759–67] 2003), 185.
16. "Political" in the sense of being by nature animals that live in *poleis*. *Politics*, 1253a3–4. See also *Politics*, 1278b20 and *Nicomachean Ethics*, 1097b12 and 1169b19.

17. TJ to John Adams, 5 July 1814.
18. Zuckert mistakenly takes the sentences as an argument for the existence of a moral sense, given that we were made by a wise artisan, not a pitiful bungler. The conditional, expressed counterfactually, implies the falsity of the antecedent, which is all Jefferson wishes to state. Jefferson aims at showing that moral conduct is independent of reason, not a matter of reason, for sharpened reason is indeed a rare thing, while moral perception is endemic to everyone to a greater or lesser extent. Michael P. Zuckert, "Thomas Jefferson and Natural Morality," *Thomas Jefferson, the Classical World, and Early America*, ed. Peter S. Onuf and Nicholas P. Cole (Charlottesville: University of Virginia Press, 2011), 66–67.
19. M. Andrew Holowchak, *Dutiful Correspondent: Philosophical Essays on Thomas Jefferson* (Lanham, MD: Rowman & Littlefield, 2012), 82–85.
20. The view expressed by Miller. Charles A. Miller, *Jefferson and Nature: An Interpretation* (Baltimore: Johns Hopkins University Press, 1988), 98–101.
21. The assertion of Mapp. Alf Mapp, Jr., *Thomas Jefferson: America's Paradoxical Patriot*, 244.
22. The sentiment is in keeping with much of the literature of Jefferson's day. E.g., Mercier writes, "It is not so much great talents, or an extensive knowledge, that does good, as the sincere desire of an upright heart that loves it, and wishes to accomplish it." Louis-Sebastien Mercier, *Memoirs of the Year Two Thousand Five Hundred* (Philadelphia: Thomas Dobson, 1795), 267–68. For more, see M. Andrew Holowchak, "'An Honest Heart' versus 'A Knowing Head': The Myth of the Preeminency of Rationality in Jefferson's Conceptions of Man and Society," *Thomas Jefferson: The Man behind the Myths* (forthcoming).
23. It was undertaken solely to satisfy the curiosity of Head. In that instance, Heart complained of Head's amaranthine "diagrams and crotchets" and admitted that the trip to see a "parcel of sticks and chips put together in pens" would have been a waste were it not for the Cosways.
24. E.g., TJ to John Banister, 15 Oct. 1785; TJ to Dr. James Curie, 18 Jan. 1786; TJ to Thomas Mann Randolph, Jr., 27 Aug. 1786; TJ to Madam de Tessé, 8 Dec. 1813; TJ to Nathaniel Burwell, 9 Apr. 1818; TJ to Gen. John Minor, 30 Aug. 1814; TJ to Francis Wayles Eppes, 6 Oct 1820
25. Neem argues incorrectly that each person, according to Jefferson, is born virtuous. That is misleading. Each is born with a moral

instinct or knack to do what is right, but that instinct needs nurture. Johann N. Neem, "Beyond the Wall: Reinterpreting Jefferson's Danbury Address," *Journal of the Early Republic,* Vol. 27, 2007, 148.

26. David Hume, "The Skeptic," *Essays: Moral, Political, and Literary,* ed. Eugene F. Miller (Indianapolis: Liberty Fund, 1987), 164.

27. Aristotle, *On the Soul,* trans. W.S. Hett (Cambridge: Harvard University Press, 1957), III.9–10.

28. Cf. Jefferson's commonplacing of Hume, concerning the different customs of different nations. Thomas Jefferson, *Jefferson's Literary Commonplace Book,* ed. Douglas L. Wilson (Princeton: Princeton University Press, 1987), §35.

29. Gilbert Chinard, *The Literary Bible of Thomas Jefferson: His Commonplace Book of Philosophers and Poets* (New York: Greenwood Press, Publishers, [1928] 1969), 6 and 16.

30. Adrianne Koch, *The Philosophy of Thomas Jefferson* (Gloucester, MS: Peter Smith, 1957), 40.

31. Jean Yarbrough, "The Moral Sense, Character Formation, and Virtue," *Reason and Republicanism,* ed. Gary L. McDowell and Sharon L. Noble (Lanham, MD: Rowman & Littlefield Publishers, Inc., 1997), 281–2.

32. Eugene R. Sheridan, "Introduction," *Jefferson's Extracts from the Gospels,* ed. Dickinson W. Adams (Princeton: Princeton University Press, 1983), 8.

33. Johann N. Neem, "To Diffuse Knowledge More Generally through the Mass of People," *Light and Liberty: Thomas Jefferson and the Power of Knowledge* ed. Robert M.S. McDonald (Charlottesville: University of Virginia Press, 2012), 48–49.

34. Ari Helo, *Thomas Jefferson's Ethics and the Politics of Human Progress* (Cambridge: Cambridge University Press, 2014), 90.

35. For more on intention and utility, see also, e.g., Seneca, "On Benefits," *Seneca: Moral Essays,* vol. 3, trans. John W. Basadore (Cambridge: Harvard University Press, [1935] 2001), VI.xi.3.

36. E.g., TJ to Samuel R. Demaree, 4 Oct. 1809, and TJ to Bernard Moore, 30 Aug. 1814.

37. "It is beyond doubt that utility can never conflict with what is morally correct." My translation. Cicero, *De Officiis,* trans. Walter Miller (Cambridge, Harvard University Press, 2001), III.iii.11.

38. Thomas Jefferson, *Writings,* 121.

39. It was common for Scottish moralists, who greatly influenced Jefferson and who were profoundly influenced by the Stoics (see Chapter 4), to focus on intention as much as outcome. Lord Kames, for instance, writes: "In these every circumstance concurs: the fitness or unfitness of the means; the goodness or badness of the end; the intention of the actor; which gives them the peculiar character of *fit, right,* and *meet,* or *unfit, wrong,* and *unmeet.*" Lord Kames, *Essays on the Principles of Morality and Natural Religion,* 2nd ed. (London, 1758), 36.

40. In Charron's words, in keeping with Aristotle and the Greek and Roman Stoics, *"We do not want Precepts so much as Patterns,"* for "Prudence is a boundless and bottomless Sea; never limited by positive Precepts." Pierre Charron, *Of Wisdom, Vol. III,* trans. George Stanhope (London: 1729), 1016 and 1002, respectively.

41. The Stoics made use of *praecepta* and *decreta*—parochial and generic principles to guide moral decision making—but such principles were more useful guides of right actions, not determinants of it.

42. See also "Declaration concerning Ethan Allen," 2 Dec. 1775; TJ to Gov. Patrick Henry, 27 Mar. 1779; TJ to David Williams, 14 Nov. 1803; TJ to Caesar A. Rodney, 10 Feb. 1810; TJ to John Adams, 11 Jan. 1816; TJ to John Adams, 12 Sept. 1821; and TJ to Cornelius Blatchly, 21 Oct. 1822.

43. Helo et al. make the point thus, "Utility was not a moral maxim by itself, but a practical maxim for an individual already committed to the notion of justice." Ari Helo and Peter Onuf, "Jefferson, Morality, and the Problem of Slavery," *William and Mary Quarterly,* Vol. LX, No. 3, 2003, 607.

44. E.g., TJ to John Adams, 11 Jan. 1816.

45. E.g., TJ to Correa de Serra, 28 June 1815.

46. Adam Smith, *The Theory of Moral Sentiments* (Indianapolis: Liberty Fund, 1984), 159–74 and 320.

47. For further ways in which reason might assist the moral sense, see M. Andrew Holowchak, *Dutiful Correspondent,* 159–76, and "The March of Morality: Making Sense of Jefferson's Moral Sense" in *Thomas Jefferson and Philosophy: Essays on the Philosophical Cast of Jefferson's Writings,* ed. M. Andrew Holowchak (Lanham, MD: Lexington Books, 2012), 147–64.

48. M. Andrew Holowchak, *Thomas Jefferson.*

49. David Hume, "The Skeptic," *Essays: Moral, Political, and Literary,* ed. Eugene F. Miller (Indianapolis: Liberty Fund, 1987), 162.

50. David Hume, "The Skeptic," 163–66.

51. David Hume, "The Skeptic," 167–68.

52. David Hume, "The Skeptic," 169.

53. David Hume, "The Skeptic," 170–71.
54. David Hume, "The Skeptic," 172.
55. David Hume, "The Skeptic," 172.
56. David Hume, "The Skeptic," 173. What Donald Livingston calls "false philosophy" for Hume. False philosophy is speculative, abstract, and esoteric apropos of "common ways of thinking." In contrast, "true philosophy" for Hume is exoteric, "practical and eloquent." It aims to express "the common sense of mankind in more beautiful and more engaging colours." The true philosopher stands above the false philosopher in that he grasps the limits or vulgarity of false philosophical understanding. Donald Livingston, *Philosophical Melancholy and Delirium* (Chicago: University of Chicago Press, 1998), 45–47.
57. The bodily humors—a relic of Hippocratic medicine.
58. David Hume, "The Skeptic," 180.
59. David Hume, "The Skeptic," 178.
60. David Hume, "The Standard of Taste," *Essays: Moral, Political, and Literary*, ed. Eugene F. Miller (Indianapolis: Liberty Fund, 1987), 230.
61. David Hume, "The Standard of Taste," 235.
62. David Hume, "The Standard of Taste," 234–35.
63. David Hume, The History of England, From the Invasion of Julius Caesar to the Rovolution in 1688, vol. 6 (Indianapolis: Liberty Classics, 1983), 513.
64. David Hume, "Concerning Moral Sentiment" and "Some Farther Considerations with regard to Justice," *An Enquiry concerning the Principles of Morals*, ed. J.B. Schneewind (Indianapolis: Hackett Publishing Company, 1983), 83–85 and 93–94.
65. David Hume, "The Standard of Taste," 230.
66. David Hume, "The Standard of Taste," 242.
67. David Hume, "The Standard of Taste," 243.
68. E.g., TJ to Peter Carr, 19 Aug. 1785; TJ to Dr. Joseph Priestley, 21 Mar. 1801; and TJ to Charles E. Wells, 3 Dec. 1809.
69. Disrelish of reason apropos of moral judgments and knowledge of certain "metaphysical" truths—e.g., the nature of deity, the uniformity of nature, and the existence of causality in the cosmos—Kames expresses often. It is too slippery a guide and too inaccessible by the majority of humans, ill-suited for reasoning. E.g., Lord Kames, *Morality and Natural Religion*, 2nd ed. (London, 1758), 259, 265, 267, and 284.
70. I add "conveniency," because, while some intuitive perceptions are truths—e.g., the self-existence of deity—others are untruths that are of utmost usefulness for humans—e.g., the existence of good, bad, beauty, and ugliness. In that regard, human faculties are given to them by deity to be of utmost use to them in flourishing, and truth is not always suited to human flourishing.
71. Lord Kames, *Morality and Natural Religion*, 265–75 and 298–309.
72. Lord Kames, *Morality and Natural Religion*, 6–10.
73. Lord Kames, *Morality and Natural Religion*, 10–1.
74. Lord Kames, *Morality and Natural Religion*, 29–31.
75. Lord Kames, *Morality and Natural Religion*, 34–36, 44–52, 55–58, 73, and 89.
76. Knowing the moral sense entails knowing nature's laws—"rules of our conduct and behaviour, founded on natural principles, approved by the moral sense, and enforced by natural rewards and punishments," or more succinctly, "rules of action adapted to our nature." Lord Kames, *Morality and Natural Religion*, 55 and 93.
77. Lord Kames, *Morality and Natural Religion*, 103–8.
78. Lord Kames, *Morality and Natural Religion*, 108–12.
79. Lord Kames, *Morality and Natural Religion*, 46–54, 65–66, 86–87, 93–95, and 97–99.
80. Smith writes similarly. He distinguishes between "acts of beneficence" (friendship, charity, and generosity) and those of justice. The former are voluntary and less essential for social stability than acts of justice. Justice, "the main pillar that holds up the whole edifice," is in a sense involuntary in that it appeals to a human sense of duty. In all, justice "does no real positive good and might be regarded as a "negative virtue," since we see its real benefit only when the strictures of justice are vilipended. Adam Smith, *The Theory of Moral Sentiments*, 80–86.
81. Kames illustrates through self-preservation—the strongest of all human principles of action. The moral sense will not condone self-preservation in all instances, though it allows a starving man to take food wherever he can find it and the approbation of the proprietor must be assumed. Likewise, if two men in a shipwreck hang on to a plank that can only support one of them, it is within moral law for them to use force to decide who gets the plank, as each has an equal title to self-preservation. Lord Kames, *Morality and Natural Religion*, 46–54 and 59.
82. Lord Kames, *Essays on the Principles of*

Morality and Natural Religion, 2nd ed. (London, 1758), 94–97.

83. Lord Kames, *Morality and Natural Religion,* 118–122.

84. Lord Kames, *Morality and Natural Religion,* 122–28.

85. Lord Kames, *Morality and Natural Religion,* 130.

86. Lord Kames, *Morality and Natural Religion,* 131.

87. Lord Kames, *Morality and Natural Religion,* 113–14, 152–53, and 162.

88. E.g., TJ to Francis Wayles Eppes, 27 June 1821.

89. E.g., "Notes on Religion," 1776; TJ to Dr. Benjamin Waterhouse, 26 June 1822; TJ to Dr. Thomas Cooper, 2 Nov. 1822; TJ to John Adams, 11 Apr. 1823; and TJ to George Thatcher, 26 Jan. 1824.

90. Lord Kames, *Morality and Natural Religion,* 164–78

91. Adam Smith, *Theory of Moral Sentiments,* 321 and 326.

92. Jefferson dislocated his right wrist in a boyish display of failed athleticism while out with Cosway. Though the wrist was reset my physicians, it was not reset well, and Jefferson suffered from wrist pain for the remainder of his days.

Chapter 2

1. TJ to James Madison, 20 Sept. 1785.
2. Thomas Jefferson, "Tour to Some of the Gardens of England," *Writings,* 623–38.
3. Thomas Jefferson, "Travelling Notes for Mr. Rutledge and Mr. Shippen," *Writings,* 659–60.
4. A point noted by William Howard Adams. "To encourage a private interest in art was to encourage class divisions that would undermine the principles of American democracy." William Howard Adams, "The Fine Arts," *Thomas Jefferson: A Reference Biography,* Merrill D. Peterson (New York: Charles Scribner's Sons, 1986), 209.
5. JA to Abigail Adams, 9 Oct. 1774 and 25 Apr. 1778. John Adams and Abigail Adams, *The Book of Abigail and John: Selected Letters of the Adams Family, 1762–1784,* eds. Lyman Butterfield and Mark Friedlaender (Northeastern University Press, 2002).
6. The fourth stage, urbanization and overcrowding, being symptomatic of moribundity. Gordon S. Wood, *Empire of Liberty: A History of the Early Republic, 1789–1815* (Cambridge: Oxford University Press, 2009), 549.
7. William Hogarth, *Analysis of Beauty,* *Written with a View of Fixing the Fluctuating Ideas of Taste* (London: J. Reeves, 1753), iii.

8. William Hogarth, *Analysis of Beauty,* iii–iv.
9. William Hogarth, *Analysis of Beauty,* v–vi.
10. William Hogarth, *Analysis of Beauty,* 51. See also Laurence Sterne, *The Life and Opinions of Tristram Shandy, Gentleman* (New York: Penguin Books, [1759–67] 2003), 107.
11. William Hogarth, *Analysis of Beauty,* xviii.
12. William Hogarth, *Analysis of Beauty,* 3.
13. William Hogarth, *Analysis of Beauty,* 7–8.
14. William Hogarth, *Analysis of Beauty,* 9.
15. William Hogarth, *Analysis of Beauty,* 12.
16. William Hogarth, *Analysis of Beauty,* 13.
17. William Hogarth, *Analysis of Beauty,* 71.
18. William Hogarth, *Analysis of Beauty,* 16–17.
19. William Hogarth, *Analysis of Beauty,* 18–20.
20. William Hogarth, *Analysis of Beauty,* 21.
21. William Hogarth, *Analysis of Beauty,* 21–23.
22. William Hogarth, *Analysis of Beauty,* 24–28.
23. William Hogarth, *Analysis of Beauty,* 29–34.
24. Edmund Burke, *A Philosophical Enquiry into the Origin of Our Ideas of the Sublime and Beautiful* (London, 1757), vii.
25. Edmund Burke, *The Sublime and Beautiful,* 14.
26. Edmund Burke, *The Sublime and Beautiful,* 32.
27. Edmund Burke, *The Sublime and Beautiful,* 14 and 17.
28. Edmund Burke, *The Sublime and Beautiful,* 14–15.
29. Edmund Burke, *The Sublime and Beautiful,* 18–20.
30. Edmund Burke, *The Sublime and Beautiful,* 21–25.
31. Edmund Burke, *The Sublime and Beautiful,* 28–29.
32. Edmund Burke, *The Sublime and Beautiful,* 30–31.
33. Edmund Burke, *The Sublime and Beautiful,* 72.
34. Edmund Burke, *The Sublime and Beautiful,* 42–43, 43–49, 50–51, 51–52, 52–54, 53–57, 58–59, 60, 60–61, 62, 64–65, 65–66, 66, 67–68, 68, 69–71, and 71–72, respectively.
35. Edmund Burke, *The Sublime and Beautiful,* 122, 126, and 129–30.
36. Edmund Burke, *The Sublime and Beautiful,* 75–77.

37. Burke concedes the utility of all things, however, as the creator would not make anything in vain. It is merely that the utility of many things escapes human detection. Edmund Burke, *The Sublime and Beautiful*, 84–87.
38. Edmund Burke, *The Sublime and Beautiful*, 91–92.
39. Edmund Burke, *The Sublime and Beautiful*, 93.
40. Edmund Burke, *The Sublime and Beautiful*, 95.
41. Edmund Burke, *The Sublime and Beautiful*, 96–97, 98–99, 99–100, 101–2, and 102–3, respectively.
42. Edmund Burke, *The Sublime and Beautiful*, 115.
43. Henry Home, *Elements of Criticism*, 5th ed. (Dublin: Charles Ingham, 1772), ii.
44. Henry Home, *Elements of Criticism*, ii.
45. Henry Home, *Elements of Criticism*, iii.
46. Elsewhere, Kames maintains that beauty is a secondary quality, not a primary quality—i.e., it is not a property of objects, but a property of the human mind. Henry Home, *Essays on the Principles of Morality and Natural Religion, Second Edition* (London, 1758), 160.
47. Henry Home, *Elements of Criticism*, iv.
48. Henry Home, *Elements of Criticism*, iv.
49. Henry Home, *Elements of Criticism*, iii–iv.
50. Henry Home, *Elements of Criticism*, iv.
51. Henry Home, *Elements of Criticism*, iv.
52. Henry Home, *Elements of Criticism*, 9–10.
53. Henry Home, *Elements of Criticism*, 10–11.
54. Henry Home, *Elements of Criticism*, 11.
55. Henry Home, *Elements of Criticism*, 12–13.
56. Thomas Jefferson, "To the Virginia Delegates in Congress" (12 July 1785), *The Papers of Thomas Jefferson, Vol. 8, 25 February–31 October 1785*, ed. Julian P. Boyd (Princeton: Princeton University Press, 1953), 289–90.
57. Thomas Jefferson, "Memorandum from Thomas Jefferson" (29 August 1790), *The Papers of George Washington*, Presidential Series, *Vol. 6, 1 July 1790–30 November 1790*, ed. Mark A. Mastromarino (Charlottesville: University Press of Virginia, 1996), 368–70.
58. Thomas Jefferson, *Notes on Virginia*, ed. William Peden (Chapel Hill: University of North Carolina Press, 1954), 10.
59. Thomas Jefferson, *Notes on Virginia*, 138–40.
60. Edmund Burke, *The Sublime and Beautiful*, 62–63 and 148.
61. William Hogarth, *Analysis of Beauty*, 28.
62. Thomas Jefferson, *Notes on Virginia*, 19.
63. Thomas Jefferson, *Notes on Virginia*, 24–25.
64. Thomas Jefferson, *Notes on Virginia*, 25.
65. TJ to C.F.C. Volney, 8 Feb. 1805.
66. Ossian was purportedly the author of several Gaelic epics, collected by word of mouth by James McPherson and published subsequently as the works of Ossian. The poems are likely the creation of McPherson, who, scholars agree, created Ossian.
67. See also TJ to Cornelia Jefferson Randolph, 26 Dec. 1806.
68. Thomas Jefferson, *Notes on Virginia*, 140.
69. Cf. Agathon's speech in Plato's *Symposium*. Agathon has just won an important oratorical contest, and gives a eulogy to the god *Eros* in honor of his victory. The speech, Socrates says, is a feast for the ears to "ignorant listeners," but not so to any listener with knowledge. Plato, *Symposium*, trans. Alexander Nehamas and Paul Woodruff (Indianapolis: Hackett Publishing Company, 1989), 199a.
70. Modeled after the Maison Carrée in Nîmes, France—formerly a Roman temple.
71. See also TJ to Benjamin Waterhouse, 13 Oct. 1815; TJ to William Short, 31 Oct. 1819; and TJ to George Thatcher, 16 Jan. 1824.
72. H.M. Kallen, "The Arts and Thomas Jefferson," *Ethics*, Vol. 53, No. 4, 1943, 282.
73. Merrill D. Peterson, *The Jefferson Image in the American Mind* (Charlottesville: University of Virginia Press, 1998), 154.
74. William Hogarth, *Analysis of Beauty*, 71.
75. Thomas Jefferson, "Travel Journals," *Writings*, 624–25.
76. TJ to Peter Carr, 10 Aug. 1787.
77. E.g., TJ to Thomas Cooper, 10 Sept. 1814, and TJ to John Langdon, 5 Mar. 1810.
78. See also TJ to James Monroe, 28 Oct. 1795.

Chapter 3

1. The lists to Munford and Cabell are also lengthy.
2. *The Papers of Thomas Jefferson, Vol. 1, 1760–1776*, ed. Julian P. Boyd (Princeton: Princeton University Press, 1950), 74.
3. See John Minor to TJ, 8 Sept. 1814. Thomas Jefferson, *The Papers of Thomas Jefferson*, Retirement Series, Vol. 7, *28 November 1813 to 30 September 1814*, ed. J. Jefferson Looney (Princeton: Princeton University Press, 2010), 643–44.
4. For dating the letter to Moore, see Morris L. Cohen, "Thomas Jefferson Recommends a Course of Law Study," *119 University of Pennsylvania Law Review*, 823, 1971.

5. TJ to William Short, 31 Oct. 1819. See "Jefferson's Platonic Republicanism," *Polis* (forthcoming).

6. TJ to Benjamin Rush, 21 Apr. 1803; TJ to John Adams, 22 Aug. 1813; TJ to John Adams, 12 Oct. 1813; TJ to Thomas Law, 13 June 1814; TJ to Dr. Benjamin Waterhouse, 13 Oct. 1815; TJ to Charles Thomson, 9 Jan. 1816; TJ to William Short, 31 Oct. 1819; TJ to Dr. Benjamin Waterhouse, 26 June 1822; and TJ to John Davis, 18 Jan. 1824.

7. See M. Andrew Holowchak, "'This Faithful, Internal Monitor': Jefferson on the Moral Sense," *Thomas Jefferson: Uncovering His Unique Philosophy and Vision* (Amherst, NY: Prometheus Books, 2014).

8. M. Andrew Holowchak, "The Reluctant Politician: Thomas Jefferson's Debt to Epicurus," *Eighteenth-Century Studies*, Vol. 45, No. 2, 2012, 277–97.

9. E.g., dialogs such as *Charmides, Crito, Laches,* and *Euthyphro.*

10. TJ to George Logan, 20 June 1816.

11. E.g., TJ to Littleton Waller Tazewell, 5 Jan. 1805; TJ to Peter Carr, 7 Sept. 1814; and TJ to Joseph Cabell, 14 Jan. 1818.

12. E.g., TJ to Peter Carr, 10 Aug. 1787; TJ to Thomas Jefferson Randolph, 24 Nov. 1808; TJ to James Fishback, 27 Sept. 1809; TJ to Thomas Law, 13 June 1814.

13. An avowed advocate of Academic Skepticism, "the more he studied and lived, the more of a Stoic in ethics he became." G.P. Gould, "Introduction," in Cicero, *On Duties,* trans. Walter Miller (Cambridge: Harvard University Press, 1913] 2001), xiii.

14. See Stephen White, "Cicero," *Routledge Encyclopedia of Philosophy,* ed. Edward Craig (London: Routledge, 1996) 356.

15. Cicero, *Tusculan Disputations,* trans. J.E. King (Cambridge: Harvard University Press, [1927] 1945), I.6.

16. Raubitschek, Isabelle K. and Antony E., "Letter on the Composition of the Republic," *Selected Works of Cicero* (Roslyn, NY: Walter J. Black, 1948), 201.

17. E.g., Cicero, *Tusculan Disputations,* I.7.

18. TJ to John Adams, 5 July 1814. See also TJ to Francis Eppes, 19 Jan. 1821. Earlier he tells John Wayles Eppes (17 Jan. 1810) that reading any of Cicero's orations is a "piece of task-work." To John Garland (27 Feb. 1822) he says Demosthenes, more logical than Cicero, is suited for the Senate; Cicero, more imaginative, for the bar.

19. E.g., TJ to Robert Skipwith, 3 Aug. 1771; TJ to Peter Carr, 19 Aug. 1785; TJ to Philip (Mazzei, 16 Feb. 1787; TJ to Peter Carr, 10 Aug. 1787; TJ to Amand Koenig, 29 June 1789; TJ to William Green Munford, 5 Dec. 1798; TJ to Joseph C. Cabell,** Sept. 1800; and TJ to Francis Eppes, 6 Oct. 1820.

20. Cicero, *On Duties,* trans. Walter Miller (Cambridge: Harvard University Press, 1913] 2001).

21. See Cicero, "Letter 27," *Selected Works* (Roslyn, NY: Walter J. Black, Inc., 1948).

22. *Honustum* can also be grasped more generally as "moral goodness."

23. One in full possession of any one virtue, is in full possession of all (II.35).

24. For more on Jefferson's appropriation of *kairos,* see M. Andrew Holowchak, "A Heart at Ease Flies to No Extremes: Life as a Sentimental Journey," *Thomas Jefferson's Philosophy of Education: A Utopian Dream* (London: Taylor & Francis, 2014), and "A 'Convenient Defect of Vision': Jefferson's View of African Americans," *Framing a Legend: Exposing the Distorted History of Thomas Jefferson and Sally Hemings* (Amherst, NY: Prometheus Books, 2013).

25. Translations mine. Cicero, *De Senectute,* trans. William Armistead Falconer (Cambridge: Cambridge University Press, [1923] 1992).

26. *Parvulus* relates also to age and can mean "young."

27. Plato, *Apology,* 40c–41b.

28. E.g., TJ to Martha Jefferson, 28 Mar. 1787; TJ to Martha Jefferson, 5 May 1787; TJ to Martha Jefferson, 21 May 1787; TJ to Martha Jefferson Randolph, 26 Apr. 1790; and TJ to Mary Jefferson, 30 May 1791.

29. See M. Andrew Holowchak, *Framing a Legend: Exposing the Distorted History of Thomas Jefferson and Sally Hemings* (Amherst, NY: Prometheus Books, 2013), 48–54.

30. The argument in gist of Plato's *Phaedo.*

31. I have found eight references directly to the work or indirectly, under, e.g., "Cicero: moral works."

32. He had a keen mind and was a voluminous writer with over 700 publications, of which nothing but fragments survive. He also developed a formal approach to propositional logic that has only recently begun to receive due attention.

33. There are the usual dissenters, like Cleanthes, who divided philosophy into six parts: dialectic, rhetoric, ethics, politics, physics, and theology. D.L., VII.40–41.

34. There were originally eight, but only four survive.

35. Seneca, "On Benefits," *Seneca: Moral Essays,* vol. 3, trans. John W. Basadore (Cambridge: Harvard University Press, [1935] 2001), III.xviii.2.

36. Seneca, "On Providence," *Seneca: Moral Essays*, vol. 1, trans. John W. Basadore (Cambridge: Harvard University Press, [1928] 1998).
37. Seneca, "On Steadiness," *Seneca: Moral Essays*, vol. 1, trans. John W. Basadore (Cambridge: Harvard University Press, [1928] 1998).
38. Seneca, "On Anger," *Seneca: Moral Essays*, vol. 1, trans. John W. Basadore (Cambridge: Harvard University Press, [1928] 1998).
39. Cf. III.xxv.3, where he writes of "the enormous wild beast that looks back moonily at baying dogs."
40. Seneca, "To Marcia," *Seneca: Moral Essays*, vol. 2, trans. John W. Basadore (Cambridge: Harvard University Press, [1932] 2001).
41. Seneca, "To Polybius," *Seneca: Moral Essays*, vol. 2, trans. John W. Basadore (Cambridge: Harvard University Press, [1932] 2001).
42. Senece, "To Helvia," *Seneca: Moral Essays*, vol. 2, trans. John W. Basadore (Cambridge: Harvard University Press, [1932] 2001).
43. Seneca, "The Good Life," *Seneca: Moral Essays*, vol. 2, trans. John W. Basadore (Cambridge: Harvard University Press, [1932] 2001).
44. Seneca, "On Leisure," *Seneca: Moral Essays*, vol. 2, trans. John W. Basadore (Cambridge: Harvard University Press, [1932] 2001).
45. Seneca, "On Tranquility," *Seneca: Moral Essays*, vol. 2, trans. John W. Basadore (Cambridge: Harvard University Press, [1932] 2001).
46. Seneca, "On Shortness of Life," *Seneca: Moral Essays*, vol. 2, trans. John W. Basadore (Cambridge: Harvard University Press, [1932] 2001).
47. Seneca, "On Benefits," *Seneca: Moral Essays*, vol. 3, trans. John W. Basadore (Cambridge: Harvard University Press, [1935] 2001).
48. Cf. Letter LXXXI. Seneca, *Epistles*, vol. 2, trans. Richard M Gummere (Cambridge: Harvard University Press, [1920] 2001).
49. E.g., TJ to David Barrow, 1 May 1815, and TJ to John Adams, 11 Apr. 1823.
50. E.g., TJ to Mary Jefferson, 11 Apr. 1790; TJ to Ellen Wayles Randolph, 27 Nov. 1801; TJ to Thomas Jefferson Randolph, 24 Nov. 1808; TJ James Fishback, 27 Sept. 1809; and TJ to Francis Wayles Eppes, 21 May 1816.
51. E.g., TJ to Maria Cosway, 27 Aug. 1786; TJ to John Adams, 21 Jan. 1812; TJ to Gen. Thaddeus Kosciusko, 28 June 1812; TJ to James Ronaldson, 12 Jan. 1813; TJ to John Melish, 13 Jan. 1813; and TJ to Benjamin Austin, 9 Jan. 1816.
52. W.A. Oldfather, "Introduction," in Epictetus, *The Discourses as Reported by Arrian, Books I–II*, trans. W.A. Oldfather (Cambridge: Harvard University Press, [1925] 2000), xiv–xvi.
53. C.R. Haines, "Introduction," in *Marcus Aurelius*, trans. C.R. Haines (Cambridge: Harvard University Press, [1916] 1999), xiii.
54. W.A. Oldfather, "Introduction," vii–viii.
55. I follow throughout the translation of Oldfather, with certain alterations.
56. In that regard, he was much like Cicero, who disavowed Stoicism, but always seemed to embrace Stoic stances on moral issues at the end of the day.
57. Translations mostly follow Grube. Marcus Aurelius, *The Meditations*, trans. G.M.A. Grube (Indianapolis: Hackett Publishing Company, 1983). Greek from Marcus Aurelius, *Marcus Aurelius*, trans. C.R. Hanes (Cambridge: Harvard University Press [1916] 1999).
58. George Long, "The Philosophy of Antoninus," in *The Thoughts of the Emperor M. Aurelius Antoninus*, trans. George Long (New York: G.P. Putnam's Sons, 1990), 45.
59. M. Andrew Holowchak, *The Stoics*, 20.
60. E.g., TJ to John Randolph, 25 Aug. 1775; TJ to Richard Henry Lee, 17 June 1779; TJ to Marquis de Lafayette, 4 Aug. 1781; and TJ to James Madison, 28 Aug. 1789.
61. The exception might be in his youth. For instance, while greatly under the spell of Bolingbroke, he commonplaces a passage (§28) in which Bolingbroke criticizes the moral code of Jesus for being incomplete and for not being "proved from principles of reason, and by clear deductions." In those regards, Bolingbroke adds, the ancient moralists Tully, Seneca, and Epictetus were superior. Thomas Jefferson, *Jefferson's Literary Commonplace Book*, ed. Douglas L. Wilson (Princeton: Princeton University Press, 1989).
62. TA metaphor he repeats to Francis Adrian Van der Kemp, 25 Apr. 1816, and William Short, 31 Oct. 1819.
63. Plato, *The Republic of Plato*, vol. 1, ed. James Adam (Cambridge: Cambridge University Press, 1965).

Chapter 4

1. Pierre Charron, *De la sagesse*, ed. 3, trans. George Stanhope (London: 1729), 50–55 and 65–67.
2. Pierre Charron, *Wisdom*, 134–142.
3. Pierre Charron, *Wisdom*, 150–55.
4. Pierre Charron, *Wisdom*, 508–11.
5. Pierre Charron, *Wisdom*, 171–73.
6. The account shows considerable confusion. If persons only ever receive surface impressions, the best one can say is that an impression appears good and the best one can do is formulate judgments in keeping with the nature of impressions.

7. Pierre Charron, *Wisdom*, 262–64.
8. Pierre Charron, *Wisdom*, 268–69.
9. Pierre Charron, *Wisdom*, 274–77.
10. Pierre Charron, *Wisdom*, 277.
11. Pierre Charron, *Wisdom*, 277–78.
12. Pierre Charron, *Wisdom*, 277–79.
13. Pierre Charron, *Wisdom*, 282–84.
14. Pierre Charron, *Wisdom*, 476–84.
15. Pierre Charron, *Wisdom,* 487–89.
16. E.g., TJ to Peter Carr, 19 Aug. 1785; TJ to Maria Cosway, 12 Oct. 1786; TJ to James Fishback, 27 September 1809; and TJ to Thomas Law, 13 June 1814.
17. E.g., "Bill for the More General Diffusion of Knowledge," *Writings*, 365; TJ to Charles Yancey, 9 Jan. 1816; TJ to George Tickner, c. May 1817; and TJ to Joseph C. Cabell, 14 Jan. 1818.
18. See "Jefferson on War and Peace," M. Andrew Holowchak, *Dutiful Correspondent: Philosophical Essays on Thomas Jefferson* (Lanham, MD: Rowman & Littlefield, 2012), 177–200.
19. E.g., TJ to John Adams, 1 June 1822. See Chapter 10 of this book.
20. "Jefferson's Moral Agrarianism: Poetic Fiction or Moral Vision?" *Agriculture and Human Values*, Vol. 28, 2011, 497–506.
21. Francis Hutcheson, *A Short Introduction to Moral Philosophy in Three Books; Containing the Elements of Ethicks and the Law of Nature*, ed. 2 (Glasgow: Robert and Andrew Foulis, 1753), 4.
22. Francis Hutcheson, *Short Introduction*, 40.
23. Francis Hutcheson, *Short Introduction*, 4–5.
24. Francis Hutcheson, *Short Introduction*, 7–9.
25. Francis Hutcheson, *Short Introduction*, 40.
26. Francis Hutcheson, *Short Introduction*, 9–10.
27. Francis Hutcheson, *Short Introduction*, 11.
28. Francis Hutcheson, *Short Introduction*, 11–15.
29. Francis Hutcheson, *Short Introduction*, 14–20.
30. Francis Hutcheson, *Short Introduction*, 23–36.
31. Francis Hutcheson, *Short Introduction*, 27–28.
32. Francis Hutcheson, *Short Introduction*, 29–30 and 56. See Aristotle, *Nicomachean Ethics*, 1097a32–b21, 1100a6–9, 1100b25–27, and 1153b16–21.
33. Francis Hutcheson, *Short Introduction*, 34–36.
34. Francis Hutcheson, *Short Introduction*, 37–38.
35. Francis Hutcheson, *Short Introduction*, 52–60.
36. Francis Hutcheson, *Short Introduction*, 51–52.
37. Francis Hutcheson, *Short Introduction*, 55–56.
38. E.g., TJ to Mary Jefferson, 14 June 1797, and TJ to Ellen Wayles Randolph, 27 Nov. 1801.
39. E.g., *Bill for the More General Diffusion of Knowledge* (1779); TJ to Caspar Wistar, 21 June 1807; TJ to John Adams, 5 July 1814; TJ to Peter Carr, 7 Sept. 1814; and TJ to Francis Wayles Eppes, 13 Dec. 1820.
40. E.g., TJ to Dr. Benjamin Waterhouse, 26 June 1822.
41. E.g., TJ to John Adams, 18 Dec. 1825.
42. Lord Kames, *Morality and Natural Religion*, ed. 2 (London, 1758), 259, 265, 267, and 284.
43. Lord Kames, *Morality and Natural Religion*, 259, 265–75, 284, and 298–309.
44. Lord Kames, *Morality and Natural Religion*, 6–11.
45. Lord Kames, *Morality and Natural Religion*, 29–31.
46. Lord Kames, *Morality and Natural Religion*, 34–6, 44–52, 55–58, 73, and 89.
47. Lord Kames, *Morality and Natural Religion*, 55, 93, and 103–8.
48. Lord Kames, *Morality and Natural Religion*, 108–12.
49. Lord Kames, *Morality and Natural Religion*, 46–54, 65–66, 86–87, 93–95, and 97–99.
50. Lord Kames, *Morality and Natural Religion*, 58–63. Benevolence he later adds (94–95 and 98–99) is "in many circumstances, by means of peculiar connections ... an indispensable duty," for example, in the bond of parent and child, other blood relations, or in the case of a person in distress.
51. Lord Kames, *Morality and Natural Religion*, 66–67.
52. Lord Kames, *Morality and Natural Religion*, 93 and 76–85.
53. Lord Kames, *Morality and Natural Religion*, 150.
54. Lord Kames, *Morality and Natural Religion*, 118–22.
55. Lord Kames, *Morality and Natural Religion*, 122–28.
56. Lord Kames, *Morality and Natural Religion*, 130–1.
57. Lord Kames, *Morality and Natural Religion*, 134–38.
58. Lord Kames, *Morality and Natural Religion*, 134, 164–65, and 173.
59. Lord Kames, *Morality and Natural Religion*, 140–49.

60. Lord Kames, *Morality and Natural Religion*, 113–14, 152–53, and 162.
61. E.g., TJ to Charles Thomson, 20 Sept. 1787; TJ to Daniel Salmon, 15 Feb. 1808; and TJ to John Adams, 15 Aug. 1820.
62. See M. Andrew Holowchak, *Thomas Jefferson*, chap. 1.
63. E.g., TJ to Gov. Patrick Henry, 27 Mar. 1779; TJ to James Madison, 28 Aug. 1789; TJ to David Williams, 14 Nov. 1803; and TJ to Correa de Serra, 28 June 1815.
64. Thomas Jefferson, *Notes on Virginia*, XIII, 1782; E.g., TJ to James Madison, 28 Oct. 1785; and TJ to P.S. Dupont de Nemours, 24 Apr. 1816.
65. E.g., TJ to Francis Wayles Eppes, 27 June 1821.
66. E.g., "Notes on Religion," 1776; TJ to Dr. Benjamin Waterhouse, 26 June 1822; TJ to Dr. Thomas Cooper, 2 Nov. 1822; TJ to John Adams, 11 Apr. 1823; and TJ to George Thatcher, 26 Jan. 1824.
67. Lord Kames, Morality and Natural Religion, 164–78
68. E.g., TJ to John Adams, 15 Aug. 1820. See M. Andrew Holowchak, *The Philosophy of Thomas Jefferson*, chap. 1.
69. John Aikin, "Biographical Account of the Author of These Volumes," xiv–xv. William Enfield, *Sermons on Practical Subjects* (London, 1799), xvi.
70. William Enfield, *The History of Philosophy*, vi–viii.
71. William Enfield, *The History of Philosophy*, 25.
72. William Enfield, *The History of Philosophy*, 25–26.
73. William Enfield, *The History of Philosophy*, 26.
74. William Enfield, *The History of Philosophy*, 29–30.
75. This problem of anachronism today contaminates a large amount of historical scholarship on Jefferson. For illustration, Onuf's *Jeffersonian Legacies* is unabashedly a fresh look at Jefferson from the perch of modern standards. See M. Andrew Holowchak, *Framing a Legend: Exposing the Distorted History of Thomas Jefferson and Sally Hemings* (Amherst: Prometheus Books, 2013), 205–10.
76. William Enfield, *The History of Philosophy*, 27–28.
77. William Enfield, *The History of Philosophy*, 32–34.
78. For Jefferson on rigor in language, see, e.g., TJ to John Waldo, 16 Aug. 1813; TJ to John Adams, 21 Mar. 1819; and TJ to John Brazier, 24 Aug. 1819).
79. E.g., TJ to John Adams, 15 Aug. 1820.

80. See M. Andrew Holowchak, *Framing a Legend*, 163–64.
81. Condorcet, *Outlines of an Historical View of the Progress of the Human Mind: Being a Posthumous Work of the Late M. de Condorcet* (London: J. Johnson, 1795), 3–14.
82. Condorcet, *Progress of the Human Mind*, 12–15 and 18–19.
83. Condorcet, *Progress of the Human Mind*, 21–28.
84. Condorcet, *Progress of the Human Mind*, 29–39.
85. Condorcet, *Progress of the Human Mind*, 40–68.
86. Condorcet, *Progress of the Human Mind*, 69–95.
87. The ultimate cause of decline, Condorcet says, was the vulgarity of the citizenry. "At Rome the study of letters and love of the arts were never the real taste of the people." Condorcet, *Progress of the Human Mind*, 96–136.
88. Condorcet, *Progress of the Human Mind*, 137–58.
89. Condorcet, *Progress of the Human Mind*, 158–77.
90. Condorcet, *Progress of the Human Mind*, 178–223.
91. Condorcet, *Progress of the Human Mind*, 223–315.
92. Condorcet, *Progress of the Human Mind*, 316–36.
93. Condorcet, *Progress of the Human Mind*, 337–62.
94. Joseph Priestley, *An History of Early Opinions concerning Jesus Christ, Compiled from Original Writers; Proving that the Christian Church was at First Unitarian* (Birmingham: Pearson and Rollason, 1786), ix.
95. Joseph Priestley, *Early Opinions*, 9.
96. Joseph Priestley, *Early Opinions*, 11–17.
97. Joseph Priestley, *Early Opinions*, 84–85.
98. Joseph Priestley, *Early Opinions*, 22.
99. Joseph Priestley, *Early Opinions*, 57–60.
100. Joseph Priestley, *Early Opinions*, 71.
101. Joseph Priestley, *Early Opinions*, 327–32.
102. Joseph Priestley, *Early Opinions*, 385.
103. Joseph Priestley, *Early Opinions*, 383–84.
104. It must be acknowledged that there was no uniformity of opinion on the status of Christ, other than his being mortal and on a divine mission. As Zastoupil notes, "British Unitarians prided themselves on the theological heterogeneity of their congregations," not on forced uniformity of opinion. Lynn Zas-

toupil, "'Notorious and Convicted Mutilators': Rommohun Roy, Thomas Jefferson, and the Bible," *Journal of World History*, Vol. 20, No. 3, 2009, 425.

105. Joseph Priestley, *Early Opinions*, 73–79.

106. E.g., TJ to Sam Kercheval, 19 Jan. 1810, and TJ to Charles Thomson, 9 Jan. 1816.

107. Thomas Jefferson, *The Papers of Thomas Jefferson*, vol. 33, *17 February–30 April 1801*, ed. Barbara B. Oberg (Princeton: Princeton University Press, 2006), 342.

108. Constantin François de Volney, *The Ruins, or Meditations on the Revolutions of Empires* (Teddington, UK: The Echo Library: 2010), 21–22.

109. Constantin François de Volney, *Ruins*, 28 and 34–36.

110. Constantin François de Volney, *Ruins*, 38–42.

111. Constantin François de Volney, *Ruins*, 42–44.

112. Constantin François de Volney, *Ruins*, 47–50.

113. Constantin François de Volney, *Ruins*, 60–61.

114. Constantin François de Volney, *Ruins*, 63–64.

115. Constantin François de Volney, *Ruins*, 66–69.

116. Constantin François de Volney, *Ruins*, 70–72.

117. Constantin François de Volney, *Ruins*, 73.

118. Constantin François de Volney, *Ruins*, 75.

119. Constantin François de Volney, *Ruins*, 79–109.

120. Constantin François de Volney, *Ruins*, 141.

121. Constantin François de Volney, *Ruins*, 152.

122. Constantin François de Volney, *Ruins*, 154 and 162.

123. Constantin François de Volney, *Ruins*, 165–171.

124. Constantin François de Volney, *Ruins*, 174–94.

125. Constantin François de Volney, *Ruins*, 192.

126. M. Andrew Holowchak and Amy J. Barbee, "Why Have Jefferson Biographers Largely Overlooked His Love Affair with Laurence Sterne?" *History News Network*, 160587.

127. Laurence Sterne, *The Sermons of Mr. Yorick*, vol. 4 (London, 1776), 1–3.

128. Laurence Sterne, *Sermons*, Vol. 4, 11–20.

129. Laurence Sterne, *Sermons*, Vol. 4, 21–25.

130. Laurence Sterne, *Sermons*, Vol. 4, 153–63.

131. Laurence Sterne, *Sermons*, Vol. 4, 163–72.

132. TJ to Gen. Thomas Nelson, 21 Feb. 1781; TJ to Thomas Jefferson Grotian, 10 Jan. 1824; and TJ to Thomas Jefferson Smith, 21 Feb. 1825.

133. See Rev. Fernand Cabrol, "Introduction," *Great French Sermons from Bossuet, Bourdaloue, and Massillon*, ed. Rev. D. O'Mahony (London: Sands and Co., 1917), xiv–xv.

134. Rev. D. O'Mahony (ed.), *French Sermons*, 118–19.

135. Rev. D. O'Mahony (ed.), *French Sermons*, 119–20.

136. Rev. D. O'Mahony (ed.), *French Sermons*, 120–21.

137. E.g., TJ to John Adams, 1 Aug. 1816; TJ to Henry Dearborn, 17 Aug. 1821; TJ to John Adams, 1 June 1822; and TJ to Francis Adrian van der Kemp, 11 Jan. 1825.

138. Rev. Fernand Cabrol, "Introduction," *French Sermons*, ed. Rev. D. O'Mahony (London: Sands and Co., 1917), xv–xvi.

139. Rev. D. O'Mahony (ed.), *French Sermons*, 254–55.

140. Rev. D. O'Mahony (ed.), *French Sermons*, 257–58.

141. Following the lead of Plato, Aristotle, and the Stoics.

142. Rev. D. O'Mahony (ed.), *French Sermons*, 260–61.

143. Rev. D. O'Mahony (ed.), *French Sermons*, 271.

144. Rev. D. O'Mahony (ed.), *French Sermons*, 271–74.

145. Rev. D. O'Mahony (ed.), *French Sermons*, 275–76.

146. TJ to Thomas Jefferson Randolph, 24 Nov. 1808. See also TJ to Francis Wayles Eppes, 21 May 1816, and TJ to John Saunderson, 31 Aug. 1820.

147. E.g., TJ to Elbridge Gerry, 29 Mar. 1801; TJ to James Fishback, 27 Sept. 1809; TJ to William Canby, 18 Sept. 1813; TJ to John Adams, 22 Aug. 1813; TJ to Miles King, 26 Sept. 1814; TJ to George Logan, 12 Nov. 1816; TJ to John Adams, 11 Jan. 1817; and TJ to John Adams, 5 May 1817.

148. E.g., TJ John Hancock, 11 Oct 1776; TJ to Miles King, 26 Sept. 1814; TJ to Mrs. Samuel Harrison Smith, 6 Aug. 1816; TJ to George Logan, 12 Nov. 1816; and TJ to John Adams, 11 Jan. 1817.

149. TJ to James Fishback, 27 Sept. 1809.

150. Thomas Jefferson, First Inaugural Address, *Writings*, 494.

Chapter 5

1. Lord Kames, *Essays on the Principles of Morality and Natural Religion*, 2nd ed. (London, 1758), 12.
2. David Hume, "Of the Study of History," *Essays: Moral, Politcial, and Literary*, ed. Eugene F. Miller (Indianapolis: Liberty Fund, 1987), 565.
3. David Hume, "Of the Study of History," 567.
4. See M. Andrew Holowchak, *Thomas Jefferson's Philosophy of Education: A Utopian Dream* (London: Taylor & Francis, 2014), chap. 5.
5. Tacitus, *Annals*, III.27. *Complete Works of Tacitus*, trans. Alfred John Church and William Jackson Brodribb (New York: McGraw-Hill, [1864–1877] 1964).
6. Thomas Jefferson, "Bill for the More General Diffusion of Knowledge," *Thomas Jefferson: Writings*, ed. Merrill D. Peterson (New York: Library of America, 1984), 365.
7. Together they offer an account of the Roman Empire from the death of Augustus (14 A.D.) to the death of Domitian (96 A.D.). Much of what has been written is now lost.
8. Tacitus, *The Agricola and Germany of Tacitus*, trans. Alfred John Church and William Jackson Brodribb (London: MacMillan and Co., 1868)..
9. Irene Coltman Brown, "Tacitus and a Space for Freedom," *History Today*, Vol. 31, No. 4, 1981, 14.
10. Tacitus, *Complete Works of Tacitus*.
11. Irene Coltman Brown, "Tacitus and a Space for Freedom," *History Today*, Vol. 31, No. 4, 1981, 11–15.
12. TJ to Joseph Delaplaine, 12 Apr. 1817.
13. Thomas Jefferson, "Bill for Establishing a System of Public Education," in Roy J. Honeywell, *The Educational Work of Thomas Jefferson* (Cambridge: Harvard University Press, 1931), 237–38.
14. M. Andrew Holowchak, *Thomas Jefferson's Philosophy of Education: A Utopian Dream* (London: Taylor & Francis, 2014), chap. 4.
15. Thomas Jefferson, *Notes on Virginia*, ed. William Peden (Chapel Hill: University of North Carolina Press, 1954), 133.
16. Thomas Jefferson, *Notes on Virginia*, 147.
17. See also TJ too John Adams, 15 Aug. 1820.
18. See M. Andrew Holowchak, *Thomas Jefferson's Philosophy of Education*, chap. 4.
19. Plutarch, *The Parallel Lives*, vol. 3, trans. Bernadotte Perrin (Cambridge: Harvard University Press, [1916]).
20. Francois Jean Chastellux, *Travels in North-America, In the Years 1780–81–82*, vol. 1 (New York, 1828), 84–85. See TJ to John Adams, 5 May 1817.
21. "Only speak well of the dead."
22. TJ to Col. William Duane, 12 Aug. 1810.
23. See also TJ to John Adams, 25 Nov. 1816.
24. Roger P. Mellen, "Thomas Jefferson and the Origins of Newspaper Competition in Pre-Revolutionary Virginia," *Journalism History*, Vol. 35, No. 3, 2009, 152–56.
25. E.g., TJ to 29 Aug. 1791; TJ to George Hammond, 2 Feb. 1792; TJ to Edward Rutledge, 27 Dec. 1796; TJ to Samuel Smith, 22 Aug. 1798; TJ to Peregrine Fitzhugh, 23 Feb. 1798; TJ to Elbridge Gerry, 29 Mar. 1801; TJ to Gen. Thaddeus Kosciusko, 2 Apr. 1802; TJ to Marc Auguste Pictet, 5 Feb. 1803; TJ to Thomas Seymour, 11 Feb. 1807; TJ to John Norvell, 14 June 1807; TJ to James Madison, 19 Apr. 1809; TJ to James Madison, 19 Apr. 1809; TJ to David Howell, 15 Dec. 1810; TJ to John Adams, 21 Jan. 1812; TJ to Dr. Walter Jones, 2 Jan. 1814; TJ to James Monroe, 1 Jan. 1815; TJ to Mr. Maury, 15 June 1815; TJ to President James Monroe, 4 Feb. 1816; and TJ to Nathaniel Macon, 12 Jan. 1819.
26. TJ to George Washington, 9 Sept. 1792; Report to the Spanish Commissioners, 1793; TJ to Archibald Stuart, 14 May 1799; TJ to James Madison, 5 Feb. 1799; TJ to Thomas Cooper, 29 Nov. 1802; TJ to Thomas McKean, 19 Feb. 1803; Second Inaugural Address, 1805; TJ to William Wirt, 30 Mar. 1811; TJ to Monsieur Paganel, 15 Apr. 1811; and TJ to Charles Yancey, 6 Jan. 1816.
27. TJ to Archibald Stuart, 14 May 1799.
28. For more on Ebeling, see Gordon McNett Stewart, *The Literary Contributions of Christoph Daniel Ebeling* (Amsterdam: Rodopi, 1978).
29. Christoph Daniel Ebeling to TJ, 30 July 1795.
30. See also TJ to William Duane, 12 Aug. 1810.
31. David Hume, *The Letters of David Hume*, vol. 1, ed. J.Y.T. Greig (Oxford: Clarendon Press, 1954), 237.
32. Douglas Wilson, "Jefferson and Hume," *The William and Mary Quarterly*, Vol. 46, No. 1, 1989, 50–51.
33. For more, see Douglas Wilson, "Jefferson and Hume," *The William and Mary Quarterly*, 62.
34. Now called the "Virginia Records."

35. For more on Hening, see Kent C. Olson, "The Law Givers: Heroes of Virginia Statutory History," *Virginia Lawyer,* Vol. 60, 2011, 50–54.
36. Thomas Jefferson, *Notes on Virginia,* 147.
37. Thomas Jefferson, *Notes on Virginia,* 148.
38. Thomas Jefferson, *Notes on Virginia,* 147–48.
39. Sterne's manner of writing is loose and unstructured. The chapters of his *Sentimental Journey,* if they can be called chapters, comprise short, generally uneventful, episodes, whose merit is mostly that they are peppered with moral insights, democratic in nature— viz., accessible to all.
40. Lord Kames, *Principles of Morality and Natural Religion,* 12–13.
41. David Hume, "On the Study of History," 567.

Chapter 6

1. I grasp "scientific" here more flexibly and broadly, as did Jefferson, to include, for example, morality, architecture, invention, and military technology.
2. TJ to George F. Hopkins, 5 Sept. 1822.
3. See M. Andrew Holowchak, *Dutiful Correspondent: Philosophical Essays on Thomas Jefferson* (Lanham, MD: Rowman & Littlefield, 2012), 131–56.
4. Lucia Stanton, "Jefferson's People: Slavery at Monticello," *The Cambridge Companion to Thomas Jefferson,* Frank Shuffleton, ed. (New York: Cambridge University Press, 2009), 87.
5. Adams says, "Jefferson's frequent use of *virtue* and *virtuous,* watchwords of republican ideology, had far greater resonance than we now give them. Honest work and virtue are frequently linked to his vision of the ideal society. Moral and physical discipline would make Americans superior both to the benighted savage and to the indolent few in civilization's most advanced stages." William Howard Adams, *The Paris Years of Thomas Jefferson* (New Haven, CT: Yale University Press, 1997), 166.
6. TJ to Thaddeus Kościusko, 1810. To Henry Dearborn (22 June 1807), he says, "The field of knowledge is the common property of mankind, and any discoveries we can make in it will be for the benefit of yours and of every other nation, as well as our own." Cf. Franklin, who said that circumstances often require a scientist to give up science for political service. "Had Newton been Pilot but of a single common Ship, the finest of his Discoveries would scarce have excused or attoned for his abandoning the Helm one Hour in Time of Danger" (BF to Coldwallader Colden, 11 Oct. 1750). *The Papers of Benjamin Franklin, Vol. 4, July 1, 1750, through June 30, 1753,* ed. Leonard W. Labaree (New Haven: Yale University Press, 1961), 67–69.
7. Edward T. Martin, *Thomas Jefferson: Scientist* (New York: Henry Schuman, Inc., 1952), 216–17.
8. David Daggett, *Sun-Beams May Be Extracted from Cucumbers, But the Process Is Tedious* (New Haven, CT: Thomas Green and Son, 1799), 8–9.
9. Charles Brockden Brown, "Review of 'The Claims of Thomas Jefferson to the Presidency, Examined at the Bar of Christianity' (Philadelphia: Dickins, 1800), 361–62. [http://brockdenbrown.cah.ucf.edu/xtf2/view?docId=1800–11354.xml], accessed 14 Nov. 2011.
10. Washington Irving, *Knickerbocker's History of New York,* Book IV, Chapter I. http://www.gutenberg.org/files/13042/13042-h/13042-h.htm#I_CHAPTER_I, accessed 17 Nov. 2011.
11. Washington Irving, *Knickerbocker's History of New York,* Book IV, chapters 4 and 5.
12. Clement Clarke Moore, "Observations upon Certain Passages in Mr. Jefferson's Notes on Virginia, which Appear to Have a Tendency to Subvert Religion and Establish a False Philosophy" (New York, 1804), 5–6.
13. TJ to Charles F. Wells (3 Dec. 1809).
14. TJ to Benjamin Rush, 23 Sept. 1800.
15. Dumas Malone, *Jefferson & His Time, Vol. 3: Jefferson and the Ordeal of Liberty* (Boston: Little, Brown and Company, 1962), 418.
16. TJ to John Tyler, 28 June 1804.
17. George Tucker, *The Life of Thomas Jefferson, Third President of the United States,* vol. 2 (Philadelphia: Carey, Lea & Blanchard, 1837), 522.
18. TJ to Spencer Roane, 6 Sept. 1819.
19. TJ James Madison, 6 Sept. 1789 and Thomas Jefferson, Query XIII, *Notes on Virginia,* ed. William Peden (Chapel Hill: University of North Carolina Press, 1954), 120–21.
20. Richard K. Matthews, "The Radical Political Philosophy of Thomas Jefferson: An Essay in Retrieval," *Midwest Studies in Philosophy,* Vol. 28, No. 1, 2004, 48.
21. Dumas Malone, *Jefferson & His Time, Volume 6: The Sage of Monticello* (Charlottesville, VA: University of Virginia Press, 1981), 138. See also *Jefferson & His Time, Vol. 4: Jefferson the President, First Term, 1801–5* (Boston: Little, Brown & Company, 1970), 31.

22. Henry F. May, "The Enlightenment," *Thomas Jefferson: A Reference Biography*, ed. Merrill D. Peterson (New York: Charles Scribner's Sons, 1986), 52.
23. Gilbert Chinard, *Thomas Jefferson: The Apostle of Americanism* (Ann Arbor, MI: The University of Michigan Press, [1929] 1962), 132–35.
24. Philipp Ziesche, "Exporting American Revolutions: Gouverneur Morris, Thomas Jefferson, and the National Struggle for Universal Rights in Revolutionary France," *Journal of the Early Republic*, Vol. 26, No. 3, 2006: 442.
25. Adrienne Koch, *The Philosophy of Thomas Jefferson* (Gloucester, MA: Peter Smith, 1957), 132.
26. Otto Vossler, *Jefferson and the American Revolutionary Ideal*, C. Philippon and B. Wishy (trans.) (Lanham, MD: University Press of America, 1982), 85, 117, and 181–86.
27. See M. Andrew Holowchak, *Thomas Jefferson: Uncovering his Unique Philosophy and Vision* (Amherst, NY: Prometheus Books, 2014), chap. 2.
28. TJ to John Adams, 28 Oct. 1813.
29. TJ to Henry Lee, 8 May 1826.
30. John Locke, *Two Treatises on Government*, ed. Peter Laslett (New York: New American Library, 1965), II.ii.4.
31. TJ to John Adams, 15 Aug. 1820.
32. Thomas Jefferson, "First Inaugural Address," *Writings*, 492–93.
33. TJ to Samuel Kercheval, 12 July 1816.
34. See also TJ to Count de Moustier, 17 May 1788, TJ to Elbridge Gerry, 26 Jan. 1799, and TJ to William Green Munford, 18 June 1799.
35. Feb. 1826. Thomas Jefferson, *The Works of Thomas Jefferson*, vol. 12, ed. Paul Leicester Ford (New York: G.P. Putnam's Sons, 1904–5), 273.
36. TJ to Thomas Mann Randolph, 3 May 1798.
37. E.g., Conor Cruise O'Brien, "Thomas Jefferson: Radical and Racist," *Atlantic Monthly*, October 1996, 53–74, and Michael Hardt, "Jefferson and Democracy," *American Quarterly*, Vol. 59, No. 1, 58–65.
38. John Howe, "Republicanism," *Thomas Jefferson: A Reference Biography*, ed. Merrill D. Peterson (New York: Charles Scribner's Sons, 1986), 63.
39. Thomas Jefferson, "First Inaugural Address," *Thomas Jefferson: Writings*, ed. Merrill D. Peterson (New York: Library of America, 1984), 493.
40. TJ to Pierre Samuel Dupont de Nemours, 24 Apr. 1816.
41. See also TJ to Tench Coxe, 1 June 1795.
42. TJ to George Wythe, 13 Aug. 1786.
43. Alf Mapp, Jr., *Thomas Jefferson: America's Paradoxical Patriot* (Lanham, MD: Rowman & Littlefield, 1987), 141–42.
44. Dumas Malone, *Jefferson & His Time, Volume 1: Jefferson the Virginian* (Boston: Little, Brown and Company, 1948), 275.
45. Thomas Jefferson, Query XVII, *Notes on Virginia*, 159.
46. Thomas Jefferson, "A Bill for Establishing Religious Freedom," *Writings*, 346–47.
47. Thomas Jefferson, "A Bill for Establishing Religious Freedom," 347.
48. Thomas Jefferson, "A Bill for Establishing Religious Freedom," 348.

Chapter 7

1. See also, e.g., TJ John Hancock, 11 Oct 1776; TJ to Thomas Leiper, 21 Jan. 1809; TJ to James Fishback, 27 Sept. 1809; TJ to George Logan, 12 Nov. 1816; and TJ to Thomas Parker, 15 May 1819.
2. TJ to Ezra Stiles Ely, 25 June 1819.
3. Allen Jayne, *Thomas Jefferson's Declaration of Independence: Origins, Philosophy, & Theology* (Lexington: University of Kentucky Press, 1998), 151.
4. E.g., TJ to Thomas Leiper, 21 Jan. 1809; TJ to William Canby, 18 Sept. 1813; TJ to John Adams, 11 Jan. 1817; and TJ to Thomas Parker, 15 May 1819.
5. Owen notes that Jefferson's "primitive Christianity" aligns itself to "indifference to doctrinal questions." One wonders whether "indifference" is too tame and should not be supplanted by "disdain." J. Judd Owen, *American Political Science Review*, Vol. 101, No.3, 2007, 500. Luebke claims that Jefferson's anti-clericism was the response to the hostile clerical attacks, with his campaigned for the presidency. Fred C. Luebke, "The Origins of Thomas Jefferson's Anti-Clericism," *Church History*, Vol. 32, No. 3, 1963, 345.
6. TJ to Thomas B. Parker, 15 May 1819. Cf. Tocqueville: "A countless number of sects in the United States all have different forms of worship they offer the Creator but they all agree about the duties that men owe each other. Each sect adores God in its own particular way but all sects reach the same morality in the name of God." Alexis de Tocqueville, *Democracy in America*, trans. Gerald Bevan (New York: Penguin, 2003), 340.
7. David Hume, *Dialogues concerning Natural Religion*, ed. Richard H. Popkin (Indianapolis: Hackett Publishing, 1998), 82.
8. David Hume, *Dialogues concerning Natural Religion*, 83.

9. Allen Jayne, *Thomas Jefferson's Declaration of Independence*, 171.
10. Charles B. Sanford, "The Religious Beliefs of Thomas Jefferson," *Religion and Political Culture in Jefferson's Virginia*, ed. Garrett Ward Sheldon and Daniel Driesbach (Lanham, MD: Rowman & Littlefield, 2000), 66.
11. E.g., TJ to Benjamin Rush, 21 Apr. 1803; TJ to Sam Kercheval, 19 Jan. 1810; and TJ to John Adams, 12 Oct. 1813, and TJ to Dr. Benjamin Waterhouse, 26 June 1822.
12. TJ to Dr. Benjamin Waterhouse, 26 June 1822. See also TJ to Edward Dowse, 19 Apr. 1803; TJ to Benjamin Rush, 21 Apr. 1803; TJ to Joseph Priestley, 29 Jan. 1804; TJ James Fishback, 27 Sept. 1809; TJ to Sam Kercheval, 19 Jan. 1810; TJ to Charles Thomson, 9 Jan. 1816; TJ to Francis Adrian Van der Kemp, 25 Apr. 1816; TJ to William Short, 31 Oct. 1819; and TJ to George Thatcher, 26 Jan. 1824.
13. Arthur Scherr, "Thomas Jefferson versus the Historians: Christianity, Atheistic Morality, and the Afterlife," *Church History*, Vol. 83, No. 1, 2014, 86–89.
14. Johann N. Neem, "Beyond the Wall: Reinterpreting Jefferson's Danbury Address," *Journal of the Early Republic*, Vol. 27, 2007, 149.
15. Lord Kames, *Essays on the Principles of Morality and Natural Religion*, Second Edition (London, 1758), 265–75 and 298–309.
16. E.g., TJ to Adams, 26 May 1817 and 12 May 1820. Charles B. Sanford, *The Religious Life of Thomas Jefferson* (Charlottesville: The University of Virginia Press, 1984), 152.
17. Charles B. Sanford, "The Religious Beliefs of Thomas Jefferson," 82.
18. E.S. Gaustad, "Religion," *Thomas Jefferson: A Reference Biography*, ed. Merrill D. Peterson (New York: Charles Scribers' Sons, 1984), 290.
19. Eugene R. Sheridan, "Introduction," *Jefferson's Extracts from the Gospels*, ed. Dickinson W. Adams (Princeton: Princeton University Press, 1983), 40–41.
20. Paul K. Conkin, "The Religious Pilgrimage of Thomas Jefferson," *Jeffersonian Legacies:* (Charlottesville: University Press of Virginia, 1993), 20.
21. John Ragosta, "Thomas Jefferson's Religion and Religious Liberty," *Religious Freedom: Jefferson's Legacy, America's Creed* (Charlottesville: University of Virginia Press, 2013), 21–22.
22. TJ to John Adams, 15 Aug. 1820.
23. TJ to John Adams, 15 Aug. 1820. See also TJ to Thomas Cooper, 14 Aug. 1820.
24. Carl J. Richard, "A Dialogue with the Ancients: Thomas Jefferson and Classical Philosophy and History," *Journal of the Early Republic*, 9, 1989, 439.
25. Such observations, it seems, meant little to Adams, who wrote to Jefferson (8 Dec. 818): "I cannot conceive that such a Being could make such a Species as the human merely to live and die on this Earth. If I did not believe in a future State, I should believe in no God," and the universe would seem to be nothing more than a "swelling Pomp, a boyish Fire Work."
26. Taken from E.M. Halliday, *Understanding Thomas Jefferson* (New York: HarperCollins, 2001), 50–51.
27. Thomas Jefferson, *Literary Commonplace Book*, ed. Douglas L. Wilson (Princeton: Princeton University Press, 1989), §§14, 15, 42, 46, and 49.
28. Thomas Jefferson, *Literary Commonplace Book,* §52.
29. Jefferson here follows the lead of Middleton, Bolingbroke, and perhaps even David Hume.
30. For a reconstruction of *The Philosophy of Jesus*, see Dickinson W. Adams, "The Reconstruction of 'The Philosophy of Jesus,'" *Jefferson's Extracts from the Gospels* (Princeton: Princeton University Press, 1983), 45–47.
31. http://tjlibraries.monticello.org/tjandreading/timeline.html, accessed 14 Dec. 2013.
32. http://www.masshist.org/thomasjeffersonpapers/catalog1783/index.html, accessed 13 Dec. 2013.
33. This catalog is essential the same as that of 1789, though the number of books was increased to some 5,000.
34. Douglas L. Wilson, *Jefferson's Books* (Charlottesville: Thomas Jefferson Memorial Foundation, 1996), 43.
35. Thomas Jefferson, "Notes on Religion," 1776.
36. Joseph Priestley, *An History of Early Opinions concerning Jesus Christ, Compiled from Original Writers; Proving that the Christian Church was at First Unitarian* (Birmingham: Pearson and Rollason, 1786), 73–75.
37. Joseph Priestley, *Early Opinions concerning Jesus Christ*, 77–79.
38. Hall writes that the most prominent Unitarian of his time was William Ellery Channing, who preached the oneness and indivisibility of God; that Christ performed miracles, overcame death, and was the greatest son of God, but not a member of the godhead; that Paul was an inspired and important teacher; that miracles and immortality are genuine; and that the Apostles were sacred writers. Jefferson stated Paul and the Apostles were corruptors of Jesus's teachings, and denied

miracles and inspiration, thereby disallowing and special status to Christ, other than being a great reformist and moralist. Jefferson, thus, could not have been a Unitarian. J. Lesslie Hall, "The Religious Opinions of Thomas Jefferson," *The Sewanee Review,* Vol. 21, No. 2, 1913, 169–70.

39. See Merrill D. Peterson, *The Jefferson Image in the American Mind* (Charlottesville: University of Virginia Press, [1960] 1998), 303.

40. Onuf sensibly claims that Unitarianism for Jefferson was religious reform in keeping with his republican sentiments. "From Jefferson's perspective, Unitarianism did not represent an elite reaction to the evangelical surge, but rather the precocious fulfillment of its ultimate theological tendencies," which were democratic reforms of church hierarchies. Peter Onuf, *The Mind of Thomas Jefferson* (Charlottesville: University of Virginia Press, 2007), 157–59 and also 151.

41. Thomas Jefferson, *Notes on Virginia,* ed. William Peden (Chapel Hill: University of North Carolina Press, 1954), 160.

42. Thomas Jefferson, *Notes on Virginia,* 159.

43. Thomas Jefferson, "Notes of a Tour into the Southern Parts of France, &c., 3 March–10 June 1787," *The Papers of Thomas Jefferson,* Vol. 11, *1 January–6 August 1787,* ed. Julian P. Boyd (Princeton: Princeton University Press, 1955), 415–464.

44. Thomas Jefferson, *Notes on the State of Virginia,* ed. William Peden (Chapel Hill: University of North Carolina Press, 1954), 161.

45. Thomas Jefferson, *Notes on Virginia,* 158–59.

46. Thomas Jefferson, *Notes on Virginia,* 159.

47. Cf. Jefferson's notes on uniformity in "Jefferson's Outline of Argument in Support of His Resolutions, 11 October–9 December 1776," Thomas Jefferson, *The Papers of Thomas Jefferson,* vol. 1, *1760–1776,* ed. Julian P. Boyd (Princeton: Princeton University Press, 1950). 535–539.

48. Thomas Jefferson, *Notes on Virginia,* 159–60.

49. See also TJ to George Wythe, 13 Aug. 1786.

50. Alexis de Tocqueville, *Democracy in America,* 345.

51. Dumas Malone, *Jefferson and the Rights of Man* (Boston: Little, Brown and Company, 1951), 110.

52. Merrill D. Peterson, *Thomas Jefferson & the New Nation: A Biography* (Oxford University Press, 1970), 134.

53. Derek H. Davis, "Thomas Jefferson's Letter to the Danbury Baptist Association: The Meaning of the Famous 'Wall of Separation' Metaphor," *Thomas Jefferson and Philosophy: Essays on the Philosophical Cast of Jefferson's Writings,* ed. M. Andrew Holowchak (Lanham, MD: Lexington Books, 2013), chap. 5.

54. Robert L. Cord, "Mr. Jefferson's 'Nonabsolute' Wall of Separation between Church and State," *Religion and Political Culture in Jefferson's Virginia,* ed. Garrett Ward Sheldon and Daniel L. Dreisbach (Lanham, MD: Rowman & Littlefield, 2000), 167–88.

55. Daniel L. Dreisbach, "Religion and Legal Reforms in Revolutionary Virginia," *Religion and Political Culture in Jefferson's Virginia,* ed. Garrett Ward Sheldon and Daniel L. Dreisbach (Lanham, MD: Rowman & Littlefield, 2000), 194 and 206.

56. Johann Neem, "Beyond the Wall: Reinterpreting Jefferson's Danbury Address," *Journal of the Early Republic,* Vol. 27, 2007, 142.

57. Endorsed them not just because they were thought to be representative of the will of the people.

58. Thomas Jefferson, "Draft Constitution for the State of Virginia," *The Papers of Thomas Jefferson, Vol. 1, 1760–1776,* ed. Julian P. Boyd (Princeton: Princeton University Press, 1950), 337–347.

59. Thomas Jefferson, *Writings,* ed. Merrill D. Peterson (New York: Library of America, 1984), 702.

60. Thomas Jefferson, "Proclamation Inviting Mercenary Troops in the British Service to Desert, [2 February 1781]," *The Papers of Thomas Jefferson,* Vol. 4, *1 October 1780–24 February 1781,* ed. Julian P. Boyd (Princeton: Princeton University Press, 1951), 505–506.

61. "IV. Draft of a Model Treaty, 1784, *The Papers of Thomas Jefferson,* Vol. 7, *2 March 1784–25 February 1785,* ed. Julian P. Boyd (Princeton: Princeton University Press, 1953), 479–490.

62. Thomas Jefferson, *Notes on Virginia,* 147.

63. Galileo Galilei, *Discoveries and Opinions of Galileo* (New York: Anchor Books, 1957), 211–15.

64. Henry S. Randall, *The Life of Thomas Jefferson,* vol. 3 (New York, 1858), 672.

Chapter 8

1. Jennings L. Wagoner, Jr., *Jefferson and Education* (Chapel Hill: University of North Carolina Press, 2004), 18.

2. Roy J. Honeywell, *The Educational Work of Thomas Jefferson* (Cambridge: Harvard University Press, 1931), 9–10.

3. Wagoner states: "While they hoped that the general diffusion of knowledge would maximize happiness and assist able and deserving young men to attain positions of influence in society and government, they were in actuality much more concerned about the future of the nation than with the rise of individuals. These essayists, along with Jefferson, were searching for a system of education that would be suitable for coming generations of free and independent citizens, intent on maintaining a republican society. They sought educational arrangements that would unite Americans as a people and as an expanding union of republics bound together by ties of interest, affection, and mutual consent." Jennings L. Wagoner, Jr., *Jefferson and Education* (Chapel Hill: University of North Carolina Press, 2004), 51–52.

4. Darren Staloff, "The Politics of Pedagogy: Thomas Jefferson and the Education of a Democratic Citizenry," *The Cambridge Companion to Thomas Jefferson*, ed. Frank Shuffleton (Cambridge University Press, 2009), 128.

5. See also Roger D. Heslep, *Thomas Jefferson and Education* (New York: Random House, 1969), 50.

6. Thomas Jefferson, "Bill for the More General Diffusion of Knowledge," *Writings*, ed. Merrill D. Peterson (New York: Library of America, 1984), 371.

7. Thomas Jefferson, "Bill for Establishing a System of Public Education," in Roy J. Honeywell, *The Educational Work of Thomas Jefferson*, 238.

8. See also TJ to Joseph Priestley, 27 Jan. 1800.

9. Thomas Jefferson, *Notes on Virginia*, ed. William Peden (Chapel Hill: University of North Carolina Press, 1954), 147.

10. Thomas Jefferson, "Rockfish Gap Report," *Writings*, ed. Merrill D. Peterson (New York: Library of America, 1984), 459.

11. "Opinion on the French Treaties," 28 Apr. 1793. See also TJ to Dr. James Brown, 27 Oct. 1808, and TJ to John Colvin, 20 Sept. 1810.

12. See also TJ to Robert Skipwith, 3 Aug. 1771; TJ to James Madison, 20 Feb. 1784; TJ to Ebenezer Hazard, 18 Feb. 1791; TJ to John Norvell, 14 June 1807; TJ to Anne Randolph Bankhead, 8 Dec. 1808; TJ to Col. William Duane, 1810; TJ to Col. William Duane, 4 Apr. 1813; TJ to William Wirt, 1814; TJ to John Adams, 10 Aug. 1815; TJ to William Wirt, 12 Nov. 1816; TJ to John Adams, 5 May 1817; and TJ to William Short, 8 Jan. 1825.

13. Thomas Jefferson, *Notes on Virginia*, 147.

14. Thomas Jefferson, "Bill for the More General Diffusion of Knowledge," *Writings*, 365.

15. See also TJ to James Madison, 28 Aug. 1789; TJ to Noah Webster, 4 Dec. 1790; TJ to James Madison, 28 Aug. 1789; TJ to Thomas Mann Randolph, 30 May 1790; Report on Negotiation with Spain, 18 Mar. 1792; TJ to James Monroe, 7 Sept. 1797; TJ to Philip Norborne Nicholas, 7 Apr. 1800; TJ to Benjamin Galloway, 2 Feb. 1812; TJ to Joseph Priestley, 24 Apr. 1816; TJ to Dr. John Manners, 12 June 1817; and TJ to John Hambden Pleasants, 19 Apr. 1824.

16. See also TJ to George Washington, 4 Dec. 1788, and TJ to Richard Price, 8 Jan. 1789.

17. TJ to James Madison, 30 Jan. 1787; TJ to Abigail Adams, 22 Feb. 1787; and TJ to William S. Smith, 13 Nov. 1787.

18. Cf. Charron, who writes that a prince cannot be sure of political stability unless his advisors and officers are both men of ability and men of virtue. Pierre Charron, *Of Wisdom*, vol. 3, trans. George Stanhope (London: 1729), 1054.

19. Steele rightly notes that Jefferson's assessment of European gender reversal was "ultimately a condemnation of the artificial aristocracy." The drudgery of peasant women was contrary to nature. So too was the effeminacy of aristocratic men. Brian Steele, "Thomas Jefferson's Gender Frontier," *The Journal of American History*, June, 2008, 32–33.

20. TJ to Edmund Pendleton, 26 Aug. 1776.

21. E.g., TJ to George Ticknor, 25 Nov. 1817.

22. See also TJ to John Adams, 5 July 1814.

23. E.g., Thomas Jefferson, *Writings*, 459–60; TJ to Count Charles Van Gysbert, 13 Oct. 1785; Answers to Questions of M. de Meusnier, 24 Jan. 1786; TJ to Jean Pierre Brissot de Warville, 16 Aug. 1786; Extempore Thoughts and Doubts on Running over Bankrupt Bill, Dec. 1792; TJ to Thomas Digges, 19 June 1788; and TJ to P.S. Dupont de Nemours, 18 Jan. 1802.

24. Thomas Jefferson, *Writings*, 460–61.

25. See M. Andrew Holowchak, "The Paradox of Public Service: Jefferson, Education, and the Problem of Plato's Cave," *Studies in Philosophy and Education*, Vol. 32, No. 1, 2013, 73–86.

26. E.g., TJ to John Brazier, 24 Aug. 1819.

27. Thomas Jefferson, "Bill for the More General Diffusion of Knowledge," *Writings*, 365.

28. Thomas Jefferson, *Notes on Virginia*, 147.

29. Zuckert notes, "No special techniques of selection are necessary or desirable to bring

these men of talent and virtue into leadership positions." Free elections are sufficient. He overpasses, however, the role of education of the masses and the role of grammar schools in the education of those to be governors. Michael Zuckert, "Founder of the Natural Rights Republic," *Thomas Jefferson and the Politics of Nature*, ed. Thomas S. Engemen (Notre Dame: University of Notre Dame Press, 1998), 45.

Chapter 9

1. E.g., Peter S. Onuf, "The Scholar's Jefferson," *The William and Mary Quarterly*, Vol. 50, No. 4, 1993, 692, and Andrew Burstein, *The Inner Jefferson: Portrait of a Grieving Optimist* (Charlottesville: The University of Virginia Press, 1995), 148–49.
2. E.g., TJ to Martha Jefferson, 11 Dec. 1783; Peter Carr, 19 Aug. 1785; James Fishback, 27 Sept. 1809; and Thomas Law, 13 June 1814.
3. TJ to John Adams, 8 Apr. 1816. Smith concurs. "To the greater part of whose precepts there can be no other objection, except that honourable one, that they teach us to aim at a perfection altogether beyond the reach of human nature." Adam Smith, *The Theory of Moral Sentiments* (Indianapolis: Liberty Fund, 1984), 60.
4. A noteworthy exception is Adrienne Koch. Adrienne Koch, *The Philosophy of Thomas Jefferson* (New York: Columbia University Press, 1943), 4–7.
5. Seneca, whom he does not take to be a Stoic, is a "fine moralist, disfiguring his work at times with some Stoicisms, and affecting too much of antithesis and point, yet giving us on the whole a great deal of sound and practical morality."
6. Gilbert Chinard, *The Literary Bible of Thomas Jefferson: His Commonplace Book of Philosophers and Poets* (New York: Greenwood Press, Publishers, [1928] 1969), 6 and 16.
7. Karl Lehmann, *Thomas Jefferson: American Humanist* (Charlottesville, VA: The University Press of Virginia, [1965] 1994), 139–41.
8. Harold Hellenbrand, *The Unfinished Revolution: Education and Politics in the Thought of Thomas Jefferson* (Newark: University of Delaware Press, 1990), 63. Cicero, it is generally agreed today, was much drawn to Stoicism, but was no Stoic. He was an eclectic, who was, if anything, mostly drawn to Academic Skepticism of Plato's later Academy.
9. Harold Hellenbrand, *The Unfinished Revolution*, 49.
10. Andrew Burstein, "Jefferson and the Language of Friendship," *The Cambridge Companion to Thomas Jefferson*, ed. Frank Shuffleton (Cambridge University Press, 2009), 160.
11. Daryl Hale, "Thomas Jefferson: Sublime or Sublimated Philosopher?" *International Social Science Review*, Vol. 72, Nos. 3 & 4, 76.
12. Charles A. Miller, *Jefferson and Nature: An Interpretation* (Baltimore: The Johns Hopkins University Press, 1988), 98–101.
13. Much of the account of Stoicism is from my book, *The Stoics: A Guide for the Perplexed* (London: Continuum, 2008).
14. Diogenes Laertius, *Lives of the Eminent Philosophers*, vol. 2, trans. R.D. Hicks (Cambridge: Harvard University Press, [1925] 1991), X.87.
15. Diogenes Laertius, *Lives*, X.88.
16. See also Lord Kames, *Essays on the Principles of Morality and Natural Religion* (New York: Garland Publishing, 1976), 87–88.
17. Seneca, *Epistles*, vols. 1–3, trans. Richard M. Gummere (Cambridge: Harvard University Press, 2000–2002), CXXI.21.
18. Cicero, *On Ends*, trans. H. Rackham (Cambridge: Harvard University Press, 1994), III.62–66.
19. Seneca, *Epistles*, XCV.52–53.
20. As with spear-throwing, one's purpose is to have true aim, not necessarily to hit the target. Cicero, *On Ends*, III.vi.22.
21. Cicero, *On Ends*, III.20.
22. Seneca, *Benefits, Essays*, vols. 1–3, trans. John W. Basadore (Cambridge, MA: Harvard University Press, 1998–2001), III.xviii.2 and xxviii.1.
23. E.g., T.V. Smith, "Thomas Jefferson and the Perfectibility of Mankind," *Ethics*, Vol. 53, No. 4, 1943, 304; Horace Kallen, "The Arts and Thomas Jefferson," *Ethics*, 53, 1943, 278; Carl Becker, *The Declaration of Independence: A Study in the History of Political Ideas* (New York: Random House, 1958); Daniel Boorstin, *The Lost World of Thomas Jefferson* (New York: Henry Holt, 1948); Dumas Malone, *Jefferson in His Time*, vols. 1–6 (Boston: Little, Brown, 1948–81); Gordon Wood, *The Creation of the American Republic, 1776–1787* (Chapel Hill: The University of North Carolina Press, 1969); Merrill D. Peterson, *Thomas Jefferson and the New Nation* (New York: Oxford University Press, 1970); Joyce Appleby, "What Is Still American in the Political Philosophy of Thomas Jefferson?" *William and Mary Quarterly*, 39, 1982, 291–93 and 295–96; Jeffrey Leigh Sedgwick, "Jeffersonianism in the Progressive Era," *Reason and Republicanism: Thomas Jefferson's Legacy of Liberty*, ed. Gary L. McDowell and Sharon L. Noble (Lanham,

MD: Rowman & Littlefield Publishers, Inc.), 194–95; and Conor Cruise O'Brien, "Thomas Jefferson: Radical and Racist," *Atlantic Monthly*, October 1996, 53–74.

24. TJ to John Adams, 11 Apr. 1823.

25. TJ to Miles King, 26 Sept. 1814.

26. Adam Smith, *The Theory of Moral Sentiments*, ed. D.D. Raphael and A.L. Macfie (Indianapolis: Liberty Fund, 1984), 171.

27. Caleb Perry Patterson, *The Constitutional Principles of Thomas Jefferson* (Gloucester, MA: Peter Smith, 1953), 50.

28. Jefferson, "Opinion on the French Treaties," *Writings*, ed. Merrill D. Peterson (New York: Library of America, 1984), 423.

29. E.g., TJ to Joseph Priestley, 9 Apr. 1803; TJ to Benjamin Rush, Apr. 1803; and TJ to William Small, 31 Oct. 1819.

30. M. Andrew Holowchak, *The Stoics*, 49.

31. M. Andrew Holowchak, *The Stoics*, 75.

32. M. Andrew Holowchak, *The Stoics*, 217.

33. Literally, Zeus or an animal.

34. Addis says that Jefferson, because of his out-and-out materialism, was a committed pantheist who "continued to create and sustain the world moment by moment." How he arrives at this conclusion, which is consistent with Jefferson's always skimpy "accounts" of deity, he does not say. Cameron Addis, "The Jefferson Gospel: A Religious Education of Peace, Reason, and Morality," *Light and Liberty: Thomas Jefferson and the Power of Knowledge* (Charlottesville: University of Virginia Press, 2012), 105.

35. Seneca, *Epistles*, XX.2.

36. Epictetus, *Discourses*, IV.i.138–43.

37. Aurelius, *Meditations*, XI.15.

38. M. Andrew Holowchak, *The Stoics*, 54 and 58.

39. TJ to Peter Carr, 19 Aug. 1785. Cf. Adam Smith. *Theory of Moral Sentiments* (Indianapolis: Liberty Classics, 1969).

40. E.g., TJ to John Wayles Eppes, 17 Jan. 1810; TJ to John Adams, 5 July 1814; and Thomas Jefferson, "Prospectus," in A.L.C. Destutt de Tracy, *A Treatise on Political Economy, To which is Prefixed a Supplement to a Preceding Work on the Understanding or, Elements of Ideology*, trans. Thomas Jefferson (Georgetown, D.C., 1817), xv–xvii.

41. E.g., TJ to Judge John Tyler, 28 June 1804, and TJ to John Norvell, 14 June 1807.

42. Cf. Pierre Charron, *On Wisdom*, vol. 3, trans. George Stanhope (London, 1729), 1240, and Laurence Sterne, "The Parable of the Rich Man and Lazarus," *The Sermons of Mr. Yorick*, vol. 4 (London, 1776), 1–20.

43. M. Andrew Holowchak, *The Stoics*, 48.

44. E.g., TJ to James Madison, 28 Aug. 1789; TJ to Thomas Law, 13 June 1814; and TJ to Francis Gilmer, 7 June 1817.

45. TJ to President George Washington, 15 Dec. 1789. See also TJ to William Short, 12 Mar. 1790 and TJ to Marquis de Lafayette, 2 Apr. 1790.

46. Peterson says, "They came, most of them, to do him honor; hospitality was the custom of the country, and there was no nearby inn to which they could go." Merrill D. Peterson, *Thomas Jefferson and the New Nation: A Biography* (New York: Oxford University Press, 1970), 926. See also "Services to My Country," *Writings*, 702–4, and TJ to Thomas Law, 15 Jan. 1811.

47. See also TJ to Bishop James Madison, 31 Jan. 1800; TJ to John Adams, 12 Oct. 1813; and TJ to Benjamin Waterhouse, 26 June 1822.

48. TJ to Thomas Jefferson Gotian, 10 Jan. 1824; and TJ to Thomas Jefferson Smith, 21 Feb. 1825.

49. Thomas Jefferson, *Writings*, 423. See also Pierre Charron, *On Wisdom, Vol. 3*, trans. George Stanhope (London, 1729), 1456.

50. From Conor Cruise O'Brien, *The Long Affair: Thomas Jefferson and the French Revolution, 1785–1800* (Chicago: The University of Chicago Press, 1996), 36.

51. Robert Dawidoff, "Man of Letters," *Thomas Jefferson: A Reference Biography*, ed. Merrill D. Peterson (New York: Charles Scribner's Sons, 1986), 195.

52. Merrill D. Peterson, Thomas Jefferson and the New Nation, 309–10.

53. Epictetus, *Discourses*, III.v.14–8.

54. Epictetus, *Discourses*, IV.i.159–65. See also Aurelius' *Meditations*, VII.66.

55. See also Epictetus, *Handbook*, #33, and Plutarch, *Progress in Virtue*, 85b.

56. See also TJ to James Fishback, 27 Sept. 1809, and TJ to Thomas Law, 13 June 1814.

57. See also TJ to Francis Wayles Eppes, 21 May 1816; TJ to John Saunderson, 31 Aug. 1820; and TJ to Isaac Engelbrecht, 25 Feb. 1824.

58. Epictetus, The Discourses, I.xxviii.5–7.

59. E.g., Kames states: "By the [moral sense] certain actions are perceived to be right, and are approved accordingly as virtuous. The most illiterate rustic would [know] that to be honest or to be grateful is right; and there he would stop, never having thought of their useful tendency." Lord Kames, *Essays on the Principles of Morality and Natural Religion, Third Edition* (London, 1779), 76 and 92.

60. Epictetus, *Discourses*, II.xviii.1–5.

61. Epictetus, *Discourses*, III.xii.10–11.

62. See also TJ to Martha Jefferson Randolph, 17 July 1790. Johnstone writes: "[Jeffer-

son] possessed an amiability that proceeded from a basic optimism toward his fellow human beings and a desire to promote harmony in both his public and his private life. His advice to others was 'to take things always by the smooth handle.' A keen intelligence, a penchant for conciliation, a ready deference to others, good humor, politeness, a talent for the pen, a skill at conversation, and personal honesty and integrity provided him a formidable array of persuasive gifts." Robert M. Johnstone, Jr., "The Presidency," *Thomas Jefferson: A Reference Biography,* ed. Merrill D. Peterson (New York: Charles Scribner's Sons, 1986), 353. Dumas Malone states, "[Jefferson] abhorred controversy, ... preferred to work behind the scenes, and ... lacked the personal aggressiveness commonly associated with political leadership." Dumas Malone, *Thomas Jefferson: A Brief Biography* (Thomas Jefferson Memorial Foundation, 2001), 27.

63. E.g., Howard Temperly, "Jefferson and Slavery: A Study in Moral Philosophy," *Reason and Republicanism: Thomas Jefferson's Legacy of Liberty,* ed. Gary L. McDowell and Sharon L. Noble (Lanham, MD: Rowman & Littlefield Publishers, Inc., 1997), 86 and 89–90, and Robert Dawidoff, "The Jeffersonian Option," *Political Theory,* Vol. 21, No. 3, 1993, 438.

64. E.g., Leonard W. Levy, "Civil Liberties," *Thomas Jefferson: A Reference Biography,* ed. Merrill D. Peterson (New York: Charles Scribner's Sons, 1986), 331–47.

65. E.g., TJ to Judge John Tyler, 28 June 1804; TJ to James Sullivan, 21 May 1805; TJ to DeWitt Clinton, 24 May 1807; and TJ to William A. Burwell, 22 Nov. 1808.

66. Epictetus, *Discourses,* I.19–23.

67. E.g., TJ to Peter Carr, 19 Aug. 1785, TJ to Peter Carr, 10 Aug. 1787, and TJ to Martha Jefferson, 28 Mar. 1787.

68. TJ to William Ludlow, 6 Sept. 1824. For full discussion of the implications of this passage, see M. Andrew Holowchak, "Differences of Circumstance, Differences of Fact: Jefferson Medialist View of History," *American Studies in Scandanavia* (forthcoming).

69. Seneca, *Epistles,* XXII.12.

70. This can also mean "to prevent."

71. Seneca, *Epistles,* XVIII.11.

72. Aurelius, *Meditations,* VIII.15 and 20.

73. Seneca, *Epistles,* XCI.

74. Seneca, *Epistles,* CVIII.27, and Aurelius, *Mediations,* II.1.

75. Seneca, *Epistles,* CI.7–8.

76. Part of the mission of the American Philosophical Society at the time.

77. Aurelius, *Meditations,* V.16 and III.4.

78. Thomas Jefferson, *Writings,* 702–4.

79. Cf. Epictetus, *Handbook,* #43.

80. Epictetus, *Handbook,* #15.

81. James A. Bear, Jr., *Jefferson at Monticello: Recollections of a Monticello Slave and of a Monticello Overseer* (Charlottesville: University of Virginia Press, 1967), 71.

82. James A. Bear, Jr., *Jefferson at Monticello,* 84.

83. William D. Gould, "The Religious Opinions of Thomas Jefferson," *Mississippi Valley Historical Review,* Vol. 20, No. 2, 1933, 204–5.

84. Herbert W. Schneider, "The Enlightenment in Thomas Jefferson," *Ethics,* Vol. 53, No. 4, 1943, 251.

85. Henry F. May, "The Enlightenment," *Thomas Jefferson: A Reference Biography,* ed. Merrill D. Peterson (New York: Charles Scribner's Sons, 1986), 49 and 58.

86. TJ to John Adams, 8 Apr. 1816 and 18 Dec. 1825.

87. Seneca, *Letter to Marcia,* XVI.5.

Bibliography

Adams, Dickinson W., "The Reconstruction of 'The Philosophy of Jesus,'" *Jefferson's Extracts from the Gospels* (Princeton: Princeton University Press, 1983).
Adams, John, and Abigail Adams, *The Book of Abigail and John: Selected Letters of the Adams Family, 1762–1784,* eds. Lyman Butterfield and Mark Friedlaender (Northeastern University Press, 2002).
Adams, William Howard, *The Paris Years of Thomas Jefferson* (New Haven: Yale University Press, 1997).
Addis, Cameron, "The Jefferson Gospel: A Religious Education of Peace, Reason, and Morality," *Light and Liberty: Thomas Jefferson and the Power of Knowledge* (Charlottesville: University of Virginia Press, 2012), 96–115.
Aiken, John, "Biographical Account of the Author of These Volumes," xiv-xv. William Enfield, *Sermons on Practical Subjects* (London, 1799).
Appleby, Joyce, "What Is Still American in the Political Philosophy of Thomas Jefferson?" *William and Mary Quarterly,* 39, 1982, 287–309.
Aristotle, *On the Soul,* trans. W.S. Hett (Cambridge: Harvard University Press, 1957).
Bear, James A., Jr., *Jefferson at Monticello: Recollections of a Monticello Slave and of a Monticello Overseer* (Charlottesville: University of Virginia Press, 1967).
Becker, Carl, *The Declaration of Independence: A Study in the History of Political Ideas* (New York: Random House, 1958).
Bernstein, R.B., *Thomas Jefferson* (New York: Oxford University Press, 2003).
Boorstin, Daniel, *The Lost World of Thomas Jefferson* (New York: Henry Holt, 1948).
Brown, Charles Brockden, "Review of 'The Claims of Thomas Jefferson to the Presidency, Examined at the Bar of Christianity' (Philadelphia: Dickins, 1800), 361–62. [http://brockdenbrown.cah.ucf.edu/xtf2/view?docId=1800-11354.xml], accessed 14 Nov. 2011.
Brown, Irene Coltman, "Tacitus and a Space for Freedom," *History Today,* Vol. 31, No. 4, 1981, http://www.historytoday.com/irene-brown/tacitus-and-space-freedom, accessed 12 August 12, 2016.
Burke, Edmund, *A Philosophical Enquiry into the Origin of Our Ideas of the Sublime and Beautiful* (London, 1757).
Burstein, Andrew, *The Inner Jefferson* (Charlottesville: University of Virginia Press, 1995).
Burstein, Andrew, "Jefferson and the Language of Friendship," *The Cambridge Companion to Thomas Jefferson,* ed. Frank Shuffleton (Cambridge University Press, 2009).
Cabrol, Rev. Fernand, "Introduction," *Great French Sermons from Bossuet, Bourdaloue, and Massillon,* ed. Rev. D. O'Mahony (London: Sands and Co., 1917).
Charron, Pierre, *Of Wisdom, Vols. 1–3,* trans. George Stanhope (London: 1729).
Chastellux, Francois Jean, *Travels in North-America, In the Years 1780–81–82,* vol. 1 (New York, 1828).

Chinard, Gilbert, *The Literary Bible of Thomas Jefferson: His Commonplace Book of Philosophers and Poets* (New York: Greenwood Press, Publishers, [1928] 1969).
Chinard, Gilbert, *Thomas Jefferson: The Apostle of Americanism* (Ann Arbor: University of Michigan Press, [1929] 1962).
Cicero, *On Duties*, trans. Walter Miller (Cambridge: Harvard University Press, [1913] 2001).
Cicero, *On Ends*, trans. H. Rackham (Cambridge: Harvard University Press, 1994).
Cicero, *De Officiis*, trans. Walter Miller (Cambridge: Harvard University Press, 2001).
Cicero, *Selected Works* (Roslyn, NY: Walter J. Black, Inc., 1948).
Cicero, *De Senectute*, trans. William Armistead Falconer (Cambridge: Cambridge University Press, [1923] 1992).
Cicero, *Tusculan Disputations*, trans. J.E. King (Cambridge: Harvard University Press, [1927] 1945).
Cohen, Morris L., "Thomas Jefferson Recommends a Course of Law Study," *119 University of Pennsylvania Law Review*, 823, 1971.
Cohen, William, "Thomas Jefferson and the Problem of Slavery," *Journal of American History* 56, No. 3 (1969): 506–25.
Condorcet, *Outlines of an Historical View of the Progress of the Human Mind: Being a Posthumous Work of the Late M. de Condorcet* (London: 1795).
Conkin, Paul K., "The Religious Pilgrimage of Thomas Jefferson," *Jeffersonian Legacies:* (Charlottesville: University Press of Virginia, 1993), 1–16.
Cord, Robert L., "Mr. Jefferson's 'Nonabsolute' Wall of Separation between Church and State," *Religion and Political Culture in Jefferson's Virginia*, ed. Garrett Ward Sheldon and Daniel L. Dreisbach (Lanham, MD: Rowman & Littlefield, 2000), 167–88.
Daggett, David, *Sun-Beams May Be Extracted from Cucumbers, But the Process Is Tedious* (New Haven, CT: Thomas Green and Son, 1799).
Davis, Derek H., "Thomas Jefferson's Letter to the Danbury Baptist Association: The Meaning of the Famous 'Wall of Separation' Metaphor," *Thomas Jefferson and Philosophy: Essays on the Philosophical Cast of Jefferson's Writings*, ed. M. Andrew Holowchak (Lanham, MD: Lexington Books, 2013), 79–90.
Dawidoff, Robert, "The Jeffersonian Option," *Political Theory*, Vol., 21, No. 3, 1993, 434–52.
Dawidoff, Robert, "Man of Letters," *Thomas Jefferson: A Reference Biography*, ed. Merrill D. Peterson (New York: Charles Scribner's Sons, 1986).
Diogenes Laertius, *Lives of the Eminent Philosophers*, vol. 2, trans. R.D. Hicks (Cambridge: Harvard University Press, [1925] 1991).
Dreisbach, Daniel L., "Religion and Legal Reforms in Revolutionary Virginia," *Religion and Political Culture in Jefferson's Virginia*, ed. Garrett Ward Sheldon and Daniel L. Dreisbach (Lanham, MD: Rowman & Littlefield, 2000), 189–218.
Ellis, Joseph, *American Sphinx: The Character of Thomas Jefferson* (New York: Alfred A. Knopf, 1997).
Enfield, William, *The History of Philosophy*, Vols. 1–2 (London: 1791).
Epictetus, *The Encheiridion*, trans. W.A. Oldfather (Cambridge: Harvard University Press, [1928] 2000).
Franklin, Benjamin, *The Papers of Benjamin Franklin, Vol. 4, July 1, 1750, through June 30, 1753*, ed. Leonard W. Labaree (New Haven: Yale University Press, 1961).
Galilei, Galileo, *Discoveries and Opinions of Galileo* (New York: Anchor Books, 1957).
Gaustad, E.S., "Religion," *Thomas Jefferson: A Reference Biography*, ed. Merrill D. Peterson (New York: Charles Scribers' Sons, 1984).
Gould, G.P., "Introduction," in Cicero, *On Duties*, trans. Walter Miller (Cambridge: Harvard University Press, 1913] 2001).
Gould, William D., "The Religious Opinions of Thomas Jefferson," *Mississippi Valley Historical Review*, Vol. 20, No. 2, 1933, 164–76.
Haines, C.R., "Introduction," in *Marcus Aurelius*, trans. C.R. Haines (Cambridge: Harvard University Press, [1916] 1999).

Hale, Daryl, "Thomas Jefferson; Sublime or Sublimated Philosopher?" *International Social Science Review*, Vol. 72, Nos. 3 & 4, 2001, 75–83.
Hall, J. Lesslie, "The Religious Opinions of Thomas Jefferson," *The Sewanee Review*, Vol. 21, No. 2, 1913, 164–76.
Halliday, E.M., *Understanding Thomas Jefferson* (New York: HarperCollins, 2001).
Hardt, Michael, "Jefferson and Democracy," *American Quarterly*, Vol. 59, No. 1, 41–78.
Hellenbrand, Harold, *The Unfinished Revolution: Education and Politics in the Thought of Thomas Jefferson* (Newark: University of Delaware Press, 1990).
Helo, Ari, *Thomas Jefferson's Ethics and the Politics of Human Progress* (Cambridge: Cambridge University Press, 2014).
Helo, Ari, and Peter Onuf, "Jefferson, Morality, and the Problem of Slavery," *William and Mary Quarterly*, Vol. 60, No. 3, 2003: 583–614.
Heslep, Roger D., *Thomas Jefferson and Education* (New York: Random House, 1969).
Hogarth, William, *Analysis of Beauty, Written with a View of Fixing the Fluctuating Ideas of Taste* (London: J. Reeves, 1753).
Holowchak, M. Andrew, "Differences of Circumstance, Differences of Fact: Jefferson Medialist View of History," *American Studies in Scandanavia*, Vol. 47, No. 1, 2015: 3–21.
Holowchak, M. Andrew, *Framing a Legend: Exposing the Distorted History of Thomas Jefferson and Sally Hemings* (Amherst, NY: Prometheus Books, 2013).
Holowchak, M. Andrew, *Happiness and Greek Ethical Thought* (London: Continuum, 2004).
Holowchak, M. Andrew, "Jefferson's Moral Agrarianism: Poetic Fiction or Moral Vision?" *Agriculture and Human Values*, Vol. 28, 2011, 497–506.Holowchak, M. Andrew, *Dutiful Correspondent: Philosophical Essays on Thomas Jefferson* (Lanham, MD: Rowman & Littlefield, 2012).
Holowchak, M. Andrew, "Jefferson's Platonic Republicanism," *Polis*, Vol. 31, No. 2, 2014: 369–86.
Holowchak, M. Andrew, "The Paradox of Public Service: Jefferson, Education, and the Problem of Plato's Cave," *Studies in Philosophy and Education*, Vol. 32, No. 1, 2013, 73–86.
Holowchak, M. Andrew, "The Reluctant Politician: Thomas Jefferson's Debt to Epicurus," *Eighteenth-Century Studies*, Vol. 45, No. 2, 2012, 277–97.
Holowchak, M. Andrew, *The Stoics: A Guide for the Perplexed* (London: Continuum, 2008).
Holowchak, M. Andrew, *Thomas Jefferson: Uncovering His Unique Philosophy and Vision* (Amherst, NY: Prometheus Books, 2014).
Holowchak, M. Andrew, *Thomas Jefferson's Philosophy of Education: A Utopian Dream* (London: Taylor & Francis, 2014).
Holowchak, M. Andrew, and Amy J. Barbee, "Why Have Jefferson Biographers Largely Overlooked His Love Affair with Laurence Sterne?" *History News Network*, 160587.
Holowchak, M. Andrew, and Brian Dotts (eds.), *Thomas Jefferson: The Man Behind the Myths* (Jefferson, NC: McFarland, 2016).
Home, Henry, *Elements of Criticism*, 5th ed. (Dublin: Charles Ingham, 1772).
Home, Henry (Lord Kames), *Essays on the Principles of Morality and Natural Religion*, 2nd ed. (London, 1758).
Honeywell, Roy J., *The Educational Work of Thomas Jefferson* (Cambridge: Harvard University Press, 1931).
Howe, John, "Republicanism," *Thomas Jefferson: A Reference Biography*, ed. Merrill D. Peterson (New York: Charles Scribner's Sons, 1986), 59–80.
Hume, David, *Dialogues concerning Natural Religion*, ed. Richard H. Popkin (Indianapolis: Hackett Publishing, 1998).
Hume, David, *An Enquiry concerning the Principles of Morals*, ed. J.B. Schneewind (Indianapolis: Hackett Publishing Company, 1983).
Hume, David, *Essays: Moral, Political, and Literary*, ed. Eugene F. Miller (Indianapolis: Liberty Fund, 1987).

Hume, David, *The History of England, From the Invasion of Julius Caesar to the Revolution in 1688*, vol. 6 (Indianapolis: Liberty Classics, 1983), 513.
Hume, David, *The Letters of David Hume*, vol. 1, ed. J.Y.T. Greig (Oxford: Clarendon Press, 1954).
Hutcheson, Francis, A Short Introduction to Moral Philosophy in Three Books; Containing the Elements of Ethicks and the Law of Nature, ed. 2 (Glasgow: 1753).
Irving, Washington, *Knickerbocker's History of New York*, Book IV, Chapter I. http://www.gutenberg.org/files/13042/13042-h/13042-h.htm#I_CHAPTER_I, accessed 17 Nov. 2011.
Jayne, Allen, *Thomas Jefferson's Declaration of Independence: Origins, Philosophy, & Theology* (Lexington: University of Kentucky Press, 1998).
Jefferson, Thomas, *Jefferson's Literary Commonplace Book*, ed. Douglas L. Wilson (Princeton: Princeton University Press, 1987).
Jefferson, Thomas, *Notes on Virginia*, ed. William Peden (Chapel Hill: University of North Carolina Press, 1954).
Jefferson, Thomas, *The Papers of Thomas Jefferson*, 42 Vols. (to date), ed. Julian Boyd et al. (Princeton: Princeton University Press, 1950–).
Jefferson, Thomas, *The Works of Thomas Jefferson, ed. Paul Leicester Ford, 12 Vols. (New York: Putnam, 1902).*
Jefferson, Thomas, *The Writings of Thomas Jefferson: Being his Autobiography, Correspondence, Reports, Messages, Addresses, and Other Writings, Official and Private: Published by the Order of the Joint Committee of Congress on the Library, from the Original Manuscripts, Deposited in the Department of State*, 9 Vols., ed. Henry Augustine Washington (Washington: Taylor & Maury, 1853–4).
Jefferson, Thomas, The Writings of Thomas Jefferson, Definitive Edition, 20 Vols., ed. Andrew Adgate Lipscomb and Albert Ellery Bergh (Washington: Thomas Jefferson Memorial Association, 1907).
Johnstone, Robert M., Jr., "The Presidency," *Thomas Jefferson: A Reference Biography*, ed. Merrill D. Peterson (New York: Charles Scribner's Sons, 1986), 349–68.
Jordan, Winthrop D., *White over Black: American Attitudes toward the Negro, 1550–1812* (Baltimore: Penguin Books, 1969).
Kallen, Horace, "The Arts and Thomas Jefferson," *Ethics*, 53, 1943, 269–83.
Koch, Adrianne, *The Philosophy of Thomas Jefferson* (Gloucester, MS: Peter Smith, 1957).
Lehmann, Karl, *Thomas Jefferson: American Humanist* (Charlottesville: University Press of Virginia, [1965] 1994).
Livingston, Donald, *Philosophical Melancholy and Delirium* (Chicago: University of Chicago Press, 1998).
Locke, John, *Two Treatises on Government*, ed. Peter Laslett (New York: New American Library, 1965).
Long, George, "The Philosophy of Antoninus," in *The Thoughts of the Emperor M. Aurelius Antoninus*, trans. George Long (New York: G.P. Putnam's Sons, 1990), 27–62.
Luebke, Fred C., "The Origins of Thomas Jefferson's Anti-Clericism," *Church History*, Vol. 32, No. 3, 1963, 344–56.
Malone, Dumas, *Jefferson & His Time, Volume 1: Jefferson the Virginian* (Boston: Little, Brown and Company, 1948).
Malone, Dumas, *Jefferson & His Time, Volume 2: Jefferson and the Rights of Man* (Boston: Little, Brown and Company, 1951).
Malone, Dumas, *Jefferson & His Time, Volume 4: Jefferson the President, First Term, 1801–5* (Boston: Little, Brown & Company, 1970).
Malone, Dumas, *Jefferson & His Time, Volume 6: The Sage of Monticello* (Charlottesville: University of Virginia Press, 1981).
Malone, Dumas, *Thomas Jefferson: A Brief Biography* (Thomas Jefferson Memorial Foundation, 2001).
Mapp, Alf, Jr., *Thomas Jefferson: America's Paradoxical Patriot* (Lanham, MD: Rowman & Littlefield, 1987).

Marcus Aurelius, *The Meditations*, trans. G.M.A. Grube (Indianapolis: Hackett Publishing Company, 1983).
Martin, Edward T., *Thomas Jefferson: Scientist* (New York: Henry Schuman, Inc., 1952).
Matthews, Richard K., "The Radical Political Philosophy of Thomas Jefferson: An Essay in Retrieval," *Midwest Studies in Philosophy*, Vol. 28, No. 1, 2004: 37–57.
May, Henry F., "The Enlightenment," *Thomas Jefferson: A Reference Biography*, ed. Merrill D. Peterson (New York: Charles Scribner's Sons, 1986), 47–58.
Mellen, Roger P., "Thomas Jefferson and the Origins of Newspaper Competition in Pre-Revolutionary Virginia," *Journalism History*, Vol. 35, No. 3, 2009, 151–61.
Mercier, Louis-Sebastien, *Memoirs of the Year Two Thousand Five Hundred* (Philadelphia: Thomas Dobson, 1795).
Miller, Charles A., *Jefferson and Nature: An Interpretation* (Baltimore: Johns Hopkins University Press, 1988).
Moore, Clement Clarke, *Observations upon Certain Passages in Mr. Jefferson's Notes on Virginia, which Appear to Have a Tendency to Subvert Religion and Establish a False Philosophy* (New York, 1804).
Neem, Johann N., "Beyond the Wall: Reinterpreting Jefferson's Danbury Address," *Journal of the Early Republic*, Vol. 27, 2007, 139–54.
Neem, Johann N., "To Diffuse Knowledge More Generally through the Mass of People," *Light and Liberty: Thomas Jefferson and the Power of Knowledge* ed. Robert M.S. McDonald (Charlottesville: University of Virginia Press, 2012), 47–74.
O'Brien, Conor Cruise, *The Long Affair: Thomas Jefferson and the French Revolution, 1785–1800* (Chicago: University of Chicago Press, 1996).
O'Brien, Conor Cruise, "Thomas Jefferson: Radical and Racist," *Atlantic Monthly*, October 1996, 53–74.
Oldfather, W.A., "Introduction," in Epictetus, *The Discourses as Reported by Arrian, Books I–II*, trans. W.A. Oldfather (Cambridge: Harvard University Press, [1925] 2000).
Olson, Kent C., "The Law Givers: Heroes of Virginia Statutory History," *Virginia Lawyer*, Vol. 60, 2011, 50–54.
Onuf, Peter S., *The Mind of Thomas Jefferson* (Charlottesville: University of Virginia Press, 2007).
Onuf, Peter S., "The Scholar's Jefferson," *The William and Mary Quarterly*, Vol. 50, No. 4, 1993: 671–99.
Owen, J. Judd, "The Struggle between 'Religion and Nonreligion," *American Political Science Review*, Vol. 101, No.3, 2007, 493–503.
Patterson, Caleb Perry, *The Constitutional Principles of Thomas Jefferson* (Gloucester, MA: Peter Smith, 1953).
Peterson, Merrill D., *The Jefferson Image in the American Mind* (Charlottesville: University of Virginia Press, 1998).
Peterson, Merrill D., *Thomas Jefferson & the New Nation: A Biography* (Oxford University Press, 1970).
Plato, *The Republic of Plato*, ed. James Adam (Cambridge: Cambridge University Press, 1965).
Plato, *Symposium*, trans. Alexander Nehamas and Paul Woodruff (Indianapolis: Hackett Publishing Company, 1989).
Plutarch, *The Parallel Lives*, vol. 3, trans. Bernadotte Perrin (Cambridge: Harvard University Press, [1916]).
Priestley, Joseph, *An History of Early Opinions concerning Jesus Christ, Compiled from Original Writers; Proving that the Christian Church was at First Unitarian* (Birmingham: Pearson and Rollason, 1786).
Quinby, Lee, "Thomas Jefferson: The Virtue of Aesthetics and the Aesthetics of Virtue," *The American Historical Review*, Vol. 87, No. 2, 1982, 337–56.
Ragosta, John, *Religious Freedom: Jefferson's Legacy, America's Creed* (Charlottesville: University of Virginia Press, 2013).
Randall, Henry S., *The Life of Thomas Jefferson*, vol. 3 (New York, 1858).

Raubitschek, Isabelle K., and Antony E., "Letter on the Composition of the Republic," *Selected Works of Cicero* (Roslyn, NY: Walter J. Black, 1948).
Richard, Carl J., "A Dialogue with the Ancients: Thomas Jefferson and Classical Philosophy and History," *Journal of the Early Republic*, 9, 1989, 431–55.
Risjord, Norman K., *Thomas Jefferson* (Lanham, MD: Rowman & Littlefield Publishers, Inc., 2002).
Sanford, Charles B., "The Religious Beliefs of Thomas Jefferson," *Religion and Political Culture in Jefferson's Virginia*, ed. Garrett Ward Sheldon and Daniel Driesbach (Lanham, MD: Rowman & Littlefield, 2000).
Scherr, Arthur, "Thomas Jefferson versus the Historians: Christianity, Atheistic Morality, and the Afterlife," *Church History*, Vol. 83, No. 1, 2014, 60–109.
Schneider, Herbert W., "The Enlightenment in Thomas Jefferson," *Ethics*, Vol. 53, No. 4, 1943, 246–54.
Sedgwick, Jeffrey Leigh, "Jeffersonianism in the Progressive Era," *Reason and Republicanism: Thomas Jefferson's Legacy of Liberty*, ed. Gary L. McDowell and Sharon L. Noble (Lanham, MD: Rowman & Littlefield Publishers, Inc.), 189–204.
Seneca, *Epistles*, vols. 1–3, trans. Richard M. Gummere (Cambridge: Harvard University Press, 2000–2002).
Seneca, *Epistles*, vol. 2, trans. Richard M Gummere (Cambridge: Harvard University Press [1920] 2001).
Seneca, *Seneca: Moral Essays*, vols. 1–3, trans. John W. Basadore (Cambridge: Harvard University Press [1928–35] 1998–2001).
Sheridan, Eugene R., "Introduction," *Jefferson's Extracts from the Gospels*, ed. Dickinson W. Adams (Princeton: Princeton University Press, 1983).
Smith, Adam, *The Theory of Moral Sentiments* (Indianapolis: Liberty Fund, 1984).
Smith, T.V., "Thomas Jefferson and the Perfectibility of Mankind," *Ethics*, Vol. 53, No. 4, 1943, 293–310.
Staloff, Darren, "The Politics of Pedagogy: Thomas Jefferson and the Education of a Democratic Citizenry," *The Cambridge Companion to Thomas Jefferson*, ed. Frank Shuffleton (Cambridge University Press, 2009), 127–42.
Stanton, Lucia, "Jefferson's People: Slavery at Monticello," *The Cambridge Companion to Thomas Jefferson*, Frank Shuffleton, ed. (New York: Cambridge University Press, 2009).
Steele, Brian, "Thomas Jefferson's Gender Frontier," *The Journal of American History*, June, 2008, 17–42.
Sterne, Laurence, *The Life and Opinions of Tristram Shandy, Gentleman* (New York: Penguin Books, [1759–67] 2003).
Sterne, Laurence, *The Sermons of Mr. Yorick* (London: 1776).
Stewart, Gordon McNett, *The Literary Contributions of Christoph Daniel Ebeling* (Amsterdam: Rodopi, 1978).
Tacitus, *The Agricola and Germany of Tacitus*, trans. Alfred John Church and William Jackson Brodribb (London: Macmillan and Co., 1868).
Tacitus, *Annals*, III.27. *Complete Works of Tacitus*, trans. Alfred John Church and William Jackson Brodribb (New York: McGraw-Hill, [1864–1877] 1964).
Temperly, Howard, "Jefferson and Slavery: A Study in Moral Philosophy," *Reason and Republicanism: Thomas Jefferson's Legacy of Liberty*, ed. Gary L. McDowell and Sharon L. Noble (Lanham, MD: Rowman & Littlefield, 1997), 85–99.
Tocqueville, Alexis de, *Democracy in America*, trans. Gerald Bevan (New York: Penguin, 2003).
Tracy, A.L.C. Destutt de, A Treatise on Political Economy, To which is Prefixed a Supplement to a Preceding Work on the Understanding or, Elements of Ideology, trans. Thomas Jefferson (Georgetown, D.C., 1817).
Volney, Constantin François de, *The Ruins, or Meditations on the Revolutions of Empires* (Teddington, UK: The Echo Library: 2010).
Vossler, Otto, *Jefferson and the American Revolutionary Ideal*, C. Philippon and B. Wishy (trans.) (Lanham, MD: University Press of America, 1982).

Wagoner, Jennings L., Jr., *Jefferson and Education* (Chapel Hill: University of North Carolina Press, 2004).
White, Stephen, "Cicero," *Routledge Encyclopedia of Philosophy*, ed. Edward Craig (London: Routledge, 1996).
Wilson, Douglas, "Jefferson and Hume," *The William and Mary Quarterly*, Vol. 46, No. 1, 1989, 49–70.
Wilson, Douglas L., "Jefferson and the Republic of Letters," *Jeffersonian Legacies*, ed. Peter S. Onuf (Charlottesville: University Press of Virginia, 1991), 50–76.
Wilson, Douglas L., *Jefferson's Books* (Charlottesville: Thomas Jefferson Memorial Foundation, 1996).
Winthrop, D. Jordan, *White over Black: American Attitudes toward the Negro, 1550–1812* (Baltimore: Penguin Books, 1969).
Wood, Gordon, *The Creation of the American Republic, 1776–1787* (Chapel Hill: University of North Carolina Press, 1969).
Yarbrough, Jean, "The Moral Sense, Character Formation, and Virtue," *Reason and Republicanism*, ed. Gary L. McDowell and Sharon L. Noble (Lanham, MD: Rowman & Littlefield Publishers, Inc., 1997) 271–303.
Zastoupil, Lynn, "'Notorious and Convicted Mutilators': Rommohun Roy, Thomas Jefferson, and the Bible," *Journal of World History*, Vol. 20, No. 3, 2009: 399–434.
Ziesche, Philipp, "Exporting American Revolutions: Gouverneur Morris, Thomas Jefferson, and the National Struggle for Universal Rights in Revolutionary France," *Journal of the Early Republic*, Vol. 26, No. 3, 2006: 419–47.
Zuckert, Michael, "Founder of the Natural Rights Republic," *Thomas Jefferson and the Politics of Nature*, ed. Thomas S. Engemen (Notre Dame: University of Notre Dame Press, 1998), 11–58.
Zuckert, Michael P., "Thomas Jefferson and Natural Morality," *Thomas Jefferson, the Classical World, and Early America*, ed. Peter S. Onuf and Nicholas P. Cole (Charlottesville: University of Virginia Press, 2011), 56–77.

Index

Academic Skepticism 70, 76, 113
Adams, Abigail 224
Adams, Henry
Adams, John 16, 17, 18, 20, 21, 23, 36, 55, 76, 92, 103, 116, 124, 136, 146, 151, 162, 163, 166, 167–68, 169, 170, 175, 176, 177, 198, 199, 207, 208, 212, 215, 219, 224, 241n25
Adams, Samuel 138
Adams, William Howard 231n4, 239n5
Addis, Cameron 245n34
Agricola 130
Aiken, John 109
Alexander of Macedon 112
anger 80
Antipater 21, 74
Antoninus 64, 65, 66, 70, 78, 79, 88–90, 171, 207, 212
Archimedes 113
Aristippus 73, 77
Aristotle 16, 19, 39, 56–58, 65, 66, 76, 83, 94, 103, 113, 209, 229n40, 237n141
Arrian 79, 84
ataraxia 12–13
Athanasius/Athanasian Creed 173
Aurelius *see* Antoninus

Bacon, Edmund 224
Bacon, Francis 114, 145, 146–47
Banister, John 35–36
Bankhead, Anne Randolph 132, 144
Baxter, John 138
Bellini, Charles 35, 62
benevolence 14, 17, 20, 25, 29, 30, 73, 93, 105, 106, 107, 160, 164, 173, 175, 189, 212, 214, 224, 235n50
benevolence vs. justice 107
Bernstein, R.B. 8
Bible 2, 65, 95, 96, 148, 150, 164, 171
Bill for Establishing a System of Public Education 193–94

Bill for Establishing Religious Freedom 158, 181–85, 189
Bill for the More General Diffusion of Knowledge 129, 132, 140, 193, 195, 204, 243n3
Bill of Rights 198
Blatchly, Cornelius 156
Blue Mountains 52
Bolingbroke, Lord 1, 55, 64, 145, 170, 171, 175–78, 234n61, 241n29
Bonaparte, Napoleon 17
Bourdaloue, Lewis 65, 96, 97, 123–24, 171, 205
Boyd, Julian 9, 18, 217
Brazier, John 196
Brown, Irene Coleman 130, 131
Burk, John W. 143
Burke, Edmund 34, 37, 40–44, 50, 53, 54, 55, 56, 61, 232n37
Burke, John D. 54
Burstein, Andrew 9, 209
Burwell, Nathiel 144, 215
Burwell, Rebecca 8

Cabanis, Pierre Jean George 169
Cabell, Joseph C. 63, 200
Caesar, Julius 147
Calvin, John 173
Calvinism 31–32, 108, 109, 167, 173, 174, 175
Canby, William 162
Carey, Matthew 138
Carr, Peter 16, 17, 21
Cato, Marcus Porcius 74
Cervantes, Miguel 27
Charron, Pierre; 65, 95, 96, 97–101, 171, 205, 229n40, 243n18
Chastellux, Marquis de 134
Chinard, Gilbert 20, 152, 209
Christianity 113
Chrysippus 74, 78

255

INDEX

Cicero, Marcus 3, 21, 64, 65–66, 69–78, 83, 94, 124, 141, 171, 205, 207, 209, 212, 214, 229n37, 244n8
Clark, Sheldon 153
Cleanthes 78, 233n33
Commonplace Book, Literary 170, 176, 212
Condorcet, Marquis de 65, 95, 96. 97, 111–115, 166, 171, 205, 220, 236n87
Conkin, Paul 167
consolation 80–81
Cooper, Thomas 175, 205
Copernicus, Nicholas 114
Cord, Robert 185
Cosway, Maria 2, 7–33, 52, 53, 56, 209, 224, 228n23, 231n92, 233n18, 233n31, 234n56
courage 77, 81
Crantor 78
criticism 45–46
Cumberland, Richard 101
Currie, James 55

Daggett, David 148
Danbury Baptists 183–85
Davis, Derek 184, 185
Dawidoff, Robert 9, 217
Dearborn, Henry 239n6
Declaration of Independence 136, 217
Demarre, Samuel R. 63
Démeunier, Jean Nicholas 175
Demosthenes 70
Descartes, Réne 114, 177
Destutt de Tracy, ALC 1, 1, 109, 116, 169, 176, 177
Dickens, Asbury 149
Dickinson, Charles 136–137
Diodati, Comte 129, 205
Diogenes Laertius 09
Diogenes the Stoic 74
Driesbach, Daniel 185
Duane, William 133
Dupont de Nemours, P.S. 155

Ebeling, Christoph Daniel 137
Edgeworth, Maria 143
Ellis, Joseph 4, 9
Enfield, William 64, 95, 96, 97, 109–11, 171, 205
England 35–36
Enlightenment 30, 145, 148
Epictetus 2, 4, 64, 66, 70, 78, 79, 84–88, 91, 171, 207, 208, 212, 213, 214, 215, 216, 218, 219, 220, 224, 234n61
Epicurus 1, 2, 5, 9, 12–13, 14, 18, 19–20, 33, 52. 66, 69, 70, 77, 113, 207–9, 212, 213, 228n13, 228n14
Eppes, Francis 55, 216, 222
eukairia/kairos 72, 76, 83, 136, 156, 23n24

Federalism 137, 138, 145, 146, 147, 148, 149, 150, 151, 153, 156

Fenno, John 137
Findley, William 150
Fishback, James 23, 92, 163
Fitzhugh, Peregrine 49, 135
France 35–36
Franklin, Benjamin 217, 239n6
free will 30–31, 107–9
Freud, Sigmund 58

Galileo 188
Gallatin, Albert 56
Gassendi, Pierre 228n14
Gaustad, E.S. 167
Gerry, Eldbride 147
George III, King 21, 22, 134
Gilmer, Francis 211
Gould, William 225

Hale, Daryl 9, 209
Hall, J. Lesslie 241n38
Hamilton, Alexander 146–47
Hancock, John 162
happiness 9, 10, 12, 14, 15, 18, 19, 20, 22, 27, 29, 35, 46, 47, 61, 81, 82, 98, 99, 100–5, 110, 11, 112, 118, 119, 120, 121, 122, 126, 129, 133, 140, 146, 148, 150, 154 156, 186, 191, 192, 193, 197, 200, 202, 2205, 208, 216, 220, 221, 243n3
Hazard, Ebenezer 139
Heaton, James 24
Hecaton 82
Hellenbrand, Harold 208
Helo, Ari 20, 22, 229n43
Hening, William Waller 139
Henley, Samuel 63
Henry, Patrick 54, 134, 220
Hierocles 213–14
Hieronymous 77
Hilliard, William 63
Hippocratic medicine 113
Hobbes, Thomas 153, 211
Hogarth, William 34, 37–40, 43, 45, 49, 49, 50, 56, 59, 60
Holowchak, M. Andrew 233n24
homologia 210
Honeywell, Roy 192
Howe, John 156
Hubbell, Harry 69
Hume, David 1, 18, 25–32, 64, 105, 107, 128, 133, 134, 138–39, 143, 145, 163, 171, 176, 229n28, 230n56, 241n29
Hutcheson, Francis 1, 65, 95, 97, 101–5, 171, 205, 221

imitation 36, 42, 57, 58, 133
Irving, Washington 149

Jarvis, William 201
Jefferson (Randolph), Martha 1, 7, 48, 170, 222, 223

Index

Jefferson, Thomas: on aesthetic sense 2, 5, 34–62, 142; and afterlife 161, 165, 167–71; on atheism 189; on beauty 47–50, 142; bible 2, 66, 91–94, 117, 164, 172, 176, 177, 178; on blacks 49–50, 132, 145; and constitutional renewal 146, 152; cosmopolitanism of 216–17; on crimes and punishments 132; on death 1, 13, 15, 25, 30, 31, 43, 75–78, 80, 82, 85, 88, 89, 90, 99, 100, 105, 106, 108, 112, 117, 123–24, 136, 167–71170, 188, 213, 218, 222, 241n38; and deity 16, 17, 23, 57, 161, 162, 168, 169, 174, 175–79, 182; and education 3, 35, 115, 133, 140, 146, 156, 187, 191–202; as Epicurean 19–20, 207–9; and equality 36, 109, 115; eudaemonism of 19; on fiction 140–44; freedom of religion 179–86; hagiography of 3–4; on history 25, 128–40, 204; on husbandry 101, 148, 178; as hypocrite 3–4; and Jesus 1, 5, 20, 22, 49, 55, 91–94, 97, 116, 117, 164–66, 167, 171–72, 174, 175, 178, 188, 221, 234n61, 241n38; liberal eudemonism of 202; and liberty 30, 31, 73, 84, 103, 107, 108, 109, 112, 113, 119, 120, 121, 122, 135, 140, 147, 148, 150, 156, 183, 186, 198, 201, 202, 225; library catalogs of 172–73; materialism of 158, 172; on miracles 187–88; and moral cynosures 22–23, 126, 218; and moral progress 23–24, 109, 115, 220–21; as moral relativist 5, 19, 20, 24; on moral sense and reason 3, 22–25, 100, 161, 204; and Native Americans 54, 132, 145; and natural *aristoi* 153, 191–206; and neoterism 133; and newspapers 135–36; not political relativist 152–55; *Notes on Virginia* 49, 50, 54, 61, 132, 140, 145, 150, 157, 179, 180, 186, 197; as philologist 131–32; on poetry 54, 126; political philosophy of 145–60; and progress 23–24, 145–60; as rationalist 3; reading lists of 171–72; on religion 96, 97, 107, 109, 115, 126, 157, 161–90; and science 28, 101, 145–46, 147, 148, 154, 159; on slavery 24–25; as Stoic 1, 2, 5, 20–21, 29, 65, 66, 75, 76, 93–94, 97, 207–26; on sublimity 50–56; and truthfulness 214–16; and war 100; and wealth 123, 124; as Whig 139; and wisdom 123
Jesus 1, 3, 20, 22, 49, 55, 91–94, 97, 115, 117, 164–66, 167, 170, 172, 174–75, 178, 188, 221, 234n61, 241n30, 241n38
Johnson, Richard Mentor 63
Johnson, William 139
Johnstone, Robert M. 245n62
justice 14, 19, 20, 27, 30, 43, 46–47, 67, 71, 77, 89, 93, 98, 104, 106, 107, 112, 120, 121, 123, 125, 130, 132, 164, 167, 175, 176, 198, 211, 214, 218, 222, 230n80

Kames, Lord 1, 3, 26–32, 33, 34, 37, 44–46, 47, 58, 59, 61, 64, 96, 97, 105–9, 128, 133, 142, 143, 145, 166, 171, 176–77, 205, 220, 229n39, 230n69, 230n76, 230n80, 230n81, 232n46, 235n50, 245n59
Koch, Adrienne 20, 22, 153

Lamozzo, Gian Paolo 37
Law, Thomas 17, 19, 20, 21, 47, 104, 215, 217, 218
Lee, Richard Henry 132, 216
Leiper, Thomas 126
Lepidus, Marcus 130, 131
liberty 31
Linn, William 150
Livingston, Donald 230n56
Livy 92, 133, 134, 7
Locke, John 31, 64, 95, 96, 109, 145, 146–47, 153–54, 169, 171, 177, 205
Logan, George 21, 167
Lucilius 79

Madison, James 23, 36, 134, 152, 159, 162, 181, 198
Malone, Dumas 8, 150, 152, 157, 182
Mapp, Alf 8, 157, 228n21
Martin, Edward T. 148
Massillon, Jean Baptise 3, 65, 96, 97, 124–26, 171, 205
Matthews, Richard 152
Maury, Rev. 196
Maury, Walker 63
May, Henry 152, 225
McPherson, Charles 53
McPherson, James 53
Mercier, Louis-Sébastien 228n22
Michelangelo 37
Middleton, Conyers 171
Miller, Charles 209
Milligan, Joseph 133
Minor, John 63, 78, 127, 172
moderation 77
Monroe, James 54
Montesquieu 154
Monticello 11, 53, 62, 83, 146, 172, 181, 217, 224
Moore, Bernard 63, 64, 69, 122, 123, 232n4
Moore, Clement Clarke 150
moral expediency 72–73, 86, 88, 218
moral goodness 70–72, 73–74, 85, 87, 88, 218
moral sense 103, 106, 109
Munford, William Green 63, 211, 222

Napoleon, Bonaparte 134
Native Americans 24
Natural Bridge 11, 51, 52
Neem, Johann 20, 22, 185, 228n25
Neoplatonism 65
New Testament 3, 49, 65–66, 91, 92, 95, 115, 171, 177, 188
Newton, Isaac 30, 146–47, 149, 153, 154, 178, 239n6

258 INDEX

Niagara Falls 11, 52
Nicholas, Wilson C. 195
Norvell, John 129, 138, 205

occasio 72
Oldfather, W.A. 84
Onuf, Peter 4
Owen, Judd 240*n*5

Page, John 62, 169
Paige, Mann 198
Paine, Thomas 55
Panaetius 21, 70–72, 76, 78, 82, 86, 218
Parker, Thomas 162
Patterson, Caleb Perry 211
Pendleton, Edmund 158
Peterson, Merrill 4, 57, 182, 217, 245*n*46
Phalaris 73
Plato 19, 65, 67, 68, 74, 75, 76, 78, 94, 113, 116, 168, 202, 209, 232*n*69, 237*n*141, 244*n*8
Plutarch 133
Polemo 78
Posidonius 78
Priestley, Joseph 55, 65, 95, 96, 97, 115–117, 150, 155, 171, 173, 174
Priscus, Caius Lutorius 131
prudence 77

Quakers 175
Quinby, Lee 9

Ragosta, Paul 167
Randall, Henry 189
Randolph, Peyton 22, 218
Randolph, Thomas Jefferson 22, 189, 218, 219
Raymondis, Paradis de 65, 95, 171
Revolution, American 24, 136, 193
Richard, Carl 168
Risjord, Norman 8
Rittenhouse, David 148
Rockfish Gap Report 197, 200
Roman Republic 113
Rousseau, Jean Jacques 211
Rush, Benjamin 22, 55, 90, 91, 146, 165, 177
Russell, Benjamin 137
Rutledge, Edward 49

Sallust 133, 134
Sanford, Charles 164, 167, 168
Schneider, Herbert 225
Seneca 65, 66, 70, 78, 79–84, 124, 141, 171, 205
Services to My Country 186
Seymour, Thomas 135
Shaftesbury, Lord 101
Shakespeare, William 58, 142, 144
Sheridan, Eugene R. 20, 22, 167
Sherlock, Thomas 65, 171

Short, William 65, 70, 87, 92, 132, 136, 172, 174, 177, 207, 208, 213
Siculus, Diodorus 92
Skipwith, Robert 18, 37, 47, 58, 59, 61, 63–65, 68, 78, 79, 142, 143, 144, 171, 204
Slavery 24–25
Small, William 3, 20, 218
Smith, Adam 25, 32, 145, 176, 211, 221, 230*n*80, 244*n*3
Smith, James 175
Smith, Margaret Bayard 162
Smith, Thomas Jefferson 2, 223
Socrates 64, 65, 66–69, 87, 91, 112, 218, 232*n*69
Staloff, Darren 193
Stanton, Lucia 147
Steele, Brian 243*n*19
Sterne, Laurence 3, 58, 64, 65, 96, 97, 121–23, 141, 142, 170, 171, 205, 221, 239*n*39
Stewart, Dugald 31, 169
Stilpo 78
Stoics 18, 19, 21, 33, 65, 66, 69, 70, 71, 72, 74, 76–90, 97, 99, 102, 103, 104, 105, 113, 123, 178, 207–226, 228*n*14, 229*n*39, 229*n*40, 229*n*41, 233*n*13, 234*n*56, 237*n*141, 244*n*5, 244*n*8
Story, Isaac 168
Stuart, Archibald 63, 116
Stuart, Josephus B. 134
Summary View 21
Syllabus 22
sympathy 14, 29, 32, 42, 46, 102, 105, 217

Tacitus, Publius Conelius 3, 129–31, 132, 133, 134, 187
Taylor, Hugh P. 136
Taylor, Paul 139
Tessé, Madame La Comtesse de 48, 154
Thompson, James 49
Thomson, Charles 48, 49
Tocqueville, Alexis de 182, 240*n*6
Tracy, A.L.C. Destutt de 1, 31, 109, 116, 169, 176, 177
Trinitarianism 31, 109, 115–17, 157, 173, 174, 175, 180

Unitarianism 1, 109, 115, 117, 167, 173–75, 236*n*84, 236*n*104, 241*n*38, 242*n*40
University of Virginia 60, 84, 101, 195, 202, 205
Utley, Vine 84, 126, 223

Van der Kemp, Francis Adrian 169, 170
virtue 3, 8, 9, 12, 13, 18, 19, 20, 21, 22, 26, 27, 29, 30, 36, 43–44, 46, 47, 58, 61, 63, 67, 70–72, 73, 76, 77, 78, 79 80, 81, 85, 89, 94, 98, 100, 101, 103, 104–5, 106, 107, 108, 112, 113, 118, 121, 123, 128, 133, 142, 143, 148, 153, 156, 166, 186, 188, 191, 192, 193, 194, 195,

198, 199, 200, 202, 209, 210, 213, 214, 128, 220, 221, 222, 223, 225, 230*n*80, 233*n*23, 239*n*5, 243*n*18, 243*n*29
Volney, Comte de 3, 65, 96, 97, 117–121, 171, 228*n*12
Vossler, Otto 153

Wagoner, Jennngs L. 243*n*3
Waldo, John 133
Washington, George 24, 90, 134, 149, 216
Waterhouse, Benjamin 167, 173, 217
Webster, Noah 137
Whittemore, Thomas 162
Willard, Joseph 148
William and Mary College 157, 192, 193, 195, 205

Wilson, Douglas 8, 139, 172
Wirt, William 54, 134, 136
Wyche, John 63
Wythe, George 3, 22, 35, 48, 126, 132, 139, 157, 158, 179, 181, 218

Xenocrates 78
Xenophon 64, 66–69, 70, 91, 141, 171

Yarbrough, Jean 20, 22

Zastoupil, Lynn 236*n*104
Zeno 77, 78
Ziesche, Philipp 153
Zuckert, Michael P. 228*n*18, 243*n*29

www.ingramcontent.com/pod-product-compliance
Lightning Source LLC
Chambersburg PA
CBHW051215300426
44116CB00006B/583